Shame and the Anti-Feminist Backlash

Shame and the Anti-Feminist Backlash examines how women opposed to the feminist campaign for the vote in early twentieth-century Britain, Ireland, and Australia used shame as a political tool. It demonstrates just how proficient women were in employing a diverse vocabulary of emotions—drawing on concepts such as embarrassment, humiliation, honour, courage, and chivalry—in the attempt to achieve their political goals. It looks at how far nationalist contexts informed each gendered emotional community at a time when British imperial networks were under extreme duress. The book presents a unique history of gender and shame, which demonstrates just how versatile and ever-present this social emotion was in the feminist politics of the British Empire in the early decades of the twentieth century. It employs a fascinating new thematic lens to histories of anti-feminist/feminist entanglements by tracing national and transnational uses of emotions by women to police their own political communities. It also challenges the common notion that shame had little place in a modernising world by revealing how far groups of patriotic womanhood, globally, deployed shame to combat the effects of feminist activism.

Sharon Crozier-De Rosa is a senior lecturer in history at the University of Wollongong.

Routledge Research in Gender and History

20 **Women and the Reinvention of the Political**
   Feminism in Italy, 1968–1983
   Maud Anne Bracke

21 **Women in Higher Education, 1850–1970**
   International Perspectives
   Edited by E. Lisa Panayotidis and Paul Stortz

22 **Gendering the Settler State**
   White Women, Race, Liberalism and Empire in Rhodesia, 1950–1980
   Kate Law

23 **Women in Magazines**
   Research, Representation, Production and Consumption
   Edited by Rachel Ritchie, Sue Hawkins, Nicola Phillips and S. Jay Kleinberg

24 **New Perspectives on European Women's Legal History**
   Edited by Sara L. Kimble and Marion Röwekamp

25 **Gender and the Representation of Evil**
   Edited by Lynne Fallwell and Keira V. Williams

26 **Transgressive Women in Modern Russian and East European Cultures**
   From the Bad to the Blasphemous
   Edited by Yana Hashamova, Beth Holmgren and Mark Lipovetsky

27 **Catastrophe, Gender and Urban Experience, 1648–1920**
   Edited by Deborah Simonton and Hannu Salmi

28 **Women in International and Universal Exhibitions, 1876–1937**
   Edited by Myriam Boussahba-Bravard and Rebecca Rogers

29 **Shame and the Anti-Feminist Backlash**
   Britain, Ireland and Australia, 1890–1920
   Sharon Crozier-De Rosa

Shame and the Anti-Feminist Backlash

Britain, Ireland and Australia, 1890–1920

Sharon Crozier-De Rosa

NEW YORK AND LONDON

First published 2018
by Routledge
711 Third Avenue, New York, NY 10017

and by Routledge
2 Park Square, Milton Park, Abingdon, Oxon OX14 4RN

Routledge is an imprint of the Taylor & Francis Group, an informa business

© 2018 Taylor & Francis

The right of Sharon Crozier-De Rosa to be identified as author of this work has been asserted by her in accordance with sections 77 and 78 of the Copyright, Designs and Patents Act 1988.

All rights reserved. No part of this book may be reprinted or reproduced or utilised in any form or by any electronic, mechanical, or other means, now known or hereafter invented, including photocopying and recording, or in any information storage or retrieval system, without permission in writing from the publishers.

Trademark notice: Product or corporate names may be trademarks or registered trademarks, and are used only for identification and explanation without intent to infringe.

Library of Congress Cataloging-in-Publication Data
Names: Crozier-De Rosa, Sharon, author.
Title: Shame and the anti-feminist backlash : Britain, Ireland and
　Australia, 1890–1920 / by Sharon Crozier-De Rosa.
Description: New York : Routledge, 2018. | Series: Routledge research in
　gender and history ; 29 | Includes bibliographical references and index. |
　Identifiers: LCCN 2017045020 (print) | LCCN 2017050139 (ebook) |
　ISBN 9780203086032 () | ISBN 9780415635868 (hbk : alk. paper)
Subjects: LCSH: Anti-feminism—Great Britain—History. | Anti-feminism—
　Australia—History. | Patriotism—Great Britain—History. | Patriotism—
　Australia—History. | Women—Political activity—Great Britain—History. |
　Women—Political activity—Australia—History. | Women—Psychology. |
　Women—Identity.
Classification: LCC HQ1593 (ebook) | LCC HQ1593 .C77 2018
　(print) | DDC 305.420941—dc23
LC record available at https://lccn.loc.gov/2017045020

ISBN: 978-0-415-63586-8 (hbk)
ISBN: 978-0-203-08603-2 (ebk)

Typeset in Sabon
by Apex CoVantage, LLC

 Printed and bound by CPI Group (UK) Ltd, Croydon, CR0 4YY

For my mum and dad,
Kate and Sean.

Contents

	Acknowledgments	viii
	Introduction	1
1	Shaming Unwomanly Women	35
2	Reversing the Shame of British Colonisation	61
3	Embarrassing the Imperial Centre	87
4	Shaming British-Australia	107
5	War and the Dishonourable British Feminist	131
6	Shaming Manhood to Embody Courage	165
7	The Shame of the Violent Woman	193
	Conclusion	231
	Bibliography	242
	Index	255

Acknowledgments

In the course of writing this book, I have benefitted from the encouragement and support of many people.

The staff at Routledge have been a pleasure to work with, in particular Max Novick and Jennifer Morrow.

As a member of the School of Humanities and Social Inquiry at the University of Wollongong, I have been fortunate to be surrounded by generous colleagues who have gladly offered encouragement, advice, and feedback on my ideas and writing, despite the many demands on their time. Firstly, thank you to Sarah Sorial for her generosity and advice as she provided commentary on my draft manuscript in a very compressed amount of time. I would also like to extend a thank you to Julia Martinez for her constant advice and support. I have benefitted from the collegiality of, among others, Ian Buchanan, Rowan Cahill, Jane Carey, Georgine Clarsen, Leigh Dale, Debra Dudek, Sarah Ferber, Di Kelly, Sukhmani Khorana, Claire Lowrie, Vera Mackie, John McQuilton, Robyn Morris, Ben Maddison, Brian Martin, and Frances Steel. I also acknowledge the camaraderie of members of the university's Contemporary Emotions Research Network, Colonial and Settler Studies Network, and the Feminist Research Network.

I have also been the grateful recipient of support and advice from those outside my institution. I thank David Lowe for mentoring me as an Alfred Deakin Postdoctoral Research Fellow. It was during my brief time at Deakin University that the nucleus of this book took shape, and I conducted my first overseas research trip to gather the sources I needed. I also acknowledge the support of others including Frank Bongiorno, Gemma Clark, Louise D'Arcens, Victoria Haskins, David Lemmings, Louise Ryan, Michelle Smith, and Margaret Ward. This book has profited from the insightful comments of audiences at seminars and conferences. There are too many to mention, but I would like to acknowledge those regularly attending the conferences and seminars of the Australian Women's History Network, Australasian Association of European Historians, Irish Studies Association of Australia and New Zealand, Australian Historical Association, and the Centre for the History of Violence at the University of Newcastle.

My heartfelt thanks goes to the staff of the libraries I visited while undertaking this research including the Women's Library (then at the London Metropolitan University and now at the London School of Economics), the National Library of Ireland, the National Library of Australia, the British Library, the State Library of Victoria, the State Library of New South Wales, and the University of Wollongong Library. I received funding from the University of Wollongong and Deakin University to conduct this research. I have also benefitted from the experience of having brief sections of this research published as journal articles: 'The National and the Transnational in British Anti-Suffragists' Views of Australian Women Voters', *History Australia*, vol. 10, no. 3 (2013) pp. 51–64, and 'Shame and Anti-Feminist Politics in Britain and Ireland: Drawing Women Back into the Fold?', *Australian Journal of Politics and History*, vol. 60, no. 3 (2014) pp. 346–359.

My final thank you goes to my family. My mum and dad, Kate and Sean, flew in to look after my children as I flew out to archives and conferences. Thank you. I thank Bernie Crozier, Róisín Manley, Daniel Fox, and Michele Steenkamp for sending me morsels of Irish and British women's history via social media. You helped to keep me in touch. To my sons, Oisín and Lorcán, I say a great big sorry for being absent as I indulged in shame and feminisms and anti-feminisms. But I also say a great big thank you for listening to me on this topic on countless occasions, asking quirky questions that challenged me to see things differently, and for making me laugh, often. Justin, thank you for all your support. I have needed and greatly appreciated it.

Introduction

> For Great Britain is already too rapidly losing many of the noble ideals and institutions which once made her the unrivalled mistress of the world ... and if the mothers of the British race decide to part altogether with the birthright of their simple *womanliness* for a political mess of pottage, then darker days are in store for the nation than can yet be foreseen or imagined. For with woman alone rests the Home, which is the foundation of the Empire. When they desert this, their God-appointed centre, the core of the national being, then things are tottering to a fall.[1]

In 1907, Marie Corelli—phenomenally popular novelist, celebrity, and self-appointed 'guardian of the public conscience'[2]—published her much-quoted anti-suffragist text, *Woman, or—Suffragette?* As the pamphlet's title indicates, the radical suffragist's transgressions were so great that the line dividing woman and radical feminist was an unbridgeable one. As an incredibly successful writer and public persona, Corelli's fame was predicated on the sales of 500- or 600-page novels that capitalised on descriptions of the loose and decaying morality of late nineteenth- and early twentieth-century British society. A particular feature of her writing was her condemnation of the women at the centre of that decaying moral fabric.

Who were these women? In Corelli's world—and that of her vast army of readers—they were modern or 'new' or feminist women. These were the author's 'distracted, man-fighting sisters', who were inspired to go 'clamouring like unnatural hens in a barn-yard about their "rights" and "wrongs"', intentionally attempting to 'neutralise their sex', and at the very least robbing that sex of its dignity.[3] These were shamelessly deviant women, like the notorious New Woman[4] and the violent suffragettes,[5] who while fighting publicly for the vote and other such worldly gains only invoked disgrace. Their dangerous and indecorous behaviour, Corelli assented, was 'a degradation to the very name of woman'.[6] Devoid of the womanly feelings of modesty and shame, these gender abominations alienated their respectable non-feminist sisters. Even more than that, their deviant actions harmed the nation and empire to which they owed allegiance. These feminist women were, then, 'a scandal to the nation' because they made 'England a laughing-stock to the rest of the world'.[7] Their selfish desires for political power exposed their inability to be guided by feminine emotional values. Their continued campaigns also threatened to dismantle the entire emotional regimes underpinning the gender relations of the nation and the Empire, and indeed, of the civilised world.

Corelli's attacks on the feminist woman were steeped in shame. She attempted to shame transgressive women into abandoning their disruptive activities. As a moral and social emotion, shame worked by instilling in individuals a fear of losing the love or respect of someone or some community they were attached to or to whom they attached value. If women valued the communities to which they belonged—gendered and national communities—then they would desist from these acts. Otherwise, they risked being ostracised. However, as feminist theorist Jill Locke explains, shame has its limitations.[8] If feminists did not honour their connection with the community of 'good' patriotic womanhood, then they were unlikely to be motivated by Corelli's shaming. Therefore, shame performed a number of ideological functions in her writing. It existed to inspire reform. If it could not do this, it was assigned a protective role. It was used to highlight the boundaries existing between the true community of English womanhood and its transgressive other. For anti-suffragist women such as Corelli, shame was a versatile political tool.

Corelli and her fellow female anti-suffragists did not use shame without articulating their wider understanding of the nature and workings of this emotion and related emotional concepts, such as honour, courage, chivalry, and embarrassment. Rather, their collective body of writing reveals much about the complexities of early twentieth-century deliberations on the make-up of gendered emotional regimes. Feminists were considered scandalous because they threatened the nature of the emotional regimes which guided men's and women's behaviour. Men and women were expected to adhere to different sets of emotional standards—those appropriate to their sex. For example, men were required to be honourable in their daily dealings. They were expected to enact the emotional qualities underpinning honour: courage, chivalry, honesty, and fairness. Women, on the other hand, were directed to behave according to a different set of emotional rules. They were expected to be sensitive, loving, and nurturing. Each set of emotional rules reflected the proper place of the sexes in society: men's emotional regimes guided their participation in the public realm and women's were much more suited to their place in the private sphere. When feminists committed public outrages—such as staging mass demonstrations or damaging property in the name of 'Votes for Women'—they threatened to appropriate men's emotional regimes. In doing so, they jeopardised the integrity and operation of those gendered regimes. As Corelli pointed out, this was detrimental to two intersecting communities: womanhood and the nation.

In this book, I undertake the much-neglected task of examining how women deployed emotions in their attempts to regulate the behaviour of other women. In particular, I analyse how politically minded women understood and used shame in their discussions about women's empowerment and disempowerment. I address a series of questions relating to women's articulations and manipulations of shame and related emotions. For example, was shame an empowering tool for the politically disempowered? Did women's deployment of shame accord with their wider understanding of the gendered nature of emotions and emotional regimes? That is to say, shame and its antithesis, honour, were profoundly gendered emotions: shame was regarded as inescapably feminine, whereas only men could actively pursue honour. Therefore, when defending the integrity of the nation from the perceived feminist onslaught, did 'good' patriotic women act to appropriate a distinctly masculine remit? Did they erode the masculine nature of honour? If so, how did they rationalise such an incursion into masculine emotional regimes? My study of shame extends beyond the question of how women used shame in the attempt to ensure compliance. It also analyses how these women understood the wider nature of emotions and emotional regimes—that is, the emotional context in which shame and shaming operated.

I adopt a national and a transnational approach in this book by drawing on the political writings of patriotic women in other sites of empire—namely, Ireland and Australia. Historians of empire have long had cause to embrace transnational approaches to the past. The essence of empire involves movements and exchanges across national and colonial borders.[9] How far did concerns about gender, nationalism, and emotions connect or disconnect patriotic women across the British Empire? For example, in the first decades of the twentieth century, all three countries—England, Ireland, and Australia—were undergoing significant degrees of political upheaval uniquely linked to their relative places on the British imperial spectrum. Across these separate but related national sites, concepts of female citizenship diverged. Patriotic women used these varying concepts of female citizenship to maintain or reconstruct their gendered communities. I analyse how far understandings and uses of shame intersected or diverged across these disparate sites. I look at how each community of patriotic womanhood articulated the nature of the emotional contexts in which shame and shaming operated.

Gendered Emotional Regimes and Communities

This book adds to the expansive fields of gender history and the history of nationalisms and imperialism. It also contributes to the more recent, but ever-burgeoning, field of emotions history. Much has been written over the past few decades about what has been termed a history of emotions.[10] The works of prominent scholars such as Barbara Rosenwein and William Reddy are of particular relevance to this study of the emotional values of different communities of patriotic womanhood. In the early 2000s, Rosenwein argued that a given society accommodated numerous emotional communities and that individuals moved through multiple emotional communities daily. The emotional styles, rules, standards, and expectations varied from community to community. Members of each emotional community were expected to adhere to 'the same valuations of emotions and their expression'.[11] They were expected to amend their emotional styles to suit the relevant emotional environment. Women connected by their intertwining views on the relationship between gender and the nation formed a type of emotional community. They identified specific emotional values and styles that women should adhere to in order to be regarded as bona fide members of that gendered national community.

At around the same time, William Reddy formulated the term emotional regimes. He understood emotional regimes to be the set of normative emotions prescribed by societies and governments and the codes of expression and repression (emotives) designed to inculcate and manage those emotions. He argued that such prescribed emotions and codes were required to underpin any stable political regime.[12] Since then, other scholars of emotions have added to and amended those theories. Benno Gammerl, for example, has extended the study of emotional regimes and communities to argue that far from being restrictive or rigidly prescribed, many of these emotional communities were fluid enough to variously cut across or bridge distinctions of class, race, nationality, or gender.[13] How fluid or rigid were the emotional regimes directing women's participation in nationalist politics? Did groups of patriotic womanhood construct emotional communities that were open and flexible in the face of feminist demands?

In this book, I am concerned with how emotional communities and emotional regimes intersected with national and gendered politics. Despite the obvious presence of emotions in politics, Jeff Goodwin, James M. Jasper, and Francesca Polletta argue that there has been some hesitation on the part of academic observers to admit to the place of emotions in political life. Instead, they have managed to 'ignore the swirl of passions all around them in political life'.[14] In accounting for this relative absence, political scientist Carol Johnson cites the perceived gendered nature of emotions generally. Traditionally, emotion was associated with the feminised private sphere of home and family, while emotion's supposed antithesis, reason, was associated with the masculinised public world of business and politics.[15] I add to the emerging body of literature that works to reject this binary by analysing how women used emotions strategically to achieve political ends. By concentrating on women active in protest movements at the beginning of the twentieth century, I perform the much-needed task of historicising political emotions, specifically shame and its close family of emotions—negative (for example, disgrace, embarrassment, and indignation) and positive (including honour, courage, and chivalry).

A Transnational History of Shame?

Shame is a social and moral emotion. It is the fear of being judged defective by an individual or group to whom one attaches value. It is not simply outwardly directed as, for example, embarrassment might be. It is not the temporary feeling brought about by an accidental violation of social norms as embarrassment is. Rather, shame is internalised. The fear of shame is the fear of failing not only one's valued community, but through that one's sense of self. Sociologist Thomas Scheff argues that shame is 'the feeling of a *threat to the social bond*'.[16] It is the master emotion, he claims, because people always anticipate failing themselves and their group. Shame is ever-present because as social beings, people fear an erosion of the bonds that tie them to their community.[17] Transgressive subjects could shame themselves by dishonouring their bond with their community. They could also bring shame to that collective if, through their deviant behaviour, they corrupted the values, and therefore the bonds, of that community.

In this book, I look at early twentieth-century women's communities of belonging. I also examine these women's understandings of the perceived threats to their social bonds. Therefore, shame is at the heart of this study. Patriotic women consistently articulated their impressions of shame and its kin as they negotiated these perceived threats. Their communications also reveal that they were adept at identifying shame's complex workings. Shame was a highly versatile social emotion. It had the capacity to act as a motivational tool. If transgressive subjects confronted their shame and reformed their behaviour, they could be accepted back into the fold of their once valued community. However, as a social or political tool, shame was also limited in that it relied on the deviant's ability and desire to accept shame and embrace reform.

Still, and further demonstrating shame's versatility, while accepting the limitations of the reformative power of this emotion, early twentieth-century women also identified the possibility of a positive outcome arising from this process of shaming. If the attempt to inflict shame on transgressive subjects did not have the desired effect of bringing about their reform, then exposing the presence of these shameful transgressors could at least be used to draw a tighter, more defined border around the rightful members of that community. It served to clarify group values and group belonging. It had the potential to induce greater group solidarity.

As much as scholars agree on a general definition of shame and its workings, shame is not ahistorical. Reasons for feeling shame and manifestations of it vary from time to time and place to place. Shame has a history. Recent research into past accounts of shame has produced a growing collection of histories of the emotion.[18] This body of work includes research into shame and crime; shame and family relations; shame, gender, and the body in political protest movements; and national consciousness and the 'stains' of the past, including indigenous dispossession in New Zealand and the Great Famine in Ireland.[19] This is a growing body of scholarship. However, historians argue that much more research into past attitudes to shame is needed to understand how the meaning and manifestation of this emotion varied across time and space. More research is required to comprehend the multifaceted features of this uncomfortable, complex, and ever-changing emotion.[20]

In this book, I expand historical understandings of the complexity and versatility of shame through examining its gendered and national and/ or transnational dimensions. I analyse how three communities of patriotic women opposed to feminist campaigns for the vote articulated their understanding of the emotional styles—standards, regulations, and expressions—making up their specific gendered and emotional community. I undertake this task by focusing particularly on their attitudes towards shame and its related emotions. By adopting a transnational as well as national approach, I help to identify nationally specific understandings of shame as well as trace circulating discussions of shame as they cross a number of the national borders that comprise the British Empire. In doing so, this study contributes to a body of scholarship that Ida Blom has identified as transcultural histories of 'the interactions between gender orders, nationalisms and nation building'.[21] Blom asserts that multi-national investigations of this kind allow historians to more substantially understand the 'cross-cultural parallels' that sit alongside 'decisive culturally determined differences' in gendered constructions of the nation and nationalisms.[22] This framework is also pertinent to the task of revealing how attitudes towards the place of gendered emotional regimes in nationalist processes variously connected and disconnected diverse communities of patriotic womanhood.

Being opposed to campaigns for the vote connected many of the groups of women studied here. However, each group's reasons for opposing enfranchisement varied in line with national priorities. This had consequences for how each group constructed its emotional communities and for the nature of the deployment of emotional tools for political ends. For example, the Australian women I look at were reluctant suffragists. That is, they opposed their own enfranchisement. However, once the new Australian Commonwealth inducted them into formal citizenship, they took on the task of educating other reluctant patriotic women about how to vote in a manner that was beneficial to the integrity of Australian womanhood and the honour of the Australian nation. In many ways, the British women opposed to the vote harboured similar concerns to pre-enfranchised Australian women. The major difference was that British women were laden with the worries of the imperial centre, and Australian women had only the welfare of the relatively insignificant former colonies to care about. To bring shame on the colonies, then, meant something very different to dishonouring the centre of a vast imperial network. In Ireland, matters were different again. Many of the women who opposed the campaign for the vote did so because they put the needs of the aspiring Irish nation before those of the feminist community. They were not necessarily against feminist advancement. Rather, they wanted to prevent their nationalist sisters from asking British men for concessions that they should be asking Irish men for. To fail in this endeavour, they believed, was to compound the emasculated colonised Irish man's shame.

Political women's relationships with shame and related emotions were multi-dimensional. Patriotic women were highly attuned to the negative impact that rogue members could have on their community of womanhood. To bring shame on that community risked its disintegration. As patriots, they were also painfully aware of the reputation of their nation. To shame the nation—to bring it into disrepute—could have catastrophic consequences for the national community. This was certainly the case for women in the imperial centre, where a reputation for stability and supremacy helped ensure ongoing control over a vast, disruptive empire. However, it was also true of patriotic women in smaller national units. Nationalist women in Ireland and Australia often assumed the role of guardian of the aspiring or fledgling nation's honour, whether they were invited to do so or not. Through examining patriotic women's approaches to shame and shaming, can we ascertain how far allegiance to the national community trumped that to the community of womanhood? What can an analysis of shame in women's politics reveal about competing national and gender anxieties and loyalties?

Before attempting to answer these questions, it is necessary to trace the intersecting national and gender anxieties in early twentieth-century England, Ireland, and Australia.

Britain's Intersecting Anxieties and 'Good' Patriotic Womanhood

During the late nineteenth and early twentieth centuries, when the British Empire was at its height, England—at the centre of that vast international network—articulated its understanding of itself largely within an international framework: as the standard bearers of civilisation, modernity, and progress globally.[23] Covering perhaps a quarter of the world's land mass and overseeing at least 400 million subjects scattered across 80 to 100 separate territorial units who acknowledged the sovereignty or accepted the protection of the British Crown, the British Empire was a formidable imperial power.

However, even at the height of empire, the imperial centre was beset by intersecting political anxieties which reflected the turbulent political conditions around the Empire at the time.[24] Well-publicised military defeats, such as those at the hands of the Afghanistanis, Zulus, Boers, and Sudanese, promoted fears about national and imperial decline. At the same time, growing awareness of the fierce competition from countries such as Germany and Italy for global sites not yet occupied by Western imperial powers spurred a new sense of urgency in the imperial project.[25] Ironically, Britain's imperial success at this stage fed further worries 'at home'. As Britain continued to acquire vast new territories, anxieties about the corresponding increase in associated responsibilities and costs grew.[26] Doubt about the reasons for assuming this extra cost and responsibility surfaced. Questions abounded: Was it about continuing to bring civilisation to the less fortunate or maintaining the protection of trade routes or acquiring more territories and thereby greater profit and power? Whatever the specific nature of the uncertainty, this growing sense of imperial ambivalence contributed to what Bradley Deane, in his study of masculinity and imperial identity, has termed the 'ideological fog' that permeated late Victorian society.[27]

Perceived threats emanating both from outside and from within the Empire added to those uncertainties about the state of Britain's imperial mission. In the decades preceding the end of the First World War, and certainly by the time of the Russian Revolution in 1917, the growing stature of socialism was to be a cause of grave concern to dedicated imperialists in the British centre and the colonial peripheries. Increasingly, as the twentieth century progressed, socialism was seen to be a major challenge to the supremacy of imperialism as the dominant international ideology. The threat that this ideology represented internally was no mere spectre. Within Britain, more working-class men were acquiring new political power thanks to the campaigns that led to the Parliamentary Reform Acts of 1867 and 1884, which expanded the British electorate from 1.3 million to 5.6 million.[28] Males from the working class were increasingly drawn into the metropole's imperial concerns as their vote was courted.

As early twentieth-century British feminists began to agitate more visibly and more forcefully for the franchise to be extended to women, national, imperial, class, and gender anxieties intertwined. Such entangled anxieties were only heightened by the decision taken to adopt violent methods by a small but influential section of the British suffrage movement in 1905. British women had been campaigning for the vote since the 1860s.[29] Little progress was made, however, until many of the smaller influential suffrage societies across Britain gathered under the umbrella organisation, the National Union of Women's Suffrage Societies (NUWSS), which was established in 1897 and was led for the most part by Millicent Garrett Fawcett. Emmeline Pankhurst and her daughter, Christabel Pankhurst, who were dissatisfied with the NUWSS's lack of progress, formed the Women's Social and Political Union (WSPU) in 1903. The 'confrontational, assertive and "unladylike" tactics' of the new militant WSPU re-energised the suffrage campaign by forcing the feminist issue into the limelight.[30] From 1905 to 1912, the campaign took the form of heckling politicians and noisily disrupting political meetings, as well as a willingness to go to prison rather than paying fines for 'unruly' behaviour. From 1912 until their cessation with the beginning of the Great War in 1914, suffragettes,[31] as members of the WSPU were labelled, moved on to more violent and often illegal forms of activity such as mass window-breaking raids; vandalising post boxes; attacking public property, including setting fire to buildings; and going on hunger strike.[32] In 1918, a small section of British and Irish women were granted the right to vote for a Westminster parliament. British women had to campaign for another decade before they were granted the same voting rights as British men in 1928.

The unladylike tactics of the militant wing of the suffrage movement only exacerbated existing gender anxieties. By the turn of the century, many in England were intellectualising about how degenerate, decadent, and over-civilised the increasingly middle-class and bureaucratic imperial centre was. A significant aspect of this degeneracy was the blurring of gender divisions. The existence of manly women—epitomised by the iconic feminist transgressor, the New Woman—and unmanly men—exemplified by the 'bogey' of the 'hen-pecked, lower middle-class clerk'[33]—called into doubt the naturalness of the gender divisions underpinning middle-class notions of respectability. Respectability dictated that men were the active doers—what Anne McClintock deems the 'the forward-thrusting agency of national progress'.[34] Women were the inactive, metaphorical holders of the nation's values: the conservative repository of the national archaic.[35] When transgressive feminists agitated for what seemed to be the right to ape or even supplant the British man's role as embodiment of national progress—by challenging a national narrative that positioned women as 'inherently atavistic'—they jeopardised the relevancy of the moral and social codes that underpinned and justified the so-called imperial civilising mission.[36] They threatened the stability of the Empire, for how could the metropole transport and transplant British notions of middle-class respectability—those on which the Empire depended—if its own women were unsettling these very values?

Not surprisingly, feminist agitation in the imperial centre provoked a very passionate, heated, even violent, exchange between those keen for reform and those protective of the status quo. Many British men were against women getting the vote. The reasons for some of this opposition are straightforward. Further expansion of the electorate would carry with it increasing complications. A greater diversity of voters and their interests would now have to be courted and catered to. The very real possibility also existed of men being forced to share power if women followed their demand for the vote with that of the right to stand for parliament.

However, what is perhaps surprising is the level of vitriolic opposition to the female franchise emanating from the community of 'good' patriotic

British women.[37] If women were granted the right—and the duty—to vote, then everyday practices would change. Patriotic women would feel compelled to fulfil their political duties—educating themselves more closely in the political affairs of the nation and physically lining up at polling booths to submit their votes—thereby adding to the large volume of responsibilities that women already bore (chief among these was, of course, giving birth to and rearing the country's future generations).

More significantly, though, many anti-suffragist women articulated their opposition to the granting of the franchise in terms of the corruption or complete dismantling of existing gendered emotional regimes. They were anxious not only about the possibility of a changed physical landscape—again, one which would now see women lining up at polling booths or even walking the corridors of parliament—but also about the very likely prospect of an altered emotional landscape. If women demanded a place in the public sphere, they would have to conform to masculine emotional standards. They would have to demonstrate that they could embody honour, for example. If they were to prove capable of doing this, what would happen to those aspects of traditional honour codes that protected women from male acts of aggression? What would happen to chivalry? Such a drastically changed physical landscape would mean that the emotional rules or codes governing the behaviour of each sex would no longer be maintained. Emotional standards would no longer be relied on to govern relations between the sexes. Emotional chaos threatened.

Communities of 'Good' Patriotic Women: Ireland and Australia

Women in the imperial centre were, of course, not the only women around the Empire to feel that their gendered emotional communities were under threat from radical feminist demands. Many in Ireland too were campaigning for the female franchise. They had been doing so since the 1870s.[38] Not only were many in Ireland campaigning for the vote but by 1912, the Irish suffrage campaign had also entered into a militant phase. The difference with Ireland was its positioning on the imperial spectrum and the reactions of its population to this positioning.

Ireland was England's oldest imperial possession and since the 1800 Act of Union it was either an equal partner in the United Kingdom of Great Britain and Ireland or, in the eyes of Irish nationalists certainly, an inferior member of the kingdom and a continued colonial possession. In the early decades of the twentieth century, there was a re-energised, organised push for national recognition in Ireland that was countered by strident Unionist opposition. However, as re-invigorated as the nationalist movement was, it was also a fractured one. On one side, there was the moderately nationalist

Irish Parliamentary Party led by John Redmond who wanted a home-based parliament in Ireland—a Commonwealth parliament still subservient to the Westminster imperial parliament. On the other side of the nationalist debate there were the radicals who wanted complete separation from Britain—an independent Ireland free of all imperial ties, equal or subservient. These latter activists were represented in the main by Sinn Féin, whose aspirations for complete autonomy were clearly present in its title, translated from the Gaelic as 'We, Ourselves'.

Not surprisingly, feminist activists in Ireland were as divided on the national question as Irish men. There were feminists who were loyal to the union with Britain and who played a pivotal role in Unionist politics of the time. However, by the early twentieth century, a large proportion of Irish feminists were nationalist in outlook: either those supporting the more popular moderate Home Rulers, or the minority of more extreme separatists supporting or being supported by Sinn Féin.[39]

Women on both sides of the Irish Sea were connected by the fact that they were ruled by the same male British parliament over which they had no control. British and Irish feminists' desires to empower women through enfranchising them made them part of the same network of suffrage activists. British and Irish feminists referenced each other's campaigns; exchanged funding, ideas, and approaches; and travelled across national spaces. British organisations on both sides of the suffrage debate established branches in Ireland, including the NUWSS, the WSPU, and the Anti-Suffrage League (later the National League for Opposing Woman Suffrage (NLOWS)).[40] Those activists who shared a commitment to using militant tactics were also arrested and imprisoned across both national spaces.[41] However, these various ties with the British movement complicated suffrage politics in Ireland even further. For example, whereas some, mainly Unionist, women welcomed British organisations on Irish soil, others, nationalist in outlook, increasingly considered the presence of dominating, imperialist organisations in anti-colonial Ireland to be highly problematic.[42] Divisions between the two national feminist communities were to grow more pronounced as the Irish nationalist campaign picked up pace and as British resentment of demands for separatism became more manifest.

The existence of links, however tenuous or fluid, between the Irish and the British suffrage movements—including the combined pressure exerted by Irish and British suffragists on Irish nationalist politicians—complicated Irish nationalist politics more generally.[43] While the moderate Irish Parliamentary Party, which held the balance of power in the Westminster parliament, was trying to push through a Home Rule Bill to secure a home-based parliament in Ireland, Irish feminists were campaigning for a clause for the female franchise to be inserted into that bill. Nationalist politicians largely opposed such a move on the grounds that inserting such a clause might give British politicians opposed to Irish Home Rule further reason for delaying its inception. Many nationalist women also saw wisdom in delaying the introduction of female suffrage until Home Rule had been secured. Not only that but also a number of Irish nationalist women were vehemently opposed to Irish women campaigning for the vote in an English parliament—what these radical nationalists saw as an enemy parliament. And so, for the purposes of this study of shame and gendered emotional regimes, what is so interesting about the Irish context is that some of the most strident anti-suffragism in Ireland—seemingly paradoxically—emanates from these Irish nationalist feminist women. Despite their strong, almost oppositional ideological preferences, conservative British female imperialists and radical Irish nationalist women had at least their opposition to women getting the vote in British parliament in common. These communities of Irish and British women patriots were bound together by their resort to shame and shaming to protect their respective nationalist priorities.

Across the far reaches of the Empire, in Australia, patriotic women were fighting a different battle. The Australian colonies were some of the first to grant women the right to vote globally and, in the case of the newly federated Australian Commonwealth, one of the first to simultaneously grant women the right to vote and to stand for parliament (1902). Therefore, those women who did not want the burden of the vote had no choice but to exercise that responsibility. Patriotic women then took it upon themselves to educate fellow women in their new duties as voting citizens. Knowing the eyes of the world—and certainly those of Britain, the Mother Country[44]— were on them, their fight, as they saw it, was to prove themselves loyal citizens of the Commonwealth and the Empire.

Despite feminist scholars' attempts to dispel it, in some quarters, the myth still persists that Australian men gave their womenfolk the vote as a kind of 'gift'.[45] However, the pathway to female enfranchisement in the Australian colonies was not straightforward or uniform. In 1901, Australia transformed from a group of six British colonies to a federated Commonwealth of Australia. A new federal parliament that dealt with matters pertaining to the Commonwealth as a whole was established. But, in keeping with a federal structure, the former colonies, now states, kept their separate parliaments. Most campaigns for the vote in the colonies (later states) began in the 1880s, although the character of each campaign differed. None were militant, and most took the form of lobbying politicians, raising petitions, sending deputations to parliament, and arranging lectures, public meetings, and speaking tours (usually across vast distances). The intensity of opposition differed in each colony/state too. Therefore, whereas women in South Australia won the vote in 1894, Western Australia followed in 1899. In 1902 and 1903, respectively, women were granted the right to vote in New South Wales and Tasmania. Queensland granted suffrage in 1905. After an acrimonious campaign, Victorian women were only enfranchised in 1908. This meant that Victorian women had to endure the frustrating experience of already voting in two Commonwealth elections before they could do so in their own state.[46]

Importantly, the vote in Australia was racialised. Aboriginal women and men were disenfranchised whether through informal means or formal legislation. For example, indigenous people in Queensland and Western Australia were not enfranchised in 1902.[47] They were not to be granted the right to vote until 1962. The Australian woman's vote, therefore, was a predominantly white vote. The majority of suffragists failed to prioritise the voting rights of non-white women in this white settler-colonial society. In failing to do this, they proved themselves complicit with reigning views about the racial superiority of the Anglo-Saxons and the inevitability of the demise of the indigenous race.[48] This complicity of white feminists in racial exclusion has rendered complicated and uncomfortable some discussions about the legacies of the early feminist movement. At the time, whiteness and the task of not only carrying on the so-called British race but also using the unadulterated air of the 'new' world to rejuvenate that 'race' was a charge that white women in Australasia took very seriously.[49]

To a large degree, then, white women voters' priorities chimed with the political aspirations and values of the newly federated Commonwealth. These national priorities were bolstered by perceived threats—territorial and racial—both from within and outside of Australia's borders. For instance, Australia harboured sub-imperial ambitions in the Pacific region.[50] And so, like Britain, it experienced the threat of imperial competition from Western powers, including France, Germany, and the United States, who had territorial designs on the region. Australia pressed Britain to protect its interests in the area but found that Britain itself was under pressure to maintain its imperial dominance in the scramble for territory seemingly unclaimed by the Western powers. In light of this increased pressure, the imperial centre expected its Dominions, including Australia, to become more self-sufficient.[51] Given its loyalty to the Empire, Australia also worried about the spread of international socialism. Socialism represented a threat to Western forms of imperial control. Therefore, in the early decades of the twentieth century, Australia shared a number of political aspirations and anxieties with the Mother Country: it worried about its imperial aspirations and about the perceived threat international socialism represented to traditional models of imperialism, especially from 1917 onwards.

Australian concerns also diverged from those of Britain. In contrast to the imperial centre whose race 'problems' were largely confined to the colonial outposts of the Empire, Australia was home to ever-intensifying racial anxieties.[52] Racial tensions had always been present in Australia given the nature of British colonisation in the region and the frontier violence between the incoming white settlers and the indigenous inhabitants. However, at this time, the new white Commonwealth was more concerned with Asia than it was with its depleting indigenous population. It looked warily towards

Japan as Japanese expansionary intentions with regard to places such as China, Korea, and Russia were imagined as a threat to Australia's borders. This perceived external danger was bolstered by the apparent threat from within represented primarily by the presence of cheap Chinese labour in the Australian colonies.

The move for Federation, then, was accompanied by that for a supposedly racially pure Australia—a White Australia.[53] Australia's racial policies were given formal recognition in the new Commonwealth parliament's 1901 Immigration Restriction Act, which allowed for selective immigration based on language tests. Other laws followed that discriminated against the non-white population already living in Australia by denying them rights to citizenship, welfare benefits, certain occupations, and, in some instances, land.[54] Australian politics and culture may have shared racial ideologies with the imperial centre, but its affairs were directed by policies of racism that were significantly different from any enacted in the British metropole. The unique nature of Australian women's racial anxieties were clearly evident in their political writings after enfranchisement.

On the issue of feminist militancy, Australian society avoided such violent disruptions, but some Australian women still managed to have a hand in them in Britain. For example, a number of prominent Australian suffragists— many of whom were born in the United Kingdom—travelled to Britain and either supported or directly participated in the militant movement there. Among these were Dora Montefiore, Nellie Martel, Jessie Street, and the more spectacular Muriel Matters (who is renowned for an infamous escapade during which she threw out suffrage pamphlets from an airship over London not long after she had been released from prison for chaining herself to the Ladies' Gallery grille in the House of Commons). Perth-based Bessie Rischbieth, who became very conservative in later life, was also swept up by the energy of the militant movement when she visited London in 1913. Victoria's Vida Goldstein toured Britain and championed the movement there in 1911.[55]

As mentioned earlier, the issue of the woman vote affected relations between the Irish and the British. So too did it affect colonial-imperial relations between Australia and Britain. Although now a Commonwealth parliament, the Australian parliament was still in a subordinate position to the Westminster parliament. Yet Australian women had managed to trump their sisters in the Mother Country by obtaining the right to vote decades before them. These factors combined to alter the nature of the relationship between feminists in the metropole and those in the peripheries. As Australian historian of British and Australian feminism Barbara Caine elucidates, the international woman suffrage movement allowed antipodean women their first opportunity 'to turn the imperial tables as it were, and to offer their unfortunate British sisters help, guidance and advice'.[56] The Australian example certainly worked to challenge metropolitan assumptions about the superior positioning of women in the imperial centre compared with those in the Empire's outposts. This turning of the tables can be seen in London's Great Suffrage Procession of June 1911. Many of the Australian women participating in the suffrage movement in Britain took part in the procession and in doing so they instructed their imperial mother to 'Trust the women Mother as I have done' via a banner carried by Margaret Fisher and Vida Goldstein. The very words of this banner reveal a collective belief in the advanced state of Australia's approach to relations between the sexes on the matter of citizenship. This was a sense of superiority that extended to other facets of society. For instance, activists such as Goldstein and Rischbieth certainly believed that the influence of the woman's vote on issues such as prostitution and employment in Australia was far in advance of conditions prevailing in the metropolitan centre.[57]

The pressure that newly enfranchised female patriots in Australia placed on themselves to exercise the vote in a manner befitting rational, loyal women of the Empire, while cognisant that they were in many ways in a position of superiority in comparison to the women of the imperial centre, is evident in their political discourse. As in Britain and Ireland, awareness of national anxieties intersected with those about gender to produce a passionate body of political writing that acknowledged the important role that emotions played in the attempt to protect and police gendered emotional communities.

Imperial ties connected women across Britain, Ireland, and Australia, whether those women wanted them to or not. Whether loyal or disloyal, each group of national womanhood operated within the same imperial framework. They were affected by similar, if not the same, legislations. They had to frame their aspirations by referencing existing assumptions, for instance, about their country's position on the hierarchical imperial spectrum or about the nature of British or non-British values. Knowledges were shared as ideas and values circulated around the Empire. Therefore, despite the many different circumstances shaping their individual national existences, these separate but linked communities of patriotic womanhood were often compelled to refer to each other when asserting their particular political aspirations. In this book, I look at both the national and the transnational dimensions of patriotic women's interactions with political emotions and national and international anxieties. I use their political writings to trace how these women understood the unique and the shared elements of their political and emotional experiences.

Women's Political Writing: The Sources

In the nineteenth century, the issue of women's rights received abundant attention in the pages of the British periodical press.[58] However, by the beginning of the twentieth century, as the campaign for suffrage intensified and grew increasingly contentious, the overwhelmingly male press either omitted reporting about the women's movement or did so in a highly skewed manner. Therefore, some feminist organisations decided to establish their own suffrage presses. Historian of feminist media Maria DiCenzo asserts that print media was the most effective way of circulating ideas at the beginning of the twentieth century. It was, therefore, the most suitable vehicle for attempting to influence public opinion.[59]

Feminist publications were established to accommodate discussions taking place around the issue of women's rights, but they were also intended to mobilise readers—predominantly female readers—for political activism.[60] In the case of the suffrage movement, suffrage periodicals and pamphlets were aimed at harnessing the energies of confirmed or aspiring suffrage activists. Suffrage publications were, then, a crucial part of the suffrage movement's strategy.[61] They were also to become an integral aspect of the anti-suffrage campaign, too, as anti-suffragist women, who felt they had a lot to lose if the vote was foisted on them, were moved to establish their own dedicated publication outlets. Women on both sides of the suffrage divide used the women's press to foster a firmer sense of an appropriate gendered political community.

These papers were dedicated to the issue of women's suffrage, but they produced articles that were also much broader in scope. As DiCenzo iterates, granting women citizenship on an equal basis with men was seen by many in turn-of-the-century society to have the potential to dramatically alter national life: law, marriage, family, educational institutions, and professions, as well as the political affairs of the state.[62] Discussions taking place within women's political publications reflected the breadth of the women's rights debate.

These papers also worked to accommodate diverging points of view. In the United Kingdom, the feminist community, for example, was not homogenous. Rather, it was varied, even fractured. The feminist press mirrored the multifaceted nature of the movement. In some instances, this was more prominent than in others. For example, the highly fractured nature of the Irish feminist movement was reflected in the pages of its press as feminist nationalists and nationalist feminists jostled for position.[63]

These women's papers also referenced and responded to the views of their political opponents. For instance, the WSPU's official organ, *Votes for Women*, strategically kept abreast of developments taking place in anti-suffragist politics. The paper frequently referred to comments made by prominent anti-feminists or referenced articles published in their opponents' press, such as the NLOWS organ, the *Anti-Suffrage Review* (the *Review*). The *Review* did likewise.[64] These publications offer historians access to sites of struggle both within and between feminist organisations.[65] Looking across a selection of suffragist and anti-suffragist media also allows historians to gain insight into the debates taking place at the feminist/anti-feminist crossroads.

In its first edition in 1908, the British paper, the *Review*, declared that the body it represented—the Women's National Anti-Suffrage League, which was to amalgamate with the men's anti-suffrage league two years later to become the National League for Opposing Woman Suffrage—was driven to organise itself in response to the undignified actions of campaigning suffragists, particularly those adopting aggressive or violent tactics.[66] The *Review* explained that it had two overarching aims: one was to inspire and gather wide public support for opposition to woman suffrage through extra-parliamentary propaganda; the other was to 'exert direct pressure on parliamentary decision-makers'.[67] In the period preceding the war at least, male members of the League—including Lord Curzon and Lord Cromer—preferred pursuing a single-minded campaign to persuade male politicians of the dangers of female suffrage, while leading female members—such as Lady Jersey and the renowned novelist, Mary Ward—favoured using public appearances, speeches, and articles in the popular press and in the *Review* to garner mass public support for their cause and hopefully stimulate debate about the wider 'Woman Question'.[68] The paper had a wide readership drawn from members of the League. The League boasted 42,000 subscribing members and 15,000 adherents by 1914. Members were drawn from branches in England, Wales, and Ireland, and the affiliated Scottish League for Opposing Woman Suffrage.[69]

In contrast to Irish feminist papers, which I discuss next, the pages of the *Review* contained political commentaries that were substantially uniform. That is to say, few contributors to the paper expressed views that were at odds with the majority opinion. They were united in their condemnation of feminist actions and feminist demands, and shared many reasons for doing so. This is not to argue that the views they articulated were in any way superficial or simplistic. Nor is it to claim that anti-suffragists were lacking in individuality. Brian Harrison, an early historian of the anti-suffrage campaign, warned against taking such a position. All too often, he argued in 1978, the efforts of the anti-suffrage movement have been presented as 'misguided and unimportant', or their ideals have been dismissed on the basis of their eventual failure, thereby consigning this unsuccessful movement to 'history's rubbish-heap'. This conservative mindset, he asserted, was not singular, shallow, or uncomplicated.[70] Since then, Julia Bush has added her cautions. In 2007, Bush argued that modern histories of suffragism 'all too often ignore its committed female critics, and fail to evaluate the widespread support for their views'. Thus, she said, 'The women anti-suffragists have become eclipsed within an opposition which was itself marginalized by historical failure'.[71]

A much larger body of research exists on the triumphant flank of the British suffrage campaign than on the losing side, although interest in anti-suffrage politics and anti-feminism more generally has grown. From the 1990s onwards, more historians and literary scholars—including Lucy Delap, Valerie Sanders, Julia Bush, Tamara Wagner, and David Thackeray—have broadened current understandings of the sheer diversity of late Victorian and Edwardian conceptions of female citizenship from the point of view of women writers and activists. In doing so, they have challenged simple applications of the label 'anti-feminist' to women involved in anti-suffrage and other related campaigns.[72] In this book, I sometimes adopt the term anti-feminist, but I do not do so uncritically. Women anti-suffragists were situated on the anti-feminist side of gender politic, but their reasons for adopting such a stance were deep, complex, and multilayered.

As I aim to show, women had many reasons for opposing the female franchise, and much of the time this came down to protecting a much-cherished set of gendered emotional standards and a gendered emotional community. Therefore, whereas I contribute to the still relatively small body of scholarship focusing on the women of the anti-suffragist movement, I do so in a manner that departs from existing histories. These histories explain the reasons women had for opposing female enfranchisement. They also highlight some of the strategies employed by these women. However, they do not examine in detail the emotional techniques deployed by anti-suffragist women in the attempt to reform or ostracise the aberrant feminist. Nor do they analyse anti-suffragist objections through the lens of gendered emotional communities and regimes, the concern for which, I argue, lay at the heart of many of their arguments.

The Irish feminist movement exemplifies the difficulties of attaching the 'anti-feminist' label to women opposed to the campaign for the vote much more obviously than even the British anti-suffrage campaign. As outlined previously, the Irish feminist movement was highly fractured. Not only that but also some of the most strident opposition to Irish women gaining the vote in British parliament came from other Irish feminist groups rather than simply emanating from self-professed, anti-feminist organisations. Therefore, to access the views of women opposed to the campaign for the vote there, I have had to consult feminist rather than anti-feminist periodicals.[73] As the preeminent organisation opposed to the British parliament granting women the right to vote, the NLOWS had claimed the right to establish branches in Ireland, which, like the rest of the United Kingdom of Great Britain and Ireland, was ruled directly by the Westminster parliament. The views expressed by the Irish members of this organisation mirror those of fellow members across the Irish Sea. The League's paper, the *Review*, accommodated the opinions of all members, British and Irish. Therefore, in order to access a specifically Irish response to the campaign for the vote in British parliament, I have looked to nationalist women's papers produced there. My interest is in patriotic women. I interpret 'patriotic' in the early twentieth-century Irish sense, as demonstrated by the intensifying majority anti-colonial nationalist campaign, to be Irish nationalist rather than British Unionist.

The volatile nature of politics in early twentieth-century Ireland, including the wars it engendered, produced a fractured feminist movement and, consequently, a fractured feminist archive. Therefore, I have chosen to examine a number of publications with short publication runs. In particular, I have selected *Bean na hEireann* (the *Bean*), translating as *Woman of Ireland*, which ran from 1908 to 1911 and which pronounced itself the first Irish nationalist feminist paper, and the *Irish Citizen* (the *Citizen*), a suffrage journal that emerged in 1912 in response to widening divisions among British and Irish suffragists and lasted until 1920 when its presses were destroyed by British forces in the Anglo-Irish War (Irish War of Independence).

The *Bean* was the organ of Inghinidhe na hEireann (Daughters of Ireland), a radical nationalist, pro-militant women's group that was to later merge with Cumman na mBan, the women's wing of the Irish Republican Army. The *Bean* labelled itself 'the first and only Nationalist Woman's paper'.[74] It promoted itself as a paper advocating separatism, feminism, and 'the interest of Irishwomen generally'. As Karen Steele explains, it 'quickly developed into an important platform for advanced nationalist women seeking a voice in the growing liberation movements of nationalism, feminism and socialism'.[75] Written mostly by women assuming strong Celtic personae, the paper also found room for commentary by male nationalists including Arthur Griffith, James Stephens, and Bulmer Hobson.[76] For the most part, the *Bean* was opposed to Irish women asking British men for political concessions. It was, therefore, anti-suffragist, though by no means anti-feminist.

The *Citizen* was the paper of the Irish Women's Franchise League (IWFL), the 'most active and most militant of all the suffrage groups in Ireland'.[77] It was certainly feminist in outlook and grew increasingly nationalist, although it initially stated that it was open to all suffragists, nationalist and Unionist.[78] Like the British WSPU, the IWFL was born out of frustration and discontent with the ineffectiveness of the older non-militant suffrage movement. This suffrage association was not typical of other organisations in Ireland. Not only was it militant but also largely intellectual in nature in that a number of the organisers held university degrees.[79] The *Citizen*, established in 1912 by Margaret and James Cousins and Hanna and Francis Sheehy Skeffington, avowed that it was a paper whose intentions were to represent Irish suffragism, as distinct from the campaign in England. Within months of its establishment, the paper reported that it was selling perhaps 3,000 copies per week with a readership of over 10,000.[80] It functioned as a paper that would give a distinctly Irish voice to the suffrage campaign, thereby distinguishing it further from the British movement. However, by giving that campaign a distinctively Irish voice, it also operated as a retort to those anti-suffrage nationalists who had argued all along that the suffrage movement was an English and therefore a foreign and an un-Irish movement.[81]

Although a feminist paper, the *Citizen* suits the purposes of this book, which is to access how communities of patriotic womanhood understood the interconnections between gender and national politics and emotions. In its pages, the paper accommodated divergent views—those from across the divided Irish feminist community—even if the editors allowed their voices to have the final say. Therefore, it is useful for capturing a range of women's voices on issues of importance to patriotic women and to the Irish nation.

The Australian Women's National League (AWNL) was established in 1904 in the state of Victoria. The League listed as its four objectives to support loyalty to the throne and empire, to combat socialism, to educate women in politics, and to safeguard the interests of the home, women, and children.[82] At this stage, Victoria was the only state not to have given women the vote, even though these women were already voting in federal elections. The AWNL was initially opposed to the woman vote. However, by 1906, it pledged support for enfranchisement.[83] It was an expansive and influential body of patriotic women. During the First World War, AWNL membership grew to 54,000, across 420 branches, making it the largest body of organised women in Australia and perhaps even 'the largest explicitly women's political organisation in the world' at that time.[84] In 1907, on the eve of Victorian women being enfranchised, the League established its paper, the *Woman* (*Woman*).

The paper dedicated itself to educating the women of the country who now had the right to vote in federal parliament in their new duties as enfranchised citizens of the new Commonwealth, whether they welcomed those duties or not.[85] In the first issue of *Woman*, the editors stated that it was 'an Australian magazine, owned, managed, and edited by women' and designed 'to enlist the influence and the sympathies of women throughout the Commonwealth'.[86] The overarching aims of the paper were 'to encourage the work of Australian women, to promote unity of thought on subjects of national moment, and to form a factor in interesting and amusing women in wholesome and common-sense directions' and all from 'an anti-socialistic standpoint'.[87] The large majority of women may well have opposed the granting of the female franchise—they may well have had it 'thrust upon them'—but now that they had it, patriotic women had to be willing to accept the duty as a serious responsibility.[88]

Woman expressed the necessity for unity. The disparate Australian states had to have a unity of purpose. Therein lay the best means of protecting Australia's welfare. The paper promoted a similar unity of purpose among the new female electorate. The AWNL was a state-based organisation in Victoria. Nevertheless, it issued the call to all Australian women to act as a unified whole in order to fortify the new nation. The interests and needs of individual states were still important, the paper instructed, but 'there should be union on those matters of joint importance which affect us as citizens, not merely of a State, but of a Commonwealth'.[89] In the pages of *Woman*, patriotic Australian women articulated their understandings of intersecting national, imperial, and gender anxieties. They used the paper as a vehicle for their attempted construction of a patriotic and unified community of dedicated newly enfranchised political women.

The sets of political publications analysed in this book were produced in different national sites and accordingly responded to different national priorities. However, they were also linked by a number of factors. As previously mentioned, the three communities of patriotic womanhood were linked by their ties to the British Empire. The women leading these political organisations and writing for their particular papers were educated and sometimes privileged or renowned members of their societies. It can be assumed that they were largely Christian in outlook—certainly, a Christian ethos pervades much of their discourse—although they rarely specified denomination in their writing. Given that their shared remit was to produce or protect a community of patriotic or nationalist womanhood from the feminist threat, it makes sense that they did not exclude potential members on the basis of religious denomination.[90] Each group of patriotic womanhood had the best interests of their respective nations at heart amid transforming imperial conditions and connections. Moreover, although men contributed to the periodicals in question, these journals were dedicated to discussing women's issues, specifically the woman vote. The papers were endorsed by women's political organisations. Therefore, I tend not to discern between female and male writers (even where the sex of the writer is known, which is frequently not the case). Instead, I take the collection of articles produced by each organisation as one body of writing representing the interests of discreet groups of national womanhood. In the rare instances when I do single out the sex of the author, I do so because I think a distinctly male contribution adds to my understanding of gendered emotional regimes.

Locating Emotions in Women's Political Writing

In this study, I argue that early twentieth-century women who participated in the political lives of their nations—willingly or only reluctantly—articulated and used emotions in a way that is revealing of just how cognisant they were, not only of the place of emotions in political life but also of the need for a strategic deployment of emotions for political ends. More than this, these women also acknowledged the specifically gendered nature of these emotions and their deployment of them. This self-awareness helps historians to locate the emotions in their texts.

I adopt a number of approaches to locating and analysing the emotions in women's past political writings. These include identifying emotional vocabularies and ascertaining active emotional processes. In the first place, I analyse the vocabulary of emotions as it relates to shame and related emotions, including honour, courage, chivalry, embarrassment, and indignation. Often anti-suffragist women wrote using direct or clear emotional expressions. Marie Corelli, for example, made direct reference to disgust, shame, indignation, and humiliation. Often anti-suffragist women writing for the *Review* used similar variants of shame to express their opposition to feminist demands. Sometimes they referred to affective responses to feminist behaviour too. For example, some writers professed to blush or burn with shame. I detail these as I come across them.

Secondly, I seek out descriptions of active emotional processes—of emotions in action. This is about unearthing more embedded understandings of emotions. It involves reading into the text for the purpose of understanding how women used emotions to further their political intentions. Such a process requires commencing with a definition of a particular emotion and then forming an understanding of how that emotion performs. The issue of definition is important here. Historians disagree on the matter of how rigid our definitions of individual emotions have to be before beginning the search for them in historical documents. German historian Ute Frevert has called for rigidly defined emotions. Fellow scholar of German history Alon Confino has countered that 'a tight definition of "emotions"' can actually be counter-productive. 'With such a definition', he asserts, 'we cannot capture the looseness and fluidity of emotions, which is precisely what characterized them'. A broad definition of emotions is enough, he argues, to start the historian on her or his research. 'Ultimately', Confino states, 'what is important is how people in the past defined emotions; the historian's best move is to start with their understandings.'[91] Once a partial definition is achieved, my aim is to understand how the emotion worked.

Shame—that fear of being judged deficient—for example, was about threatening to remove a potential transgressor from a community to which she or he attached value. Therefore, shame was present in a text where anti-suffragist women pointed out feminists' lack of worthiness as women—where they attempted to remove them from the community of 'good' womanhood that they had defined. I discuss this further in Chapter 1. Embarrassment is another case in point. As I discuss in Chapter 3, embarrassment is brought about when someone transgresses an accepted rule—when they should have known better. When British anti-suffragists expressed surprise, even dismay, at antipodean women daring to place themselves on an equal footing with their metropolitan sisters, they revealed that they felt vicarious embarrassment for Australian women who should have known better than to compare themselves with their superiors. Having the franchise in the insignificant colonies, for instance, was not comparable with having voting power in the centre of a vast imperial network. Shame or embarrassment might not have been cited directly in these instances, but they were both at work in the text.

My intention is not to judge how effective these emotional processes were. I keep Jill Locke's caution about the limitations of shaming in mind. Rather, I am keen to gauge just how effective early twentieth-century political women considered shame and shaming to be, given the abundance of it in their writings. I am also concerned with accessing what these women understood of the emotional milieu in which they—and their shaming strategies—operated.

Defining particular emotions and understanding how they operated in the early twentieth century is a complex task. I deal with the complications of this task in two ways. Firstly, I often quote lengthy passages from women's political writing to enable the reader to access how women at the time understood particular emotions and to discern how the emotions worked within the text. Secondly, I deal with definitions of distinct emotions related to shame and explanations of how they function in the relevant individual chapter. For example, whereas I explain in detail the workings of shame in Chapter 1 'Shaming Unwomanly Women' and embarrassment in Chapter 3 'Embarrassing the Imperial Centre', I delve into understandings of specific virtues such as honour and chivalry and courage in the chapters relevant to those virtues. I elaborate on nationalised concepts of honour in Chapter 2 'Reversing the Shame of British Colonisation' and Chapter 4 'Shaming British-Australia'. In Chapter 5 'War and the Dishonourable British Feminist', I examine how masculinised honour codes fared in wartime. I analyse moral and physical courage in Chapter 6 'Shaming Manhood to Embody Courage' and chivalry in Chapter 7 'The Shame of the Violent Woman'. The ever-present and ever-versatile emotion of shame—connected as it is to all of the aforementioned emotional virtues—threads through and links every chapter.

The Structure of the Book

One immediate concern for anti-suffrage women when contemplating the possibility of female enfranchisement was the impact it would have on accepted concepts of womanhood and notions of femininity. They worried that taking so much time away from the family and the home to participate in a public campaign—marching in the streets and participating in public meetings and political deputations—would adversely affect the well-being of the family. It would, therefore, paint a negative picture of womanhood as a community of individuals who were selfish enough to abandon the sex's primary duty as carer for and guardian of the family. Womanhood, anti-suffragist women argued, was not made for the cold, harsh, and competitive world of politics. The emotional regimes guiding men's and women's experiences were not the same. Women were not emotionally prepared to participate in the masculinised public realm. This was not in keeping with feminine norms. For feminists to attempt to force their sisters to take on this foreign and anxiety-inducing obligation was cruel and unwomanly. That too was not in keeping with feminine norms. In Chapter 1, I examine how British anti-suffragist women understood the shame of the feminist transgressor. I analyse how and why they attempted to shame their suffragist sisters into abandoning their political crusade. How did they understand shame as a politicised emotion and shaming as a gendered political tool? Did Irish feminists opposed to the Irish suffrage campaign adopt similar tactics for similar reasons? How did enfranchised women in Australia—those who had not wanted the vote—respond to the portrait of the shamelessly unfeminine political woman?

Patriotic women across the British Empire were keenly attuned to discussions about national honour and its antithesis, shame. However, their concerns about this issue assumed different forms, reflecting different national priorities. Whereas Irish women situated across the intersecting branches of nationalist politics lamented the emasculation of the once proud Irish nation, Australian women were anxious that their young virile Commonwealth would prove itself a worthy member of the Empire's family of nations. At the centre of that vast imperial network, British women worried that any slur cast on their national reputation would mean the fall of a noble and enriching empire. In Chapter 2, I examine how patriotic Irish women approached the issue of the gendered nature of national honour. These women were painfully attuned to the shame of the colonised nation and colonised manhood. They were also aware that modern society directed that only men were equipped to restore the nation's honour. These gender restrictions and the perceived abject state of their menfolk frustrated enthusiastic female patriots. How did these nationalist women respond to the existence of physical impediments and emotional regulations that prevented them from actively restoring their country's pride? How did they challenge the gendered nature of prevailing honour codes?

In Chapter 3, I look specifically at the relationship between Britain and Australia from the point of view of the two communities of patriotic womanhood. Australian women had already been granted the right to vote. Loyal British-Australian women desired that women in the imperial centre would be likewise enfranchised. That way, they could all form part of a transnational community of enfranchised loyal empire womanhood. Anti-suffragists in Britain considered that experiments in the insignificant colonial outposts had no bearing on affairs at the heart of the vast and troublesome imperial network. How, then, did those British anti-suffragists respond to antipodean women's attempts to advise the Mother Country about how to treat its womanhood? How did Australian women respond to claims emanating from the imperial centre that they were guilty of transgressing emotional rules guiding relations between the metropole and the former colonies? What do these exchanges reveal about the nature of embarrassment, vicarious or otherwise?

Loyal British-Australians may have deflected metropolitan assertions of embarrassment, even shame, over their promotion of enfranchised models of womanhood, but they were not free from the effects of core-periphery anxieties of a more general nature. Of all the Empire's women, patriotic Australian women considered themselves to be uniquely burdened with the responsibility of guarding against national shame. Many of them had not wanted the vote. But now, as voting citizens, they had a direct hand in choosing how the honour of the young white nation was protected. Their anxieties, therefore, were twofold. On the one hand, they worried that the new nation would not prove itself a mature and loyal member of the imperial family of nations and would instead bring shame upon itself and the Empire. On the other hand, patriotic women expressed a deep concern that women citizens would not perform this new role with the level of political wisdom and patriotic zeal required of them. In Chapter 4, I examine how patriotic Australian women used shame in their attempts to protect the integrity of their identity as loyal British-Australians.

In Chapter 5, I extend the discussions of national honour found in previous chapters. While patriotic women in the Australian outposts worried that they were not proving themselves worthy of the beneficence of the Motherland, women in that Motherland were to be found besmirching the name of that great imperial centre with impunity. The disruptive public actions of pre-war militant and non-militant British suffragists had brought shame to the nation. Their deviant behaviour only intensified with the onset of the Great War. Before the war, anti-suffragists opposed women's entry into the public sphere on the grounds that these women were not trained to adhere to the masculine honour codes that directed men's participation in that realm. Inexperienced women would only affect a corruption of those gendered codes with their unwarranted and unwanted intrusions. Now, with the outbreak of war, these same deviant women were demanding expanded access to public roles. They were partially successful in securing this access. For anti-suffragists witnessing the debacle, the only outcomes secured by this dubious success seemed to be the appearance of duplicitous women politicians who could not honour wartime truces and vampirish battlefield nurses who preyed on sick and wounded soldiers for political favours. In this chapter, I analyse the use of shame to oppose the dishonourable wartime feminist and her efforts to degrade the moral and emotional fabric of wartime British society.

In the final two chapters of the book, I address the gendered and emotional dimensions of violence. Courage and chivalry were integral aspects of masculine honour codes. Violence underpinned these codes. Men could resort to male-on-male violence publicly to restore any lost honour. Women could not claim any active relationship with honour. They could not act in its name. Therefore, they could not enact violence publicly. They existed beyond the masculine realms of honour and violence. This was to be particularly pertinent when it came to World War One. Men were required to perform violence and abide by honour codes in the name of the State. Women were not. In Chapter 6, I analyse women's attitudes towards the gendered emotional virtue of courage. How did patriotic women who respected the boundaries dividing men's and women's emotional regimes react to men's displays of cowardice? Did they justify transgressing those boundaries in order to shame their menfolk into enlisting for the war? How did they use shame to motivate men to overcome cowardice at this crucial time in the histories of their respective nations? Did they challenge the gendered nature of courage, even during wartime?

In Chapter 7, I focus on women's violence, or their threats to embody violence, whether for feminist or nationalist reasons. The emotional virtue I draw on most in this chapter is chivalry. Chivalric codes emphasised manly attributes such as courage under fire, well-honed military skills, generosity in victory, and honour in victory or defeat. In an early twentieth-century context, such codes also placed an emphasis on exercising courtesy towards women. Many anti-suffragist women interpreted this courtesy in terms of protection from male acts of aggression. Adherence to notions of chivalry meant men, the physically stronger sex, promising women, the physically weaker sex, protection from violence (a promise of protection that was often more ethereal than real given the prevalence of domestic violence). What happened to those codes and promises when it was women perpetrating acts of violence—whether disruptive and unruly suffragettes or overly patriotic women agitating to fight alongside men on the frontlines of war? How did those women opposed to modern feminism's insistence on sexual equality—even physical equality—react to this seemingly supremely dangerous dismantling of gendered emotional regimes? What impact did national priorities and national narratives have on acceptances of or challenges to female acts of militancy? Did any of these patriotic women construct what might be called a feminist ethics of violence? How was violence used to attack the gendered nature of emotional regimes?

Notes

1 Marie Corelli, *Woman, or—Suffragette? A Question of National Choice* (London: Arthur Pearson, 1907) pp. 3–4.
2 Brian Masters, *Now Barabbas Was a Rotter: The Extraordinary Life of Marie Corelli* (London: Hamish Hamilton, 1978) p. 10. For other readings on Corelli, see Annette R. Federico, *Idol of Suburbia: Marie Corelli and Late-Victorian Literary Culture* (Charlottesville and London: University Press of Virginia, 2000); William Stuart Scott, *Corelli: The Story of a Friendship* (London: Hutchinson, 1955); Eileen Bigland, *Corelli: The Woman and the Legend* (London: Jarrolds, 1953); George Bullock, *Corelli: The Life and Death of a Best-Seller* (London: Constable, 1940); and Teresa Ransom, *Miss Marie Corelli, Queen of Victorian Bestsellers* (Gloucestershire: Sutton, 1999). Shorter readings include: Margaret B. McDowell, 'Marie Corelli', in Thomas F. Staley, ed., *Dictionary of Literary Biography, vol. 34: British Novelists, 1890–1929: Traditionalists* (Detroit: Gale Research Company, 1985) pp. 82–89; John Lucas, 'Marie Corelli', in James Vinson, ed., *Great Writers of the English Language: Novelists and Prose Writers* (London and Basingstoke: Macmillan, 1979) pp. 281–283; and Sandra Kemp, Charlotte Mitchell, and David Trotter, "Corelli", in *Edwardian Fiction: An Oxford Companion* (Oxford and New York: Oxford University Press, 1997) p. 77.
3 These quotations are taken from a selection of Corelli's fiction and non-fiction. For a more detailed discussion of Corelli's criticism of British feminists, see Sharon Crozier-De Rosa, 'Marie Corelli's British New Woman: A Threat to

Empire?', *The History of the Family*, vol. 14, no. 4 (2009); and Sharon Crozier-De Rosa, 'Marie Corelli, Shame and the "New Woman" in Fin-de-Siècle Britain', in David Lemmings, Ann Brooks, eds., *Emotions and Social Change: Historical and Sociological Perspectives* (Oxford: Routledge, 2014).

4 It is widely accepted that the term 'New Woman' was first coined in 1894 by the novelist Sarah Grand, pseudonym of Frances Elizabeth Belleuden Clarke, author of *The Heavenly Twins*, 1893. Grand's article entitled 'The New Aspect of the Woman Question,' in which she uses the term 'New Woman,' was published in 1894, in the *North American Review* (David Rubinstein, *Before the Suffragettes: Women's Emancipation in the 1890s* (Brighton: Harvester, 1986) pp. 15–16). See also Barbara Caine, *Victorian Feminists* (New York: Oxford University Press, 1992) p. 252. For an extensive discussion of Grand and the New Woman novel, see Teresa Mangum, *Married, Middlebrow, and Militant: Sarah Grand and the New Woman Novel* (Ann Arbor: The University of Michigan Press, 2001). Exact definitions of the term, New Woman, vary. For discussions of definition, see Sally Mitchell, 'New Women, Old and New', *Victorian Literature and Culture*, vol. 27, no. 2 (1999) pp. 579–588. Also see Crozier-De Rosa, 'Marie Corelli's British New Woman', pp. 416–429.

5 Early twentieth-century commentators tended to capitalise the term, Suffragette. However, since then, the word has entered into common usage, therefore I do not capitalise unless within quotations.

6 Corelli, *Woman, or—Suffragette?*, p. 20.

7 Corelli, *Woman, or—Suffragette?*, p. 18.

8 Jill Locke, 'Shame and the Future of Feminism', *Hypatia*, vol. 22, no. 4 (2007) pp. 146–162.

9 Here I am applying an understanding of transnationalism as the movement of people, institutions, and ideas across and through national boundaries. See Akira Iriye, 'Transnational History', *Contemporary European History*, vol. 13, no. 2 (2004) pp. 211–222, p. 212; Ian Tyrrell, 'Comparative and Transnational History', *Australian Feminist Studies*, vol. 22, no. 52 (2007) pp. 49–54, p. 49, and Ann Curthoys and Marilyn Lake, 'Introduction', in Ann Curthoys and Marilyn Lake, eds., *Connected Worlds: History in Transnational Perspective* (Canberra: ANU E-Press, 2005) pp. 6–20.

10 For a guide to the development of this area of historiography, see Susan Matt, 'Current Emotion Research in History: Or, Doing History from the Inside Out', *Emotions Review*, vol. 3, no. 1 (2011) pp. 117–124.

11 Barbara Rosenwein, 'Problems and Methods in the History of Emotions', *Passions in Context I: International Journal for the History and Theory of Emotions*, no. 1 (2010) pp. 1–32, p. 1. Also see Barbara Rosenwein, 'Worrying About Emotions in History', *The American Historical Review*, vol. 107, no. 3 (2002) pp. 921–945.

12 William M. Reddy, *The Navigation of Feeling: A Framework for the History of Emotions* (Cambridge: Cambridge University Press, 2001) p. 129.

13 See 'introduction' to a special edition of the journal *Rethinking History* on emotional styles, edited by Benno Gammerl, 'Emotional Styles—Concepts and Challenges', *Rethinking History*, vol. 16, no. 2 (2012) pp. 161–175, pp. 163-4.

14 Jeff Goodwin, James M. Jasper, Francesca Polletta, 'Introduction: Why Emotions Matter', in Jeff Goodwin, James M. Jasper, Francesca Polletta, *Passionate Politics: Emotions and Social Movements* (Chicago: University of Chicago Press, 2001) pp. 1–24, pp. 1–2. Since then, numerous scholars have produced research findings on the role of emotions in political life, whether current or historical. For example, see the work of political scientist Carol Johnson, including her article 'From Obama to Abbott: Gender Identity and the Politics of Emotion,' which provides a succinct appraisal of recent scholarship on emotions and politics. See

Carol Johnson, 'From Obama to Abbott: Gender Identity and the Politics of Emotion', *Australian Feminist Studies*, vol. 28, no. 75 (2013) pp. 14–29.

15 See Johnson, 'From Obama to Abbott', p. 15. A preoccupation with assigning passion and reason their rightful place in the political realm is not new. The increasingly visible incursion of women into the public affairs of the early twentieth-century state, for example, was responsible for sparking sometimes heated discussion about the place of emotions in politics. In January 1910, in 'The Women's Parliament' page of the moderately feminist Irish periodical, *The Lady of the House*, for example, one correspondent claimed that the actions of militant feminists had halted the progress of the mainstream suffrage movement because of 'people naturally feeling that hysteria has no place in political life': 'a more well-balanced mental attitude must be the portion of those who seek to help control the destinies of our country' (*The Lady of the House*, 15 January 1910, p. 15). More radical publications, such as the feminist periodical, *The Irish Citizen*—while acknowledging that conservative politicians had 'a great objection to emotion in politics'—did not mind admitting the emotional into the political; indeed, in one article in that publication, at least they strenuously declared that all life was emotional and so it was natural and right for both emotion and reason to be allowed to inform political life (*The Irish Citizen*, vol. 1, no. 1, 25 May 1912, p. 2).

16 Thomas J. Scheff, 'Shame and the Social Bond: A Sociological Theory,' *Sociological Theory*, vol. 18, no. 1 (2000) pp. 84–99, p. 97.

17 I discuss shame in much greater detail in Chapter 1. See Thomas J. Scheff, 'Shame in Self and Society', *Symbolic Interaction*, vol. 26, no. 2 (2003) pp. 239–262, p. 256.

18 For a discussion of the challenges facing historians of shame, see Peter N. Stearns, 'Shame, and a Challenge for Emotions History', *Emotion Review*, vol. 8, no. 3 (2015) pp. 197–206.

19 See, for example, David Nash and Anne-Marie Kilday, *Cultures of Shame: Exploring Crime and Morality in Britain 1600–1900* (Basingstoke: Palgrave Macmillan, 2010); Deborah Cohen, *Family Secrets: Shame and Privacy in Modern Britain* (Oxford: Oxford University Press, 2013); Begoña Aretxaga, *Shattering Silence: Women, Nationalism, and Political Subjectivity in Northern Ireland* (Princeton: Princeton University Press, 1997); Barbara Brookes, 'Shame and Its Histories in the Twentieth Century', *Journal of New Zealand Studies*, no. 9 (2010) pp. 37–54; and Vincent Comerford, 'Grievance, Scourge or Shame? The Complexity of Attitudes to Ireland's Great Famine', in Christian Noack, Lindsay Janssen and Vincent Comerford, eds., *Holodomor and Gorta Mór: Histories, Memories and Representations of Famine in Ukraine and Ireland* (London: Anthem Press, 2012).

20 See Nash and Kilday, *Cultures of Shame*, pp. 173–174. For a more detailed discussion of the need for further historicisation of shame, see Nash, 'Towards an Agenda for a Wider Study of Shame'.

21 Blom identifies this as an emerging area of scholarship but she also highlights, 'Much more comparative research is needed to reach a better understanding of the gendered meaning of duties to the nation.' See Blom, 'Gender and Nation in International Comparison', p. 5 and p. 17. For an example of Blom's contribution to the field, via her comparison of nation-building processes and the role of gender in Norway, Japan, India, and Sweden, see Ida Blom, 'Feminism and Nationalism in the Early Twentieth Century: A Cross-Cultural Perspective', *Journal of Women's History*, vol. 7, no. 4 (1995) pp. 82–94.

22 Blom, 'Gender and Nation in International Comparison', p. 14.

23 This inextricable merging of the English nation and the British Empire means that Englishness and Britishness merged. Although they were not exactly

synonymous terms, they were often used interchangeably. In this book, I tend to use English when referring only to the inhabitants of England. I use British more expansively, however, when I am referring to British values or a sense of a global British peoples or, more contentiously, 'race'. For more on the interconnections between the British metropole and its empire, see Bernard Porter, *The Absent-Minded Imperialists: Empire, Society, and Culture in Britain* (Oxford: Oxford University Press, 2004) pp. 243–244; Shula Marks, 'History, the Nation and Empire: Sniping from the Periphery', *History Workshop Journal*, vol. 29, no. 1 (1990) pp. 111–119, pp. 115–117; and Krishan Kumar, 'Nation and Empire: English and British National Identity in Comparative Perspective', *Theory and Society*, vol. 29, no. 5 (2000) pp. 575–608, pp. 575 and 591.

24 See Porter, *The Absent-Minded Imperialists*, p. 252; Bradley Deane, 'Imperial Barbarians: Primitive Masculinity in Lost World Fiction', *Victorian Literature and Culture*, vol. 38, no. 1 (2008) pp. 205–225, p. 213, and see Andrew Thompson, *The Empire Strikes Back: The Impact of Imperialism on Britain from the Mid-Nineteenth Century* (Harlow: Pearson Longman, 2005) for an extended discussion of what the empire meant to various sections in England including the elites, middle- and lower middle class, and the working class.

25 Porter, *The Absent-Minded Imperialists*, pp. 165–167.

26 Deane, 'Imperial Barbarians', p. 213, and Iveta Jusová, *The New Woman and the Empire* (Columbus: The Ohio State University Press, 2005) p. 4.

27 See Deane, 'Imperial Barbarians', p. 213. Deane argues that the popularity of 'Lost World' novels, those novels that explored forgotten cities, empires, or civilisations and the ambiguous relationship between the modern adventurer and the 'primitive' man, between the 'barbarian' and the civilised, reveals the existence of 'a significant uncertainty about late Victorian imperialist ambitions and their relationship to "barbarism"' (Deane, 'Imperial Barbarians', p. 205).

28 Porter, *The Absent-Minded Imperialists*, p. 167.

29 Susan Kingsley Kent asserts that the period from 1866—when the first mass petitions were collected and presented to parliament—to 1870 has been labelled the first phase of the organised movement and was characterised by 'optimism and spirited activity'. The second phase of the movement, stretching from the 1870s until 1905, was characterised by substantial feminist reform but little progress regarding the vote. See Susan Kingsley Kent, *Sex and Suffrage in Britain, 1860–1914* (Princeton: Princeton University Press, 1987) p. 184.

30 June Purvis, 'Fighting the Double Moral Standard in Edwardian Britain: Suffragette Militancy, Sexuality and the Nation in the Writings of the Early Twentieth-Century British Feminist Christabel Pankhurst', in Francisca de Haan, Margaret Allen, June Purvis and Krassimira Dasklova, eds., *Women's Activism: Global Perspectives from the 1890s to the Present* (New York: Routledge, 2013) pp. 121–135, p. 121.

31 Members of the militant Women's Freedom League (WFL) were also referred to as suffragettes in the anti-feminist press; however, the tactics of the WFL, although militant, were not violent. This is discussed further in Chapter 7.

32 Purvis, 'Fighting the Double Moral Standard in Edwardian Britain', p. 121.

33 Deane, 'Imperial Barbarians', p. 213.

34 Anne McClintock, 'No Longer in a Future Heaven: Gender, Race and Nationalism', in Anne McClintock, Aamir Mufti and Ella Shohat, eds., *Dangerous Liaisons: Gender, Nation and Postcolonial Perspectives* (Minneapolis: University of Minnesota Press, 1997) pp. 89–112.

35 McClintock, 'No Longer in a Future Heaven', pp. 89–112.

36 McClintock, 'No longer in a Future Heaven', p. 93.

37 I write 'good' because many of the women on both sides of the suffrage debate couched their defences of their relative positions in terms that were very

nationalistic. However, in discounting the patriotism of radical feminists, those on the anti-suffragist side tended to construct a community of female patriots who were 'good' rather than manipulative, false, or misguided.

38 Activists such as the Dublin-based Quaker Anna Haslam and Belfast Presbyterian Isabella Tod had been campaigning for the vote in Ireland since the 1870s. Nationalist and Unionist women formed part of the same movement for women's emancipation, although until the twentieth century, Protestants and Unionist women formed the majority of active suffragists. See Mary Cullen, 'Feminism, Citizenship and Suffrage: A Long Dialogue', in Louise Ryan and Margaret Ward, eds., *Irish Women and the Vote: Becoming Citizens* (Dublin: Irish Academic Press, 2007) pp. 1–20, p. 12. For more on Irish emancipation campaigns generally, see Mary Cullen, 'The Potential of Gender History', in Maryann Gialanella Valiulis, ed., *Gender and Power in Irish History* (Dublin: Irish Academic Press, 2009) pp. 18–38.

39 For a detailed discussion on the differences of women's nationalism in Ireland, see Margaret Ward, *Unmanageable Revolutionaries: Women and Irish Nationalism* (London: Pluto Press,1983); Margaret Ward, 'Conflicting Interests: The British and Irish Suffrage Movements', *Feminist Review*, vol. 50, no. 1 (1995) pp. 127–147; Louise Ryan, 'Traditions and Double Moral Standards: The Irish Suffragists' Critique of Nationalism', *Women's History Review*, vol. 14, no. 4 (1995) pp. 487–503; Cliona Murphy, 'Suffragists and Nationalism in Early Twentieth-Century Ireland', *History of European Ideas*, vol. 16, nos. 4–6 (1993) pp. 1009–1015; and Senia Pašeta, *Irish Nationalist Women, 1900–1918* (Cambridge: Cambridge University Press, 2013).

40 Cliona Murphy, *The Women's Suffrage Movement and Irish Society in the Early Twentieth Century* (New York; London: Harvester Wheatsheaf, 1989) p. 75. For a history of the Irish suffrage movement, also see Rosemary Cullen Owen, *Smashing Times. A History of the Irish Women's Suffrage Movement, 1889–1922* (Dublin: Attic Press, 1984).

41 The first group of Irish women to be imprisoned in Ireland for their militancy consisted of eight women: Hanna Sheehy Skeffington, Margaret Murphy, Jane Murphy, Marguerite Palmer, Marjorie Hasler, Kathleen Houston, Maud Lloyd, and Hilda Webb. They were arrested in Dublin in June 1912 for throwing stones through the windows of government offices. However, prior to this, in 1910 and then again in 1911, Irish women, including IWFL co-founder, Margaret Cousins, were imprisoned in England for participating in protests organised by the WSPU. See William Murphy, *Political Imprisonment and the Irish, 1912–1921* (Oxford: Oxford University Press, 2016) p. 14.

42 Cliona Murphy points out an irony in the growing tensions between the British and the Irish suffrage movements by drawing attention to the fact that it was not only Unionist suffragists that benefited from the links to the British movement. The fiercely nationalistic suffragists, Hanna and Francis Sheehy Skeffington and Margaret and James Cousins established the nationalist suffrage paper, the *Irish Citizen*, with 200 pounds received from their English suffragist friends, Emmeline and Frederick Pethick Lawrence, who established the militant paper, *Votes for Women*. See Murphy, *The Women's Suffrage Movement and Irish Society in the Early Twentieth Century*, p. 76.

43 The degree to which Irish and British suffrage movements were linked is debated. Cliona Murphy, for example, argues that, despite the proximity of these campaigns, the Irish campaign's substantive connections to the British movement 'amounted to little more than its connections with the American or Australian movements'. See Murphy, *The Women's Suffrage Movement and Irish Society in the Early Twentieth Century*, p. 7.

44 The politically conservative Australian women whose works I examine in this book referred to England and Britain as the Mother Country. Therefore, I use that term throughout to exemplify their view of their relationship with the imperial centre.
45 For an excellent appraisal of the 'gift or struggle' debate, see Audrey Oldfield, *Woman Suffrage in Australia: A Gift or a Struggle?* (Cambridge: Cambridge University Press, 1992). Also, drawing on the works of Anne Summers, Beverley Kingston, Katie Spearitt and Audrey Oldfield, Susan Magarey stresses the point that the women's movement in Australia in later decades of the nineteenth century was a 'struggle', however optimistic the vision of a new identity for women and a new world in which to situate that identity. See Susan Magarey, 'History, Cultural Studies, and Another Look at First-Wave Feminism in Australia', *Australian Historical Studies*, vol. 27, no. 106 (1996) pp. 96–110, p. 101.
46 See Oldfield, *Woman Suffrage in Australia*, p. 15.
47 For a discussion of the exclusion of indigenous subjects and inclusion of white female subjects in the citizenship of the newly federated Australia, see, for example, Patricia Grimshaw, Marilyn Lake, Ann McGrath, and Marian Quartly, eds., *Creating a Nation, 1788–1900* (Ringwood: McPhee Gribble, 1994) p. 2.
48 Jane Carey argues that within the Australian women's movement of the 1900s and 1910s, there was remarkably little discussion of the so-called Aboriginal problem. Marilyn Lake asserts that it was the maternalist orientation of the women's movement in inter-war Australia that led feminists there to champion the rights of Aboriginal women, including calling for an end to the removal of Aboriginal children from their mothers, recognition of Aboriginal citizen rights, education, an end to the sexual abuse of indigenous women, and the return of Aboriginal land. See Jane Carey, 'White Anxieties and the Articulation of Race: The Women's Movement and the Making of White Australia, 1910s–1930s', in Jane Carey and Claire McLisky eds., *Creating White Australia* (Sydney: Sydney University Press, 2009) pp. 195–213, pp. 210–213, and Marilyn Lake, *Getting Equal: The History of Australian Feminism* (St Leonards, NSW: Allen & Unwin, 1999) pp. 13–15.
49 For a discussion of indigenous people and the female franchise, see Oldfield, *Woman Suffrage in Australia*, pp. 64–66.
50 Duncan S. A. Bell, 'Dissolving Distance: Technology, Space, and Empire in British Political Thought, 1770–1900', *The Journal of Modern History*, vol. 77, no. 3 (2005) pp. 523–562.
51 Stuart Macintyre, *A Concise History of Australia*, 3rd ed. (Cambridge: Cambridge University Press, 2009) p. 140.
52 For a discussion of how decolonisation brought the race 'problem' home to Britain, see Evan Smith and Marinella Marmo, *Race, Gender and the Body in British Immigration Control: Subject to Examination* (Basingstoke: Palgrave Macmillan, 2014) pp. 22–44.
53 Macintyre, *A Concise History of Australia*, pp. 142–143.
54 Macintyre, *A Concise History of Australia*, pp. 143–145.
55 Barbara Caine, 'Australian Feminism and the British Militant Suffragettes', Paper presented to the Department of the Senate Occasional Lecture Series at Parliament House, Canberra, Australia, 31 October 2003: www.aph.gov.au/binaries/senate/pubs/pops/pop41/caine.pdf, accessed 21 January 2016. For an account of an exchange Goldstein had with a British commentator over the comparative value of the Australian women's and British man's vote, see Sharon Crozier-De Rosa, 'The National and the Transnational in British Anti-Suffragists' Views of Australian Women Voters', *History Australia*, vol. 10, no. 3 (2013) pp. 51–64.
56 Caine, 'Australian Feminism and the British Militant Suffragettes'.

32   Introduction

57 See Caine, 'Australian Feminism and the British Militant Suffragettes'.
58 Hilary Fraser, Stephanie Green and Judith Johnston, *Gender and the Victorian Periodical* (Cambridge: Cambridge University Press, 2003) p. 145.
59 Maria DiCenzo, Lucy Delap and Leila Ryan, *Feminist Media History: Suffrage, Periodicals and the Public Sphere* (Basingstoke and New York: Palgrave Macmillan, 2011) p. 2.
60 DiCenzo, Delap and Ryan, *Feminist Media History*, p. 2.
61 DiCenzo, Delap and Ryan, *Feminist Media History*, p. 13.
62 DiCenzo, Delap and Ryan, *Feminist Media History*, p. 3.
63 Feminist nationalist prioritised their feminists aspirations over their nationalist ones, whereas nationalist feminists prioritised their nationalist aspirations over their feminists objectives. Both subscribed to feminist and nationalist politics; they just varied in the order of priority.
64 DiCenzo, Delap and Ryan asserts, 'One need only see how often the *Anti-Suffrage Review* or other monthly reviews like the New Age regularly cited suffrage organs and other feminist publications to appreciate how closely opponents and other observers monitored movement media.' See DiCenzo, Delap, and Ryan, *Feminist Media History*, p. 83.
65 DiCenzo, Delap and Ryan, *Feminist Media History*, p. 78.
66 See the first edition of the *Anti-Suffrage Review*, no. 1, December 1908, pp. 1–2
67 Julia Bush, 'National League for Opposing Woman Suffrage (*act.* 1910–1918)', *Oxford Dictionary of National Biography*, online ed. (Oxford: Oxford University Press, 2008) www.oxforddnb.com/view/theme/92492, accessed 13 November 2011.
68 Bush, 'National League for Opposing Woman Suffrage'.
69 Bush, 'National League for Opposing Woman Suffrage'.
70 See Brian Harrison, *Separate Spheres: The Opposition to Women's Suffrage in Britain* (London: Croom Helm, 1978) pp. 13–24.
71 Julia Bush, *Women Against the Vote: Female Suffragism in Britain* (Oxford: Oxford University Press, 2007) p. 2.
72 See, for example, Valeria Sanders, *Eve's Renegades: Victorian Anti-Feminist Women Novelists* (London: Macmillan Press, 1996); Julia Bush, 'British Women's Anti-Suffragism and the Forward Policy, 1908–14', *Women's History Review*, vol. 11, no. 3 (2002) pp. 431–454; Lucy Delap, 'Feminist and Anti-Feminist Encounters in Edwardian Britain', *Historical Research*, vol. 78, no. 201 (2005) pp. 377–399; Bush, *Women Against the Vote*; and David Thackeray, 'Home and Steele Politics: Women and Conservatism Activism in Early Twentieth-Century Britain', *Journal of British Studies*, vol. 49, no. 4 (2010) pp. 826–848. See also Tamara S. Wagner, 'Introduction: Narratives of Victorian Antifeminism', in Tamara S. Wagner, ed., *Antifeminism and the Victorian Novel: Rereading Nineteenth-Century Women Writers* (Amherst, New York: Cambria Press, 2009) pp. 1–15.
73 For recent works examining the women's press in Ireland around this time, see C. L. Innes, ' "A Voice in Directing the Affairs of Ireland": *L'Irlande Libre, The Shan Van Vocht* and *Bean na h-Eireann*', in Paul Hyland and Neil Sammells, eds., *Irish Writing: Exile and Subversion* (Basingstoke: Palgrave Macmillan, 1991) pp. 146–158; Louise Ryan, 'The Irish Citizen, 1912–1920', *Saothar*, vol. 17 (1992) pp. 105–111; Karen Steele, *Women, Press and Politics During the Irish Revival* (Syracuse: Syracuse University Press, 2007); Sonja Tiernan, 'Tabloid Sensationalism or Revolutionary Feminism? The First-Wave Feminist Movement in an Irish Women's Periodical', *Irish Communications Review*, vol. 12, no. 1 (2010) pp. 74–87; and Brittany Columbus, '*Bean na h-Éireann*: Feminism and Nationalism in an Irish Journal, 1908–1911', *Voces Novae: Chapman University Historical Review*, vol. 1, no. 1 (2009) pp. 3–30.

74 This was pronounced in an editorial by Helena Moloney later in the journal's life. See Innes, '"A Voice in Directing the Affairs of Ireland"', p. 146.
75 Steele, *Women, Press, and Politics During the Irish Revival*, p. 109.
76 Steele, *Women, Press, and Politics During the Irish Revival*, p. 110. For a discussion of the complex nature of the so-called Celtic Revival—one feature of which was the mentioned adoption of Celtic personae—see, among others: Declan Kiberd, *Inventing Ireland: The Literature of the Modern Nation* (London: Vintage, 1996); and Gregory Castle, *Modernism and the Celtic Revival* (Cambridge: Cambridge University Press, 2001).
77 Murphy, *The Women's Suffrage Movement and Irish Society in the Early Twentieth Century*, p. 29.
78 Murphy, *The Women's Suffrage Movement and Irish Society in the Early Twentieth Century*, pp. 32–34.
79 For example, organisers Francis and Hanna Sheehy Skeffington had university degrees. Hanna had a master's degree and taught at a girl's school (a position she lost after being imprisoned during the militant part of the movement). Margaret Cousins was awarded a music degree and went on to teach music. There were three professors in the movement: Professor Mary Halden, first woman professor of Irish History; Professor Oldham; and Professor Tom Kettle. See Murphy, *The Women's Suffrage Movement and Irish Society in the Early Twentieth Century*, p. 29.
80 See Murphy, *The Women's Suffrage Movement and Irish Society in the Early Twentieth Century*, p. 34.
81 Murphy, *The Women's Suffrage Movement and Irish Society in the Early Twentieth Century*, p. 76.
82 Australian Women's National League, *History of the Australian Women's National League*, 50th Anniversary Publication, Melbourne, 1954, p. 4.
83 Marian Simms, 'Conservative Feminism in Australia: A Case Study of Feminist Ideology', *Women's Studies International Quarterly*, vol. 2, no. 3 (1979) pp. 305–318, p. 306.
84 Eva Hughes's claim was that it was the largest body globally. Quoted in Marian Quartly, 'Defending "The Purity of Home Life" Against Socialism: The Founding Years of the Australian Women's National League', *Australian Journal of Politics and History*, vol. 50, no. 2 (2004) pp. 178–193, p. 178, and Judith Smart, 'Hughes, Agnes Eva (1856–1940)', *Australian Dictionary of Biography*, National Centre of Biography, Australian National University, http://adb.anu.edu.au/biography/hughes-agnes-eva-6755/text11675, published first in hardcopy 1983, accessed online 29 May 2017.
85 Judith Smart, 'Eva Hughes: Militant Conservative', in Marilyn Lake and Farley Kelly, eds., *Double Time: Women in Victoria—150 years* (Melbourne: Penguin, 1985) pp. 179–189.
86 *Woman*, vol. 1, no. 1, 21 September 1907, pp. 4–5.
87 *Woman*, vol. 1, no. 1, 21 September 1907, pp. 4–5.
88 *Woman*, vol. 1, no. 10, 25 June 1908, p. 233.
89 *Woman*, vol. 1, no. 1, 21 September 1907, pp. 4–5.
90 The Australian paper, the *Woman*, refers to the Irish Catholic 'problem' once the war commences and some Irish-Australians show allegiance to Irish nationalism and oppose moves for conscription for wartime service. Although Australia had no established religion, the many different Protestant denominations dominated the religious scene at this time. (For a brief discussion of the Australian religious scene just before the turn of the twentieth century, see Macintyre, *A Concise History of Australia*, pp. 115–117.) Irish nationalist and Unionist women were largely Catholic, Anglican, or Presbyterian, if they were members of any religious

organisation. Here, too, in the papers I look at, religion was rarely specified in the interests of championing gender and national politics over sectarian divisions. Certainly, Christian values direct much of the *Review's* sentiments in a religiously diverse Britain. For a brief discussion of the religious scene in Britain, see François Bédarida, *A Social History of England 1851–1990*, translated by A. S. Forster and Geoffrey Hodgkinson (London and New York: Routledge, 1990) pp. 85–92.

91 See Frank Biess, Alon Confino, Ute Frevert, Uffa Jensen, Lyndal Roper, and Daniela Saxer, Forum: 'History of Emotions', *German History*, vol. 28, no. 1 (2010) pp. 67–80, especially pp. 79–80.

1 Shaming Unwomanly Women

In 1915, the feminist nationalist paper, the *Irish Citizen* (the *Citizen*), published the views of a Catholic priest who had observed women exercising their right to vote in New Zealand:

> Father Malloy notes that the 'antis' of this country are the women of the protected leisure class, the selfish women who have everything they want themselves, and can't imagine why every other woman is not satisfied.[1]

The women who do not use their vote here, he was recorded as saying, 'have not the soul or the vision to see that the less fortunate need their help and their protection'.[2] They were not womanly women.

This was an instance of suffragists accusing anti-suffragists of shameful behaviour. Yet I would argue that accusations of selfishness aimed at suffragists, not by suffragists, had much more hold on the public imagination in the early twentieth century. An avalanche of British propaganda material—visual and literary—attacked campaigning feminists for abandoning home and family to fulfil their selfish desires for power and notoriety. Suffragists were labelled selfish because they desired the vote simply because they coveted what men had. They were deemed selfish because they were attempting to foist upon their sisters a new burden unsuited to their character and temperament, thereby adding to their already heavy load of responsibilities. Since the Enlightenment and birth of the modern nation-state, a new conceptualisation of womanly citizenship had developed. This ideal of female citizenship—one that endorsed the legitimacy of the 'separate but equal' spheres ideology—was one that truly womanly women cherished. Anti-suffragists, then, were fighting to protect a precious notion of womanhood and treasured feminine virtues from further modernisation.

Similarly, across the Irish Sea, women opposed their Irish sisters' demands for the vote in order to protect a cherished notion of womanhood. However, the idea of womanliness that they invoked was different from that in Britain. Irish anti-suffragists drew on a well-worn transnational trope—that of woman as man's moral anchor—and adapted it to reflect Irish conditions. In this case, they implored the anti-colonial Irish woman to work to restore the pride and masculinity of the Irish man, which had been depleted by the process of British colonisation. Their condemnation of the suffrage movement, therefore, was predicated on the more urgent need to foster and protect a conceptualisation of womanly citizenship uniquely suited to the emerging Irish nation.

In Australia, the situation was dire, for women already had the vote in the newly federated Commonwealth. The Enlightenment idea of patriotic womanhood had already been further modernised. As Australian women, therefore, they were under the dual pressure of proving themselves loyal to womanhood as well as to nation and empire. The eyes of the world, and certainly of the Mother Country, were fixed on Australian women as they exercised what was a revolutionary right at that stage. Their womanliness—as enfranchised citizens of what was emerging as a new modern nation—was on trial.

Scholars of shame have noted that shame has had a complicated relationship with modernising forces. In this chapter on shaming unwomanly women, I look at how patriotic women understood and articulated the relationship between shame and modernising concepts of womanhood.

Modernising Concepts of Womanhood

Following on from the Enlightenment-inspired French Revolution, new ideas about nationhood and citizenship became entwined with those about sexual difference.[3] The rights of citizenship—including the right to participate in public debates, to vote, and to bear arms in defence of the nation—were masculinised. Women's bodies were increasingly tied to the performance of conventional female roles: domestic, reproductive, and social.[4] Middle-class ideas of respectability grew alongside those of gendered spheres. Men belonged to the public sphere, women to the private. The 'public man' was considered a man deserving of respect. The 'public woman' referred to the prostitute. As Barbara Caine and Glenda Sluga note, the modern State and modern politics were predicated on separate gendered spheres. Therefore, when women demanded access to the public sphere, they threatened to undermine the ideological basis of modern nation-state politics. They also contravened codes that deemed respectable femininity and publicity as incompatible.[5]

Documents, such as the French Revolution's *Declaration of the Rights of Man and Citizen* (1789), paradoxically offered both the promise of universal human rights and instituted the exclusionary practice of the gendering and racialising of those rights. From the time of the Revolution, when it became clear that women were being written out of citizenship, there were dissenting voices.[6] In France, Olympe de Gouges's *Declaration of the*

Rights of Woman and Citizen (1791) and in England, Mary Wollstonecraft's *Vindication of the Rights of Woman* (1792) readily come to mind here. The women who protested angrily against their exclusion from the political sphere ushered in modern feminism. By the 1840s, women in the United States of America had organised a campaign to demand voting rights for women. They were joined by women in Britain and Ireland in the 1860s and 1870s, and Australian women in the 1880s. By demanding access to the public world of politics—and by taking to the public streets in the process—they challenged the Enlightenment-derived concept of the private woman citizen. They attacked the concept of respectable womanhood and its place in relation to the modern nation-state. In their attempts to modernise female citizenship—to bring it up to the same level as men's—they attacked what were for some much-cherished notions of femininity. To defenders of traditional concepts of womanhood and the womanly citizen—members of the community of 'good' patriotic womanhood—these attacks were shameful. They shamed rather than emancipated womanhood.

Shame and Gender in History

Shame is an emotion that connects the personal to the social. In his groundbreaking 1939 study of shame and the civilising process, German sociologist Norbert Elias defined shame as fear of social degradation or, more generally, of other peoples' gestures of superiority.[7]

> It takes on its particular coloration from the fact that the person feeling it has done or is about to do something through which he comes into contradiction with people to whom he is bound in one form or another, and with himself, with the sector of his consciousness by which he controls himself. The conflict expressed in shame-fear is not merely a conflict of the individual with prevalent social opinion; the individual's behaviour has brought him into conflict with the part of himself that represents this social opinion.[8]

Sixty years later, sociologist Thomas Scheff extended this understanding of the relationship between internal and external factors, arguing that the 'large family of emotions' included under the term shame, a family that includes cognates and variants such as embarrassment, humiliation, feelings of rejection and failure, all have in common 'the feeling of a *threat to the social bond*'.[9] Cultural anthropologist Richard Shweder agrees. Shame, he argues, is

> the deeply felt and highly motivating experience of the fear of being judged defective. It is the anxious experience of either the real or anticipated loss of status, affection or self-regard that results from knowing

that one is vulnerable to the disapproving gaze or negative judgment of others. It is a terror that touches the mind, the body, and the soul precisely because one is aware that one might be seen to have come up short in relationship to some shared and uncontested ideal that defines what it means to be a good, worthy, admirable, attractive, or competent person, given one's status or position in society.'[10]

As a 'highly motivating experience', shame worked on individuals by instilling in them a fear of losing the love or respect of someone or some community they were attached to or to whom they attached value. Shame connected internal anxieties to external influences, inner values to social standards. All psychologically 'normal' people, Shweder avows, feel some sort of fear about being judged defective.[11] Therefore, shame deserves the title of the social emotion—the master emotion—because, whether real or simply anticipated, it is always present.[12]

Scholars may agree on how shame functions, but shame is not ahistorical. Rather, it is historically and culturally contingent. Shweder writes that shame has '[s]ocially shared and valued ego ideals, notions about a well-developed self, and ideas about what it means to be a good, worthy, admirable, attractive, or competent person' at its core.[13] However, these shared ideals about what it is to be a 'good' person vary across time and space. It is these shared values that lend specific or unique colour to 'the character, substance, and meaning of "shame"'.[14] Historians can look through the prism of shame to access a past community's shared values, and they can plot a history of attitudes to and understandings of this social emotion through examining those shared values. Analysing how different groups of 'good' patriotic womanhood approached the emotion of shame offers insight into historical notions of shame, but it also casts light on the priorities that these female communities and their respective nations held dear.

Shame has been regarded as a highly gendered emotion.[15] Commentators from Aristotle to Freud have characterised it as an emotion 'suitable for youth', 'womanish', and as a 'feminine characteristic *par excellence*'.[16] In this book, I not only address the need to further historicise shame but also contribute to the relatively small body of literature that examines the emotion in its historical and gendered form. I respond to the deficit of historicisations of the relationship between gender and shame by examining the neglected place of it and related emotions in early twentieth-century women's protest movements.

As mentioned in the book's introduction, scholars have argued that there has been a reluctance to admit the centrality of emotions in the political realm and 'understand both the intersecting reason and passion of political life'.[17] And yet emotions like shame played a pivotal role in political affairs, especially in protest movements. In many instances, shame has been a versatile component of the 'moral, cognitive, and emotional package of attitudes' that forms the successful political activist's toolkit.[18] Activists have used shame to variously bind members of a group closer together, to confirm the exclusion of outsiders, or to draw those outsiders into the fold.[19] However, relying on shame to achieve political ends has its limitations. For, as feminist theorist Jill Locke has argued in relation to feminist shaming, realisation of how shame and shaming function brings with it recognition of the limited effects of shame as a form of social control, for shaming relies on the target's or intended recipient's 'ability to engage in shameful self-assessment'.[20] Shaming, then, as criminologist John Braithwaite adds, may produce uncertain outcomes. Again, whereas in some instances it may act to bind the recipient to the group or community to which she or he belongs—bringing that person back to the fold as it were—in others, it may do the opposite, alienating and ostracising the shaming target.[21] In line with Locke's and Braithwaite's cautions, early twentieth-century shaming of unwomanly radical feminists or disloyal female nationalists would only be successful if those unwomanly or disloyal women valued the connections they had with the community of 'good' national womanhood to which they were supposed to belong.

Womanhood Corrupted by Politics

As mentioned at the outset of the book, in her 1907 anti-suffrage pamphlet, *Woman, or—Suffragette?*, renowned bestseller Marie Corelli asserted that militant feminists were 'a scandal to the nation', making 'England a laughing-stock to the rest of the world'.[22] Devoid of the womanly feelings of modesty and shame, they alienated their sisters. They induced affective displays of shame. One disaffected sister, for example, was reported as saying that she 'burn[ed] with shame at being associated, as members of a common sex' with women like the suffragettes who behaved more like 'drunken men than even the worst feminist viragos'.[23] Such undignified behaviour, Corelli assented, was 'indeed a degradation to the very name of woman'.[24] If these women had understood the idea of 'proper' womanhood, they would have realised that woman's greatest power lay not in her obtaining the vote, and certainly not in her running about the streets yelling and defacing property, but rather in her exercising her influence over men. To illustrate this point further, Corelli produced her own version of separate spheres ideology:

> The clever woman sits at home, and, like a meadow spider, spreads a pretty web of rose and gold spangled with diamond dew. Flies, or men, tumble in by scores, and she holds them all prisoners at her pleasure with a golden strand as fine as a hair. Nature gave her, at her birth, the 'right' to do this, and if she does it well, she will always have her web full.[25]

Not everyone was convinced by Corelli's imagined scenario. The feminist periodical *Votes for Women* used this occasion to sardonically draw attention to what it said was this infamous anti-feminist's obsession with 'the idea of fascinating women inveighing helpless men into their toils'.[26] Yet Corelli's point—shared by many anti-suffragists—was that women were the manufacturers of their own demise.[27] Whatever the 'folly and the tyranny of man in regard to woman', she sensationally stated, 'woman alone is in fault for his war against her'.[28]

None of this is to say that Corelli marked the beginning of femininity's demise at the point at which the suffragette entered national politics. Rather, she argued that the erosion of British femininity was already underway at least a decade before feminist militancy with the masculinising of national womanhood. For example, in her 1898 pamphlet *The Modern Marriage Market*, she complained:

> Some men still make 'angels' out of us in spite of our cycling mania,— our foolish 'clubs,' where we do nothing at all,—our rough games at football and cricket, our general throwing to the winds of all dainty feminine reserve, delicacy, and modesty,—and we alone are to blame if we shatter their ideals and sit down by choice in the mud when they would have placed us on thrones. It is our fault, not theirs. We have willed it so. Many of us are more 'mannish' than womanly; we are more inclined to laugh at and make mock of a man's courtesy and reverence than we are to be flattered by it.[29]

Women, she declared, were 'free' 'to assert their modesty, their sense of right, their desire for truth and purity, if only they will'.[30] It was a sad indictment of the state of British womanhood that they refused to do so. The militant feminist only compounded the slur cast on that womanhood with her very public unruly and indecorous behaviour.

In 1908, the *Anti-Suffrage Review* (the *Review*) mirrored Corelli's sentiments when it explained that the Women's National Anti-Suffrage League (later the National League for Opposing Woman Suffrage (NLOWS))[31] had been driven to establish itself as an organised body because of the 'shock of repulsion' and 'wave of angry laughter' rocking England due to the recent and much publicised actions of militant suffragists there.[32] The paper asked, 'Have not the spectacles of the last few weeks shown conclusively that women are not fit for the ordinary struggle of politics, and are degraded by it?' All militant feminists had done was to render 'the calm and practicable discussion of great questions impossible; a feeling and antagonism disastrous to women, disastrous to England'.[33]

The fear for female anti-suffragists was that the actions of suffragists, particularly those of the militant feminists, would be disastrous for all women because the aberrant behaviour of a few would stigmatise the whole community of national womanhood. They worried that British womanhood as a collective would be judged and be found wanting on the basis of the existence of unwomanly women. Therefore, anti-suffragist women, like Corelli and the organisers and members of the NLOWS, displayed a heightened sensibility to shame throughout the length of the feminist campaign.

Contributions to the *Review* often directly referenced shame or its variants, such as embarrassment or humiliation. However, the paper also revealed a multitudinous approach to the emotion and to its motivational potential. For example, in line with Locke's caution about shame's effectiveness as a reformative technique, articles in the *Review* reveal that anti-suffragist women were often ambivalent about whether or not the transgressive women they were targeting would honour their bond with 'good' women and take on board their shaming. At times, anti-suffragists tried to protect the honour of British womanhood by appealing to their wayward sisters to abandon their disruptive campaigns. They attempted to convince them to reform through revealing to them the shameful consequences of their actions. Other times, they exposed just how shameless and therefore lacking in devotion to concepts of 'good' womanhood female suffragists were. Drawing attention to the transgressor's shame, in this instance, worked to confirm the boundaries existing between true members of the community and those existing beyond its pale. It reconfirmed group membership. In this way, those writing for the *Review* alternated between exhibiting faith in the potentially transformative powers of shame, on the one hand, and affirming that the transgressive female subject's shamelessness irrevocably ostracised her from the group whose values she did not adequately value, on the other.

The *Review* may have varied its use of and articulations of faith in shaming techniques, but it was unequivocal about the feeling of shame that 'good' women felt when they thought about their connection—on the basis of shared sex—with radical feminists. In 1909, it echoed Corelli's earlier depictions of affective shame generated by the actions of radical feminists:

> Women, especially, are burning with a deep latent shame at the behaviour of the unwomanly women who disgrace the sex while purporting to 'emancipate' it. Emancipation from the Suffragettes, not by them, is felt to be the need of the present.[34]

Women had received the 'great heritage of womanhood'. It was their privilege and responsibility to protect that heritage. The plea to suffragists, then, was to honour not shame that responsibility, to dedicate their energies to 'the upholding and maintenance of the honour of womanhood' not bring about its demise.[35]

42 Shaming Unwomanly Women

As I will discuss in much greater detail in later chapters, honour was gendered. A woman's honour was located in the private sphere, men's in the public. A woman did not protect women's honour by joining men in the public world. They were not protecting the honour of womankind when they adopted man's typical resort to physical force and violence. Such a recourse was an act of weakness not strength as reported in the suffragist press. The *Review* made this clear to its readers:

> Women—womanly women—and womanliness does not necessarily imply weakness, nor need femininity spell frivolity—though again to our shame be it said, if oft-times it does—women *need* the chivalry of men (a quality which Suffragettes are doing their level best to destroy), and are not ashamed to own it.[36]

Womanly women knew that a sense of integrity compelled them to acknowledge their need for the protection of the stronger sex. They were being true to themselves and the proper nature of womanhood by admitting this.

True womanhood was being depleted by modernising notions of gender. In 1909, to clarify the distinction between proper traditional notions of womanhood and false newer models, the *Review* conjured up a scenario it said was typical of the Middle Ages. In the Middle Ages, if a woman could not marry or was unhappy in her marriage, she 'happily' went to a nunnery. Back then, there 'were no faded and soured spinsters, no bustling, mannish women, no shouting, noisy creatures with a grievance, no blighted and lifeless drudges—there were nuns'.[37] This lifestyle may appear 'distasteful' to the modern woman. However,

> it is difficult to deny that a nun was more beautiful and useful than a Suffragette (at least more feminine), and that the nunnery was a dignified solution to the problem of the unnecessary woman, who in this manner was made not so unnecessary and given a grace by her withdrawal from the world her energetic descendants wholly lack.[38]

Retreat to the private offered the 'unnecessary woman' refuge from the possibility of public shame. In this way, the nun of the Middle Ages 'venerated' her sex, whereas the modern woman only 'ridiculed' hers. The paper reiterated this point. A suffragette was a 'restless, discontented creature who employs her unvalued time in noisy declamation, foolish assertion, and ungentle behaviour that only degrades the sex she pretends to exalt'.[39]

Five years later, the *Review* felt compelled to highlight again the corrosive effect that modernising concepts of womanhood were having on the community of true women. Through this modernising process, the 'ideal of womanhood' was being lost. It was being abandoned by the many modern women who live only for pleasure, amusements, and the gratification of self—a striking contrast to the older type of woman who delighted in ordering their households, who were learned in matters of health, and in the training of children.[40]

This 'older type of womanhood' had been depicted in an earlier article as 'a type of woman who has been rather cavalierly treated in the discussion of this Suffrage question'.[41]

> She is not a very spectacular woman; she is not a very interesting woman perhaps; she does not make a very good heroine for a problem play or a sex novel; she does not much adorn processions or frequent meetings; she is just the ordinary common or garden married woman living with her husband and her family.[42]

This model of femininity was very far removed from the 'superfluous' frustrated spinster or 'unhappily' married feminist that the *Review* implied made up the ranks of the suffrage campaign.[43]

The shameless, unwomanly behaviour of campaigning suffragists threatened to unravel the bonds that tied members of the community of British womanhood together. The damage wrought by their transgressive behaviour did not stop there. It also threatened the integrity of another emotional community, that of British manhood. Suffragists jeopardised the existence and operation of proper notions of sexual difference through abnormal acts of gender mimicry and the creation of a so-called a *middle* sex.[44] In the years leading to the Great War, the *Review* warned against the calamitous consequences of woman attempting to 'invade his [man's] province, to think his thoughts and to do his work'.[45] Man accepts woman as a 'mother, sweetheart, inspirer and friend', but once he sees that 'she despises these relations, once she ceases to be what he thinks and wishes', she will feel the full effects of his 'resentment'.[46] Woman, another article asserted, should not crave man's place in the world. To do so is to 'arrest progress'.[47] When she 'insists on trying to be a poor imitation of man, or else a mere neuter, possessing neither the virility of manhood nor the charm of womanhood', she demonstrates that she has neither the knowledge nor the wisdom to understand how relations between the real sexes work. This, the *Review* declared, is the inescapable outcome of 'the strange phenomenon of the unsexed woman'—a woman

> who in striving for what she calls her rights is aggressiveness personified; whose instincts are so perverted that she cannot distinguish between right and wrong; and mistakes criminality for heroism; who appears to think that hatred of man, and her assertion of equality with, while weakly imitating him, is the appropriate relation of the sexes.[48]

The unsexed woman owed no allegiance to either sex and so did not feel compelled to guard against dishonouring either sex.

The worst thing was that it appeared that feminists eroded relations between the sexes—and in the process, jeopardised the very nature of those sexes—simply to sate a selfish desire. In a 1910 meeting, leading anti-suffragist Violet Markham was recorded as saying,

> I was struck by this argument, brought forward by a lady on the suffrage side. 'We want the vote because we consider it would be good for us to have it.' As a woman I was sorry to hear any woman take so narrow and selfish and individualistic a view of a great public issue, because a woman is not a woman unless she is standing for a higher and more spiritual expression of any matter, public or private.[49]

To want the vote to fulfil individual desires contravened one of the basic characteristics of the 'ideal of womanhood', which was 'unselfishness'.[50] Besides, the needs of the nation trumped that of the individual, or even the sex.[51] The bonds of womanhood were important but, as we will see in the next chapter, patriotic women tended to prioritise the needs of the national community.

Like Corelli, Markham drew a rigid boundary around the community of true womanhood. Bringing shame to that collective meant ostracism. Women were no longer 'women' if they attacked the integrity of that gendered community. They were no longer fit to be called women if they refused to abide by the emotional regimes guiding that community. Selfishness was not a feminine emotional virtue. Aping men's behaviour by performing public acts of militancy was not feminine. These women, then, existed beyond the pale of the emotional community of good British womanhood.

This emphasis on 'British' is an important one. The *Review*'s invocations of a community of womanhood was underpinned by a notion of Britishness, supported by British values. However, the paper promoted its brand of womanhood as a transnational rather than a nationally specific concept. As befits a notion of womanhood emanating from the centre of a vast empire with the self-appointed task of bringing civilisation to the world, this was a mobile concept. British imperialists argued that it could—and should—be overlaid on women of other nationalities or ethnicities. However, not all women of other nationalities or ethnicities agreed. For example, in Australia, patriotic women only partially accepted this concept of femininity and womanly duty. In Ireland, it was deemed irrelevant to local conditions and historical trajectory, and so it was rejected—by nationalist women, at least.

Womanhood and the National Question in Ireland

British anti-suffragists were not the only group of patriotic women to deplore the prioritising of satisfying women's individual desires over the needs of the national collective. In 1909, the editors of the Irish nationalist women's paper, the *Bean na hEireann* (the *Bean*), expressed disappointment that the Irish Women's Franchise League (IWFL) had stated that its members wanted the vote because men had it.[52] Such a glaringly selfish desire at a time when the nation was embroiled in an intensifying nationalist movement was not becoming of Irish womanhood.

In 1910, the *Bean* proudly reasserted that it was 'the first and only Nationalist Woman's paper' in the country. However, it was keen to deny the existence of any sex antagonism in its pages. It was a woman's paper that 'did not regard men—Irishmen in any case—as her natural foe'. This did not mean it accepted that 'the sphere of women is bounded by frying pans and fashion plates'.[53] Politics was the Irish woman's sphere as much as the kitchen. As a nationalist paper, the *Bean*'s remit was to foster the sense of a nationalist community, which meant creating or confirming a sense of comradeship among nationalist men and women, while specifically targeting women in the process. It supported political women, but opposed the move by Irish suffragists to gain the vote in a British parliament. National independence was its priority. Once this was achieved, the newly freed Irish nation could then turn its attention to the critical issue of gender equality.

For the *Bean*, the concept of womanhood was intricately tied up with the concept of the Irish nation. There were few discussions, then, that mirrored those taking place in British women's periodicals, such as the *Review*, about the nature of womanhood more generally. The closest the paper came to referencing the general nature of womanhood—that is to say, a concept of womanhood that was not tied only to the national context—was when it defended the right of Irish women to champion nationalist politics: 'We deliberately assert that such doctrine is not unbecoming to a woman, and an Irishwoman'.[54] Even here, the dominant community evoked was still that of national womanhood.

Indeed, gender politics in Ireland were so entrenched in nationalist politics that even the feminist *Citizen* rarely discussed the idea of womanhood without explaining its relation to the national collective. One departure from this was when Irish women were granted the right to vote in 1918. Some women who had previously dedicated themselves to the feminist campaign for the vote were seemingly refusing to let themselves be co-opted or herded by male politicians, especially by those politicians who had who previously opposed the enfranchisement of women.[55] One contributor to the *Citizen* chided women in Ireland who refused to take a side and pledge allegiance to a particular political party, however male-dominated. These 'non-party' women were naïve citizens. 'To me', the writer asserted, 'she is a helpless, cowardly kind of being who asks for benefits she is unable or unwilling to earn.'[56]

> To say that women ought to be non-party means that you shrink from the hard work and rough knocks of politics—a contemptible effort to

combine old-fashioned womanliness with the advantages of a political career.[57]

Here, the *Citizen* permitted the attempted shaming of political women who were dedicated to feminist ideals but who did not want to participate in nationalist-Unionist politics, thereby remaining untainted by male-dominated party politics. The attitude adopted by newly enfranchised Irish women towards taking up their new political duties was unacceptably gendered. If women wanted to truly form part of the political fabric of any nation, then they had to first declare their allegiances within the existing political structures. They could not exist beyond the realities of that real political world, untouched by its sordidness and difficulties. To desire this was to be guilty of coveting an unrealistic and selfish compromise between the hidden world of femininity and the public world of masculinity. It was to be guilty of wanting to retain their previous untainted political innocence—the reserve of the traditional womanly woman—while claiming the rewards of those capable of performing the more manly virtues of courage, honesty, integrity, and decisiveness in the public realm. There was no room, the *Citizen* expounded, for the sentimental female. Rather, it was the new political woman's business to 'train up a generation of cold, unemotional, business-like young girls who enjoy and understand work', presumably including political work.[58] This was the girl who would embody the concept of the new Irish female citizen.

Australian Women Voters Rejecting the Shame of the Political Woman: Physical Appearance and Emotional Make-Up

In Australia, it was in the interests of a significant proportion of the community of patriotic womanhood to demonstrate just how womanly a woman could be while faithfully carrying out her political duties. The women of the Australian Women's National League (AWNL) were intensely aware that the eyes of the Western world, and certainly those of the imperial centre, were on them as they enacted what many considered to be a radical social experiment. They were also keenly mindful of the accusations emanating from metropolitan anti-suffragists that voting was ill suited to the exhibition of true womanly characteristics. Many of these Australian women had not wanted the vote but they would not shirk the new responsibilities foisted upon them. They had determined that it was in the interest of the Commonwealth and the Empire to educate themselves and other Australian women about their new duties so that they could discharge them ably. Therefore, these women dedicated a very significant proportion of their time to repelling the notion that voting women were unwomanly, that they represented any sort of a gender abomination. In the journal, *Woman*, they

Shaming Unwomanly Women 47

worked diligently to deny the stigma attached to the enfranchised female. Yet the fear that Australian womanhood would be judged and found to be defective was present in a lot of their discussions. Consequently, and perhaps more than any of the groups of patriotic women studied here, it was these women in the antipodes who demonstrated that shame was indeed the master emotion, that it was ever-present if only because it was anticipated.[59]

One of the first steps taken by *Woman* in its move to deny the shame attached to the modern political woman was to prove the irrelevancy of the stereotype of the modern or 'new' woman in the Australian context. In an article covering the first Commonwealth Conference of Women's Anti-Socialistic Organisations held in 1907, the fervently anti-socialist *Woman* declared that 'the "new woman" was conspicuous only by her absence':

> 'Seven hundred of us,' said a South Australian delegate, looking around the throng in the 'Cliveden' ball-room, 'and not one with a stiff collar—not one with a pocket!' Even while refusing to admit that the linen collar is necessarily 'mannish'; even while deploring that the absence of a pocket should seem a sine quâ non of femininity, there was yet convincing proof in the well-dressed gathering that the claims of women to high standards of thought and an intelligent interest in the affairs of her country need infer no sacrifice of her most womanly attributes.[60]

The paper continued to provide 'proof' of the enfranchised woman's womanliness over the following years. In 1909, it stated that it was completely possible for the Australian woman to be a political woman without exhibiting any desire to usurp men's positions or any need to lose 'our most valuable asset, our womanliness'.[61] By the time the 1912 Conference of Women's Liberal Organisations had come around, *Woman* proudly asserted that the political woman had 'come into her kingdom, and she has done so without sacrificing any of her womanliness'. As in 1907, the 'so-called typical political woman was conspicuous by her absence'. At these political events, *Woman* continued, 'the Australian political woman stands as a gracious, capable, and withal, womanly figure, taking her turn at the wheel that must guide the ship of her country's destiny'.[62] What all this affirmed, *Woman* professed a year later, is that voting women were attune to the ongoing validity and desirability of sex difference in modern times. 'A mannish woman and a womanish man', it declared, were 'rank innovations on the Almighty's plan'.[63]

The New Woman was renowned for the challenge she represented to man's station in society. She was depicted by those opposed to feminist advancement as power grabbing—as man's competitor. Therefore, *Woman* not only denied accusations of the manly appearance and dress of the political woman but also rejected any claims that she wanted to compete with or usurp men's positions. The political woman, it assured readers, did not have a voracious appetite for all that men possessed. They did not have the 'slightest desire to dominate or control'. On the contrary, their wish was 'merely to have a due and proper share in the direction of the business of the Federation'.[64]

Woman assured its audience that voting would not alter women's moral and emotional make-up. However, it denied the relevancy of anti-suffragist claims that women were innately emotional, even over-emotional. Anti-suffragists declared that the presence of enfranchised women in the public world of politics would bring extreme emotionalism into that world. A lack of reason would, therefore, characterise a space that was once renowned for its rationality. The British *Review* testified that the entry of women onto the political stage at home had affirmed the truth of these claims.

Year after year, the pages of the *Review* were rife with indictments of the women's suffrage campaign on the grounds that women were far too emotional to exercise political reason. In 1909, for instance, it asserted that women formed 'opinions more quickly, less patiently, less coolly than do men'. 'Emotion, prejudice, sentiment, play a larger part in their decisions than in those of men', it affirmed.[65] By 1912, the intensifying militant campaign led the anti-suffrage paper to draw attention, again, to the folly and destructiveness of permitting emotions to enter into the political arena. Suffragettes had been 'swept away by the waves of emotionalism which have engulfed many women', the *Review* stated. These political women 'unsex themselves and plead as an excuse for their wicked and foolish actions their pathetic belief in the power of the vote'.[66] In 1917, as it looked likely that parliament was going to give in to the demands of feminists, the paper pointed out that now the entire country—dedicated anti-suffragists excluded—was being caught up in unthinking emotionalism. What would transpire for the political life of the nation was a reign of emotionalism. The danger, one article declared, is 'that women with votes may more easily than men be stampeded in a given direction on emotional grounds'.[67] Yet another article affirmed the accuracy of this. If women voters were to outnumber men, then emotions would dominate politics:

> All that is needed is a sudden wave of emotion, a catch vote, or some political intrigue, and the country will find itself committed to a policy which the robust section of its manhood on reflection will not endorse.[68]

Although *Woman* rejected the accuracy of these observations, it also acknowledged that some women fell back on this assertion of the inextricable connections between femininity and emotionalism to resist the new political responsibilities foisted on them. Far from agreeing with anti-feminist claims that the woman exercising her vote brought shame to womanhood, *Woman* argued that the cowardly woman who hid behind outmoded, inaccurate concepts of femininity disgraced that community. These irrelevant and archaic women threatened the integrity of true womanhood. Those who diligently educated themselves about their new duties and exercised them in an appropriately feminine manner did not.

In 1914, for example, in the early months of the World War One, *Woman* asserted that old-fashioned notions of femininity—those characterised by 'sentimentality, weakness, want of self-reliance, a narrow outlook on life'—no longer had a place in the modern world, if they ever had one before that.[69] Enfranchised or not, women across the Empire were affected by expanding opportunities. They were committed to war work. Some voted. Others capitalised on wider access to education and employment. *Woman* declared that shifting economic and demographic conditions meant that many women had to confront the fact that marriage was not always an option; therefore, they had to undertake paid employment. Woman's terrain was shifting.

Yet the paper had confidence that women could embrace all these changes without sacrificing true feminine values. Femininity still meant 'tenderness, intuition, quick and comprehensive sympathy, kindliness, refinement', it assured readers.[70] This is not, the paper instructed, to confuse 'sympathy' with 'sentiment'. Femininity was characterised by 'sympathy' not 'sentiment'.[71] No one wanted a woman to be too logical because a woman 'who is too logical often becomes unsympathetic, and loses a great deal of her charm'.[72] But neither was it helpful if she was too emotional. Excess emotion would not help the modern woman citizen to perform her new range of duties—if it had ever helped her in the past, which the paper claimed it doubted. Such a redundant notion of femininity shamed real womanhood. It demeaned real women's worth. It attacked the integrity of womanhood's contribution to and place in modern society. Women who clung to such damaging notions of femininity did not belong within *Woman*'s clearly defined gendered community.

Ever-Present Fear of New Australian Womanhood Being Found Defective

Through the early twentieth century, *Woman* continued to issue fervent denials that femininity was the necessary trade-off for enfranchisement. The fact that if felt compelled to repeat such declarations though is revealing of just how tenacious accusations of unwomanliness targeting the new woman voter were. Therefore, articles in the paper alternated between encouraging women to use their vote, on the one hand, and expressing a growing sense of dissatisfaction and frustration that old myths persisted, causing women to prove themselves to be shamefully inadequate, on the other.

These old myths of the masculinised political woman, *Woman* declared, were used as justification by women who refused to adapt to their new political responsibilities. In the face of fears about the perceived manliness of the political woman, some Australian women were pledging allegiance to what they thought were ultra-feminine notions of womanliness. They were adhering to outmoded ideas of gendered temperaments and responsibilities. For instance, in 1910, amid election campaigning, the paper accused the 'average woman' of being 'too much occupied with the trivialities of "the daily round, the common task"' to understand that she possessed 'a giant weapon for good or ill'—namely, the power of influencing legislation in social matters.[73] The 'average' Australian woman refused to vote because she prioritised protecting her family and her 'womanliness' over contributing to national politics. *Woman* pointed out that this was a selfish and misguided decision. This was also a misdirected understanding of womanliness.

Later, the paper lamented that its recourse to encouraging women to embrace their new wider duties and responsibilities was not working. It bemoaned the fact that 'so few of our women have yet risen to the height of their opportunities; have yet awakened to a full sense of their "National and Imperial responsibilities"'.[74] Too many women, it claimed, were justifying their self-imposed exile from the political sphere by uttering the old maxim that 'A woman's duty is in her own home'.[75] Woman's duty began in the home, but it did not end there. The paper attempted to reassure women that by exercising their right and duty to vote, they would not lose their womanliness. Women could 'rise to their new responsibility', all the while being secure in the knowledge that 'in so doing, they need not fear that they will lose the attributes of True Womanhood'.[76]

The following year, however, some writers adopted a more strident and less conciliatory tone. Many women, *Woman* explained, had felt indignant that they had been ranked with 'children, lunatics, and criminals' before they were granted suffrage. They will now rank themselves 'with the Greek class of "idiots" if they refuse to take interest in public affairs', it warned.[77] 'Let no one be afraid that a widening of their outlook and increase of responsibility will make them less feminine.' One only had to look back upon a history of noble women 'whom circumstances have forced into exceptional positions to realise that true womanliness shines forth more brightly side by side with the fuller development of mental and moral qualities', the writer continued.[78] Australian women were the modern version of these noble women of the past, for they too had been forced to assume an exceptional position in their domestic society and in the wider empire. On account of this, these uniquely encumbered women had been required to further develop their 'mental and moral qualities', while simultaneously proving their intrinsic womanliness. In a way, by coupling noble women of the past with dignified women voters in the present, *Woman* worked to deny the associations that many anti-suffragists had established between shame and modernising concepts of womanhood.

Yet, amid *Woman*'s protestations of the assured femininity of the political woman, too many Australian women citizens were refusing to embrace the responsibilities of their unique citizenship. Their insistence on not voting on the basis that voting was shamefully unwomanly had, ironically, brought shame down on the community that these apolitical women thought they were protecting. 'Are we doing our duty to the great heritage entrusted to our keeping?' the paper asked in 1911.[79] The response was negative. 'No other women in the world have so great power and responsibility placed in their hands, but so far nearly half of our women have been politically asleep.'[80] Women who had not taken the time to go to the polls, and so who had been responsible for the socialists taking control of the country (for the socialistic Labor Party successfully formed a majority government after the 1910 elections), were apparently boasting that they were 'not at all interested in politics'. No woman, the paper stated, could afford to say that she was not interested in politics any longer, for politics were very much interested in women.[81] By refusing to exercise her political responsibilities, the apolitical woman had threatened the integrity of the entire Australian community as a loyal member of the family of nations that composed the British Empire. In Chapter 4, I will elaborate on the Australian woman's duties to the nation and the Empire.

Fear of Australian womanhood being judged defective—of being shamed—lurked in the pages of *Woman*. However, this fear was less about being found unwomanly for voting—in line with accusations emanating specifically from pre-enfranchised British women—and more about Australian womanhood adhering to an anachronistic and embarrassing model of femininity. This state led AWNL president Eva Hughes to make an exasperated plea to fellow women to exercise their political rights and responsibilities. 'We have had the Franchise in Australia long enough to know that it is a false and silly plea "that it is unwomanly to vote"', Hughes decreed in 1911. Rather, she argued, it is 'unwomanly *not* to take the fullest share possible to us in the legislation of our country'.[82] It frustrated Hughes and other AWNL members that their fellow women citizens could not see and accept the truth of this. Womanhood, certainly in Australia, had modernised. It was now more useful than it had been in its previously disenfranchised state. To refuse to conform to that more useful concept of woman's mission while stubbornly paying homage to a redundant old-world model was impractical and wasteful. The apolitical woman's habit of desperately clinging to obsolete and ineffective notions of femininity embarrassed the community of patriotic Australian women.

By the end of the Great War, however, the ongoing stubbornness of the apolitical woman was more than embarrassing. It was treacherous. These women had endured the massive political upheaval that the war had produced in Australia. The intensely divisive conscription referenda—discussed in Chapter 4—exemplified this. Two referenda, in 1916 and 1917, failed to conscript men for war. Australia had been tainted with the stain of empire disloyalty. Female citizens had not done enough to prevent this. Therefore, if Australian women had not realised how crucial their political responsibilities were at the outset of the war, they should have known by its close. Yet two years after the war's end, *Woman* declared, 'The woman non-voter is ubiquitous'. 'One meets her everywhere—no, not everywhere. She is never to be seen in the polling booth or at 349 Collins-street', referring to the AWNL's headquarters in Melbourne.[83] Whatever type of woman she is—young, old, fat, thin, charming, morose—one thing is certain and that is that 'she is patronisingly superior when she informs you that she didn't bother to vote, that she takes no interest in politics', the paper pronounced.

> She has other interests; politics are for men, or for fusty women who have nothing better to do. Golf, tennis, dress, anything is more interesting; or she trots out the old story of how a woman is better employed looking after her home and her babies, etc., etc. 'My husband didn't care whether I voted or not,' she says, with the conscious virtue of the wife who always does what her husband wishes her to do. 'His man was sure to get in.' 'It was too hot, too wet, too cold, or too dusty, besides Saturday is an awkward day.' 'What's the use? Never see any good in these elections. What does the Government do for me, anyway, when it does get in.' 'There's too much quarrelling for me. If I vote, I'm sure to offend somebody, and so I stay at home,' and so the absurd nonsense goes on.[84]

The writer's frustration was palpable. 'It is incredible that these women, educated, well informed in most matters, are yet not shrewd enough to see that politics are their first business', *Woman* argued, 'because on politics depend, to a very large extent, the happiness of the home, the success of the business, and the prosperity of the country.'[85] The government was women's business, and no woman had a right to opt out of the responsibility for electing that government—not in 1908 and not now in 1920. The apolitical woman brought dishonour on Australian womanhood because her insistence on not voting meant that she neglected the expanded womanly duties of the modern Australian woman. Consequently, the private and the public communities to which she was attached suffered. By 1920, it did not feel as if she was sufficiently attached to those communities to undertake a shameful self-assessment and alter her ways.

Irish Women Endorse the Womanliness of the Australian Woman Voter

It was in the best interests of suffragists around the Empire, of course, to affirm that the woman voter would be womanly and that she would continue to prioritise her domestic and familial responsibilities. Irish suffragists did this by drawing on eyewitness testimony to affirm that the Australian woman voter fulfilled both these criteria. In 1915, the IWFL paper, the

Citizen, recorded an interview with Mrs Keane, a member of the League, who had returned from a visit to Australia. Keane informed readers that she had been eligible to register to vote in Australia because she had been in residence there for over six months before the election was held.[86] Therefore, she witnessed first-hand the behaviour and proclivities of actual women voters, of which she was one.

Throughout her interview, Keane denied assertions made in anti-suffragist propaganda that exercising the vote eroded feminine values, introduced political dissent into otherwise unified family lives, and influenced women to neglect their domestic and familial responsibilities. The interviewer asked Keane if she had witnessed any quarrelling between men and women voters on the day of the election. Was there any sign that homes were breaking up because of the woman vote? Families all voted alike, she said. Therefore, families remained intact. The question of whether or not children were starved or ignored on the day of the election elicited the response that there was no separation of mothers and children because women brought children with them to the polling booths. Australian women also participated in the political realm without ignoring their domestic responsibilities, she avowed. Perhaps at pains to point out just how undamaging the vote was, Keane then made the unsubstantiated assertion that Australian women were more diligent with regard to their domestic duties than women in Britain and Ireland.[87]

Far from conforming to the anti-feminist image of the manly, power-hungry feminist voter propagated by the anti-suffragist press, the Australian woman voter was in fact rather benign. She disappointed feminists, Keane added, because she voted less as a woman advocating women's interests and more as an ordinary member of society adhering to typical party allegiances.[88] This last remark may well have been intended to mollify anti-suffragists who had long argued that women's interests would swamp those of the rest of the electorate if a large body of women were to be enfranchised.

Keane also passed remarks that were intended to mollify a particular group of anti-suffragists—namely, those in her Irish and increasingly Catholic nationalist homeland.[89] She asserted that nuns—the epitome of sanctified womanliness—were seen voting in Australian elections. All non-enclosed Orders voted, she added. Moreover, they seemed quite keen to do so.[90] This voting nuns theme was to be repeated in the pages of the *Citizen*. Later that year, for example, the paper reported that nuns in New Zealand thought nothing of voting either. Here they were citing the testimony of a Father Molloy—testimony that had previously been published in *The Philadelphia North American* and the *Maryland Suffrage News*—who asserted that these voting nuns were 'not considered unfeminine or unladylike'. Voting did not have a corrosive effect on these religious women. 'They don't neglect their prayers, or their schools, or charities while they go to the polls; and, on the other hand, they keep in closer touch with the affairs of the country and reap the benefits of its government.'[91] If these paragons of womanly purity were able to exercise the vote without any sense that their womanliness or purity was corrupted, then surely all Irish women were safe from any threat of degradation should they be similarly enfranchised.

In a way, Molloy's comments about the distinct lack of dishonour associated with the woman vote chimed with those of Keane in her *Citizen* interview. Keane asserted that Australian men honoured and respected their women more than men in Britain and Ireland did. Her evidence for this was her observation that women's votes were seen to be as important as men's votes over there.[92] She concluded that the woman vote had not altered masculine and feminine emotional standards. This was a sentiment that the AWNL was likely to endorse in its efforts to persuade fellow Australian women to exercise their new political right. However, the changes to women's lives introduced by the onset of the Great War shook the AWNL's confidence in continuing to assert that the emotional standards underpinning women's roles had not changed.

Australian Woman Voter's Fears About the Erosion of Sex Difference

Woman rejected outmoded notions of femininity and embraced many expanding opportunities for women to participate in the public life of the country, but it did not endorse an obliteration or even a substantial erosion of sex difference. It did not, for example, endorse a model of sex relations where women and men competed equally for traditionally masculine positions. In 1918, the paper assured readers that true women did not want to compete with men or usurp their positions. 'I trust', Eva Hughes said, 'that the time may be ever far distant when women will strive to usurp the place of men in our Parliaments.'[93] 'Woman's strongest power lies in the fact of her womanhood', she argued.

> Let us lose sight of that and our influence in home and public life, will be diminished to perhaps vanishing point. I love my sex—and I realise what a tremendous power lies in our hands. To compete with men in the political world would kill it. Let us leave places in our legislature to our men. Let ours be the power behind the throne, and we shall not fail.[94]

Hughes's assertions about women's greatest power lying in her ability to influence men resonated with that of anti-suffragists such as Marie Corelli and the women of the NLOWS in Britain. Drawing on a well-established Victorian model of femininity,[95] the AWNL president intertwined traditional ideals with modern realities. In this way, belief in sex difference was maintained, even amid expanding political opportunities for Australian women.

Woman continued to promote the desirability of sex difference, but it also accepted that gendered emotional regimes were not inviolable. Those regimes were open to incursions. They were, to a degree, malleable. The experience of the Great War proved the truth of this for those contributing to the paper. The war had created a type of Australian 'girl' who was categorised as a 'modern girl'. This 'girl' was a blend of 'of all the best and most worthy of permanence, in the woman of the just-passing, old-fashioned types and the one in transition to the new'.[96] This girl had worked through the war. She had emerged from that experience robustly prepared for a changed post-war world where the costs of living would be high and prospects for marriage small. To protect her interests, *Woman* said, she now needed 'equal opportunities with men in the professional and industrial world'.[97]

The problem with the necessity for ensuring equal opportunities with men, a later article clarified, was acceptance of the fact that whether they desired it or not, woman was fast becoming man's competitor. *Woman* was adamant that women should not compete with men for political positions, but there was little they could do about women's needs to compete with them for paid employment. Still, the pronouncement was that, instead of being his 'helpmeet', she was fast becoming his 'rival'.[98]

Materially, the boundaries between men's and women's experiences were blurring. However, there was also the fear that men's and women's emotional regimes would also fade into each other. Through providing work for women as nurses and doctors, *Woman* said that the war had allowed women opportunities for proving themselves 'the equals of men in bravery and self-sacrifice'.[99] Serving as nurses and doctors in the field hospitals were examples of such opportunities. Women had acquitted themselves honourably. They had proven themselves capable and competent. They had demonstrated their capability for embodying the more masculine emotional virtue of courage. This, one *Woman* article declared, had produced the 'the unfortunate but certain result that the chivalrous and protective feeling of man towards woman was fast disappearing'.[100] Women's wartime capability for performing like men—to an extent, physically and emotionally—was threatening to dismantle emotional codes that protected women from men's excesses. In Chapter 7, I discuss the poignant anxieties about unleashed male violence that many anti-suffragist women harboured at the thought of dismantling codes of chivalry.

Conclusion

In opposing the woman vote, British anti-suffragists drew on a concept of womanhood that was underpinned by British middle-class values. Guided by Victorian ideals of 'separate but equal' spheres, they affirmed that women entering into the public fray would find their femininity tainted and corrupted. Women's collective emotional make-up was not made for the sordid world of business, politics, and war. That public world was not ready for women's inherent emotionalism. Women campaigning to enter the political field destabilised reigning gendered emotional regimes.

Anti-suffragists cited a particularly British brand of womanhood but, given Britain's place at the centre of a vast imperial network and its self-appointed role as international bearer of civilisation, this was also a model of femininity that it was willing to transport and transplant around the globe. This was both a national and a transnational understanding of 'proper' feminine womanhood. However, not all women around the Empire accepted the universal claims of this model. For example, Irish nationalist women fiercely repelled such transnational claims. As we will see in the next chapter, they asserted that the only model of womanhood suited to their predicament was a uniquely, ethnically Irish model.

Patriotic women in the antipodes did not necessarily disagree with the purported transnational nature of this model of womanhood, but they did challenge the relevancy of its more antiquated aspects to the 'modern girl' and certainly to the modern Australian voting woman. Rejecting the relevancy of these obsolete and ineffective aspects of traditional notions of womanhood helped them to further deny accusations of shame targeting the political woman. These were accusations that had emanated not only from more conservative quarters at home but also, more sensationally, from vociferous anti-suffragists in the imperial metropole. The patriotic Australian women of the AWNL declared that voting did not attack the integrity of the emotional community of good womanhood. Rather, it strengthened the bonds of that collective.

At the centre of these intersecting discussions were reigning understandings of gendered emotional regimes. Whereas British anti-suffragists argued that the emotional standards and rules guiding men's and women's interactions with each other would be corrupted by feminists' incursions into typically masculine spheres of thought and action, Australian women voters contended that the boundaries protecting these gendered regimes need not be infringed by exercising the right to vote. Voting was a duty that aligned with women's enlarged domestic responsibilities. Shame belonged to the women who refused to grow with these enlarged responsibilities. It was these anachronistic women who degraded empire womanhood through their cowardly refusal to adapt to modernising conditions. National duty was paramount.

Notes

1 *Irish Citizen*, vol. 3, no. 50, 1 May 1915, p. 388.
2 *Irish Citizen*, vol. 3, no. 50, 1 May 1915, p 388.
3 For a more nuanced discussion of how man came to be equated with 'reason, masculinity, truth and intellect', which was contrasted to woman as 'sensuality, femininity, error and emotion', and how citizenship became masculinised as the

'man of reason' was constructed as the only being entitled to political rights, see Barbara Caine and Glenda Sluga, *Gendering European History 1780–1920* (London: Continuum, 2004) especially Chapter 1 'Citizenship and Difference: The Age of Revolution', pp. 7–31.
4 Caine and Sluga, *Gendering European History 1780–1920*, pp. 7–8.
5 Caine and Sluga, *Gendering European History 1780–1920*, p. 57. For other discussions of gender and nationalism, see Joan Wallach Scott, *Only Paradoxes to Offer: French Feminists and the Rights of Man* (Cambridge, MA: Oxford University Press, 1997), and Lyn Hunt, *The Family Romance of the French Revolution* (Berkeley: University of California Press, 1993). For a detailed discussion of middle-class, masculinised notions of separate spheres and respectability, see Catherine Hall, *White, Male and Middle-Class: Explorations in Feminism and History* (New York: Routledge, 1992).
6 Caine and Sluga, *Gendering European History 1780–1920*, p. 3.
7 Norbert Elias, *The Civilizing Process: The History of Manners and State Formation and Civilization*, Transl. by Edmund Jephcott (Oxford, UK and Cambridge, USA: Blackwell, 1994 [1939]) p. 492.
8 Elias, *The Civilizing Process*, p. 492. Since the publication of this seminal text, there have been many critiques of Elias's approach to shame. John Braithwaite identifies this book as an extremely important text on shame; however, he disagrees with the extent to which Elias identifies an increasing democratisation of shame, arguing that even today, shame remains class structured as well as 'profoundly gendered'. See John Braithwaite, 'Shame and Modernity', *The British Journal of Criminology*, vol. 33, no. 1 (1993) pp. 1–18, p. 2 and 4. Thomas Scheff argues that this definition of shame in *The Civilizing Process* is flawed. Indeed, more than that, he argues that such a definition was absent: 'Elias offered no definition of shame in either book, seeming to assume that the reader would understand the concept of shame in the same way that he did.' See Thomas Scheff, 'A Taxonomy of Emotions: How Do We Begin?' www.soc.ucsb.edu/faculty/scheff/main.php?id=47.html, accessed 26 January 2017. Others disagree with the seemingly unproblematic progressive narrative—that is, that the progression of civilization was a product of the advancing 'frontier of shame and repugnance'. One commentator who disagrees with this 'judgemental chronology from primitive to civilised' is historian David Nash. See David Nash, 'Towards an Agenda for a Wider Study of Shame. Theorising from Nineteenth-Century British Evidence', in Judith Rowbotham, Marianna Muravyeva and David Nash, eds., *Shame, Blame and Culpability. Crime and Violence in the Modern State* (New York: Routledge, 2014) pp. 43–59, pp. 44–45.
9 Thomas J. Scheff, 'Shame and the Social Bond: A Sociological Theory,' *Sociological Theory*, vol. 18, no. 1 (2000) pp. 84–99, p. 97.
10 Richard A. Shweder, 'Toward a Deep Cultural Psychology of Shame', *Social Research*, vol. 70, no. 4 (2003) pp. 1109–1130, p. 1115.
11 Shweder, 'Toward a Deep Cultural Psychology of Shame', p. 1116.
12 Thomas J. Scheff, 'Shame in Self and Society', *Symbolic Interaction*, vol. 26, no. 2 (2003) pp. 239–262, p. 256.
13 Shweder, 'Toward a Deep Cultural Psychology of Shame', p. 1120.
14 Although, Shweder reiterates that cultural and historical contexts are not entirely free to give meaning to shame. It is still bound to the idea of what it means to be a 'good' person. See Shweder, 'Toward a Deep Cultural Psychology of Shame', p. 1120.
15 Even today, shame remains 'profoundly gendered'. Braithwaite, 'Shame and Modernity', p. 4.

16 See Jill Locke, 'Shame and the Future of Feminism', *Hypatia*, vol. 22, no. 4 (2007) pp. 146–162, p. 148; Scheff, 'Shame and the Social Bond', p. 86; and Thomas J. Scheff, 'Elias, Freud and Goffman: Shame as the Master Emotion', in Steven Loyal and Stephen Quilley, eds., *Sociology of Norbert Elias* (New York: Cambridge University Press, 2004) pp. 229–242, p. 231.
17 Jeff Goodwin, James Jasper and Francesca Polletta, 'Why Emotions Matter', in Jeff Goodwin, James Jasper and Francesca Polletta, eds., *Passionate Politics: Emotions and Social Movements* (Chicago: University of Chicago Press, 2001) pp. 1–24, p. 5.
18 Goodwin, Jasper and Polletta, 'Why Emotions Matter', p. 16.
19 Some today continue to believe that a healthy dose of shame has the power to inspire political action for the good of the community (in the case of philosopher Michael L. Morgan's work, to motivate people to work towards eliminating genocide from the modern world). See Michael L. Morgan, *On Shame* (New York and London: Routledge, 2008), for example, p. 43.
20 Locke, 'Shame and the Future of Feminism', p. 156.
21 Braithwaite, 'Shame and Modernity,' pp. 15–16.
22 Marie Corelli, *Woman, or—Suffragette? A Question of National Choice* (London: Arthur Pearson, 1907) p. 18.
23 Corelli, *Woman, or—Suffragette?*, p. 18.
24 Corelli, *Woman, or—Suffragette?*, p. 20.
25 See Corelli, *Woman, or—Suffragette?*, p. 31.
26 *Votes for Women*, November 1907, p19.
27 Corelli, *Woman, or—Suffragette?*, p. 5.
28 Corelli, *Woman, or—Suffragette?*, p. 16.
29 Marie Corelli, Flora Annie Webster Steel, Lady Susan Hamilton Ardagh and Baroness St Helier Susan Elizabeth Mary Stewart-McKenzie Jeune, *The Modern Marriage Market* (London: Hutchinson, 1898) pp. 16–17.
30 Corelli, Steel, and Jeune, *Modern Marriage Market*, pp. 38–39.
31 For the purposes of continuity and simplicity, throughout the book, I will refer to the National League for Opposing Woman Suffrage as the body that represents female anti-suffragists. However, it is to be remembered that from 1908 to 1910, when the NLOWS was established as an amalgam of the women's and men's leagues, the *Review* represented the interests of the women's organisation the Women's National Anti-Suffrage League.
32 *Anti-Suffrage Review*, no. 1, December 1908, p. 1.
33 *Anti-Suffrage Review*, no. 1, December 1908, p. 1.
34 *Anti-Suffrage Review*, no. 11, October 1909, pp. 5–6.
35 *Anti-Suffrage Review*, no. 47, September 1912, p. 219.
36 *Anti-Suffrage Review*, no. 47, September 1912, p. 219.
37 *Anti-Suffrage Review*, no. 10, September 1909, pp. 4–5.
38 *Anti-Suffrage Review*, no. 10, September 1909, pp. 4–5.
39 *Anti-Suffrage Review*, no. 10, September 1909, pp. 4–5.
40 *Anti-Suffrage Review*, no. 66, April 1914, p. 48.
41 *Anti-Suffrage Review*, no. 21, August 1910, pp. 18–19.
42 *Anti-Suffrage Review*, no. 21, August 1910, pp. 18–19.
43 *Anti-Suffrage Review*, no. 10, September 1909, pp. 4–5.
44 *Anti-Suffrage Review*, no. 47, September 1912, p. 219.
45 *Anti-Suffrage Review*, no. 14, January 1910, pp. 4–5.
46 *Anti-Suffrage Review*, no. 14, January 1910, pp. 4–5.
47 *Anti-Suffrage Review*, no. 31, June 1911, pp. 121–2.
48 *Anti-Suffrage Review*, no. 66, April 1914, p. 48.
49 *Anti-Suffrage Review*, no. 21, August 1910, pp. 18–19.
50 *Anti-Suffrage Review*, no. 66, April 1914, p. 48.

51 *Anti-Suffrage Review*, no. 21, August 1910, pp. 18–19.
52 *Bean na hEireann*, vol. 1, no. 4, February 1909, p. 1.
53 *Bean na hEireann*, vol. 1, no. 18, May 1910, p. 8.
54 *Bean na hEireann*, vol. 1, no. 18, May 1910, p. 8.
55 *Irish Citizen*, vol. 6, no. 6, November 1918, pp. 630–631.
56 *Irish Citizen*, vol. 5, no. 54, January 1918, p. 394.
57 *Irish Citizen*, vol. 5, no. 54, January 1918, p. 394.
58 *Irish Citizen*, vol. 5, no. 54, January 1918, p. 394.
59 Scheff, 'Shame in Self and Society', p. 256.
60 *Woman*, vol. 1, no. 3, 23 November 1907, pp. 61–62.
61 *Woman*, vol. 2, no. 11, 28 July 1909, pp. 491–493.
62 *Woman*, vol. 5, no. 1, 1 March 1912, p. 295.
63 *Woman*, vol. 5, no. 13, 1 February 1913, p. 330.
64 *Woman*, vol. 3 no. 4, 24 March 1910, pp. 592–593.
65 *Anti-Suffrage Review*, no. 6, May 1909, p. 4.
66 *Anti-Suffrage Review*, no. 48, October 1912, p. 235–236.
67 *Anti-Suffrage Review*, no. 107, September 1917, pp. 65–67.
68 *Anti-Suffrage Review*, No 107, September 1917, p. 67.
69 *Woman*, vol. 7, no. 10, 1 December 1914 pp. 255–256.
70 *Woman*, vol. 7, no. 10, 1 December 1914, pp. 255–256.
71 *Woman*, vol. 7, no. 10, 1 December 1914, pp. 255–256.
72 *Woman*, vol. 5, no. 10, 1 November 1912, pp. 249–250.
73 *Woman*, vol. 3, no. 4, 24 March 1910, p. 606.
74 *Woman*, vol. 3, no. 7, 1 September 1910, p. 658.
75 *Woman*, vol. 3, no. 9, 1 November 1910, pp. 696–697.
76 *Woman*, vol. 3 no. 6, 1 August 1910, p. 648.
77 *Woman*, vol. 3, no. 12, 1 February 1911, p. 757.
78 *Woman*, vol. 3, no. 12, 1 February 1911, p. 757.
79 *Woman*, vol. 4, no. 1, 1 March 1911, pp. 1–2.
80 *Woman*, vol. 4, no. 1, 1 March 1911, pp. 1–2.
81 *Woman*, vol. 4, no. 1, 1 March 1911, pp. 1–2.
82 *Woman*, vol. 6, no. 5, 2 July 1913, pp. 97–100.
83 *Woman*, vol. 12, no. 12, 1 February 1920, p. 481.
84 *Woman*, vol. 12, no. 12, 1 February 1920, p. 481.
85 *Woman*, vol. 12, no. 12, 1 February 1920, p. 481.
86 *Irish Citizen*, vol. 3, no. 44, 20 March 1915, p. 339.
87 *Irish Citizen*, vol. 3, no. 44, 20 March 1915, p. 339.
88 *Irish Citizen*, vol. 3, no. 44, 20 March 1915, p. 339.
89 For a discuss on the nature of Irish nationalism, see Sean Cronin, *Irish Nationalism: Its Roots and Ideology* (New York: Continuum, 1980) and Robert Kee, *The Green Flag: A History of Irish Nationalism* (London: Penguin, 2001).
90 *Irish Citizen*, vol. 3, no. 44, 20 March 1915, p. 339.
91 *Irish Citizen*, vol. 3, no. 50, 1 May 1915, p. 388.
92 *Irish Citizen*, vol. 3, no. 44, 20 March 1915, p. 339.
93 *Woman*, vol. 11, no. 9, 1 November 1918, p. 364.
94 *Woman*, vol. 11, no. 9, 1 November 1918, p. 364.
95 Victorian gender ideals were often represented by the works of John Ruskin and Coventry Patmore. See John Ruskin, Lecture II: 'Of Queens' Gardens', in *Sesame and Lilies: The Two Paths: & The King of the Golden River* (London: Dent, 1970 [1865]) and Coventry Patmore, *The Angel in the House* (1854–1856) (London: Cassell, 1887). For a discussion of the nuances of these gender ideals, see Sharon Aronofsky Weltman, ' "Be No More Housewives, but Queens": Queen Victoria and Ruskin's Domestic Mythology', in Margaret

Homans and Adrienne Munich eds., *Remaking Queen Victoria* (Cambridge: Cambridge University Press, 1997) pp. 105–122.
96 *Woman*, vol. 11, no. 7, 1 September 1918, p. 283.
97 *Woman*, vol. 11, no. 7, 1 September 1918, p. 283.
98 *Woman*, vol. 11, no. 11, 1 January 1919, p. 447.
99 *Woman*, vol. 11, no. 11, 1 January 1919, p. 447.
100 *Woman*, vol. 11, no. 11, 1 January 1919, p. 447.

2 Reversing the Shame of British Colonisation

In 1909, the Irish nationalist women's periodical the *Bean na hÉireann* (the *Bean*) lamented the fact that the Irish think it is a shame to be Irish. They had not always thought this way. Ancient Ireland was a proud place. Irish people were descendants of a proud 'race'. However, British colonisation from the seventeenth century onwards had changed all of that. British imperialists attempted to train the Irish people to scorn all things Irish as being 'native', 'low and vulgar', and to revere all things modern.[1] The erosion of Irish nationalism was part of this process, as modernity was constructed as the antithesis of nationalism. Taught to hate their nation and feel ashamed of their nationalism, the Irish made what the *Bean* said was 'a servile, imitative, inglorious attempt to bring itself up to the foreign standard of happiness, which might be described, not unjustly, as ostentatious discomfort'.[2] The Irish bought into a narrative imposed on them during colonisation that celebrated the great 'intellectual advance from the dark ages of Irish barbarism'.[3] It was clear to those writing for this nationalist feminist paper that someone had to deliver this once proud nation from its current state of shameful dejection. That task fell to Irish women.

The *Bean* charged Irish women with restoring pride to the Irish nation and reinjecting honour into national affairs:

> Let us, Irishwomen, be inspired with it, and we will take our place in the world no less worthily than the rest. Our obvious duty is to our country, to the task of strengthening her spiritually, morally, materially, infusing into her a new soul, or rather the old hero soul she has gone nigh to losing. To restore our language, literature, and industries; to accentuate national distinctiveness, to enliven and purify our national spirit—in a word to regain our individuality as a people is our work, and all this we can accomplish if we but will it, and bring the necessary enthusiasm and determination to bear on it.[4]

Women should set to the task of recovering their country's cultural knowledge. They should inspire their menfolk to actively fight for Ireland's liberty and therefore its honour. It was the patriotic woman's responsibility to reverse her country's shame. Yet what of those women who resisted this honourable vocation? More than that, what of those women who colluded with the source of Ireland's shame, Britain, in their attempt to gain voting rights in a British parliament? Weren't they guilty of compounding that shame?

Patriotic women across the British Empire were keenly attuned to discussions about national honour and its antithesis, shame. However, their concerns about this issue assumed different forms, reflecting different national priorities. Whereas Irish women situated across the intersecting branches of nationalist politics lamented the emasculation of the once proud Irish nation, Australian women were anxious that their young virile Commonwealth would prove itself a worthy member of the Empire's family of nations. At the centre of that vast imperial network, British women worried that any slur cast on their national reputation would mean the fall of a noble and enriching empire.

Significantly, the notion of honour that lay at the heart of these interconnecting nationalist concerns was highly gendered. As a traditionally masculine concept, honour regulated relations between men in the public worlds of business, politics, and war.[5] Honour codes were meant to ensure that men treated each other with respect. It was about protecting men's individual reputations for honesty, fairness, courage, and loyalty. Certainly, at the beginning of the twentieth century, women were deemed to have no place in the public honour system. Why then did patriotic women in Ireland feel that they had the ability or power to protect, police, or restore the honour of their nation? How did patriotic women who respected gendered emotional regimes respond to the issue of national dishonour? In this chapter, I examine how nationalist women in Ireland understood their role in relation to national honour and shame. I look at how they deployed shame in the quest to restore national honour.

Honour, Gender and the Nation

Honour, Robert Nye argues, has traditionally 'regulated relations among men, summed up the prevailing ideals of manliness, and marked the boundaries of masculine comportment'.[6] The notion of honour was distinctly gendered. Men's honour was tied to their performance in the public realm. Women's honour was located in the private sphere because honour meant chastity for most women.[7] This explained the history of women's exclusion from public forms of citizenship. Women could not possess public forms of honour; therefore, they could not participate in the public realms, such as those of business, politics, and war, which were guided by codes of honour.[8]

The gendered nature of honour remained constant. However, concepts of what specifically constitutes honour and applications of honour codes have developed over time. When honour as a concept originated in the context of knighthoods and oaths of loyalty, it was tied to performance in military, political, and national matters. As industrialism emerged and the middle classes expanded in the Western world, honour came to be applied to behaviour in the sporting, business, and sexual realms too.[9] Charles Stewart asserts that in the seventeenth century, honour meant a general social reputation. By the nineteenth century, it had taken on 'a more interiorized sense of integrity or moral dignity'.[10] Pieter Spierenburg adds that over that time, honour moved increasingly away from being associated with the body and more towards spiritualisation, as exemplified by the reduction in honour-related violence in Western societies.[11] Nye argues that honour never lost its association with old martial values of courage and strength; however, bourgeois and modernising influences did imbue it with a sense of moral dignity and contractual or personal integrity.[12] By the beginning of the twentieth century, then, honour had evolved to act as an umbrella term for emotional virtues such as courage, chivalry, fairness, and honesty.

Traditionally, honour regulated relations between members of the social elite. Therefore, many members of society were excluded from having to abide by honour codes. However, by the dawn of the twentieth century, due to shifts such as the expansion of the male franchise, the criteria for possessing honour had broadened sufficiently to include most men.[13] More members of society could now possess honour, but this meant that many more could now also lose it. To be without honour now meant something different. To be bereft of honour invited scorn and disdain. Dishonour brought with it a sense of shame, as honour and shame were increasingly constructed as a binary.[14]

Through modernity, honour also came to be increasingly linked to the reputation of the nation. Spierenburg explains that by the turn of the twentieth century, honour had become less of a personal attribute. Before this time, an individual could dishonour the collective to which he belonged through his actions. At the very least, he argues, the individual could bring shame to his family. However, by the end of the nineteenth century, as nation-states proliferated, an individual's actions were linked to the reputation of a much larger group: the nation.[15] The honour of the nation-state and the nation had to be protected at all costs.

Ute Frevert elaborates on this. She points out that at the beginning of the twentieth century, honour, shame, and humiliation were well-known concepts within international relations.[16] Experts on moral laws informing politics argued that the State, as the dominant bearer of sovereign power, had to be protected by all means, including through recourse to war.[17] The State, then, was viewed as possessing and displaying 'a highly developed sense of honour'. Any insult to the State, real or symbolic, threatened the honour and therefore the legitimacy of that State. For the State to continue to exist, it had to maintain the respect of fellow States.[18] Honour, it follows, became a marker of State sovereignty. As Frevert extrapolates, war was justified if a state or nation's honour or reputation was besmirched. Certainly, national honour—or what sociologist Max Weber referred to as 'prestige' and 'reputation' in an attempt to modernise what he considered an anachronistic term—was cited by many of the States entering into war in 1914 as their reason for joining the conflict.[19] War was the unavoidable response to dishonour. It was a means of restoring national honour.

Not surprisingly, given its martial underpinnings, the gendered division of honour and shame continued into wartime. In many ways, it became more pronounced. Man's personal honour was tied to the nation's honour. If a man lacked courage, he shamed both himself and the nation to which he belonged.[20] I will discuss the notions of honour, courage, and chivalry as they applied to war and combat in more detail in the final two chapters of the book. However, for the purposes of this chapter on national honour and shame, I want to re-emphasise the point that the highly gendered nature of honour regimes meant that a woman could not assume an active relationship with honour in the way that a man could. Even if she lost her private form of honour—namely, her chastity—she could not act to reverse her shame. Her menfolk could fight in her name, but, as Frevert points out, strictly speaking, they fought to restore their own male reputations from the taint of association with her lost honour. They could not restore hers.[21]

Conversely, and importantly for this discussion, if a woman's menfolk lacked courage, her reputation was also compromised. Her association with dishonoured masculinity—man or nation—brought her shame. It follows, then, that patriotic women would feel the threat and fear of national dishonour keenly. It was in their interests to protect the manly qualities of the nation: its integrity, courage, dignity, and pride. Yet the gendered relationship between womanhood and honour made it clear that the only role she was supposed to assume in relation to this task was a passive one. She was only intended to influence and guide her menfolk to carry out their active responsibilities. How could she direct men to acquit themselves ably in this regard without transgressing the boundaries existing between the emotional regimes that guided their separate spheres? How could she command them to be honourable when she had no public honour herself and therefore no experience with or knowledge of the honour expected of them? Women's complicated relationship with the nation and the nationalist project introduced a further degree of ambiguity.

Woman, the Nation and Nationalism

The history of women's relationship with the nation and their participation in nationalist projects is complicated and contested. Throughout the 1980s, eminent scholars of nationalism, including Ernest Gellner and Anthony D. Smith, produced a body of scholarship that theorised about nationalisms and nation-building processes. However, it did not take long for feminist historians to note that gender, more generally, and women, specifically, were largely absent from these accounts.[22] In her groundbreaking 1989 study, *Bananas, Beaches and Bases*, Cynthia Enloe argued that it was largely assumed that men and women experienced nationalism in the same way. She also noted that research on nationalism tended to assume that nationalist projects took femininity and masculinity into account when 'defining and critiquing nationalist goals'.[23] However, Enloe, alongside other notable feminist theorists, including Nira Yuval-Davis, Floya Anthias, Sylvia Walby, and Anne McClintock, pointed out that women's relationships with nationalism were not uncomplicated; they were distinctly uneasy.[24] Some nationalist movements offered women opportunities for public representation and participation that they could rarely find elsewhere. Yet, overwhelmingly, the nationalist project cast women in a reductive symbolic role: the nation as allegorical woman who relied on the protection of her masculine other. This led many historians of nationalisms to obscure, if not omit, acknowledgment of the participation of women in nationalist movements and in resulting nation-building projects. What resulted were historical narratives that depicted nationalism as typically springing from 'masculinized memory, masculinized humiliation, and masculinized hope'.[25] These were the gendered assumptions that feminist historians hoped to overturn.

Given the prodigiously masculinsed view of nation-building, Enloe argued, 'Living as a nationalist feminist is one of the most difficult projects in today's world'.[26] Being a nationalist feminist in an anti-colonial nationalist context was even more fraught. As historians of colonised women have attested, such women were doubly enslaved, viewed by colonising forces as second-class citizens by virtue both of their gender and their colonised status.[27] In such circumstances, feminists had to articulate their emancipatory goals amid simultaneous moves for political autonomy, the assertion of a distinctive national identity, and a modernising agenda.[28] In line with the nationalist agenda, conceptualisations of womanhood had to develop to incorporate both the modern and the traditional. That is, women had to be seen to embody the traditional values of their specific culture or ethnicity as well as the modern values of their forward-looking nations.[29]

In many ways, then, the nationalist agenda ran counter to feminist objectives. Being cast in a reductive symbolic role—again the nation as allegorical woman who relied on the protection of her masculine other—was hardly emancipatory for feminists. Therefore, dedicated nationalist feminists had to work hard to align what were often conflicting ideologies and paradoxical views of womanhood. Consequently, some feminists—nationalist feminists—prioritised nationalist goals while still maintaining an allegiance to feminist ones. Other feminists—feminist nationalists—fought for their legal rights as women so that they could assume an equal footing with their national manhood when it came to constructing the nation. Historians Margaret Ward and Louise Ryan have argued that this state of conflict was certainly true for early twentieth-century Irish feminists who supported moves for national autonomy.[30] These nationalist feminists and feminist nationalists also had to decide how to deal with the issue of the emasculation of colonised Irish manhood by the ever-virulent British coloniser. The task of restoring Ireland to its previously independent state required a multifaceted approach to emotional regimes and gendered communities of national belonging.[31]

Irish Women Painfully Aware of the Shame of the Colonised Nation

Although it was not yet a nation-state, patriotic Irish women considered the task of protecting Ireland's honour to be a weighty responsibility. They demonstrated how seriously they took this duty in the pages of a variety of politically diverse Irish women's periodicals. Two of these papers, the *Bean* and the *Irish Citizen* (the *Citizen*), shared the same objectives. They desired the Irish nation to be free from British rule, and they wanted Irish women to assume a prominent role in directing the affairs of that independent nation. Yet they differed markedly on the program they endorsed for realising those aims. The *Bean* believed that Irish women should prioritise the nationalist campaign, and then they should petition their menfolk to grant them equal citizenship in the new Irish nation. The *Citizen* largely advocated women winning the vote from Britain and then using that power to stand alongside their brothers to secure their country's freedom. The divergent ways of envisioning the pathway to Ireland's and Irish women's freedom by feminist nationalists and nationalist feminists reflected the most significant divide in Irish women's nationalist politics.

As nationalist papers, the *Bean* and the *Citizen* were united in their lament over Ireland's loss of honour. They each decried the colonising process that had imposed shame on the once proud Irish nation through emasculating its manhood. British colonists had achieved this by constructing the Irish as a childlike Celtic 'race' that was erratic, irrational, and emotional.[32] Robbed of his manliness, the Irish man had no rights to national autonomy. However, the two papers diverged when it came to attempts to align support for women's political aspirations with the need to restore honour to the Irish man and the Irish nation. This division was exemplified by their competing views on the campaign for the vote in the British parliament. Whereas the *Bean* accused the women of the *Citizen* of compounding the Irish man's shame by begging his enemy to grant Irish women's political rights, the *Citizen* countered that the women behind the *Bean* were guilty of slavishly obeying Irish men's directives to abandon their feminist aspirations in favour of those of the male-led nationalist campaign. Consequently, the nationalist feminists writing for the *Bean* attempted to shame their feminist sisters into prioritising Ireland's honour over their own political ambitions. Feminist nationalists writing for the *Citizen* tried to show their nationalist sisters the shame of their subservience to Irish manhood and exclusively masculinised notions of the nation.

Initially, this mutual shaming was about inviting aberrant women back into the fold of good Irish womanhood. Members of the fractured community of patriotic womanhood understood that their broader political aims aligned and that unity strengthened their movement. However, as the nationalist campaign intensified and grew ever more violent—and certainly by the time the Great War had exposed the rawness of Irish political divisions over whether or not to continue serving British agendas—this shaming grew less inviting and more exclusionary. Shame was pulled into the service of defining the boundaries existing between these two seemingly irreconcilable factions of patriotic womanhood.

In this chapter, I trace some of the divergent views of feminists variously devoted to actively restoring the emasculated Irish nation's honour themselves and bolstering Irish men's capabilities for doing so. What do the divergent views of members of this fractured community of patriotic womanhood reveal about women's attitudes towards the gender of honour and shame in the national context? Shame occupied a complex and contested place in Irish political culture at the time. Widespread perceptions about the shameful state of the nation prompted dedicated nationalist women to assess how far Irish manhood and Irish womanhood contributed to or ameliorated that shame. The results of those assessments further divided that gendered community. The intense emotional energy that all Irish nationalist women invested in the question of how to restore Ireland's honour—or help Irish men to do so—is exemplified by the lengthy discussions of their efforts in the pages of their political journals.

Calling on Women to Reverse the Shaming Process

Whatever their differences, the *Bean* and the *Citizen* agreed that Ireland had fallen into a pitiful state characterised by collective shame. Too many Irish thought it a shame to be Irish. The *Bean* and the *Citizen* were not the first Irish woman's papers to say this. For example, the nationalist women's paper, the *Shan Van Vocht*—run by two poets, Alice Milligan and Anna Johnson, in the north of the country during the 1890s—was unequivocal about the source of the country's shame.[33] British colonisation had emasculated the Irish man and convinced the Irish woman to abandon her post as the guardian of national culture.

In 1897, the *Shan Van Vocht* used the occasion of Queen Victoria's Jubilee and her proposed visit to Ireland to oppose what it identified as further 'de-Celtifying' and 'Anglicising' of Ireland by those from across the Irish Sea.[34] Why would Ireland accept a visit from the monarch who was responsible for obliterating Irish culture? It was during Victoria's reign, the *Shan Van Vocht* argued, that England had almost succeeded in realising its aim of supplanting native Irish habits with those from its own land, thereby spoiling 'what civilization might have naturally grown up among the people'.[35] Labelling this era 'an anti-Celtic period', the paper asserted that more of the Irish character had been lost during these years than ever before. However, the process of cultural annihilation was not quite complete. Remnants of

Irish culture remained, but so did the British desire to get rid of those remnants.[36] Therefore, the paper warned, Irish people needed to be on guard against further cultural erosion.

An important element of this process of cultural erosion was the transplantation of British cultural values and practices in Ireland. For example, the *Shan Van Vocht* declared that the Irish felt that they were 'behind the times' if they were not informed enough to discuss the latest 'problem novel' coming out of England, such as those of Thomas Hardy, or those of renowned bestsellers Marie Corelli or Grant Allen. Any 'trash bearing the imprimatur of English approbation is assured of permanent favour' over the excellence of Irish writers, the paper complained.[37] In this way, the Irish had bought into the notion that the English were indeed the standards bearers of all things modern and civilised. They bought into the notion that to be 'behind the times' or out of step with modernity was shameful. The only thing that could save Irish culture from its shameful state, then, was Irish unity. Colonisation had divided the Irish. It had set them against one another. Unity of purpose was what was needed if they were to resist the 'strong tide of Saxon influence'—if the country was to 'cast off the shackles of her debasement'.[38]

The *Shan Van Vocht* was highly sensitised to Ireland's debasement. On this point, those writing for the paper proved themselves complicit with the racial ideals of its dominant imperial neighbour. This ignominious state was the result of 'a struggle of six or seven centuries, after many bloody wars and sweeping confiscations'.[39] A once proud, rich, and strong people had been reduced to a mere state of slavery through imperial exploitation. Consequently, the paper appealed to its cousins in the United States—who were, of course, familiar with the institution of slavery via black chattel slavery: 'Can the American mind picture a race of white men reduced to this condition? White men! Yes, of the highest and purest blood and breed of men.'[40] Ireland's shame was the emasculation and debasement of its once proud, white manhood.

One decade later, in 1909, the *Bean* reiterated *Shan Van Vocht*'s point about cultural erosion and Ireland's humiliation. The 'success of England's far-seeing and deliberate policy of blotting out from the memory of Ireland all records and traces of our native civilisation was practically assured', the paper proclaimed.[41] It instructed readers not to promote English fashions and English aspirations in Ireland where conditions were ill suited to accommodate them.

The paper's concerns were specifically gendered. It worried that the dissemination of such inappropriate foreign cultural material would corrupt Irish femininity. Through these cultural materials, the English set 'paltry ideals' before 'our young Irish women'.

> Before OUR women! Before the women of THIS nation—Eire—who have such a civilisation behind them, and would have such a glorious

ideal of Life and of their destiny if they could only be again awakened to a conception of it. This is the work that BEAN NA H-EIREANN has set out to do, and we need the help of all our readers.[42]

Through this appeal, the *Bean* implicated Irish women in the project of recovering Ireland's lost honour:

> Let us, Irishwomen, be inspired with it, and we will take our place in the world no less worthily than the rest. Our obvious duty is to our country, to the task of strengthening her spiritually, morally, materially, infusing into her a new soul, or rather the old hero soul she has gone nigh to losing. To restore our language, literature, and industries; to accentuate national distinctiveness, to enliven and purify our national spirit—in a word to regain our individuality as a people is our work, and all this we can accomplish if we but will it, and bring the necessary enthusiasm and determination to bear on it.[43]

The *Bean* asked Irish women to help restore the nation's honour. They were expected to do so by conforming to a traditional model of womanhood and womanly duties. That is to say, they were implored to reposition themselves as the guardians of the nation's cultural repertoire. That way, the boundary between gendered emotional regimes remained intact. Irish women could restore that aspect of national honour that fell within the woman's remit—namely, the protection of the nation's culture and values. Irish men then could be left to perform the more active duty of restoring the nation's political honour.

However, the sense that Irish women might fail in their endeavour because of their own indifference pervaded the pages of the *Bean*. In a plea entitled 'To Our Sisters', the journal called on 'the great unthinking majority' of Irish women to abandon their present collective state of apathy:

> We Irishwomen must learn to throw off our present diffidence, and assume our natural position in Irish life, and men will soon have to frankly admit that that it is only by working hand in hand that we can hope to make Ireland free.[44]

'Our *rasion d'etre*', the article emphasised, was 'to awaken Irishwomen to their responsibilities and long neglected duties'.[45] The *Bean's* ambivalence about the strength of Irish women's nationalist convictions was reflected in its alternating recourse to providing encouragement, on the one hand, and attempted shaming on the other. For example, in another 1909 article, 'Irishwomen's Duty', the author moved from inspiring fellow women to take up the cause of freeing the nation and rearming it with a sense of honour to shaming those women for not looking like they were up to the task. 'It has long been a reproach to Irish women of this generation', the paper stated, 'that they are, to a very great extent, out of touch with the tradition of Irish Nationalism, and are more emphatically strangers in their own land than even their brothers.'[46] The fear that Irish women were not up to the task of reinvigorating the nationalist movement persisted. If they were not, then Ireland's state of abject shame would continue as its cultural repertoire continued to be eclipsed by that imposed on them by the British coloniser and as its manhood continued without the camaraderie of its national womanhood.

The Use of Nostalgic Visions of Equality to Re-masculinise Irish Manhood

Irish women needed to get a sense of themselves as a national collective. They needed to reconstruct a community of patriotic womanhood to replace that which had been lost as a result of the process of colonisation and the imposition of British notions of modernity. However, the competing aspirations of feminist nationalists and nationalist feminists, as well as the political indifference of too many Irish women, rendered that task a difficult one. In many ways, these differences were reflected in Irish nationalist women's uneven approach to the gendered nature of national honour. On the one hand, some nationalist women argued that Irish men needed to reclaim the country's honour, thereby reversing their emasculation and that of the nation. Only then could the Irish stand proud. On the other hand, other nationalist women challenged the gendered nature of honour by asserting that Irish women could actively restore the nation to its former state of glory alongside or even in place of Irish men. Whatever their differing views on honour and masculinity, nationalist women were connected by their waning confidence in the Irish man's ability or desire to reassert his masculinity in the face of that of the ever-virulent British coloniser.

Patriotic Irish women had charged themselves with the task of delivering a vital component in the construction of a nationalist identity—namely, the uncovering of a glorious past of national autonomy that would also act as a blueprint for the future.[47] This vision of a glorious past also served the purpose of promoting Irish women's feminist aspirations. In the past, the *Bean* proclaimed, women were not 'the least among our patriots'. Back then, Irish women had assumed the role of protector of all that stirred 'the people to a remembrance of their common kinship'.[48] It was up to women of the present generation to get back in touch with that heritage. By moulding their individual memories into a collective consciousness—one that traced its origins back to the women of the ancient order—it was only then that a community of good nationalist Irish women could once again be formed. It was then that a truly proud Irish nation could once again be formed.

This strategy of evoking a nostalgic vision of an ancient and glorious Ireland where equality reigned between the sexes to motivate Irish women to politicise was one that connected nationalist feminists and feminist nationalists. Nationalist feminist Constance Markievicz instructed fellow Irish women to 'arm your minds with the histories and memories of your country and her martyrs, her language, and a knowledge of her arts and her industries'.[49] 'Arm your souls with noble and free ideas', she directed. 'And if in your day the call should come for your body to arm, do not shirk that either.'[50] Markievicz's call to arms was a little out of synch with other contributors to the *Bean* who emphasised the primacy of women's cultural roles. By invoking such an active response, she threatened the appropriation of masculine notions of honour. As discussed in Chapter 7, she enacted this appropriation by assuming a leading role in an armed insurrection against Britain in 1916.

Feminist nationalist Hanna Sheehy Skeffington, who was given room to voice her opinions in the pages of the nationalist women's paper, summoned up a similar nostalgic vision and juxtaposed it to Ireland's present-day degradation. However, she was more ambivalent about the power of such imagery to reverse the shameful place of women in Irish society. 'It is barren comfort for us Irishwomen', she wrote, 'to know that in ancient Ireland women occupied a prouder, freer position than they now hold even in the most advanced modern states, that all professions, including that of arms, were freely open to their ambitions.'[51]

Irish women occupied positions of authority and power in the past, Sheehy Skeffington asserted, continuing, 'Our ancestresses were the state-recognized arbiters in matters under dispute between rival factions, forming a final court of appeal, a permanent Hague Tribunal'.[52] However, now Irish men stood alongside British men as obstacles in the way of Irish women ever resuming that ancient position of privilege. Where now, she asked, is 'the glory and the dream?' 'Does the vision of the past mitigate the abject present? Is the degradation of the average Irishwoman the less real?'[53] Sheehy Skeffington doubted the reformative ability of stories of past glory to re-energise the feminist or nationalist movement.

For the most part, the *Bean* endorsed the notion that honour was a masculine concept. Women could lead the cultural branch of the nationalist movement. They could safeguard the nation's cultural repository from further foreign incursions. However, the distinctly political dimension of the nationalist project was the Irish man's responsibility. It was his duty to lead the country from the depths of degradation to which it had plummeted. Therefore, the paper pleaded with Irish men to uphold the honour of the nation. However, while in the process of doing so, it also revealed just how little confidence it had in the Irish man's ability to raise its sex and its nation from those humiliating depths.

The *Bean* compounded feminist nationalist views that Irish men—as exemplified by their politicians—had bought into a relatively new tradition of embarrassing, even humiliating, 'flunkeyism'.[54] The political games being played around the pivotal issue of Home Rule demonstrated that England was holding the Irish nation—and Irish masculinity—to ransom. English politicians repeatedly promised the possibility of a home-based parliament being re-established in Ireland without fulfilling that promise. In 1911, when Home Rule was again on the table for discussion and another royal visit was being scheduled, the *Bean* reported angrily,

> Whenever Home Rule is reported to be almost in our grasp, we are invited to take a dose of English royalty, with the promise that if we take it without wincing and all the time keep smiling, we will be given our freedom.[55]

Another 1911 article likewise asserted that Home Rule was to be 'put on our nose, as a lump of sugar on a dog's'.[56] Nationalist women well understood that offering the possibility of Home Rule was a tactic intended to sweeten Irish views of Britain and engender a conciliatory form of imperial loyalty. What Ireland needed was not sweet appeasement, however. It needed to recall its own strength. The call, then, was for nationalists to unite and to 'remember our self-respect, our nationality, and who is our enemy. Let us remember what is Ireland's'.[57]

In many ways, the *Bean* continued the *Shan Van Vocht's* tradition of reproaching the Irish people, politicians included, for their subservience while exhorting them to reconnect with the glorious Ireland of old. 'Think of the ideals of manhood and chivalry she has cherished through the long ages', the *Shan Van Vocht* had directed in the final years of the nineteenth century.[58]

> We could not read a page of such history, save with a blush of shame, if we had abandoned the strife for freedom which has come down to us sanctified by the blood of martyrs, who in dying bequeathed it to us, firm in the hope that succeeding generations in Ireland would be as noble as those gone by. We dare not belie this faith, nor stoop to the coward's wish, that the destiny of our land may be solved by the juggling and trickery of party politicians, and a system of wheedling England to an unwilling granting of certain measures for reform.[59]

Irish men needed to prove themselves worthy of the grand legacy they had inherited. Otherwise, they shamed themselves and the entire national community to which they belonged. The nationalist Irish woman took it upon herself to remind him of this further threat of shame.

Irish men needed to prove their mettle, but the fear that they would not be able to do so was ever-present both in the *Bean* and in its predecessor. Irish men were exhorted to drop their naïve approach to Irish-British entanglements. 'We need a sterner race, who will not be bribed, bought and sold by England for concessions—messes of Imperial pottage', the paper stated.[60] 'Public life in Ireland', it continued, 'has degenerated into a scramble for English political soup, and at the present time eighty influential Irishmen are spending their whole time in the English Parliament loudly asking for more.'[61]

The *Bean* saw no honour in Irish men's subservient attitude to the imperial parliament, in its 'flunkeyism'. This led it to publish Constance Markievicz's exasperated plea:

> Oh! Men of Ireland, where were you? Were you all asleep? Or getting married? Or what? Truly a few women are needed in your ranks, to rouse you from the lethargy which is overtaking you, and both by their example and by competition with their bright intelligence to make you drag yourselves from the slough of indifference into which you seem to be slipping ... Must it be left to a woman's paper to ask the men of Ireland have they lost all memory of the history of '98?[62]

Markievicz said that she understood that the Irish warrior spirit was 'not dead and gone forever, but like winter, sleeping, cold, and frost-bound, waiting for the magic touch of spring to blossom anew in brave deeds and beautiful deaths and to bear fruit in the freedom of our nation'. Her remit, and that of all other nationalist women, she declared, was to rouse the Irish man's passion and his sense of historic indignation at the 'horror' of their past treatment at the hands of the British.[63]

The *Bean* claimed that it was not its 'intention to countenance any sex antagonism between Irish women and Irish men'. It protested that it shrank from accusing countrymen of 'slavishness'. Yet it persisted in chiding Irish men for their propensity to 'talk very big and do very little'.[64] It is likely, the paper claimed, that men would benefit from 'a little of women's unselfishness and spirituality' and the 'loftier idealism and a purer atmosphere' that women's participation in the country's public life could bring.[65] Indeed, this is what was already happening. Through the women's nationalist group the Inghinidhe na h-Eireann, Irish women had 'exploded forever that silly "woman's sphere" idea, which always stifles the high courage and patriotism which is in every Irishwoman's heart'.[66] More than that, the Inghinidhe had done its best to 'make Ireland a very disloyal and troublesome part of the Empire', thereby ending 'the reign of flunkeyism in the capital of Ireland'.[67]

Irish women's historic equality with Irish men was evoked by the *Bean*. This past demonstrated that women were as capable of honour as their menfolk. However, those contributing to the paper were pragmatic enough to realise that, in the early twentieth century, only Irish men had the means to actively restore honour to the nation. Only they had access to political power. Yet Irish men had demonstrated that they sometimes lacked the moral strength or moral courage to stand up for themselves and their country. Therefore, the *Bean* charged nationalist women with the task of inspiring their nationalist brothers. Many women endorsed this method. However, other nationalist women who were frustrated that Irish men were not using their political power to re-establish the nation's honour sought the power to do so themselves. They sought a vote in the British parliament because they believed this would allow them to actively seek to restore honour to the country.

The Shame of the Misguided Feminist Nationalist Woman

It seemed, then, that there was no end to Ireland's humiliation. Not only were Irish men guilty of begging the British man for the right to rule over their own country but also Irish women were now following their menfolk 'into the supreme folly of recognising the English Parliament and begging for concessions'.[68] At a time when her country was rising up to take back its liberty, the Irish suffragist was asking Ireland's enemy—more embarrassingly, she was pleading with it—to grant her a say in the affairs of an enemy parliament: the British parliament. Here was a woman who was

> scrambling for her mess of pottage, and willing to join in with her country's conquerors and worst enemies to gain her end, but from the point of view of an Irish Nationalist. A woman who knows the truth, knows that in an independent Ireland alone can the men and women who compose the Irish Nation ever hope to find justice and liberty, peace and prosperity.[69]

The *Bean* may have harboured ambivalent feelings about how to approach the issue of gendered communities and the extinguishing of national shame, but they were unequivocal about the need to draw a protective boundary around Irish manhood when it seemed to be under attack from women who should have been on its side. Feminist nationalists were guilty of continuing Britain's emasculation of colonised manhood. If these feminists cherished the bonds they shared with fellow nationalists—men and women—they would abandon their misguided campaign for political power.

The problem with the suffrage campaign was that Irish women acknowledged the British man's ascendancy over the Irish man by appealing to him for the rights of citizenship. The *Bean* was adamant that Irish men would give their sisters the vote once they had control of their own country.[70] If women were to receive the vote because they believed it was 'the hall-mark of equality', then it was 'from Irishmen that this must be won', it said.[71]

> The rights of Irishwomen are in Ireland and must be won in Ireland, not in England or any foreign country. If Irishwomen have time and energy to use, and the will to make sacrifices and risk liberty, let it be for a nobler and greater end than the right to send hostages to England.[72]

The campaign for the vote was 'humiliating', the paper asserted, because it contributed to the emasculation of the Irish man.[73]

The *Bean* attacked Irish men for being misguided and naïve in their dealings with the British, but at least their embarrassing servility was dedicated to the cause of securing Home Rule. Nationalist women who joined the campaign for the British vote were guilty of prioritising the needs of their sex over those of Irish men. More importantly, they were guilty of prioritising their own needs over those of the national collective. Granting British suffrage to Irish women, the paper declared,

> would only mean another chain linking yet another section of the Irish to England. Another confusion of Irish with English ideas. A connection established along which the thoughts and interests of the newly awakened women of Ireland are to be carried away to Westminster.[74]

By working to strengthen the links between Ireland and its oppressor, suffragists were culpable of furthering a process whereby the Irish national spirit was being 'gradually absorbed into Imperial Jingoism'. The Irish nation was at risk of becoming 'a servile and contented West British Province'.[75] 'Do our Nationalist men consider themselves free while Ireland lies in chains?' the *Bean* asked. It was not a question of prioritising sex over nation or vice versa, the paper asserted. Although these causes looked at odds, they were in fact intertwined.[76] It directed that the best way to serve the feminist cause in Ireland was to ignore England. Then, in a tone that was more shaming than motivating, it continued, 'At all events, women should first set their own house in order'.[77] Truly patriotic Irish women should not have required such instructions.

Irish Feminist Nationalists Hit Back: Nationalist Men as Dishonourable

Not surprisingly, feminist nationalists in the country denied accusations that they were guilty of compounding the Irish man's and the Irish nation's shameful and dejected state. They said that Irish men were doing a fine job of that themselves. When the Irish Parliamentary Party played a pivotal role in the defeat of the Conciliation Bill in 1912—a bill that would have seen eligible women enfranchised across Britain and Ireland—the *Citizen* announced,

> Whatever the private opinions of individual members may have been, shame of the judgement of Ireland and the world, shame of the judgement of posterity, ought to have stayed the hand of the leader and of his followers before committing themselves to the tyrannous rejection of the plea of politically helpless women to a minor share in the making of the laws which they have to obey and which control and interfere with their power of livelihood.[78]

It was not Irish feminists but their nationalist brothers who should be engaging in what theorist Jill Locke termed shameful self-assessment.[79] Only then, the *Citizen* assumed, would they honour their connection with other members—including the female members—of their national community. However, Irish politicians were only likely to undertake such an assessment and honour their commitment to Irish women if they valued their connection to their national community over that to their gender community.

Prior to 1912, women writing for the *Bean* criticised the Irish man for his deficient nationalism. After the Conciliation Bill debacle, Irish feminists had further reason for exposing his flawed nationalism, especially through his betrayal of his Irish sisters. At this stage, the *Citizen* proclaimed Irish men were not demonstrating an allegiance to their womenfolk, even those who supported their nationalist aims. This prompted the women's paper to attempt to rationalise this omission. The 'gloomy spells of misogynist Downing Street', the *Citizen* declared, had 'entered into the souls of Nationalist members of Parliament at Westminster'.[80] These 'gloomy spells' had left the Irish delegates with 'no thought for Erin's honour and Erin's pride'.[81] Infected by foreign emotions, Irish men had lost a sense of their true selves. They had forgotten to adhere to the emotional standards underpinning Irish notions of honour, including chivalry. They had been disloyal to 'the ideals of manhood and chivalry' that Ireland had cherished through the long ages, as previously outlined by contributors to the *Shan Van Vocht*.[82] Consequently, they were to be found mistakenly honouring a connection with a transnational community of manhood—even though they were unequally positioned within that collective—over the bonds they shared with the female element of their national community.

Further evidence existed that demonstrated for the *Citizen* that Irish politicians honoured their relations with other men—even if these men existed beyond the pale of the nationalist community that these nationalist politicians claimed to prioritise—over allegiance to Irish women. In 1912, the *Citizen* declared that the nationalist man was now to be found 'slobbering' all over Ulster.[83] He was working hard to appease the British Unionist in the North, offering political concessions in the desperate hope that Home Rule might prevail. He was grovelling before this small though powerful group at the expense of half of the island's population. 'It would be ludicrous, were it not shameful', the paper complained, 'to contrast the feverish anxiety shown to proffer "safeguards" to the Protestant minority with the much more important feminine element, Catholic and Protestant.'[84] Nationalist politicians seemed to lack the self-respect that would have seen them stand up to Ulster, the so-called lion in their path. They also lacked loyalty to the women who actually supported them in their campaign for national autonomy. In the minds of feminist nationalists, then, Irish politicians had failed to embody Irish honour codes on two levels: they were cowardly and servile in the face of stronger men, and they were unchivalrous to the women they ought to have been protecting.

Perceived servility in the company of stronger men robbed Irish politicians of their masculinity. In 1915, the *Citizen* noted that Irish men still had not been granted Home Rule.[85] Britain was fighting for its honour and proving its masculinity on the battlefields of the Great War. It was also using that war as a reason for holding out on delivering its promise of Home Rule. Accordingly, the paper drew attention to the Irish politician's shameful proclivity to wait for handouts instead of taking what was due to him. His lack of action was truly unmanly. He had lost his integrity as a man.

In 1915, the *Citizen* also pointed out that the Irish man's lack of chivalry amounted to an act of 'treachery to Irish women in their fight for political freedom'.[86] Whatever the status of the Home Rule Bill, Irish women were still not to be enfranchised. In their treatment of the Woman Question, Irish politicians had 'interpreted their "mandate" in the spirit of schoolboys bartering in marbles, instead of in terms of the chivalry of Erin'.[87] 'Let them look to it', one writer warned. 'Their honour as Irishmen is at stake.'[88] Then, like the *Bean* a few years before, the paper cautioned the men of Ireland to restore the nation's honour before their womenfolk did it for them, before Irish women undertook 'the real work of rebuilding the shattered Irish nation on an unbeatable foundation of justice, honour, and intelligence'.[89]

The issuing of this challenge revealed that nationalist feminists (through the *Bean*) and feminist nationalists (writing for the *Citizen*), divided as they were on other issues, shared the view that restoring national honour was primarily a man's job. But there was some ambivalence as to whether it was a man's job because only men were enfranchised and therefore endowed with the power to affect political change or because only they were equipped to be guided by masculine emotional standards. This ambivalence was displayed in the nationalist woman's alternating recourse to invoking the Irish man's sense of chivalry—awakening his desire to protect the disenfranchised woman—and threatening to actively take on his role, thereby performing manliness in the public sphere in his stead. Either way, nationalist women hoped that a sense of shame—at not being chivalrous enough or not being manly enough—would spur Irish men into action on their behalf.

The Shame of the Auxiliary Nationalist Woman

Nationalist feminists and feminist nationalists pursued similar political goals. Each group of women believed that Irish women had a particular role to play in directing the affairs of the Irish nation. Again, however, the order in which they prioritised their feminist and nationalist goals differed. They each understood that unity of thinking was paramount to the success of the intersecting nationalist and the feminist movements; therefore, they used a mixture of encouragement, cajoling, and shaming to motivate the other to come around to their way of thinking.

References to shame and honour formed a regular part of their intercourse. Nationalist feminists writing for the *Bean* had accused feminist nationalists of dishonouring Irish men by begging British men for the vote. Those feminist nationalists writing for the *Citizen* reversed the flow of such accusations. They insisted that by championing the rights of an exclusively masculinised concept of the nation and a male-led nationalist movement to the detriment of Irish women, these misguided or servile female patriots were guilty of dishonouring the bond that they naturally shared with that womanhood—the community of patriotic womanhood to which subscribers to the *Citizen* belonged. By accepting a subservient position, they were guilty of dishonouring a historic concept of Irish nationalism that framed men and women as equals. The charge was that these nationalist women were guilty of paying homage to a false model of nationalism that bought into British-imposed notions of separate spheres

In 1914, the links between the armed male Irish Volunteers—connected to John Redmond's Irish Party—and Irish nationalist women were formalised with the establishment of the Cumman na mBan, the women's council of the nationalist Irish Volunteers. Nationalist women who had previously prioritised the feminist campaign were tempted to join a body that promised an active outlet for women's nationalist energies. The creation of the Cumman na mBan, therefore, intensified the competing interests of women of the nationalist community. Not only that but also the support that the women's council gave Irish men who decided to fight in the Great War on the side of the British exacerbated existing tensions.

The Cumman na mBan was not a homogenous group. It was rife with divisions over the degree to which female members' remit was to serve the Irish Volunteers or to have full engagement in male-dominated affairs.[90] For instance, were women supposed to arm men only or were they to arm themselves too? However, whatever the reality of conflicting interests within the women's organisation, it suited the purposes of some writing for the feminist nationalist *Citizen* to present the nationalist feminist women's council of the Volunteers as slavishly devoted to men's interests. It was at this point—through the convergence of the establishment of a formal nationalist women's organisation and that organisation's support for Irish men's participation in the British war effort—that the *Citizen* abandoned its previous reliance on lighter forms of motivational shaming. Instead, its references to shame and shaming in relation to the leanings of nationalist women grew heavier. Its tone became more vitriolic than inviting.

In August 1914, for example, radical Irish suffragist M. K. Connery declared that women who called themselves suffragists while attaching themselves to men's political parties were 'acting slavishly whether they realise it or not'.[91] She was targeting members of the Cumman na mBan. Focusing on the sex question, Connery asserted that Irish women were slaves just like English women. However, women in Ireland reacted to their enslaved situation in radically different ways. There was a difference, for example, between the slave in revolt and the one 'who joyfully hugs her chains and deems that she is thereby serving the best needs of her country and her generation'.[92] The Irish 'party woman'—attached to Redmond's Irish Party through her affiliation with the Cumman na mBan—joyfully hugged her chains. The suffragist knew that the party woman was deluded. Only the suffragist seemed to understand that that woman was only helping her country to regress further when she refused to prioritise gender equality. Only the Irish feminist, then, was free from men's controlling influences.[93]

Adopting a mocking tone, Connery suggested that the women of the Cumman na mBan officially recognise their status as 'slaves and camp-followers' by changing their name from 'Cumman na mBan to—Cumman na-John'.[94] Here she was suggesting that the Irish word for woman be replaced with Redmond's first name. This seemed fitting, she said, for a group of women who were guilty of displaying an 'anxiety to efface themselves and their sex in the interests of men, which they falsely believe to be the interests of the Nation'. In doing so, they were complicit with men in the act of 'forgetting that a Nation consists of men and women'.[95]

Two years into the war, and the *Citizen* was to be found again pointing to the 'slavish' mentality of the nationalist woman. While acknowledging that the Cumman na mBan was a 'spirited' organisation, the paper condemned it for continuing

> to work for the Irish Volunteers in a purely subordinate capacity, without any voice in the control of the organisation, without any official declaration from the Irish Volunteers that the rights and liberties for which they stand include the rights and liberties of women.[96]

If the spirited and dedicated women of the nationalist organisations had not enough self-respect—or rather sex-dignity and pride—to demand their just desserts, then what hope was there for all others? More than that, if nationalist women continued to work freely and without any demand for rewards, then how could feminist organisations levy their support of nationalist politics on the promise of reciprocal support? Feminist activists would be rendered an irrelevant presence. Their anxiety with regard to this, as well as their growing indignation and anger, led to accusations of shame: 'There is only one word for this attitude of unconditional subordination to men's movements: it is slavish'.[97] Through exhibiting a blatant lack of self-respect—and sex-respect—nationalist women were guilty of devaluing the contributions politically active women made to the nation.[98] They were complicit with political men, therefore, in the act of shaming the community of strong patriotic Irish womanhood with which Connery and other feminist nationalists identified.

The *Citizen* added to the nationalist woman's shame by declaring that she was doubly enslaved. Not only was she was she a slave to male priorities but also now a slave to British views of the Irish. Women of the Cumman na mBan served a party, Redmond's Irish Parliamentary Party, that accepted the inferior status that British imperialists had conferred on those of Irish nationality. The male Volunteer movement, the paper claimed, had 'degenerated into the mere adjunct of a thoroughly discredited political faction, "steeped (to the lips) in English traditions"'. The evidence for this was to be found in Irish men's slavish obedience to the English policy of 'coercion against women', referring to British authorities' violent treatment of campaigning suffragists. Redmond was, after all, the 'leading anti-suffragist politician in Ireland'.[99] He had adopted British anti-feminist values in a superlative fashion.

Contrary to accusations discussed earlier in the chapter, then, it was not the radical Irish suffragist but rather her non-suffragist nationalist sister who should have been ashamed of the fact that her political energies were being carried away to serve the purposes of the metropole rather than her nation. Through her support of the servile Irish Party, she was guilty of endorsing British-imposed notions of Irish inferiority. The nationalist feminist woman was not feminist enough. Now, she was not nationalist enough.

Unionist Women Under Attack

Nationalist women were not the only politically motivated women in Ireland to be led astray by their deference to the masculine community. On the other side of nationalist politics, Unionist women were to be found serving as Unionist men's lackeys. At the outset of the war, the *Citizen* appealed to Unionist women to band together with nationalist women, via membership of Irish suffrage societies, so that all Irish women could create a force that nationalist and Unionist men could not ignore. Rather than 'simply backing up the claims of their menfolk', Unionist women were implored to have pride in their political work and to press for their own amendments.[100]

However, the project of trying to unite women of all political persuasions, which had been difficult before the war, was now largely untenable as the imperial war campaign advanced and divisions between nationalists and Unionists intensified. In 1915, for example, the *Citizen* accused Unionist women of being particularly subservient and devoid of all self-respect. In reference to Unionist women's celebrations of 'Empire Day', the paper declared that the Dublin Women's Unionist Club had celebrated the day in

> the usual manner in which this Club generally celebrates all things, that is, by listening to men—generally anti-suffragist men—talking. These women were guilty of sitting by and letting Unionist men instruct them as to what they should do in order to help the men of their party; in how they should sacrifice themselves unconditionally to male Unionists.[101]

'Are there not to be found amongst the members of this club', the writer asked, 'any women with sufficient self-respect to ask—"If we do all this for you, what will you do for us?"'[102] Little hope was expressed that Unionist women would be sufficiently shamed by this nationalist woman's paper to motivate them to amend their ways and demonstrate sex-pride and loyalty.

Yet it was not only nationalist women who were to be found exposing the Unionist women's apparent lack of integrity. They were also attacked by those on their side of Irish nationalist politics. Prior to the war, British anti-suffragists accused Unionist suffragists of betraying the Unionist community to which they belonged. The *Anti-Suffrage Review* had asserted that 'professedly Unionist women' who joined the suffrage campaign in Ireland—'a campaign which, having no political ballast whatever'—were guilty of treachery to the Unionist community.[103] These women, by 'dashing wildly at any chance for advertisement', had lent support to a campaign that would have seen a clause for woman suffrage added to a Home Rule Bill. That Home Rule Bill could have resulted in the establishment of a Dublin-based parliament. The Unionist community in the north of the country was adamant that it was not being ruled by a hostile Dublin parliament. This move on the part of Unionist suffragists led the *Review* to declare that the Unionism of Unionist suffragist women seemed to be 'non-existent'.[104] These women undermined the collective identity of a political and cultural community that already perceived its identity and existence to be under attack from an intensifying nationalist campaign. The Ulster lion, the *Review* said, was being dishonoured only by the feminist element of its womanhood. If Unionist women were refusing to be shamed on the grounds of their broken allegiances to the general community of women suffragists, perhaps they would prove more susceptible to shaming on the grounds of betraying their national community of belonging—namely, Unionism.

By the war's end, women across Britain and Ireland had eventually been granted the right to vote. To nationalist women, Unionist women's exercise of that vote served to confirm that they were, beyond all doubt, slaves to their male leaders' wishes. They had, the *Citizen* said, supported Ulster Unionist leader Edward Carson—a man who had been guilty of duplicity with regard to the issue of the woman vote well before the war. 'One can feel as a woman nothing but contempt and pity for Unionist women who follow such a leader', the paper asserted.[105] On the eve of a war against the combined forces of Britain and the Irish Unionists, nationalist women observed that, whatever the comments of the British *Review* in the pre-war years, Unionist women now existed beyond the pale of the community of Irish womanhood. Drawing attention to their shame served only to confirm their exclusion from that community.

Conclusion

Patriotic women across Ireland demonstrated an often ambivalent attitude towards the role that they believed women should assume in relation to protecting the gendered nature of existing emotional regimes and guarding against national shame. This caused them to variously call for the safeguarding of masculine emotional regimes so that men could perform the task of protecting national honour and to issue threats to invade those regimes in order to restore national honour themselves if men seemed unwilling or unable.

The Irish nationalist women's community was a highly fractured one. Nationalist feminists and feminist nationalists jostled for position. They alternatively coaxed and shamed members of the opposing faction in the attempt to establish their brand of national womanhood as the legitimately Irish brand. Those who prioritised their nationalist aspirations over their feminist goals shamed their opponents for compounding the Irish man's shame when they begged his British counterpart for political concessions. It was their manhood that should have offered such concessions. National autonomy should have been the primary goal. Those who advocated gender equality so that they could fight for national liberty alongside Irish men shamed their opponents for their slavish obedience to men's priorities. If those women were to continue to support Irish men's regimes without demanding any rewards for themselves, those men would have no need to alter the status of their womenfolk. Those women demonstrated that they had no sex-dignity.

No matter how divergent many of their views were, these political women were joined in their basic belief that the task of actively restoring the honour of the emasculated colonised Irish nation was the Irish man's remit. Yet they were also linked by their increasing dissatisfaction with the performance of their national manhood. An exasperating sense of frustration at the Irish politician's ongoing weakness and servility—his 'flunkeyism'—in the face of the ever-virulent British coloniser's seeming supremacy led the women of both factions to partially renege on earlier claims that men were solely responsible for national honour. Their threats to invade men's emotional territories were limited, however. All nationalist women were pragmatic enough to understand that only Irish men had access to the avenues of power that would allow them to prove Ireland's mettle. This caused them to rely on traditional understandings of the place of gender in honour codes. It led many of these strong-minded women to resort to pleading with the national manhood to protect the interests of their womenfolk through adhering to codes of chivalry.

Notes

1 *Bean na hEireann*, vol. 1, no. 3, January 1909, p. 10.
2 *Bean na hEireann*, vol. 1, no.3, January 1909, p. 10.
3 *Bean na hEireann*, vol. 1, no. 3, January 1909, p. 10.
4 *Bean na hEireann*, vol. 1, no. 3, January 1909, p. 10.
5 Robert Nye, *Masculinity and Male Codes of Honor in Modern* France (Oxford: Oxford University Press, 1993) p. vii.
6 Nye, *Masculinity and Male Codes of Honor in Modern France*, p. vii. Ute Frevert asserts that acting in the name of honour is always a male prerogative. See Ute Frevert, *Emotions in History—Lost and Found* (Budapest and London:

Central European University Press, 2011) p. 67.
7 See Nye, *Masculinity and Male Codes of Honor*, p. vii, and Ute Frevert, 'Wartime Emotions: Honour, Shame, and the Ecstasy of Sacrifice', *International Encyclopedia of the First World War (1914–1918 Online)* encyclopedia.1914–1918-online.net/article/wartime_emotions_honour_shame_and_the_ecstasy_of_sacrifice, accessed 15 June 2017.
8 Nye, *Masculinity and Male Codes of Honor*, p. vii.
9 Nye, *Masculinity and Male Codes of Honor*, p. vii.
10 Charles Stewart, 'Honor and Shame', in James D. Wright, ed., *International Encyclopedia of the Social and Behavioral Sciences*, 2nd ed., vol. 11 (Amsterdam: Elsevier, 2015) p. 181.
11 See Pieter Spierenburg, 'Masculinity, Violence, and Honor: An Introduction', in Pieter Spierenburg, ed., *Men and Violence: Gender, Honor, and Rituals in Modern Europe and America* (Columbus: Ohio State University Press, 1998) pp. 1–29, p. 6. This is not to claim a linear move away from honour-related violence. Both Spierenburg and Stewart advocate an uneven global story of waves and troughs of incidences of honour-violence, whether, for example, 'honour killings' or gang-related violence. See Spierenburg, 'Masculinity, Violence, and Honor' and Stewart, 'Honor and Shame'. Research into honour, violence, emotions, and gender is expanding. See, for example, Carolyn Strange, Robert Cribb, Christopher E. Forth, eds., *Honour, Violence and Emotions in History* (London: Bloomsbury Academic, 2014). For a specific discussion of honour and violence in relation to the construction of modern masculinity, see Robert Shoemaker, 'Male Honour and the Decline of Public Violence in Eighteenth-Century London', *Social History*, vol. 26, no. 2 (2001) pp. 190–208.
12 Nye, *Masculinity and Male Codes of Honor*, p. 16.
13 Nye, *Masculinity and Male Codes of Honor*, p. vii.
14 Nye, *Masculinity and Male Codes of Honor*, pp. 16–17. John Hollander likewise argues that shame is honour's antithesis. See John Hollander, 'Honor Dishonorable: Shameful Shame', *Social Research*, vol. 70, no. 4 (2003) pp. 1061–1074.
15 Pieter Spierenburg, 'Masculinity, Violence, and Honor', pp. 11–12.
16 Frevert, 'Wartime Emotions'.
17 Frevert was referring to the theories of one German scholar in particular, Heinrich von Treitschke (1836–1894). For the role of honour in war, particularly in terminations and negotiated settlements (for example, the Falklands War and World War One's battle of the Somme), see Thomas Dolan, 'Demanding the Impossible: War, Bargaining, and Honor', *Security Studies*, vol. 24, no. 3 (2015) pp. 528–562.
18 Frevert, 'Wartime Emotions', p. 4.
19 Frevert presents a sample of belligerents' references to national honour in wartime discussions. See Frevert, 'Wartime Emotions', pp. 5–6.
20 Frevert, 'Wartime Emotions', p. 9.
21 Frevert, *Emotions in History*, p. 88.
22 Ernest Gellner, *Nations and Nationalism* (Ithaca: University of Cornell Press, 1983); Anthony D. Smith, *Theories of Nationalism* (London: Gerald Duckworth & Co., 1971) and Anthony D. Smith, *The Ethnic Origins of Nations* (London Wiley, 1991 [1986]). Among a small number if notable exceptions to the omission of gender was George L. Mosse, *Nationalism & Sexuality: Respectability and Abnormal Sexuality in Modern Europe* (New York: Howard Fertig Inc., 1985). In 2000, Ida Blom continued to assert that gender had long been a 'neglected category of analysis in the flowering field of historical research on nation-building'. (Ida Blom, 'Gender and Nation in International Comparison', in Ida Blom, Karen Hagemann and Catherine Hall, eds., *Gendered Nations: Nationalisms and Gender Order in the Long Nineteenth Century* (Oxford: Berg, 2000) pp. 3–26, p. 3.)

84 *Reversing the Shame of Colonisation*

23 Cynthia H. Enloe, *Bananas, Beaches and Bases: Making Feminist Sense of International Politics* (Berkeley: University of California Press, 2014) p. 100.
24 Nira Yuval-Davis and Floya Anthias, eds., *Woman, Nation, State* (Basingstoke: Palgrave Macmillan, 1989); Sylvia Walby, 'Woman and Nation', *International Journal of Comparative Sociology*, vol. 32, nos. 1–2 (1992) pp. 81–100; Nira Yuval-Davis, 'Gender and Nation', *Ethnic and Racial Studies*, vol. 16, no. 4 (1993) pp. 621–632; and Anne McClintock, 'Family Feuds: Gender, Nationalism and the Family', *Feminist Review*, vol. 44 (1993) pp. 61–80.
25 Enloe, *Bananas, Beaches and Bases*, p. 106.
26 Enloe, *Bananas, Beaches and Bases*, p. 109.
27 See Kumari Jayawardena, *Feminism and Nationalism in the Third World* (London, and Atlantic Highlands, NJ: Zed Books, 1994). See also Chatterjee on India, Partha Chatterjee, 'Colonialism, Nationalism, and Colonialized Women: The Contest in India', *American Ethnologist*, vol. 16, no. 4 (1989) pp. 622–633, and Joyce M. Chadya on Africa, Joyce M. Chadya, 'Mother Politics: Anti-Colonial Nationalism and the Woman Question in Africa', *Journal of Women's History*, vol. 15, no. 3 (2003) pp. 153–157.
28 Jayawardena, *Feminism and Nationalism in the Third World*, p. 3.
29 Jayawardena, *Feminism and Nationalism in the Third World*, p. 14.
30 Margaret Ward, *Unmanageable Revolutionaries: Women and Irish Nationalism* (London: Pluto Press, 1983); Margaret Ward, 'Conflicting Interests: The British and Irish Suffrage Movements', *Feminist Review*, vol. 50, no. 1 (1995); Louise Ryan, 'Traditions and Double Moral Standard: The Irish Suffragists' Critique of Nationalism', *Women's History Review*, vol. 4, no. 4 (1995). Both historians argue that the history of women actively involved in social and political movements in early twentieth-century Ireland has more in common with that of women in other sites engaging in anti-colonial nationalist activities than with those in European or other Western nations. This was a view that many early twentieth-century female nationalists—in Ireland and in other anti-colonial nationalist sites—shared. For example, as Jayawardena pointed out in the 1980s—and Robert J. C. Young has expounded since—men and women involved in Asian and African anti-colonial campaigns at the time frequently referred to Ireland as an inspiration and model for their own movements. See Jayawardena, *Feminism and Nationalism in the Third World*, p. 7, and Robert J. C. Young, *Empire, Colony, Postcolony* (Hoboken: John Wiley & Sons Inc., 2015), pp. 88–91.
31 In Ireland's sense, 'nation' refers to a group that identifies as community of belonging on the basis of shared ethnicity and culture. In Australia's case, it means this, but it also means the political entity that by this stage is the Commonwealth of Australia. For more on the distinctions between different understandings of 'nation', see Eric Hobsbawm, *Nations and Nationalism Since 1780* (Cambridge: Cambridge University Press, 1990) for example, pp. 18–22.
32 Begoña Aretxaga has argued that this pattern of emasculation was premised on different factors in different national sites. For example, whereas in Ireland it took the form of the construction of the colonised as 'childlike', in India, native men's treatment of their womenfolk was held up by the imperialists as evidence of their inferior, barbaric status (referring here to practices such as sati or widow burning). See Begoña Aretxaga, *Shattering Silence: Women, Nationalism, and Political Subjectivity in Northern Ireland* (Princeton: Princeton University Press, 1997), and Robert J. C. Young, *The Idea of English Ethnicity* (Oxford: Blackwell, 2008).
33 The *Shan Van Vocht*, translating as *Poor Old Woman*—referring to the title of a nationalist song—was published from 1896 to 1898. C. L. Innes explains that it was a product of the desire of Irish women to 'have a voice in directing the affairs of Ireland'. It was a cultural-nationalist and often explicitly feminist paper that sought to avoid party politics. A large proportion of the contributors

were women. See C. L. Innes, ' "A Voice in Directing the Affairs of Ireland": *L'Irlande Libre*, *The Shan Van Vocht* and *Bean na h-Eireann*', in Paul Hyland and Neil Sammells, eds., *Irish Writing: Exile and Subversion* (Basingstoke: Macmillan, 1991) pp. 146–158, pp. 150–151. For more on the paper, see Virginia Crossman, 'The Shan Van Vocht: Women, Republicanism, and the Commemoration of the 1798 Rebellion', *Eighteenth-Century Life*, vol. 22, no. 3 (1998) pp. 128–139, and Karen Steele, 'Editing out Factionalism: The Political and Literary Consequences in Ireland's "Shan Van Vocht"', *Victorian Periodicals Review*, vol. 35, no. 2 (2002) pp. 113–132.

34 *Shan Van Vocht*, vol. 2, no. 6, 7 June 1897, pp. 108–109.
35 *Shan Van Vocht*, vol. 1, no, 10, 2 October 1896, p. 197–198.
36 *Shan Van Vocht*, vol. 2, no. 6, 7 June 1897, pp. 108–109.
37 *Shan Van Vocht*, vol. 2, no. 6, 7 June 1897, pp. 108–109.
38 *Shan Van Vocht*, vol. 2, no. 6, 7 June 1897, pp. 108–109.
39 *Shan Van Vocht*, vol. 3, no. 3, 7 March 1898, pp. 47–48.
40 *Shan Van Vocht*, vol. 3, no. 3, 7 March 1898, pp. 47–48.
41 *Bean na hÉireann*, vol. 1, no. 3, January 1909, p. 10.
42 *Bean na hÉireann*, vol. 1, no. 6, April 1909, p. 8.
43 *Bean na hÉireann*, vol. 1, no. 3, January, 1909, p. 10. I have written on the *Bean*'s use of shame to invite Irish women into the fold of the community of nationalist womanhood in Sharon Crozier-De Rosa, 'Shame and the Anti-Suffragist in Britain and Ireland: Drawing Women Back into the Fold?', *Australian Journal of Politics and History*, vol. 60, no. 3 (2014) pp. 346–359.
44 *Bean na hÉireann*, vol. 1, no. 3, January, 1909, p. 1.
45 *Bean na hÉireann*, vol. 1, no. 3, January, 1909, p. 1.
46 *Bean na hÉireann*, vol. 1, no. 3, January, 1909, p. 10.
47 For more on the use of myths to construct new national identities, see, for example, John Hutchinson, 'Myth Against Myth: The Nation as Ethnic Overlay', *Nations and Nationalism*, vol. 10, nos. 1–2 (2004) pp. 109–123.
48 *Bean na hÉireann*, vol. 1, no. 3, January, 1909, p. 10.
49 Markievicz quoted in *Bean na hÉireann*, vol. 1, no. 9, July 1909, p. 8.
50 *Bean na hÉireann*, vol. 1, no. 9, July 1909, p. 8.
51 *Bean na hÉireann*, vol. 1, no. 13, November 1909, pp. 5–6.
52 *Bean na hÉireann*, vol. 1, no. 13, November 1909, pp. 5–6.
53 *Bean na hÉireann*, vol. 1, no, 13, November 1909, pp. 5–6.
54 *Bean na hÉireann*, vol. 1, no. 20, October 1910, p. 8.
55 *Bean na hÉireann*, vol. 2, no. 24, February 1911, pp. 9–10.
56 *Bean na hÉireann*, vol. 2, no. 25, March 1911, p. 8.
57 *Bean na hÉireann*, vol. 2, no. 24, February 1911, pp. 9–10.
58 *Shan Van Vocht*, vol. 1, no. 8, 7 August 1896, pp. 150–151.
59 *Shan Van Vocht*, vol. 1, no. 8, 7 August 1896, pp. 150–151.
60 *Bean na hÉireann*, vol. 1, no. 18, May 1910, pp. 11–12.
61 *Bean na hÉireann*, vol. 1, no. 18, May 1910, pp. 11–12.
62 '98 refers to the failed United Irishman's uprising in 1798. See *Bean na hEireann*, vol. 1, no. 7, May 1909, pp. 6–7.
63 *Bean na hÉireann*, vol. 1, no. 7, May 1909, pp. 6–7.
64 *Bean na hÉireann*, vol. 1, no. 7, May 1909, p. 8, and *Bean na hÉireann*, vol. 1, no. 3, January 1909, p. 1.
65 *Bean na hÉireann*, vol. 1, no. 3, January 1909, p. 1.
66 *Bean na hÉireann*, vol. 1, no. 20, October 1910, p. 8. As explained in the book's introduction, the *Bean* was the organ of Inghinidhe na hEireann (Daughters of Ireland), a radical nationalist, pro-militant women's group that was to later merge with Cumman na mBan, the women's wing of the Irish Republican Army.
67 *Bean na hÉireann*, vol. 1, no. 20, October 1910, p. 8.

68 *Bean na hEireann*, vol. 1, no. 7, May 1909, p. 13–14.
69 *Bean na hEireann*, vol. 1, no. 14, December 1909, p. 13.
70 *Bean na hEireann*, vol. 1, no. 4, February 1909, p. 1.
71 *Bean na hEireann*, vol. 1, no. 4, February 1909, p. 1.
72 *Bean na hEireann*, vol. 1, no. 4, February 1909, p. 1.
73 *Bean na hEireann*, vol. 1, no. 6, April 1909, p. 15.
74 *Bean na hEireann*, vol. 1, no. 14, December 1909, p. 13.
75 *Bean na hEireann*, vol. 1, no. 14, December 1909, p. 13.
76 *Bean na hEireann*, vol. 1, no. 4, February 1909, p. 1.
77 *Bean na hEireann*, vol. 1, no. 4, February 1909, p. 1.
78 *Irish Citizen*, vol. 1, no, 2, 1 June 1912, p. 10.
79 Jill Locke, 'Shame and the Future of Feminism', *Hypatia*, vol. 22, no. 4 (2007) pp. 146–162, p. 156.
80 *Irish Citizen*, vol. 1, no. 2, 1 June 1912, p. 10.
81 *Irish Citizen*, vol. 1, no. 2, 1 June 1912, p. 10.
82 *Shan Van Vocht*, vol. 1, no. 8, 7 August 1896, pp. 150–151.
83 *Irish Citizen*, vol. 1, no. 2, 1 June 1912, p. 10.
84 *Irish Citizen*, vol. 1, no. 3, 1 July 1912, p. 17.
85 The bill had been placed on the statute books but was suspended for the duration of the war.
86 *Irish Citizen*, vol. 3, no. 47, 10 April 1915, p. 365.
87 *Irish Citizen*, vol. 4, no. 3, 5 June 1915, p. 20.
88 *Irish Citizen*, vol. 3, no. 46, 3 April 1915, p. 356.
89 *Irish Citizen*, vol. 4, no. 3, 5 June 1915, p. 20.
90 For a discussion of the tensions reigning within the Cumman na mBan see, for example, Ríona Nic Congáil, 'Agnes O'Farrelly's Politics and Poetry, 1918–27', in Tina O'Toole, Gillian McIntosh, and Muireann Ó'Cinnéide, eds., *Women Writing War: Ireland 1880–1922* (Dublin: University College Dublin Press, 2016) pp. 103–117.
91 *Irish Citizen*, vol. 3, no. 12, 8 August 1914, p. 90.
92 *Irish Citizen*, vol. 3, no. 12, 8 August 1914, p. 90.
93 *Irish Citizen*, vol. 3, no. 12, 8 August 1914, p. 90.
94 *Irish Citizen*, vol. 3, no. 12, 8 August 1914, p. 90.
95 *Irish Citizen*, vol. 3, no. 12, 8 August 1914, p. 90.
96 See *Irish Citizen*, vol. 4, no. 37, May 1916, p. 215.
97 See *Irish Citizen*, vol. 4, no. 37, May 1916, p. 215.
98 See *Irish Citizen*, vol. 4, no. 37, May 1916, p. 215.
99 *Irish Citizen*, vol. 3, no. 12, 8 August 1914, p. 90.
100 *Irish Citizen*, vol. 3, no. 22, 17 October 1914, p. 172.
101 *Irish Citizen*, vol. 4, no. 2, 29 May 1915, p. 10.
102 *Irish Citizen*, vol. 4, no. 2, 29 May 1915, p. 10.
103 *Anti-Suffrage Review*, no. 37, December 1911, p. 247.
104 *Anti-Suffrage Review*, no. 39, February 1912, pp. 28–29.
105 *Irish Citizen*, vol. 6, no. 7, December 1918, p. 635.

3 Embarrassing the Imperial Centre

At the end of 1916, the feminist nationalist paper the *Irish Citizen* (the *Citizen*) reported that opposition to the woman vote continued in Britain but that it amounted to a 'feeble wail' only.[1] It even seemed that suffragists there might have made some progress, for British authorities announced that they would be establishing an Electoral Reform Conference, despite the war campaign. An integral part of establishing this Electoral Reform Conference was to examine the franchise systems of countries which had already granted women the right to vote, the *Citizen* explained. New Zealand and Australia, which had granted women the right to vote in 1894 and 1902, respectively, were included in this number. The British centre, then, was making efforts to learn from the experiences of those at the far reaches of its vast empire. In observing this reversal of the usual protocol—one which dictated that the superior metropolitan centre would lead the inferior colonial peripheries in matters of political importance—the *Citizen* issued the mock-celebratory directive: 'Bravo John Bull; Wake up and get a hustle on! Is the colony to be the father of the Homeland?'[2]

Irish feminist nationalists were keenly aware that in making these comments, they were capitalising on well-publicised metropolitan anxieties about the links between England's international reputation and preservation of the Empire. Many in England feared that any decline in the country's esteem could mean the fall of the entire British imperial network. This was because the Empire was seen as a direct extension of the English nation and support for imperialism an intrinsic aspect of English nationalism. To be English was to be charged with the task of bringing civilisation and progress to the far corners of the globe. England assumed a position of privilege and superiority over its vast imperial holdings, black and white. The idea, then, that the imperial metropole needed to learn something from the peripheries was an unsettling one. It jeopardised Britain's reputation.

This claim of regional parity was unsettling, but anti-suffragists argued that it was also embarrassing for those making the assertion. Everyone knew that the metropole was vastly superior to the peripheries. This superior status could be demonstrated through the relative idea of the British and the Australian woman voter. For example, although anti-suffragists worldwide did not welcome the appearance of the enfranchised woman in the antipodes, they understood that she did not represent the same level of threat as a woman voter in the British metropole. The antipodean woman voted on provincial matters, those concerning the operation of relatively unimportant former colonies. A woman voter in the imperial centre would have a say in the affairs of a vast and increasingly troublesome empire. To equate the relative positions of British and Australian women was an embarrassing oversight. Australian women—loyal to the Empire as they were—should have known better.

In this chapter, I examine British reactions to claims emanating from its former colonies that Australians could teach the British about modernity through their views on gender equality. Specifically, I look at embarrassment. Embarrassment has been labelled 'shame's next of kin'.[3] These emotions are connected by virtue of their status as moral and social emotions. They are about the fear of being judged defective. However, embarrassment is regarded as less painful than shame because it is externalised more than internalised. That is to say, whereas shame denotes the feeling of humiliation resulting from a sense of one's inadequacy, embarrassment is more about the indignity of realising that one has broken a rule that one ought to have abided by.

Australian women directing their Mother Country to bestow the same rights on its women that Australian men had given their women were guilty of committing an awkward *faux pas*. They should have known better than to have presumed they were on the same footing as British women. They embarrassed themselves; however, they seemed to refuse to acknowledge this embarrassment, as they persisted in advising the Motherland on the matter. Therefore, they forced their more knowing kin in the imperial centre—those witnessing their clumsy transgressions—to feel embarrassment on their behalf. They forced them to undergo the uncomfortable and unnecessary process of vicarious embarrassment. In this chapter, I analyse how patriotic women 'at home' set about reminding the Empire's subjects of their relative position within the hierarchy of the Empire nations. I trace the means by which they repelled any attempts to equate the honour of the English nation with that of any of the other national entities connected to the Empire. Their articulations of embarrassment rather than shame when discussing the Australian woman voter reveals how relatively unthreatening this model of modern womanhood was compared with that clamouring for the vote at home.

Embarrassment: Shame's Next of Kin

Embarrassment has been classified as a negative moral emotion, alongside shame and guilt.[4] Indeed, all three emotions have a number of broad characteristics in common. They all occur 'when the rules, norms or social agreements, defining what is right or wrong, are broken'.[5] Yet they are also distinct from one another. So, whereas shame is usually defined as that feeling of humiliation when an individual feels that he or she has failed or proven him or herself inadequate, 'shame's next of kin', embarrassment, is often more 'outwardly directed'.[6] As noted earlier, scholars of emotions argue that embarrassment is less painful than shame because it only affects 'one's presented self'. It is always played out before an 'audience'—real or imagined—prompting targets to worry 'about their social image as a result of their behavior being directly witnessed'.[7] In contrast to shame, embarrassment 'appears to be associated with more sudden and accidental violation of social conventions'.[8]

People experience embarrassment when they feel that they have behaved inappropriately. In analysing prominent sociologist Erving Goffman's definition of embarrassment, Michael Schudson explains that this is an emotion that results from failure to enact roles with poise or failure to abide by rules with tact.[9] The slightest discrepancy in poise and tact, Schudson argues, causes embarrassment, as does misguided allegiance to the wrong values or practices. Quoting Goffman, Greg Morgan adds that embarrassment is 'a normal part of normal social life'. It has been built into the 'framework of obligations' that constitutes the 'substance of any modern society'.[10] Following from this, embarrassment results when a social actor fails to fulfil obligations that his or her peers recognise as legitimate. Not surprisingly, most people try to avoid the emotional discomfort of embarrassment.[11] It was doubtless British anti-suffragists' awareness of the discomfort of embarrassment that caused them to puzzle over Australian claims to national equality. Did Australians not wish to avoid the embarrassment of being deemed ignorant, naïve, or just plain impudent that would inevitably accompany claims of colonial equality with the metropole?

Psychologists and neuroscientists argue that people who are guilty of a public indiscretion tend to be more embarrassed when the person or group witnessing that indiscretion are close members of a shared community or are considered of higher social standing.[12] Such knowledge elicits higher embarrassment. Similar assertions can be made of those witnessing the transgression. Those witnessing the deviant event can feel embarrassed on behalf of the transgressor; they can experience a vicarious form of embarrassment. The closer they are to the transgressor, the stronger their feelings of embarrassment are likely to be.

These feelings of embarrassment on behalf of a person with whom one identifies tend to fall into two categories: empathetic embarrassment and vicarious embarrassment. For example, having a close relationship with a person who has just committed a deviant act can mean having the ability to imagine exactly how that person is feeling. It can mean having a richer capacity to represent that person's pain or discomfort.[13] This is empathetic embarrassment (encapsulated by the German term 'fremdscham').[14] On the other hand, such a close relationship with the transgressor could also induce anxiety that his or her 'public flaws, blunders or norm violations' might reflect badly on the person witnessing the incident too. The other's embarrassing act could damage the witness's reputation or social image.[15] This is vicarious embarrassment.[16]

Citizens living in the imperial centre considered themselves to be morally superior to those in the colonial peripheries. Theirs was an old nation at the centre of a vast empire. They had centuries of worldly experience that white Australians did not. They knew to avoid public embarrassment. It seemed that their less knowing 'cousins' in the colonies did not. By committing a tactless error—such as claiming equal importance with the imperial centre—British-Australians did more than just embarrass themselves. By refusing to acknowledge their embarrassment, they risked forcing their more knowledgeable and experienced kin in Britain to feel embarrassed for them. This was not an empathetic form of embarrassment. Rather, it was a vicarious form of the emotion. At a time when the stability of the Empire was under threat, loyal British-Australians should have known better than to have contributed to that volatility by trying to upset accepted understandings of the hierarchy of empire. Those in the imperial centre hoped that by exposing colonial mistakes, and revealing the embarrassment they were feeling for their colonial cousins, they might affect a return to empire norms and conventions. They hoped that Australians would honour their relationship with their more experienced kin in the metropole and abandon their misguided behaviours.

Australian Pride Interpreted as Claims for Colonial Supremacy

There is little doubt that loyal British-Australian women would have been stung by metropolitan embarrassment on their behalf. Loyal British-Australians were not embarrassed by their failure to accept the artificially constructed binary of metropole and empire. They considered that part of their remit as loyal 'Britishers' was to re-configure imperial citizenship from the advantageous position of the 'New World'—a site free from the constraints of the old one.

Throughout its existence, the Australian Women's National League (AWNL) was certainly keen to promote Empire loyalty while also advocating for Australia as a site for the rejuvenation of the great British 'race'.[17] In 1917, for example, the League's paper *Woman* declared of Australia,

> We have a constitution fundamentally more broad-based than its model, the Imperial Parliament. We have transplanted the institutions and the freedom of the Motherland without the sacrifice of the centuries which our forebears had to undergo to secure them for ourselves and future generations. A continent, a magnificent heritage, given us generously to husband, and to till, and wherein to rear if we will, a new and a higher civilisation. Was there ever such generosity on the part of a parent to an

offspring? Was there ever such an opportunity afforded to an offspring to make good and to do better than its forebears? Let the character of our people be such as will fit us to occupy it and to lay a just and inalienable claim to its permanent occupancy. This territorial prize is worth all the effort that we as Australians can put forward. Let us prove equal to the task.[18]

Despite the organisation's unfaltering assertions of loyalty and gratitude, sometimes the AWNL's espousals of national pride crept dangerously close to those for recognition of colonial supremacy—at least in the eyes of alert imperialists in the metropole.

British anti-suffragists responded indignantly to claims emanating from the colonial peripheries that metropole and peripheries constituted equally important sites of empire. They were also utterly exasperated when they encountered proclamations not only of equality but also of colonial superiority. Such naïve assertions coming from the inexperienced colonists embarrassed those more knowing politicians in the centre of the vast imperial network because they demonstrated the colonists' ignorance of what was certainly accepted wisdom in the metropole—namely, that Britain was the essential heart of the Empire. It was the only responsible authority in the Empire. It was Britain's parental beneficence that allowed for the creation of white settler spaces in the antipodes in the first place. It was their power that held the vast, bountiful, but troublesome, imperial network together.

If anti-suffragists were astounded that such claims for equality or ascendancy were emanating from the peripheries, they were even more so when they encountered the fact that it was colonial women making these claims. Women—inexperienced politicians as they were—who had been given the power to vote on the insignificant domestic affairs of a tiny outpost, now presumed to lecture the Mother Country on matters of international importance. This was interpreted by those contributing to the *Anti-Suffrage Review* (the *Review*), the official organ of the National League for Opposing Woman Suffrage (NLOWS), as a clumsily misguided challenging of British dignity, reputation, and international standing. Through their very public indiscretion, Australian women embarrassed themselves. Their blundering reversal of accepted understandings of core-periphery flows also forced their more knowing kin in the metropole to experience vicarious embarrassment.

Australian Women Reversing the Core-Periphery Flow

As mentioned previously, Englishness and imperialism were intertwined.[19] Catherine Hall explains that empire provided 'a frame for England itself, a way of knowing what it was to be English'.[20] To be English was to be charged with the task of bringing civilisation and modernity to others. This was a mission characterised by what Shula Marks defines as ideals of 'manliness' and 'respectability' as well as 'a corroding and pervasive racism'.[21]

The nation defined itself in relation to the 'other' in Ireland, Africa, and the New World; 'by constructions of civilization and progress on the one hand and backwardness and barbarism on the other'.[22]

Empire provided a frame for the English to understand themselves, demonstrating the interconnectedness of 'home' and empire, but, as Antoinette Burton elucidates, the metropole and the peripheries have traditionally been constituted as separate and distinct entities. 'Home' was 'the source of Britishness/progress/civilization'. The empire beyond was constructed as barbaric and culturally backward. Staging Britain and its empire as dichotomous rather than as dialectic spaces was not accidental. Rather, Burton explains, it was a technique intended to convince Britons and others that Britain was indeed a great imperial power.[23] In keeping with Whig-historical notions of progress, she adds, 'the movement of ideas, culture, and improvement was presumed to flow in one direction: from home to away'.[24] Until recent decades, generations of historians of the Victorian Empire tended to maintain these artificial distinctions.[25]

Recent scholarship on transnationalism and empire has worked to challenge that assumption of separateness. It has also defied the notion that ideas flowed in one direction only, from the metropole to periphery. The essence of empire involves movements and exchanges across national and colonial borders.[26] For this reason, Fiona Paisley argues, the historiography of empire must go beyond 'discrete comparison[s]' of metropole and periphery to recognise 'the significance of circulating populations and ideas, including from "margin" to "metropolis"'.[27]

Part of this process involves accessing how those living in the colonies at the time viewed their relationship with each other and with Britons in the imperial centre. Alan Lester's research on this topic reveals that empire played host to a range of complex, interconnected, and shifting relations, not simply between metropole and periphery but also between peripheries. For example, Lester argues that white British settlers responded to metropolitan humanitarians' depictions of them as 'aberrant Britons' for their inhumane treatment of their indigenous populations by collaborating across imperial spaces to construct a 'trans-imperial discourse of colonialism'.[28] The idea that, far from being brutal land-grabbers, white British settlers were 'intrinsically racially superior', just like their counterparts in the British centre, formed a significant aspect of this discourse. White settlers, then, cast themselves as 'the means for the diffusion of an appropriate form of civilization around the world'.[29] This mantle of civiliser certainly resonated with the racial aspirations of the women of the AWNL.

Despite British conservatives' rejection of the comparative value of colonial 'experiments', there were those in the metropole who did appreciate and learn from developments taking place in the imperial peripheries and from ideas circulating around the Empire. This was particularly the case for those involved in movements for social and political reform. Burton, for example, has shown how reformers across a range of fields in Britain sought inspiration from developments and ideas emanating from the 'margins' of Empire.[30] Moreover, as Marilyn Lake has argued, reformers outside the British Empire also demonstrated an appreciation for the flow of ideas and practices across imperial spaces. The granting of female suffrage in Australasia was considered a momentous occasion in the United States, prompting well-known figures—such as renowned social reformer Jessie Ackermann, Boston suffragist Maud Park Wood, and feminist and prohibitionist Josephine Henry—to consider the potential impact of this development on their own region.[31] The physical presence of Australian suffrage campaigners on foreign soils—Britain and the United States included—provided a tangible reminder of the further possibilities for transnational exchange.[32]

British anti-suffragists attempted to refute any possibility for transnational exchange on the issue of the woman voter, but the very existence of the enfranchised woman in the antipodes meant that they were continually being forced to acknowledge her presence. Sometimes this acknowledgement took the form of publicly denying her relevance in the vastly more important imperial centre. At other times, it was to hold her up as a warning to all empire-minded people about the threat that feminism represented. Still, the fact that they had to articulate their understanding of imperial citizenship—at 'home' and 'away'—in relation to the woman voter meant that changing concepts of citizenship in the far reaches of the Empire were instrumental in shaping developing understandings of citizenship in the metropole. Whether they were willing to accept it or not, circulating ideas were influencing metropolitan anti-feminist discourse.

Repelling Claims of Equality Without Disparaging the Colonies

The first step that the British *Review* took in dismantling Australian women's claims that their situation was comparable to that of women in the imperial centre was to render the extension of the franchise to colonial women to be void of any serious meaning. Australian men, the *Review* asserted, had given their women the vote simply because they thought that it would be 'unfair' not to do so. Some states had enfranchised women already, so well-meaning but deluded men had extended the same courtesy to women nationally. 'The country maintained an attitude of indifference', the paper maintained, 'and the measure passed into law.'[33] The woman vote in the antipodes, then, was nothing more than 'an idle compliment Australian men have paid their women'.[34] In this way, British anti-suffragists diminished the importance of this revolutionary granting of political power. They also disarmed the Australian man by depicting him as well meaning, chivalrous even, but entirely lacking maturity and the manly sense of purpose that characterised male politicians in the metropole. British men had greater wisdom, the *Review* inferred, for even if they had wanted to bestow the munificent gift of the franchise on their womenfolk, as their Australian counterparts had done, they knew that it would not be prudent or sage to do so. It was only fitting that men in the metropole viewed the question of enfranchisement seriously, for theirs was a mature nation with grave responsibilities. By inference, Australia was not.

The *Review* did not rest with simply inferring that Australia was inferior to Britain. It stated so explicitly and repeatedly. In 1909, the paper labelled the idea that Britain should follow Australia's example and introduce the woman vote 'a dangerous one for it takes no note of the great difference in local conditions'.[35] It likewise omits, the *Review* went on, 'to consider that legislative experiments can be tried in the colonies, without much harm resulting, which would have very serious results, if they would not be absolutely disastrous, in this country'.[36]

British Antis were determined to remind the young Commonwealth of its relative position in the Empire's hierarchy of nations, but, initially at least, they were keen to do so without offending the periphery. In 1910, for example, the *Review* reiterated that it did not mean to be 'disparaging' to those in the colonies, but it felt compelled to remind them and others that there was 'no real analogy' between granting women the right to vote in places like Utah or Colorado or Australia and New Zealand and thinking about granting women the right to do so in a country like England.[37] The paper reminded its readers that Australia and New Zealand 'have, so far, been happily exempt from the graver problems of Empire'.[38]

Later that year, the *Review* reprinted lengthy extracts from anti-suffrage speeches made in the House of Commons which expressed a similar sentiment:

> I believe, having regard to the social and political expediency of such a country and such an Empire as ours, it is better to maintain the distinction of sex which has always hitherto been treated as lying at the root of our Parliamentary system, and which has been, and is, recognised, with exceptions trivial in number and not in any way relevant in their circumstances, by all the great civilised nations of the world.[39]

Taking the sensibilities of the colonial peripheries into account, and expressing a keenness to remind listeners that those peripheries were created by Britain, the speaker continued,

> I do not wish in the least degree to disparage the experiments which have been made by our own Dominions and Colonies. New Zealand and Australia are great fields of social and political experiment. No one who is acquainted with the circumstances of those countries, their vast areas, their sparse population, their social and economic conditions, separated by almost as great a distance as they are in point of geography from ourselves, can say that even had the experience been long enough, and the lessons taught by that experience been more generally agreed upon, they form any relevant guidance as to what is to take place here.[40]

In 1911, the paper felt compelled to reiterate once again that 'experiments' in the colonies were fine but that they had no bearing on events taking place in the imperial centre. 'Australia manages its own internal affairs for a sparse population, considerably less than the population of the County of London', it read. It went on to reaffirm for its audience that the sparsely populated periphery had 'no questions of peace or war to decide, no India dependent upon it with a population of three hundred millions, entertaining Oriental ideas regarding women'.[41] Such references to the colonised man's 'Oriental' ideas about women served to remind women at home of their privileged position—a position of privilege that was jeopardised by the transgressive behaviour of a radical few.

However, displays of patience or tolerance at suffragists citing the example of the Australian woman voter alternated with more condescending criticisms of such inappropriate comparisons. In 1911 the *Review* stated,

> Our colonies, with their minor problems, with their remoteness from the complication and danger of the Old World, with their safety under the English flag, and their simpler conditions of life, might try experiments that her children could not ask of England.[42]

Australians and New Zealanders were depicted as the pampered offspring of an over-burdened parent. They should not, the *Review* asserted, have the audacity to ask that those in the Mother Country allow themselves the same liberties that they afforded themselves.

Of course, it was not only the presence of the Australian woman voter in the far reaches of the Empire that threatened to diminish the imperial centre's reputation. As I outlined in Chapter 1, British women themselves were proving to be quite capable of jeopardising Britain's reputable name. The *Review* claimed that if anywhere between 8 and 12 million women were to be added to the British electoral roll—all because of the hysterical demands made by Britain's 'wild women', referring here to the suffragettes—then that would mean 'an immediate alteration of our place and prestige in Europe, an immediate weakening of our imperial power, an immediate diminution of security for every man and woman in these islands'.[43] Whereas suffragette outrages had eroded English women's sense of themselves to the point that some women declared that they were ashamed to be women, their actions also prompted anti-suffragist women to claim that they also 'made you ashamed to feel you were English'.[44] England would not be true to its heritage of rationality and strength if it were to be scared into granting the vote 'by a body of mildly anarchical women'.[45] England could not adopt the attitude that Australia had. This led the *Review* to implore like-minded patriots to intensify their campaign and to 'realise how dangerously near to a national disaster indifference on the subject might bring the country'.[46]

Britain was responsible for governing the entire British Empire; therefore, it could not afford to adopt the same slack attitude towards the issue of the woman vote that Australia had. In 1910, the paper granted extensive space to the coverage of prominent anti-suffragist Violet Markham's views on the subject. Markham declared that granting women the right to vote in Britain—as in places such as Australia and New Zealand—could never be in the English nation's and the British Empire's interest. It would only 'be a weakening and a disturbing element in government and in the exercise of sovereign power'.[47] As 'a woman', she declared, 'I say that it is an intolerable situation for a great nation and a great empire'.[48] The complex logistics of governing the Empire was the crucial factor. Women cannot 'take part in any share of the government of the three hundred and forty millions of coloured people who form the major portion of the population of the empire', she confirmed. All women were politically naïve. How then would they take on the responsibilities of the India Office and share in the government of 'those three hundred millions which people the great Dependency?'[49] There is 'no graver or more difficult problem which lies ahead for the British Empire than the development of the social and political relations of the coloured races under the flag', Markham asserted.[50] Whereas women in Australia had claimed or accepted the right to vote on the basis of addressing the race 'problem' there (discussed more in Chapter 4), British anti-suffragists cited the empire's race problems to justify the exclusion of women from the electorate.

To blur sex differences in the metropole—the ruling centre of the Empire—would only lead to imperial disintegration. Markham's advice was that the task of maintaining the integrity of the British Empire rested on building up 'a manhood on the one hand and a womanhood on the other which together form a nation capable of bearing worthily the great and onerous responsibilities that attach to the proud title of British citizenship'.[51] She concluded,

> To give political power without full political experience is altogether too great and dangerous an experiment for such an empire as ours, just because we are an empire and not a laboratory for the experiments of cranks and of faddists.[52]

British anti-suffragists affirmed that they had tried to avoid offending their colonial cousins with their disclaimers of core-periphery equality. They had attempted to correct Australians' inappropriate advice about British political matters and their erroneous assumptions about regional parity without disparaging the work being carried out in the Empire's outposts. However, their indignation was raised at repeated attempts by former colonists to advise the Mother Country. These former colonists seemed blind to their blunders. This was infuriating on two grounds. Australians had committed an indiscretion in full sight of those who considered themselves to be the superior relatives. As such, they should have experienced a heightened sense of embarrassment. Yet it appeared that they felt no discomfort. Also, Australians' refusal to accept the embarrassment of their position meant that their more knowing cousins, and witnesses to their *faux pas*, had to experience it for them. The misplaced pride, bordering on arrogance, emanating from a place fit only for the experiments of 'cranks and faddists' forced British anti-suffragists to experience vicarious embarrassment.

Evidence of the Australian Woman Voter's Misguided Pluck: Vida Goldstein in Britain

To the British anti-suffragist mind, enfranchised women emerging from the colonial peripheries—whether they were of the anti-suffragist or the suffragist persuasion—did not seem to understand that they were the products of a 'laboratory for the experiments of cranks and of faddists'. Nor did they understand that they should feel embarrassed by their propositions. Prominent Australian suffragist Vida Goldstein, visiting the United Kingdom in 1911, certainly exhibited no understanding of this. On the contrary, Goldstein launched a spirited attack on traditional British values via a series of conversations with her British male correspondent, David Kyles, which was reported on in the pages of the *Review*.[53] Here, in a written exchange between a female voting citizen from Australia visiting the metropolitan centre and a British male anti-suffragist on British soil and reported in a British paper, the meshing and clashing of imperial and colonial discourses and prerogatives was laid bare. The exchange also provided an effective example of an Australian refusing to accept directives about the inferior status of the colonial peripheries emanating from the imperial centre and refusing to feel embarrassed about not doing so.

Through an interestingly phrased series of questions, Kyles invited Goldstein to consider the relative merit of the British man's vote and the Australian woman's vote. He asked, 'What is the difference between the vote exercised by you in Australia and that exercised by me when I use my imperial vote in this country?' He followed this with, 'Are the votes of equal value? Do they carry the same responsibility? Are they the same or is there a difference?'[54] It is uncertain what answers he expected from a proponent of women's rights, indeed from 'an internationalist' who had travelled abroad on several occasions in support of women's suffrage.[55] Whatever response Kyles expected, he did not receive it, which led the *Review* to later draw readers' attention to 'the extraordinary opinion' expressed by Goldstein. 'The vote exercised by me', Goldstein wrote,

> is to defend my right to life, liberty, and the pursuit of happiness. Your vote represents your cash value to the nation. My vote is of infinitely greater value than yours, though the responsibility is the same, even in time of war. Adding, dividing, subtracting the samenesses, and differences, there still remains a balance in my favour![56]

The male vote in England, Goldstein was arguing, was given to men for 'property reasons'; hers was given to her on account of her 'womanhood' only. Hers, she asserted, was therefore of greater value representing, as it did, the more 'progressive' and democratic values of the so-called New World.[57] Here, Goldstein was drawing on values enshrined in the American Declaration of Independence—values that, given the context of their origin, were dangerously anti-empire. Goldstein's opinions exemplified connections across colonial sites—in this case, former colonial sites—that served to debunk the narrative of metropolitan superiority.

Kyles's difficulty in accepting Goldstein's audacious, dangerously disloyal statement was all too apparent in his response: 'I cannot fathom by what system of reasoning you reach your conclusions, nor do I understand the argument which seeks to disparage the Parliamentary franchise in this country in comparison with the Federal vote in Australia'. He declared that he could not conceive of 'anyone thinking that the Parliamentary vote in this country is not of infinitely greater importance than the Federal vote in Australia'.[58] Surely, 'not even the most enthusiastic Australian would dream of suggesting that the Imperial Parliament was not far more important than the Commonwealth Parliament'. He reaffirmed British anti-suffragist logic that repelled the notion that colonial political developments could or should be compared to those in the metropole—namely, that whereas the Imperial Parliament ruled over the Empire, the Australian Commonwealth parliament 'manages its own internal affairs for a population less than the population of the County of London'. Australia could not, he stated, decide a question of peace or war and had no dependencies like the vast and troublesome India.[59] Not surprisingly, Kyles and Goldstein did not reach an understanding by the time they ended their correspondence.

Yet here was an enthusiastic Australian doing more than dreaming of suggesting that colonial politics trumped metropolitan politics. She was stating it baldly. Kyles's exasperated response to Goldstein's claims illustrate his belief that she had transgressed widely accepted social conventions. In keeping with our earlier exposition on embarrassment, she had embarrassed herself by not behaving with poise and tact. Instead, she had demonstrated a tactless and misguided allegiance to wrong values and practices. Goldstein had not shown that she was capable of understanding what was certainly common knowledge around the Empire—namely, that politics in the British centre were vastly more important than those in the colonies. She had mistakenly placed herself on an equal footing with voters in the metropole. Kyles's intellectual puzzlement and emotional discomfort were obvious. No matter how 'enthusiastic' a member of the colonial peripheries was, this colonial 'cousin' should not have committed such a blunder. Britain and Australia, although positioned far apart on the imperial spectrum as far as national importance was concerned, were yet connected enough for colonial indiscretions to reflect badly on the imperial centre. That this naïve colonial woman did not look set to feel the embarrassment or humiliation that she should, given her *faux pas*, meant that the more knowing metropolitan man had to express it for her. He was forced to experience vicarious embarrassment.

Australian Women Voters Provide Evidence of the Inappropriateness of the Political Woman

The Australian woman voter was not simply an embarrassment because of her misguided assertions of colonial-imperial equity. Like other enfranchised women globally, she also functioned as a practical example of the inappropriateness of voting women. She was too apathetic to fully realise the extent of her political responsibilities. She did not have the ability to carry out her voting duties in tandem with her more traditional tasks. The shiny new vote distracted her from undertaking the duties expected of and suited to her sex. The vote also seemed to make her forget her place and her position. She was a colonial woman in the backward outposts of empire. She ought to be acting like a frontiers woman not as a privileged voting member of the urban elite.

British anti-suffragists painted a picture of the Australian woman voter who was undeserving of her newfound political power. Australian women were apathetic. They had also not yet grown into their new political responsibilities. The *Review* cited the example of a 'bright young woman journalist from Australia'. As 'bright' as she was, even she had not deigned to use her new voting power. Her fellow countrywomen, she said, were also not much interested in politics. Besides, they were likely to vote the same way their menfolk would vote, thereby doubling the existing male vote.[60] As the militant campaign picked up pace in the Mother Country, the *Review* affirmed that the attitude among Australian women was one of 'supreme indifference'. Women there had never shown an interest in getting the vote, it continued, not in the way women in the metropole had:

> There were never any militant suffragettes 'down under.' No Minister was attacked with a dog whip, or even heckled by women. No deputations waited on him to demand votes for women. No constable had his face slapped for merely doing his duty, neither was his helmet knocked from his head.[61]

To top this off, the writer declared that there 'was not even a quiet, self-respecting, ladylike league for the promotion of the franchise to women' in the country.[62] This erroneous claim confirmed that the paper was complicit in buying into the vote as 'gift' narrative and overlooking the complexities of the various Australian suffrage campaigns outlined earlier in the book. The naïvely disinterested enfranchised woman embarrassed those more knowing citizens who understood the privilege of their position and took their political duties more seriously.

If evidence of the disinterest of the new political woman and her negligible contribution to the maintenance of the nation-state was not enough, the *Review* also demonstrated that women in suffrage societies were not performing their actual duties to the nation in the manner they should. 'It is as wives and mothers that we women must justify our existence and value to the State', renowned anti-suffragist Mrs Archibald Colquhoun declared.[63] Women could perform their maternal duties to the State through assuming positions in local government. This is where the female sex could really embrace its civic responsibilities. Instead, she said, enfranchised women were to be found 'deliberately turning their backs on the powers that the nation has put into their hands'.[64]

> Like fretful children they want everything but what they have got. And—worst of all—their struggle for things impossible is weakening the power and destroying the influence of the women who *do* want to use what they have got, and whose voice and help are urgently wanted in the 'Enlarged Housekeeping' of the country.[65]

Later again the *Review* reaffirmed that 'the maternal woman has been for all time and will be always the mainstay of men and nations'. Maternal did not simply mean those who mothered their own children. It also encompassed those women who looked after the interests of 'the larger family of the State'.[66] However, the paper also argued that history had shown that women who were enfranchised did not adequately perform their private or public roles as mothers of the nation. Wherever 'women invade the peculiar province of men, race decay follows', the paper added.[67] To demonstrate the truth of this statement, it cited the example of female suffrage societies, Finland and Australia. Women had the vote, and as a result of this, in each site, 'the birth-rate is almost the lowest in the civilised world'.[68] Voting women abandoned public roles that demonstrated their maternal instincts. If only they were content to assume positions on local government bodies, they could ensure the welfare of the local population: men, women, and children. Voting women were also to be found denying their very real maternal instincts, as they refused to mother children, thereby contributing to the potential decay of the nation and the 'race'. On this point, universally, the women voter was more than simply embarrassing; she was shameful.

Further evidence surfaced of the shameful self-interestedness of the woman voter. 'It saddens me more than I can say to see the strife, the *idleness*, and the great degradation of womanhood which is the outcome of this question of woman's vote', one contributor to the *Review* declared. 'English women, American women, and Canadian women all have told me that much really good work has been put aside and neglected because of this foolish infatuation.' Had only one-tenth of all this feminine energy been put into doing real good for the country, 'England would be the happiest country on God's earth'.[69] England's emotional well-being—its happiness—was adversely affected by the desires and demands of women who wanted their vote just like women in Australia.

The *Review* criticised all women—suffragists and voters—who abandoned their true vocations as the nation's guardians in the face of political advancement. However, it also singled some women out for special condemnation. One woman to receive this treatment was renowned Australian suffragist, Rose Scott. Miss Scott did more than anyone to secure the right to vote in Australia, the *Review* said. Before she was enfranchised, she also did more good work than anyone else in the country to improve the lives of Australian women and children. After the vote, her reputation for looking after her fellow country people deteriorated.[70] To make its point about the degenerative effects of the vote on female citizens clearer, the paper cited the example of 'good' Japanese women. Japanese women, the *Review* averred, were putting these feminists and enfranchised women to shame. When commenting on the decision of the Japanese Association for the Advancement of Women to not attend the International Suffrage Congress in Copenhagen, it pronounced, 'The women of Japan are too fully occupied with the task of training the children of their nation as citizens and defenders to have time to spare for direct politics'.[71] The implication was, of course, that the energies of many of the women of the Empire—those who were enfranchised or those seeking enfranchisement—were not likewise gainfully employed.

These collated testimonies confirmed for the *Review*'s readership that women voters, wherever they were stationed globally, were unable to embody the emotional qualities required to exercise their political power in an appropriate manner. Their lack of emotional and political seriousness embarrassed more knowing and politically equipped male voters. But their inadequacy as a political beings also led to them further embarrassing themselves. Again, the *Review* drew on the example of the Australian woman voter to demonstrate its point.

The British anti-suffrage paper observed that the Australian woman voter was again contravening social norms. Not content to simply instruct more experienced metropolitan citizens on the issue of female enfranchisement, she was also to be found acting as if she was one of those more knowing metropolitan citizens. The enfranchised woman in the antipodes was guilty of acting above her station in life—and in the Empire. She embarrassed herself by not knowing her place. Feminism had corrupted Australian women's relationship with their country. It had instilled in their minds ideas about themselves that were ill suited to the environment they lived in. Women in the colonies needed to act like colonial women, the *Review* instructed. Instead, after the spoils of feminism—the vote and access to higher education, for example—younger generations of Australian women had transformed into the kind of females who 'who shrink from hardship, dislike country life, want town society, glee clubs, tennis and rowing clubs, and a circulating library'.[72] Feminist progress had bred colonial women 'who really have not the strength for a knock-about life in the backblocks'. Women worldwide did not have time for politics, the *Review* claimed, adding woman 'has *no time* for politics in any country, but least of all in new countries'.[73] Political power had created an aberrant model of empire womanhood. This was a woman who mistakenly thought she was destined for a metropolitan-type of life but who should have realised that her place was on the land helping her fellow colonists to eke out a living on the harsh frontiers of the Empire. The embarrassment was that British anti-suffragists understood this while colonial women seemed not to grasp that they were guilty of violating yet more empire norms.

British Women Granted the Vote

In February 1918, the *Review* announced that British women had been granted the right to vote: 'The die is cast, and Great Britain alone of the Great Powers has conferred the parliamentary franchise upon women'.[74] Now that metropolitan women had the vote, Australian women voters paled into insignificance. Their embarrassment was now irrelevant. Women 'at home' were to vote on matters of empire. They represented much more of a threat to the stability of the Empire than their peers in the peripheries.

However, the Australian woman voter's relative lack of threat in the face of the emergence of the metropolitan woman voter did not prevent the *Review* from further expounding the different hierarchal positions of Britain and Australia on the imperial spectrum. Before it disbanded its paper, the NLOWS once again affirmed the difference between the colonial and the metropolitan vote. Until now, the *Review* said, the suffrage experiment had been confined to 'the unimportant States or to self-governing portions of the British Empire'. The concerns of these small States had always been local rather than international.[75] Australia was a case in point. Australia had rejected conscription, the paper affirmed, but it could only do that because it was a minor State. Australia could have withdrawn all its troops from the war and that would not have dented the Allied cause because the Australian contribution was so insignificant.[76] Australia boasted only a small population, and it had no international commitments, therefore, it could 'indulge more or less with impunity in political experiments'. 'Not so Great Britain', was the pronouncement. The war had confirmed 'the importance of her trusteeship, held in conjunction with others, of the cause of civilization'.[77] The granting of the female franchise in Britain had done nothing to create a bond between British and Australian women in the eyes of the *Review*. Old divisions and hierarchies still held firm.

Conclusion

The emotion of embarrassment—a member of the shame family—helps us to realise the priorities and values that early twentieth-century British anti-suffragists held dear. But even more than that, British articulations of embarrassment are revealing of early twentieth-century attitudes towards the hierarchical relationships that made up the British Empire. The campaigning feminist in the imperial centre shamed the national community to which she belonged because she threatened the values and the bonds that connected that community. Australian women, although they were connected to the metropolitan centre by virtue of imperial kinship, were not sufficiently part of that community to be able to bring it to shame. Instead, their claims to equality with that centre embarrassed their imperial cousins. They should have realised what was common knowledge—namely, that Britain, situated at the heart of the vast imperial network, was infinitely more superior than the relatively unimportant peripheries. No direct comparison between the two sites could be countenanced. By presuming to be on an equal footing with women in the metropole—more than that, by thinking that she was indeed the equivalent of a metropolitan citizen instead of a member of a backward colonial outpost—the Australian woman voter embarrassed herself. If she refused to accept the embarrassing nature of her position and her claims, she forced her more knowing kin in the imperial centre to express and feel that embarrassment on her behalf.

Notes

1 *Irish Citizen*, vol. 4, no. 42, December 1916, p. 237.
2 *Irish Citizen*, vol .4, no. 42, December 1916, p. 237.
3 Harry Fox, 'The Embarrassment of Embarrassment', in Tzemah Yoreh, Aubrey Glazer, Justin Jaron Lewis and Miryam Segal, eds., *Vixens Disturbing Vineyards: Embarrassment and Embracement of Scriptures* (Boston: Academic Studies Press, 2010) pp. 5–18, pp. 5–6.
4 Coralie Bastin, Ben J. Harrison, Christopher G. Davey, Jorge Moll and Sarah Whittle, 'Feelings of Shame, Embarrassment and Guilt and their Neural Correlates: A Systematic Review', *Neuroscience and Biobehavioral Reviews*, vol. 71 (2016) pp. 455–471, p. 456.
5 Bastin, Harrison, Davey, Moll and Whittle, 'Feelings of Shame, Embarrassment and Guilt and their Neural Correlates', p. 456.
6 Fox, 'The Embarrassment of Embarrassment', pp. 5–6.
7 Bastin, Harrison, Davey, Moll and Whittle, 'Feelings of Shame, Embarrassment and Guilt and their Neural Correlates', p. 456.
8 Bastin, Harrison, Davey, Moll and Whittle, 'Feelings of Shame, Embarrassment and Guilt and their Neural Correlates', p. 456.
9 Michael Schudson, 'Embarrassment and Erving Goffman's Idea of Human Nature', *Theory and Society*, vol. 13 (1984) pp. 633–648, p. 636.
10 Greg Morgan, ' "Give Me the Consideration of Being the Bondsman": Embarrassment and the Figure of the Bond in the Sentimental Fiction of Samuel Richardson', *Eighteenth Century Fiction*, vol. 28, no. 4 (2016) pp. 667–690, p. 668.
11 Schudson, 'Embarrassment and Erving Goffman's Idea of Human Nature', p. 638.
12 Anja Eller, Miriam Koschate, Kim-Michelle Gilson, 'Embarrassment: The Ingroup—Outgroup Audience Effect in Faux Pas Situations', *European Journal of Social Psychology*, vol. 41 (2011) pp. 489–500, pp. 489–490.

13 Laura Müller-Pinzler, Lena Rademacher, Frieder M. Paulus and Sören Krach, 'When Your Friends Make You Cringe: Social Closeness Modulates Vicarious Embarrassment-Related Neural Activity', *Social Cognitive and Affective Neuroscience*, vol. 11, no. 3 (2016) pp. 466–475, p. 467.
14 Frieder M. Paulus, Laura Müller-Pinzler, David S. Stolz, Annalina V. Mayer, Lena Rademacher, Sören Krach, 'Laugh or Cringe? Common and Distinct Processes of Reward-Based Schadenfreude and Empathy-Based Fremdscham', *Neuropsychologia*, (In Press 2017), https://doi.org/10.1016/j.neuropsychologia.2017.05.030, accessed 27 June 2017.
15 Müller-Pinzler, Rademacher, Paulus and Krach, 'When Your Friends Make You Cringe', p. 467.
16 Paulus, Müller-Pinzler, Stolz, Mayer, Rademacher, Krach, 'Laugh or Cringe?', and Müller-Pinzler, Rademacher, Paulus, Krach, 'When Your Friends Make you Cringe', pp. 466–467.
17 These issues will also be discussed in the following chapter, 'Shaming British-Australia'.
18 *Woman*, vol. 10, no. 4, 1 June 1917, p. 110.
19 Krishan Kumar explains that the nation's position in relation to its 'internal' empire, Great Britain or the United Kingdom, as well as to its 'external' empire, extending to North America and the Caribbean and then to India and South East Asia, meant that there was little, if any, need to develop a specifically English national identity. See Krishan Kumar, 'Nation and Empire: English and British National Identity in Comparative Perspective', *Theory and Society*, vol. 29 (2000) pp. 575–608.
20 Catherine Hall, 'Going a-Trolloping: Imperial Man Travels the Empire' in Clare Midgley, ed., *Gender and Imperialism* (Manchester: Manchester University Press, 1998) pp. 180–199, p. 180.
21 Shula Marks, 'History, the Nation and Empire: Sniping from the Periphery, *History Workshop Journal*, vol. 29, no. 1 (1990) pp. 111–119, p. 117.
22 Marks, 1990, p. 115.
23 See Antoinette Burton, 'Rules of Thumb: British History and 'Imperial Culture' in Nineteenth and Twentieth-Century Britain, *Women's History Review*, vol. 3, no. 4 (1994) pp. 483–501, p. 484.
24 Burton, 'Rules of Thumb', p. 486.
25 Burton, 'Rules of Thumb', p. 485.
26 Here I am applying an understanding of transnationalism as the movement of people, institutions and ideas across and through national boundaries. See Akira Iriye, 'Transnational History', *Contemporary European History*, vol. 13, no. 2 (2004) pp. 211–222, p. 212; Ian Tyrrell, 'Comparative and Transnational History', *Australian Feminist Studies*, vol. 22, no. 52 (2007) pp. 49–54, p. 49, and Ann Curthoys and Marilyn Lake, 'Introduction', in Ann Curthoys and Marilyn Lake, eds., *Connected Worlds: History in Transnational Perspective* (Canberra: ANU E-Press, 2005), pp. 6–20.
27 Fiona Paisley, 'Introduction', *Australian Feminist Studies*, vol. 16, no. 36 (2001) pp. 271–277, p. 272.
28 Alan Lester, 'British Settler Discourse and the Circuits of Empire', *History Journal Workshop*, vol. 54, no. 1 (2002), pp. 25–48, p. 25.
29 Lester, 'British Settler Discourse and the Circuits of Empire', p. 44.
30 Burton, 'Rules of Thumb', p. 486. This is not to say, of course, that humanitarian reformers in the metropole were not often critical of developments and practices in the peripheries, particularly as far as the treatment of the indigenous populations were concerned. See, for example, Lester, 'British Settler Discourse and the Circuits of Empire', pp. 24–48.
31 For a more detailed discussion of American reactions to female suffrage in Australia, see Marilyn Lake, 'State Socialism for Australian Mothers: Andrew

Fisher's Radical Maternalism in its International and Local Contexts', *Labour History*, vol. 102 (2012) pp. 55–70.
32 For more on Australian suffragists in places such as the USA, see Audrey Oldfield, *Woman Suffrage in Australia: A Gift or Struggle?* (Cambridge: Cambridge University Press, 1992) pp. 231–243.
33 *Anti-Suffrage Review*, no. 103, May 1917, pp. 33–4.
34 *Anti-Suffrage Review*, no. 27, February 1911, pp. 25–6. The *Review* made similar claims of New Zealand: Mrs. Wentworth Stanley stated that she had lived in Australia and could assure her audience that the women did not work for the vote there. It was simply put in and passed. In New Zealand, it was passed by a snap decision and went through by one vote. See *Anti-Suffrage Review*, no. 5, May 1913, p. 105.
35 *Anti-Suffrage Review*, no. 3, February 1909, p. 2.
36 *Anti-Suffrage Review*, no. 3, February 1909, p. 2.
37 *Anti-Suffrage Review*, no. 16, March 1910, p. 3.
38 *Anti-Suffrage Review*, no. 16, March 1910, p. 3.
39 *Anti-Suffrage Review*, no. 21, August 1910, pp. 6–13 (report of the principle Anti-Suffrage speeches made in the House of Commons during debate on the second reading of the Parliamentary Franchise (Women) Bill). These are points made by Mr F. E. Smith.
40 *Anti-Suffrage Review*, no. 21, August 1910, pp. 6–13.
41 *Anti-Suffrage Review*, no. 27, February 1911, pp. 25–26.
42 *Anti-Suffrage Review*, no. 30, May 1911, p. 102.
43 *Anti-Suffrage Review*, no. 38, January 1912, pp. 13–14.
44 *Anti-Suffrage Review*, no. 57, July 1913, pp. 153–154.
45 *Anti-Suffrage Review*, no. 54, April 1913, p. 74.
46 *Anti-Suffrage Review*, no. 54, April 1913, p. 74.
47 *Anti-Suffrage Review*, no. 21, August 1910, pp. 18–19.
48 *Anti-Suffrage Review*, no. 21, August 1910, pp. 18–19.
49 *Anti-Suffrage Review*, no. 21, August 1910, pp. 18–19.
50 *Anti-Suffrage Review*, no. 21, August 1910, pp. 18–19.
51 *Anti-Suffrage Review*, no. 21, August 1910, pp. 18–19.
52 *Anti-Suffrage Review*, no. 21, August 1910, pp. 18–19.
53 I have written on this exchange in Sharon Crozier-De Rosa, 'The National and the Transnational in British Anti-Suffragists' Views of Australian Women Voters', *History Australia*, vol. 10, no. 3 (2013), pp. 51–64.
54 *Anti-Suffrage Review*, no. 33, August 1911, p. 163.
55 See, for example, Barbara Caine, 'Vida Goldstein and the English Militant Campaign', *Women's History Review*, vol. 2, no. 3 (1993) pp. 363–376, and Joy Damousi, 'An Absence of Anything Masculine: Vida Goldstein and Women's Public Speech', *Victorian Historical Journal*, vol. 79, no. 2 (2008) pp. 251–264.
56 *Anti-Suffrage Review*, vol. 33, August 1911, p. 163.
57 *Anti-Suffrage Review*, vol. 33, August 1911, p. 163.
58 *Anti-Suffrage Review*, vol. 33, August 1911, p. 163.
59 *Anti-Suffrage Review*, vol. 33, August 1911, p. 163.
60 *Anti-Suffrage Review*, no. 7, June 1909, pp. 1–2.
61 *Anti-Suffrage Review*, no. 27, February 1911, pp. 25–26.
62 *Anti-Suffrage Review*, no. 27, February 1911, pp. 25–26.
63 *Anti-Suffrage Review*, no. 21, August 1910, pp. 18–19.
64 *Anti-Suffrage Review*, no. 10, September 1909, pp. 1–2.
65 Colquhoun was referring to notions of civic housekeeping espoused by social worker and activist Jane Addams in the United States. See *Anti-Suffrage Review*, no. 10, September 1909, pp. 1–2.
66 *Anti-Suffrage Review*, no. 31, June 1911, pp. 121–122.
67 *Anti-Suffrage Review*, no. 31, June 1911, p. 111.

68 *Anti-Suffrage Review*, no. 31, June 1911, p. 111.
69 *Anti-Suffrage Review*, no. 58, August 1913, p. 173.
70 *Anti-Suffrage Review*, no. 58, August 1913, p. 173.
71 *Anti-Suffrage Review*, no. 32, July 1911, pp. 134–135.
72 *Anti-Suffrage Review*, no. 35, October 1911, pp. 206–207.
73 *Anti-Suffrage Review*, no 35, October 1911, pp. 206–207.
74 *Anti-Suffrage Review*, no. 112, February 1918, pp. 9–10.
75 *Anti-Suffrage Review*, no. 112, February 1918, pp. 9–10.
76 *Anti-Suffrage Review*, no 112, February 1918, pp. 9–10.
77 *Anti-Suffrage Review*, no 112, February 1918, pp. 9–10.

4   Shaming British-Australia

In 1910, Australians elected their first socialistic Labor government. The patriotic Australian women's paper, *Woman*, was gutted. This distressing political outcome confirmed that the majority of Australians were blissfully—and to the paper's mind, shamefully—unaware that that nation was their responsibility.[1] As a relatively young white nation, Australia had not yet proven that it was deserving of its privileged place within the family of nations that composed the British Empire. As newly enfranchised citizens since 1902, Australian women had not yet demonstrated that they were worthy of the distinction of being one of the first communities of national womanhood to have been entrusted with the vote. 'No other women in the world', *Woman* asserted, 'have so great power and responsibility placed in their hands, but so far nearly half of our women have been politically asleep.'[2] Australian women were charged with the special task of extending the British 'race' and Britain's democratic and civilising values to the 'new' world.[3] Therefore, by refusing to exercise their vote or by voting for the wrong party, apathetic or misguided Australian women jeopardised more than just their own integrity as patriotic Australian women. They also threatened the legitimacy of their place in the wider global British community and therefore the integrity of their British-Australian identity.

Of all the Empire's women, patriotic Australian women considered themselves to be uniquely burdened with the responsibility of guarding against national shame. Many of them had not wanted the vote. But now, as voting citizens, they had a direct hand in choosing how the honour of the young nation was protected. Their anxieties, therefore, were twofold. On the one hand, they worried that the new nation would not prove itself a mature and loyal member of the imperial family of nations and would instead bring shame upon itself and the Empire. On the other hand, patriotic women expressed a deep concern that women citizens would not perform this new role with the level of political wisdom and patriotic zeal required of them. In this chapter, I analyse how the Australian Women's National League (AWNL), through their official organ, *Woman*, worked to repel the ever-present threat of the shame of the Australian woman voter by explaining just how pivotal the political woman was to the nation and the Empire.

108 *Shaming British-Australia*

Part of the organisation's program involved convincing hesitant women that exercising their political duties was integral to maintaining the well-being of the nation. This caution was even more applicable during the Great War when Australian women experienced a heightened sense of anxiety that the new white Commonwealth was less than capable. The failure of multiple conscription referenda and the presence in Australia of disloyal Irish-Australians compounded their fears. How did the women of the AWNL understand the seemingly endless threat of shame? In this chapter, I analyse how they used shame in their attempts to protect the integrity of their identity as loyal British-Australians.

Patriotic Women and the British-Australian Nation

As I discussed in detail in Chapter 2, women had a complex and contested relationship with the highly gendered concept of the nation. Nationalism and nation-building were deemed overwhelmingly to be masculine projects. Women were often uncertain about the appropriate nature of their place and roles within those projects. Moreover, histories of nationalisms and nation-building tended to write women out of their narratives. Their participation in nationalist movements and nation-building processes were subsequently obscured. This was the case for the women of the British Empire, whether they were implicated in imperial, colonial, or anti-colonial nationalisms.

At the beginning of the twentieth century, patriotic women in Australia were confronted with a masculinisation of the newly imagined nation,[4] the Commonwealth of Australia, which was established as an independent nation-state in 1901.[5] Feminist historian Marilyn Lake argues that 'national consciousness burgeoned in the Australian colonies' late in the nineteenth century. Nationalists in the colonies were aware that they shared many characteristics with their kin in the 'Mother Country'. They spoke a common language, came from the same 'stock', and formed the same 'race'. They also shared similar racial ideologies. Therefore, to prove that the newly imagined nation was distinctive, there had to be an element of difference. For Australia, that element was the nature of its masculinity. This emerging national consciousness, then, focused on a distinct type of Australian man: the Bushman.[6] Australia's 'liberal urban bourgeois', composed of urban writers, artists, and critics, constructed the Australian myth of manliness. Reacting against the so-called model of the 'Domestic Man', with its links to British, urban and increasingly suburban middle-class Evangelical Christian respectability, they created the resourceful, independent white Bushman—a model of manliness and 'mateship' untrammelled by wife or home life.[7] The archetypal Australian Bushman was derived from Britishness but exemplary of an improved branch of the British 'race' as it had adapted to New World conditions.

As in Ireland, Australian womanhood was cast in a reductive symbolic role in the national project. The newly emerging white Australian nation was increasingly symbolised as female, as Britannia's daughter or younger cousin, for example. Actual women were removed from national imaginings, as the Australian landscape was constructed as no place for a woman. This was despite the paradoxical reality of women's active involvement in the running of the nation, for instance, as voters since 1902.[8] More than ever before in white Australian history, women were imaginatively consigned to the domestic hearth, to British middle-class notions of domestic ideology. This confinement to the private—despite the obvious public duties entrusted to white Australian women—only strengthened with the emergence of the citizen soldier, particularly the Anzac legend who had 'given birth to the nation' when he represented the young Commonwealth during the doomed Gallipoli campaign on 25 April 1915.[9] In this militarised concept of the maturing nation, Lake asserts, Australian women were to dedicate themselves to the unselfish task of mothering the nation and then sacrificing their sons to military authorities in the event of national conflict. Women were capable of breeding a population, of giving birth to babies. However, Lake added, it seemed that only Australian men 'could give birth to the political entity, the imperishable community, of the nation'.[10]

The women of the AWNL understood that it was the Australian man's job to ensure the masculine reputation of the former colonies. Guided by the emotional standards of reigning masculine emotional regimes, he was to actively promote and protect the nation's honour. As mentioned, the ensuing international war would provide an opportunity for him to do so on the world stage. However, these women also expressed concern that Australian manhood might not be up to the task of proving the young Commonwealth's manliness. They worried about the shame that would result if it did not.

The AWNL was also worried about the performance of Australian womanhood. Therefore, their anxieties about the shame of a deficient Australian manhood intersected with and fed off those about an inadequate Australian womanhood. Despite the reach of the masculinised myth of the nation, patriotic Australian women imagined themselves as intrinsic parts of the new Australian Commonwealth. Suffragists, for example, had framed their demand for the vote as a matter of patriotism.[11] Australian women, therefore, participated in 'nationalist dreams and aspirations'.[12] Some saw themselves as equal citizens, given their enfranchised state. Others constructed their citizenship more as maternal—as mothers of the nation and, more expansively, as mothers of the 'race', meaning the white, British 'race'.[13]

Patriotic women accepted the mission of extending the great British 'race'.[14] However, they worried that Australian women would not prove themselves up to the task of protecting the racial integrity of the young white nation. These concerns intermingled with more immediate anxieties about holding the Australian continent. As white settlers in a former British colony, British-Australians were, of course, aware that they were 'immigrants to a new found land and the dispossessors of the original Aboriginal custodians'.[15] They submerged some of the racial anxieties stemming from this awareness in Social Darwinist theories that assured white Australians that the Aboriginal people were a dying race, doomed to extinction in the face of modernising and civilising forces.[16] However, other aspects of their territorial worries were not so easily appeased. Geographical characteristics like the 'vast open spaces' and long, unprotected coastlines heightened 'the young nation's sense of vulnerability'. The country's proximity to Asia served to promote fears of 'Asian invasion' adding to existing racial concerns.[17]

As enfranchised citizens and as metaphorical and real mothers of the British 'race', white Australian women considered that they were doubly burdened with the task of protecting the nation's and the Empire's racial integrity. To fail to live up to this vocation meant shaming their proud racial heritage. It could potentially result in the young white Commonwealth's ostracism from the British Empire's family of nations. Therefore, patriotic women approached the task of convincing seemingly apathetic Australian men and women to exercise their vote for the good of the loyal British-Australian nation in a very serious manner.

Rousing the Dormant Patriotism of Australia

In 1909, *Woman* asked readers, 'Do we, as loyal subjects of this glorious Empire, do our full share towards maintaining it?'[18] 'We owe so much to the Motherland who has treated us so generously', it reminded them. The Motherland had been bountiful, and Australia had given little in return. 'Do we not owe her the duty of a larger-hearted patriotism?'[19] These comments arose out of discussions about how much the country should invest in the nation's and the Empire's defence forces. Every son and daughter of the Empire, the paper instructed, must risk more by way of 'personal and pecuniary sacrifice' to ensure the well-being of the Empire:

> Shall we not then call to our minds all the proud traditions of our race and stand shoulder to shoulder in the defence of our Empire, determined that not at our door shall lie 'the ordering of her disgrace'.[20]

Surely, Australians understood that Australian patriotism was inextricably intertwined with imperial loyalty. To prove themselves selfishly unpatriotic— a community of aberrant Britons or Britishers—meant shaming both the Australian nation and the British Empire.[21] The first challenge for the dutiful woman voter, then, was to address the political apathy and deficient patriotism of many within the Australian community.

Woman continued to appeal to Australian voters to use their political rights to defend British values. However, by 1913, it appeared that the Australian electorate was unwilling to respond to its pleas or directives. The nation had spawned an unfortunate culture of political apathy. The problem, *Woman* asserted, lay in the process by which Australians were granted the rights of citizenship. The fact was, the paper announced, citizenship had 'not cost the present generation anything'. If Australians had had to fight for the franchise—in the way that women in England and America were currently doing—then they might prove to be prouder of their rights and responsibilities. This pride might rouse them to protect those rights and responsibilities.[22] Instead, the country was home to repeatedly low voter turnouts and incidences of corruption in federal and state elections. Australian elections, *Woman* claimed, saw

> thousands of men and women refraining, on the paltriest of reasons, from voting at all, while others, lost to all sense of decency, voted early and often, not only has our Citizenship been abused, but the safety of our young Democracy endangered.[23]

This prompted the paper to declare, 'Australia must hang its head in shame over the flagrant abuse of Citizenship'.[24] As intolerable as it was, it seemed that the only means of arousing sufficient patriotism to motivate Australians to vote, and to vote fairly, was the fear of a punitive monetary fine. The AWNL continued with its stated mission of rousing 'the dormant patriotism of Australia'.[25] Too many, however, were refusing to respond appropriately to its message about the threat of national shame.

Shame of the Apathetic Enfranchised Woman

Woman desired to rouse all Australian citizens, but, as a patriotic woman's paper, it exerted extra pressure on female voters to perform citizenship in an appropriate manner. Year after year, the paper declared the old adage to be true: 'Show me the women of a country, and I will tell you what its history will be'.[26] Surely, it asserted, 'all women will vote for that which is for the welfare and progress of Australia, its industrial development, the increase of its population, the maintenance of the fundamental and integral part of its Constitution'.[27] By feeling compelled to even issue such a statement, the paper revealed its ambivalence about the Australian woman voter's ability or desire to put the nation's interests before her own.

Reflecting its uncertainty about the will and capabilities of the new woman citizen, *Woman* alternated between applauding Australian women for successfully carrying out their national duties and denouncing them for the inadequacy of their patriotism. In 1911, for example, the paper celebrated that the women of Australia had 'nobly risen to the occasion' when they voted to reject a referendum that would have seen the nationalisation of Australian industries—a move that the AWNL had viewed as deplorably socialistic.[28] However, other election outcomes led the paper to chastise fellow female citizens on the grounds that their sense of patriotism was lethargic, misguided, or absent and that these faults had been responsible for bringing the country to the point of collapse.[29]

112 *Shaming British-Australia*

The 1910 election campaign which resulted in the successful establishment of a socialistic Labor government had been one such case in point. As mentioned at the beginning of the chapter, *Woman* used this electoral result to argue that the majority of Australians had been blissfully unaware that the nation was their responsibility.[30] Patriotic electors had either not voted or they had voted the wrong way. International socialism challenged the supremacy of British imperialism. By voting in a socialist government, Australian voters had threatened Australia's integrity as a loyal branch of the Empire family. The direness of this situation led the paper to angrily declare that the people of Australia had been 'half asleep' during that election when their birthright—in the form of the young, white, democracy bestowed on them by the kindly Mother Country—had been 'bartered for a message of pottage'.[31]

Woman was annoyed at the performance of the entire Australian electorate, but its accusations of political torpor were particularly directed at women who formed the majority of that electorate. It was woman's province 'to raise the ideals of a country, to sow the seeds of religion, morality, of patriotism, that form the soul or the character of a nation', one *Woman* article affirmed. But the women of Australia had been found guilty of 'not doing their duty to their country'.[32] *Woman* claimed that no other women had 'so great power and responsibility placed in their hands'. And yet the paper accused women of not using this power to preserve the integrity of the nation or the Empire. It stated, 'nearly half of our women have been politically asleep'. They had refused to vote. Their indifference jeopardised the safe future of the nation. It was imperative that women woke to their new political duties because, *Woman* warned, the welfare of the country now relied on how women voters fulfilled the duties and responsibilities of her citizenship.[33]

Arming for Australia's Honour

Britain declared war in 1914. It did so without consulting the Dominions; however, it expected that Australia and all the other Dominions would follow suit.[34] Australia did. Nearly 417,000 Australians enlisted for the war out of a population of around 5 million people. Almost 330,000 men and women served overseas.[35] Over 60,000 of these were to die during the war, and a further 153,000 were wounded.[36] Of the Australian soldiers fighting in the war, 14.2 per cent died, which was a higher proportion of fatalities than other national (British, Dominion, and colonial) troops.[37]

Australia entered World War One partly out of allegiance to Britain. Loyalty to the Empire was not universal at the commencement of the war, but it was a dominant value, at least among those in positions of political, economic, and cultural authority.[38] The dominant narrative promulgated by the mainstream press was that participation in the war would prove that Australians were loyal 'Britishers'—a term that the women of the AWNL frequently drew on. Therefore, they would be deserving of British imperial protection in a region that was considered to be hostile to Australian racial policies.[39] But the war also suited the Australian Commonwealth's prerogatives. As Joan Beaumont explains, it was expedient for Australia to enter the war for a number of pragmatic reasons including

> the maintenance of British global imperial power, the protection of the White Australia Policy, the guaranteeing of Australian security in the Pacific, the defence of democracy against German tyranny and aggression, and the protection of the rights of small nations such as Belgium.[40]

The onset of the war intensified already existing anxieties about Australia's loyalty, but it also provided the young white nation with the avenue to prove its maturity and its honour on the global stage. This was an opportunity that the new Commonwealth so desperately craved, but it was also a fraught one. As in all the other belligerent nations, the pressure was on national manhood to perform nobly in the field of battle. The masculinity of the Australian man and the Australian nation was at stake. Both would be shamed if Australian men failed in this endeavour.

Australian men were certainly under extraordinary pressure by virtue of the war but so too were Australian women. As enfranchised citizens, antipodean women could vote on matters of war. More than any other group of patriotic empire womanhood, then, Australian and New Zealand women were directly implicated in the honourable or dishonourable conduct of their respective nations during the war. Their responsibilities at this time of national and international crisis were typically masculine. They could actively assert the honour of their nation, if not through arming in defence of their country, then at least through exercising their right to vote on issues related to the war. The flip side of this was that if they exercised their political power inappropriately, they could also be complicit in the act of bringing shame to their country. The threat of being found defective as loyal British-Australian women plagued these female voters as they attempted to combine their masculine wartime responsibilities with their ongoing allegiance to feminine emotional regimes.

The women of the AWNL had no qualms about directing the country to arm for war. On the contrary, *Woman* had cited not simply the desire but the need for an international war years before the war's outbreak. 'A "baptism of fire," much as it may be deplored, is *the* force, above all others, which welds a nation into one and arouses its patriotism to an effective degree', *Woman* announced in 1911.[41] Australia had been favoured by fortune, the article ran, for it had not yet been stained by blood (completely ignoring, of course, the Aboriginal blood spilt in the process of colonisation). Yet, ironically, good fortune in this respect was not always good for the welfare of the country. A lack of a crowning war, *Woman* asserted, was exactly the reason why we in Australia 'hold the many privileges we enjoy in this fair land so lightly, why so many of us are careless and indifferent to our country's well-being, why our patriotism lies dormant, instead of being active'.[42] War was necessary to bestow upon the young democracy the experience and hardship necessary to make its occupants feel gratefully aware of their privileges and therefore of their need to protect such privileges. It was essential for Australia to prove its honour.

Not only that, of course, but as touched on earlier, a display of Australian military might, backed by the greater military power of the imperial metropole, was considered of utmost importance to Australian national security. 'We in Australia are in the position of a small and isolated outpost, a weak and tempting bait (as is so often pointed out) for these countries so closely packed by the yellow races', one contributor to the paper wrote in 1912. Australia had to be careful, then, not to leave 'an open door, an unguarded territory, a standing invitation to these teeming millions'.[43] Arming the Empire and arming for the protection of that Empire was the only foreseeable way of safeguarding the interests of that global family of nations. It was also regarded as the most effective means of ensuring the continuity of Australia's exclusive racial policies.

The AWNL may have pledged unequivocal support for Australia's involvement in the international conflict but that did not mean that Australian society was unanimous in its support for all aspects of the country's wartime policies. Divisions were rife. For example, there were intense discussions about why it was pertinent to Australian national defence to send Australian soldiers overseas to fight in Europe and the Middle East. There were also uncomfortable public disputes between Australian and British authorities over the extent to which Australia, as a British Dominion, should have control over the operations of its own soldiers. There were further disagreements at the end of the war when it came to the nature of proposed peace settlements and reparations.[44]

Back on the Australian home front, there were pockets of anti-war sentiment.[45] Throughout the war, the population also felt itself increasingly divided over a range of issues, each intensifying as the war was prolonged. These issues included conscripting men for active overseas service, the labour movement and trade union activism, Irish Home Rule and the Irish-Australian section of the community, and international politics, especially the gathering socialist movement in Russia. These internal divisions had serious consequences for the integrity of the Australian community. The country may have been on the victorious side of the war campaign, but the nation that emerged out of that vast conflict was not a confident, unified one. Rather, World War One helped to produce an Australian society that was often marked by divisions, insecurity, sectarianism, and bitter suspicions and paranoias.[46] The legacies of this war have rendered this period of the history of the white Commonwealth one of its most disruptive. Patriotic women voters were encumbered with the task of attempting to inculcate a sense of domestic unity and empire loyalty as the nation underwent its most trying test of character. In the following section of the chapter, I examine *Woman*'s efforts to fend off the shame of disloyalty caused by the conscription referenda, Irish-Australian politics, and the threat of international socialism.

Australian Women Voters Deflect Accusations of Shameful Disloyalty: Conscription

In 1916, Australia moved to introduce compulsory military service. Under existing regulations, Australia could already enforce military service—but only for home defence. It could not do so for conflicts conducted internationally.[47] Therefore, the incoming prime minister, Billy Hughes, decided to put the question to the people through a referendum. Australian women would have the chance to vote directly on whether or not to force men to enlist for the war. This was an extraordinary responsibility. Accordingly, the eyes of the Empire were fixed on these enfranchised female citizens as they participated in the wartime political machine. As the Melbourne newspaper, the *Argus*, pointed out at the time, women's citizenship was on trial.[48]

Beaumont argues that discussions over conscription sparked 'a public debate that has never been rivalled in Australian political history for its bitterness, divisiveness and violence'. This was a debate that was characterised by 'raw emotional violence'.[49] Conscription implied and enacted an erosion of democratic values which incited anger. It is also no wonder that the campaigns for and against drew on the population's raw emotion, set as it was against the backdrop of mass death and mass grieving.[50] The degree of physical violence marring the conscription campaigns is demonstrative of just how highly wrought Australians were about this issue. In the eight weeks leading up to the 1916 referendum, for example, each side of the debate organised mass rallies that were characterised by chanting, booing, heckling, effigy burning, mud pelting, egg throwing, and banner destroying. At one meeting in Brisbane, fights broke out and one man was shot. Returned soldiers often exercised violence at these events. Anti-war women were not immune from such violence.[51]

The passion and the violence did not end with the defeat of the 1916 referendum. Another campaign began for the second referendum on the matter that was scheduled for 1917. The second campaign was even more emotional than the first. It was coloured by personal grief, suspicion, bitterness, hysteria, and paranoia—a mix of elements that made for a highly volatile and exceedingly passionate, often irrational, environment.[52] Violence escalated. Pro-conscriptionists—many of them women—perpetrated acts of violence against anti-conscriptionists—many of whom were female too.[53] It seemed that Australia was alone, of all the loyal Allied nations, in rejecting conscription. This was particularly so after the United States and Canada joined the other countries, such as Britain and New Zealand, who enforced compulsory service.[54] To the patriotic women of the AWNL, this was a woefully shameful situation. Australia had been tainted by its inability to demonstrate its national maturity and its empire loyalty through endorsing conscription.

The eyes of the imperial metropole were on Australian women, as they performed the unique task of voting in these crucial referenda. Their judgement was not sympathetic. Instead, anti-suffragists in Britain declared that women voters had been responsible for the defeat of both plebiscites. As we saw in Chapter 3, the Australian woman voter was regarded by British anti-suffragists as an embarrassment. These same anti-suffragists had asserted that Australia's contribution to the Allied effort was relatively insignificant. And yet, on hearing the news of the defeated 1916 conscription referenda, it suited the British *Anti-Suffrage Review*'s (the *Review*) purposes to pronounce the Australia woman voter to be a serious threat to the success of the war effort and, consequently, to the integrity of the Empire.

The 1916 referendum result proved to British anti-suffragists that female voters in the antipodes had demonstrated a dangerous propensity for direct disloyalty to the Empire. Female voters in Australia, the paper insisted, were responsible for the failure of the Conscription Referendum in October 1916. Quoting the Sydney correspondent for the *Times*, a *Review* article titled 'The Experience of Australia' maintained that the failure of the referendum was due to 'the emotionalism of the women electors, who thought they would be condemning men to death if they voted "Yes" '.[55] The paper went on to explain that it had never doubted that Labor women would vote against conscription. They would have been co-opted by their menfolk to do so. However, they were taken by surprise when they realised that a large percentage of liberal women helped to swell the 'No' vote in each of the Australian states. Australian female voters—across the political divide—'helped to swell the "anti" vote in each State'. The *Review* continued,

> Their action has dumbfounded some most ardent supporters of Woman Suffrage, because there is irrefragable evidence that they permitted their emotions to guide their pencils in the booths, and reason and patriotism appealed to them in vain. In the supreme trial of citizenship most women 'shirked their duty'.[56]

Regarding this last line, the *Review* stated, 'These are harsh words, which for our own part we should have hesitated to use'.[57] Yet it repeated them three times on the same page to wring maximum effect.

Feminine emotionalism when deciding imperial matters was a grave concern. The intrusion of feminine emotionalism into wartime imperial politics when millions of men's lives were at stake—when the very existence of liberal democracy was at risk—was unforgiveable. This explains why, for the last two years of the war at least, the Australian woman voter transformed from an object of embarrassment to one of shame. Her actions now threatened the fabric of Britishness and British political ideals. In the *Review*'s appraisal, she had turned against the community to which she had formerly pledged allegiance. She should feel the shame of such a betrayal.

Perhaps 'loyal' women in the peripheries were rendered invisible by the fact that, unlike women in Britain, they were barred from assuming any official role during the war.[58] Perhaps the *Review* chose, for strategic reasons, to overlook the war propaganda work of organisations like the Australian Women's Service Corps and war work of Australian women in the Red Cross.[59] Perhaps, again, it was the visibility of a minority of feminist pacifists in Australia, such as the Women's Peace Army, that led to the formation of this opinion about Australian woman's dereliction of duty.[60] Certainly, evidence of the anti-war work of a group of Australian feminists in the face of British suffragists' overwhelming support of the war effort served as yet another example of the potential, if not confirmed, disloyalty of Australian women voters.

By whichever pathway the *Review* reached its conclusions about Australian women's disloyalty, the outcome of the conscription referenda caused it to re-assess its approach to comparing the metropole and the periphery. As outlined in the previous chapter, British anti-suffragists denied the legitimacy of comparing the metropole to the peripheries. However, the example of the defeat of Australia's referenda was taken up by the *Review* as evidence of the universal untrustworthiness of women voters.

The patriotic women of the AWNL felt the burden of enfranchisement keenly. Therefore, they responded with anger and indignation to accusations emanating from the metropole that they had been responsible for the defeat of the conscription referenda, specifically, and that they represented a threat to the Empire, more generally. Early in 1917, *Woman* referred to the 'late saddening Referendum'. It was anxious to assure all its patriotic readers that the women of the AWNL had 'strained every nerve to help Australia to keep her honour unsullied, and we can only blush with shame for Australia's sake at the result'.[61] The paper realised that, in the eyes of the civilised world—and seemingly alone of all the loyal nations in the great family of empire—Australia had proven itself not up to the task of selfless devotion to the Empire's cause.

Woman's response to accusations of blame were twofold. On the one hand, the women of the AWNL blamed themselves for not being up to the task of convincing their more vulnerable or susceptible enfranchised sisters to vote the right way. Too many women had been persuaded by their waylaid menfolk to lend their support to the disloyal elements of the nation (namely, the pacifists, the trade unions, and Sinn Féiners—that is, those Irish-Australians who supported Irish anti-colonial nationalist aspirations[62]). On the other hand, *Woman* vehemently denied accusations emanating from outside of the country that it was Australian women voters who were responsible for Australia's new reputation for disloyalty: 'The Australian Women's National League has indignantly repudiated the assertion of [renowned British anti-suffragist] Sir Almroth Wright, "that the women of

Australia were responsible for the defeat of the Conscription Referendum in October."'[63] The shame was Australia's generally, not its loyal womanhood's specifically.

The failure of the second referendum late in 1917 only compounded *Woman's* sense that the shame was Australia's—tainted by its radical elements—but not its loyal womanhood's. The paper deemed the day of the second referendum 'a black and bitter day for all loyalists'. It continued, 'Loyalists remembered that they were still Australians—Britishers—that a Loyalist Government still controlled the destinies of the Commonwealth, and that a united effort was still required to prevent the "No" party from further wrecking its will'.[64] But the unity of the continent was not forthcoming. Therefore, *Woman* proclaimed: 'Tens of thousands of Australian women will naturally feel ashamed and sad at heart just now as they think of the abandonment of Australia's bravest sons'.[65] The call at this sad point was 'to ensure that the disloyalist and anti-British do not further humiliate the Commonwealth'. 'We are living in troubled, anxious times, in which women must be prepared to play resolutely, unflinchingly, and courageously, the part that is allotted to them'.[66] Given their awareness of international scrutiny of the Australian woman voter, *Woman* put forth the question, 'Is the Woman's Vote responsible for Australia's debacle?' Instead of reiterating their own protestations of loyalty, the paper presented the judgement of another great international power: 'America's Verdict—SOCIALISM, PACIFISM, SINN FEINISM'.[67] The undesirable, un-British, and un-Australian elements that Australia housed within its borders were the culprits, not the community of loyal Australian women voters. These were transnational culprits that had infected the national character.

Australian Women Voters Deflect Accusations of Shameful Disloyalty: Socialism

The AWNL was a fiercely anti-socialistic organisation, yet, this did not prevent anti-suffragists in the British centre from accusing them of susceptibility to socialism's pernicious doctrines. In 1909, for example, the British *Review* quoted a visiting Australian woman and her husband who had averred that female suffrage had 'done little good in the Colony'. Its chief result had been to add to the political power of the Labor Party there.[68] The *Review* declared that women had not voted for a Labor government because they bought into the pernicious doctrines of socialism. Rather, its appraisal at this time was that Australian women voters had behaved emotionally. It was not all their own doing. The 'womanhood of Australia was appealed to in a way in which it had not been appealed to before': 'The heart, not the head, was attacked'.[69] Still, the 'quite natural result' of this feminine emotional susceptibility was a socialist government.[70] If anything positive could be taken from news of socialism's successful manipulation of the woman voter, it was to remind British conservatives of the grave problems before them and of the need to avoid 'passion or emotion or hysteria' in the attempt to address these concerns.[71]

At this stage, the Australian woman voter's susceptibility to socialism—whatever the reason for this—was not regarded as anything other than inconvenient. This was to change. Developments taking place internationally cast the woman voter's supposed attraction to socialist politics into a new light. Early in 1917 when Russia was undergoing the initial stages of what would eventually be a socialist revolution, the British *Review* instructed readers to look to the 'Socialist trend of every single Suffrage State' and accept that pattern as a warning not to commit the same error in Britain. Too much was at stake in the Mother Country to allow for the female franchise experiment. A vote given now for woman suffrage in Britain, it cautioned, 'represents a dozen votes in ten or twenty years' time given to the cause of Republicanism in the British Empire'.[72] As international socialism and British imperialism looked set to collide, the woman voter was viewed with much more suspicion than formerly.

Not surprisingly, far from confirming the accuracy of the *Review*'s assertions, *Woman* fervently denied that they had any implications for loyal Australian women. Still, patriotic women in the antipodes were likewise following developments taking place in Russia. Their initially optimistic reactions to the Russian Revolution soon turned sour as revolutionary socialism replaced moderate liberalism. Therefore, *Woman* took it upon itself to join the *Review* in issuing cautions about lending any support to socialism. In doing so, it hoped to deflect any accusations of disloyalty emanating from Britain.

Immediately after the war, *Woman* directed 'the loyal women of Australia' to do their duty and prevent their country falling into the hands of 'disloyalists'.[73] The paper complained that the wider Australian electorate continued to demonstrate its susceptibility to ideologies that ran counter to those championed by Britishness. It warned that post-war chaos coupled with 'the strikes and the revolutionary tendencies and revolutions in nearly all countries in the world' meant that more than ever no woman citizen was free to shirk her political responsibilities, either in Australia or elsewhere in the Empire.[74]

It was time again for patriotic women to remind Australians where their allegiances lay:

> Australia is our great mother, and from Australia we take all our livelihood and all that stands for citizenship and good surroundings. It is for we Australian women to pay some return to Australia for all she gives us and let us be united and firm on polling day, vote for and work for those Nationalist candidates who will have courage, loyalty, and bravery, and who will at the first sign of disloyalty and disruption have the courage to stamp it out, and who will see to it that no red flag of rebellion flies from any place in this fair island of ours. The position is

fraught with so much that is serious that one false step or one error now would be disastrous to this island continent, which is part of the great British Empire.[75]

Australian women voters were instructed to make sure that they voted against the socialistic Labor Party in post-war elections thereby stamping out the threat of rebellion in at least one part of the Empire. Moreover, stemming the tide of socialism also meant protecting their returning soldiers from the insulting 'red flag of rebellion'.[76] If women were not equipped to physically defend the honour of the nation and Empire as their manhood had done, they were at least conditioned to ensure that the collective sacrifice of that manhood was not wasted. While not being called on to exhibit or embody the manly virtues of 'courage' and 'bravery' in order to protect Australia's honour themselves, women voters were directed to vote for the type of men who would.[77]

The power to actively defend the honour of British Australia lay in the hands of its male soldiers and serving politicians. However, the political power vested in the nation's womanhood also meant that it too had a hand in protecting that honour. *Woman*'s response to the threat to British-Australian values represented by international socialism revealed their position on the question of the gendered nature of national honour: it was man's remit to defend the honour of the nation, but it was also the duty of enfranchised women to actively support men in that active role. It was enfranchised women's responsibility to vote in the right men for the job. That way, the masculine character of honour, as discussed in Chapter 2, would be maintained. Masculine emotional regimes would remain intact. As for feminine emotional regimes, they too would remain integral. Women would actively exercise the traditionally masculine responsibility of voting, but they would continue to be guided by the feminine emotional standards in doing so.

Irish-Australians Shame the British-Australian Community

It was the Australian man's duty to defend the honour of the young white nation, but it seemed that there were sections of that manhood which refused to fulfil that responsibility. More than simply shirking their political responsibilities, it appeared as if certain sections of Australian manhood were actively set to attack the fabric of Australian society. They did this by attacking Australian society's adherence to British values and the nation's allegiance to the British Empire. Disloyal Irish-Australian men were one such group.

The issue of the divided loyalties of Irish-Australians exposed the limited nature of shaming as a political tool. It was unlikely that any of the AWNL's loyal members and readers of *Woman* would need to undertake any shameful self-assessment with regard to empire disloyalty. Their pledge was unremittingly to the combined interests of the nation and the Empire. However, there was little to say that radical or disloyal elements of Australian society would undertake the emotional self-assessment demanded by the community of loyal womanhood and amend their ways. Therefore, articulations of shame directed at certain members of the Irish-Australian community discussed in this section of the chapter seemed to serve the function of confirming the exclusion of disloyal subjects from the community of true British-Australians. In this instance, shame served to highlight the false nationalism of Irish-Australians as juxtaposed to the true patriotism of Australian 'Britishers'.

The war had exposed and exacerbated underlying divisions within Australian society. For example, one of the more significant legacies of the wartime conscription referenda was the sectarianism it incited. The case of the Catholic citizens who identified as Irish-Australians exemplifies this. Beaumont points out that perhaps 22 per cent of the population of Australia in the early twentieth century identified as Catholic and most were drawn from the working class and identified as Irish. On the whole, Catholic leaders refrained from taking an official stance in relation to the first conscription referenda in 1916. However, 1916 also witnessed the failed anti-colonial nationalist uprising in Dublin and the subsequent court martial and execution of the Irish nationalist leaders. This event, particularly the severe British reaction to it, radicalised many of those in Australia who identified as being Irish-Australian. The fact that pro-conscriptionists couched their demands in overwhelmingly imperialistic terms served to insert a growing wedge between those who deemed patriotism to be loyalty to the Empire first and foremost, and those who were more concerned to pledge themselves to the cause of the Australian nation. Rising tensions between Catholic and Protestant, working class and middle class, pro- and anti-imperialist, created a highly volatile milieu in which to conduct the campaign for the second conscription referendum in 1917.[78]

In 1917, the Australian Catholic Church contributed to this volatility. Whereas the Catholic Church had refrained from taking an official stance on the first conscription referendum, its views about the second referendum were in the main represented by the notorious Irish-born Archbishop of Melbourne, Daniel Mannix. There is no denying the impact that Mannix had on Australia and on the conscription campaign itself. On the one hand, he was held up as the revered champion of the underdog—the Catholic, Irish, working-class community. But, on the other, he was represented as the scourge of all that was good about loyal British Protestant Australia. His increasingly pronounced views on the necessity for Britain to grant autonomy to Ireland only served to further alienate him from loyal British-Australian. It served to intensify a sectarian split that *Woman* had not considered apparent in the years preceding conscription.

In the final years of the war and those immediately following it, *Woman* declared that some Irish-Australians were responsible for a phenomenon that it termed false nationalism. In many ways, this was a similar concept evoked by the women writing for the *Irish Citizen* who asserted that political women who did not honour Ireland's history of gender equality were guilty of paying homage to a false model of nationalism that favoured British values over those specifically Irish in origin (discussed in Chapter 2). In the case of patriotic women's claims about false nationalism in Australia, however, the Irish were the culprits, not the British.

Woman exposed what it said was the dangerous disruptiveness of the Irish in British-Australia. 'This class, while making no secret of its desire to disintegrate the Empire', the paper argued, 'lays claim to a pseudo Australian sentiment.'[79] One section of the Irish-Australian community, led by that false patriot the Irish-born Archbishop Daniel Mannix of Melbourne, was guilty of supporting radical anti-colonial nationalist aspirations in Ireland. Like all white Australians, this group benefitted from Britain's munificence. Yet they shamelessly championed a campaign that would see one arm of the Empire's family of nations viciously amputated. They represented a section of Australian society that lacked integrity and honesty on at least two grounds: they were shamelessly un-Australian and un-British. As we will see in a moment, they were also accused of being un-Irish.

Mannix claimed that the Irish were an oppressed people. Yet *Woman* assured readers that 'all the world knows that Ireland is to-day the most prosperous corner of the Empire, and her people the most pampered children of that Empire's great world-wide family'.[80] The paper illustrated just how pampered the Irish were: during the war, a time of such immense peril, were these not the only unconscripted people in the United Kingdom?[81] Therefore, Mannix and others who claimed that they represented 'the Irish-Australian sentiment towards the Throne and Empire', were deemed guilty of disseminating 'the historical half-truths and entire myths' about Irish-British relations.[82] In supporting demands for complete autonomy emanating from the Irish political party Sinn Féin, these Irish-Australians had proven that they were dangerously disloyal. Their disloyalty incensed loyal British-Australians.[83] *Woman* accused Sinn Féiners in Australia of 'loving Australia little, but hating England more'. They had demonstrated the truth of this assessment when they fervently opposed measures to introduce conscription for military service during the war—measures that were intended to illustrate Australia's empire loyalty.[84]

Woman was indignant at the false truths perpetuated by Mannix and his followers. These gross deceptions were dangerously misleading. These particular Irish-Australians were not representative of British-Australia. But *Woman* also accused them of not being representative of either Ireland or Irish-Australia. In 1918, for example, the paper declared that Ireland's 'true sons' were 'overwhelmed with shame and anger at the false counsellors, to whose bad advice and example is due the Sinn Feiner of to-day'.[85] *Woman* claimed that true Irish patriots—those who asked for Home Rule not separatism—were loyal members of the Empire. The radical nationalists were the imposters.

Citizens of Australia who propagated lies about the Empire could not be considered true members of the Australian Commonwealth because that Commonwealth owed its existence to the British Empire. Its values derived from that Empire. To masquerade as a loyal member of the Australian Commonwealth while promoting open rebellion in the Empire was to commit a shameful act of hypocrisy. It was to be duplicitous. Mannix was a representative of the British Empire due to his Irish birth, but he was a foreigner in Australia by virtue of his un-Australian and un-British points of view. How long must Australians suffer open disloyalty and rebellion on the part of men like Mannix, *Woman* asked, when these same men accept the gifts and protection of the British flag and Crown? This was a flag that had kept men like Mannix 'well-fed and softly housed while saner and braver men (including our own Australian sons) have lived, fought, suffered, and died in far distant trenches that the world, including Australia, should be free from oppression'.[86] In the face of Australian men's brave wartime sacrifices, Mannix was painted as cowardly and shamefully parasitical. 'How long,' *Woman* asked again one year later, was 'this man to be allowed to openly insult loyal people with impunity, and openly flaunt his pernicious doctrine in the face of true Australian sentiment?'[87]

The women of the AWNL vehemently denied that the shame of disloyalty was theirs. However, they feared that this false representation of Australian sentiment perpetrated by Mannix and his Irish-Australian followers would damage their reputation around the Empire. In this case, it seemed that there was little that patriotic Australian women could do to avoid the smear of disloyalty. Again, it was unlikely that any of their loyal members or readers of *Woman* would need to undertake any shameful self-assessment with regard to empire disloyalty. These references to Mannix and the Irish-Australian community's shame served only to highlight the boundary existing between the community of good patriotic Australians and the disloyal elements beyond that community's pale. As virtuous as patriotic Australian women knew themselves to be, they also understood that recent developments in Australia did nothing to appease concerns about the nature of the woman voter. The difference was that by this stage, Britain had its own woman voters to be worried about.

The pressure on Australian women to perform citizenship in an exemplary womanly manner may have lightened somewhat with the arrival of other women voters around the Empire, but that did not mean that the women did not have cause for concern about the integrity of their national community. Rather, political developments taking place beyond Australian borders accelerated the erosion of imperial ties, those that tied the Australian community to the imperial one.

Rejecting the Stain of Disloyalty in the Face of Empire Disunity

At the close of 1920, it felt as if the AWNL's fears of disunity in the Empire had been confirmed. *Woman* wrote that it was startled to hear that Great Britain and the Dominions had signed the Covenant of the League of Nations separately. Instead of a culture of separatism, the paper insisted, there must be 'closer intercourse, a continual exchange of ideas, the maintenance of a common tradition of a common type of high and progressive civilisation, finding expression in a common language and literature'.[88] They wanted imperial unity not disintegration. There 'must be a strengthening of all the moral as well as all the material ties, which may cause the Motherland and the Dominions to think alike on great international issues'.[89]

Woman reasserted that Australians had been charged with undertaking a unique mission—namely, that of extending and improving the great British 'race'. They had been extraordinarily successful to the point that the paper could now declare that this white settler-colonial society was 'more British than Britain or any other Sister Dominion'. Their evidence for this lay in the fact that this was a continent that was 'governed and inhabited solely by men of British stock, speaking one language, and owning allegiance to the same king'.[90] Conveniently disregarding the ongoing persecution of the now indigenous minority and lauding the 'successes' of the White Australia Policy that had not only prevented the inflow of 'undesirable' migrants but also oversaw the expulsion of previous inhabitants of 'undesirable' racial and ethnic backgrounds, *Woman* asserted that Australia had 'no racial, religious or color problems'.[91]

As they receded from a decade in which they had witnessed the near disintegration of the British Empire, and as they confronted evidence of the increasing separateness of the units composing the Empire, the women of the AWNL were anxious to reconfirm their intrinsic connection to the rest of the Empire, especially the metropole. They had invested so much emotional energy in creating a model of Australian nationalism that was international in character—tied as it was to the vast imperial network—that it was distressing to contemplate that model being substituted by a more parochial version. Patriotic British-Australian women were adamant that the community to which they belonged was both national and transnational. The task of guarding against shaming both interconnected entities was an onerous one. It was also a task that, to a large extent, was increasingly falling outside of the woman voter's sphere of influence. Shaming seemed to have little effect on elements in Australian society that were determined to be disloyal. By the beginning of the 1920s, then, shame presented itself as a limited political tool for good patriotic women in a national community whose identity, which was previously envisaged as homogenous, was compromised.

Conclusion

Patriotic Australia women were painfully attuned to the possibility of the new Commonwealth being endowed with a reputation for being dishonourable. Women had the vote there. In contrast to women in the imperial centre or in Ireland, they had access to real political power. Yet the women of the AWNL were adamant that the gendered emotional regimes underpinning their participation in the public world of politics—and those supporting men's actions in that sphere—had not altered. In this way, they hoped to repel British anti-suffragists' assertions that political women were manly women. The most difficult task they faced in their construction of a new community of patriotic women voters, though, was that of convincing their more apathetic sisters—those who adhered to the outmoded notions of womanhood discussed in an earlier chapter—that they needed to adapt to their new political responsibilities while protecting the integrity of feminine emotional regimes. They were required to navigate these fragile boundaries between masculine and feminine regimes for the good of the nation. If they did not, not only would they shame themselves as loyal British-Australian women but also allow the undesirable elements of the modern world—including international socialism and radical anti-colonial nationalism—to rise to the fore of Australian society.

Patriotic Australian women worked to prevent the radical elements of their society from corrupting the values of the white settler-colonial state. They endeavoured to prove their loyalty to the British Motherland. They did this all the while insisting that they had remained true to British concepts of womanhood. In this way, they could demonstrate that the political woman was an asset to both the nation and the Empire. They pledged allegiance to protecting the integrity of two intersecting communities: white Australian womanhood and loyal British-Australia. By the 1920s, however, and despite the concerted efforts of Australian women to deny imperial disintegration, it seemed that the fabric of those integrated national and imperial communities was already unravelling. Given this, it seemed that shame had lost some of its previously imagined potency for inspiring Australian men and women to rise up to protect the honour of the national collective and the integrity of that community's wider transnational identity.

Notes

1 *Woman*, vol. 4, no. 8, 2 October 1911, pp. 165–176. I also discuss the outcome of this 1910 election in Chapter 1.
2 *Woman*, vol. 4, no. 1, 1 March 1911, p. 1.
3 This idea of the New World as a site for the regeneration of humankind is not a new one. As Cecily Devereux has argued, within white settler colonies, there existed the notion that 'virgin soil' and a healthy climate brought forth 'a new and stronger race'. See Cecily Devereux, 'New Woman, New World: Maternal Feminism and the New Imperialism in the White Settler Colonies', *Women's Studies International Forum*, vol. 22, no. 2 (1999) pp. 175–184, p. 179.

4 Here I am referring to Benedict Anderson's famous formulation of the nation as an 'imagined community'. See Benedict Anderson, *Imagined Communities: Reflections on the Origin and Spread of Nationalism* (London: Verso, 1983).
5 Marilyn Lake, 'Mission Impossible: How Men Gave Birth to the Australian Nation—Nationalism, Gender and Other Seminal Acts', *Gender and History*, vol. 4, no. 3 (1992) pp. 305–322, p. 305.
6 Lake, 'Mission Impossible', p. 312.
7 Clive Moore, 'Colonial Manhood and Masculinities', *Journal of Australian Studies*, vol. 22, no. 56 (1998) pp. 35–50, p. 43–44. See also, Marilyn Lake, 'The Politics of Respectability: Identifying the Masculinist Context', in Penny Russell and Richard White, eds., *Pastiche 1: Reflections on Nineteenth Century Australia* (Sydney: Allen & Unwin, 1994) pp. 263–271.
8 Lake argues that women were 'rendered invisible or constituted as the enemy' in evocations of masculine Australia. Femininity was even represented as un-Australian in some strains of nationalism. See Lake, 'Mission Impossible', pp. 312–313.
9 Lake, 'Mission Impossible', p. 305.
10 Lake, 'Mission Impossible', p. 307.
11 Marilyn Lake quoted renowned suffragist Rose Scott as saying, 'Let us look at this question not as it concerns our Individual Interests and prejudices, but as it concerns our country and its people, their future nobility and greatness . . . we need to add to the minute and narrow truths of Partyism the lofty and more extensive Truths of Patriotism'. Rose Scott quoted in Marilyn Lake, 'Women and Nation in Australia: The Politics of Representation', *Australian Journal of Politics and History*, vol. 43, no. 1 (1997) pp. 41–52, p. 41.
12 Lake, 'Women and Nation in Australia', p. 42. For an example of a study of a woman author who identified with the newly emerging Australian nation—and with the Australian Bush—see Sharon Crozier-De Rosa, 'Identifying with the Frontier: Federation New Woman, Nation and Empire', in Maggie Tonkin, Mandy Treagus, Madeleine Seys and Sharon Crozier-De Rosa, eds., *Changing the Victorian Subject* (Adelaide: University of Adelaide Press, 2014) pp. 37–58.
13 A notion of 'Britishness' coloured the AWNL's understanding of Australia's unique racial make-up. As Marilyn Lake explains, this was different to 'Anglo-Saxonism', which pertained not only to those of British descent in Australia but also to those in the American Republic as well as to the Scandinavians, the Dutch, the Germans, and the Flemmings of Belgium. See Marilyn Lake, 'British World or New World?', *History Australia*, vol. 10, no. 3 (2013) pp. 36–50.
14 For a detailed discussion of feminist conceptions of citizenship, see Marilyn Lake, 'The Inviolable Woman: Feminist Conceptions of Citizenship in Australia, 1900–1945', *Gender and History*, vol. 8, no. 2 (1996) pp. 197–211. Recent scholars working on the issue of Australian national identity have based many of their arguments on the issue of whether Australian national identity was rooted in, co-existed with, or was hostile to, that of Britishness. Neville Meaney, for example, has argued that between the years 1870 and 1960, Australians 'thought of themselves primarily as a British people'. (Neville Meaney, 'Britishness and Australian Identity: The Problem of Nationalism in Australian History and Historiography', *Australian Historical Studies*, vol. 32, no. 116 (2001) pp. 76–90, p. 79.) Broadly supporting this assertion, although differing on other points, Russell McGregor maintains that Australian national identity was not opposed to Britishness, nor did it simply co-exist with Britishness; rather, he argues, Britishness was inherent to Australianness. It formed the repertoire of myth and symbol, the ethnic foundations necessary for the construction of a national identity. Britishness and Australianness, McGregor argues, were mutually

interactive. (Russell McGregor, 'The Necessity of Britishness: Ethno-cultural Roots of Australian Nationalism', *Nations and Nationalism*, vol. 12, no. 3 (2006) pp. 493–511.) Scholars such as McGregor and Hutchinson base their theories on those of sociologist Anthony Smith—who has written extensively on ethnicity and nationalism—to assert that although the concept of the nation may be relatively new in that it is rooted in the modern era, nations have their origins in ethnic myths that are far older than those nations. See, for example, John Hutchinson, 'Myth Against Myth: The Nation as Ethnic Overlay', *Nations and Nationalism*, vol. 10, no. 1–2 (2004) pp. 109–123.
15 See Lake, 'Mission Impossible', p. 305.
16 A good deal of scholarship exists on white Australia's views of the Aboriginal people. See, for example, Marilyn Lake, 'The Ambiguities for Feminists of National Belonging: Race and Gender in the Imagined Australian Community', in Ida Blom, Karen Hagemann and Catherine Hall eds., *Gendered Nations: Nationalisms and Gender Order in the Long Nineteenth Century* (Oxford and New York: Berg, 2000) pp. 159–176, and Amanda Nettelbeck, 'Introduction', in Catherine Martin, *An Australian Girl* (Oxford: Oxford University Press, 1999) pp. vii–xxxi.
17 See Lake, 'Mission Impossible', p. 305.
18 *Woman*, vol. 2, no. 7, 28 March 1909, p. 426.
19 *Woman*, vol. 2, no. 7, 28 March 1909, p. 426.
20 *Woman*, vol. 2, no. 7, 28 March 1909, p. 426.
21 Alan Lester argues that white British settlers were keenly attuned to accusations emanating from the imperial centre that they were somehow aberrant Britons. In particular, he refers to the outrage felt by settlers in the Cape Colony, New Zealand, and New South Wales inspired by British humanitarian interventions in the colonies. Humanitarian concern over settlers' treatment of indigenous populations, Lester explained, seemed to popularise an image of white settlers as 'acquisitive and brutal, and thus somehow, as aberrant Britons'. See Alan Lester, 'British Settler Discourse and the Circuits of Empire', *History Workshop Journal*, vol. 54, no. 1 (2002) pp. 24–48, p. 39.
22 *Woman*, vol. 6, no. 5, 2 July 1913, pp. 97–100. Here, *Woman* was complicit in perpetuating the 'gift' myth over the 'struggle' narrative outlined in the book's introduction. Again, for a discussion of the 'gift or struggle' debate, see Audrey Oldfield, *Woman Suffrage in Australia. A Gift or a Struggle?* (Cambridge: Cambridge University Press, 1992).
23 Again, for a discussion of the 'gift or struggle' debate, see Oldfield, *Woman Suffrage in Australia*.
24 *Woman*, vol. 6, no. 5, 2 July 1913, pp. 97–100.
25 *Woman*, vol. 4, no. 3, 1 May 1911, p. 43. In 1914, the paper reprinted official statistics that revealed how low the voter turnout was for the federal elections. According to official statistics, no less than 705,654 Australian electors 'cared so little or troubled so little that they did not even record their votes'. Of those who 'neglected this high privilege', 383,610 were women, and nearly a third of these, or to be accurate, 122,534, were Victorian women, referring to the AWNL heartland. See *Woman*, vol. 7, no. 5, 1 July 1914, pp. 105–108.
26 *Woman*, vol. 5, no. 12, 2 Jan 1913, pp. 290–291. For example, this maxim is repeated in vol. 3, no. 7, 1 September 1910, p. 658, and vol. 4, no. 1, 1 March 1911, pp. 1–2.
27 *Woman*, vol. 3, no. 4, 24 March 1910, p. 606.
28 *Woman*, vol. 4, no. 3, 1 May 1911, p. 43.
29 *Woman*, vol. 4, no. 3, 1 May 1911, p. 43.
30 *Woman*, vol. 4, no. 8, 2 October 1911, pp. 165–176.

31 *Woman*, vol. 3, no. 7, 1 September 1910, pp. 651–654.
32 *Woman*, vol. 4, no. 1, 1 March 1911, p. 1.
33 *Woman*, vol. 4, no. 1, 1 March 1911, p. 1.
34 Joan Beaumont, *Broken Nation: Australians and the Great War* (Sydney: Allen and Unwin, 2013) p. 12.
35 Beaumont, *Broken Nation*, p. xv.
36 Beaumont, *Broken Nation*, p. xviii.
37 See comparative table in Beaumont, *Broken Nation*, p. 589.
38 Beaumont, *Broken Nation*, p. 14.
39 This is not to argue that British authorities were entirely in sympathy with Australian racial policies. Beaumont points out that not only were many British commentators critical of the transparent racism of Australia's immigration policies but also, during the war, they were hesitant to anger Japan, which had become a partner—if a partner that induced a sense of unease—in the Allied war campaign. Moreover, the British demonstrated their deference to Japan over Australia by deeming Japan 'sensitive' enough to have been included in post-war peace talks. This inclusion and a lack of recognition of Australia's autonomy angered some Australians, notably Prime Minister Billy Hughes. Post-war Japanese designs on former German colonies in the Pacific region compounded the sense of threat felt by many in Australia. This sense of disquiet on the part of Australians was to have an impact on the nature of the Commonwealth's sub-imperial ambitions in the region and their vested interest in securing some concessions as far as retaining former German colonies in the region went. See Beaumont, *Broken Nation*, p. 147 and pp. 533–547.
40 Beaumont, *Broken Nation*, p. 14.
41 *Woman*, vol. 3, no. 12, 1 February 1911, p. 749.
42 *Woman*, vol. 3, no. 12, 1 February 1911, p. 749.
43 *Woman*, vol. 4, no. 11, 1 January 1912, pp. 263–264.
44 For a discussion of how divided Australian society was during the war, see Joan Beaumont, 'The Politics of a Divided Society', in Joan Beaumont, ed., *Australia's War 1914–18* (Sydney: Allen & Unwin, 1995) pp. 35–63.
45 For example, Vida Goldstein formed the Women's Peace Army in 1915. (Janice N. Brownfoot, 'Goldstein, Vida Jane (1869–1949)', *Australian Dictionary of Biography*, National Centre of Biography, Australian National University, http://adb.anu.edu.au/biography/goldstein-vida-jane-6418/text10975, published first in hardcopy 1983, accessed online 13 April 2017.) By the final years of the war, and certainly after the Russian Revolution, the peace and industrial labour movements in Australia were reinvigorated. In August 1917, for example, perhaps as many as 15,000 women, inspired by the Women's Peace League, the Victorian Socialist Party, and the Women's Peace Army, congregated in Melbourne to protest about food prices and war profiteers. The meeting also turned violent, with women smashing windows in city streets and throwing stones at police, spurring police retaliatory violence. Well into 1918, the wider labour movement began to agitate for an end to the war through negotiated peace, perhaps mirroring the sense of war weariness that was infecting the tired, fragile, under-resourced, and, sometimes, rebellious Australian troops at the front. Still, despite outbreaks of discontent and the ongoing presence of peace associations, anti-war elements in Australia comprised only a minority of the national population even in the final year of the war. (See Beaumont, *Broken Nation*, p. 332 and p. 457 (and for troop morale see pp. 488–492), and, p. 313.) Also see Joy Damousi, 'Socialist Women and Gendered Space: Anti-Conscription and the Anti-War Campaigns 1914–18', in Joy Damousi and Marilyn Lake, eds., *Gender and War: Australians at War in the Twentieth Century* (Melbourne: Cambridge University Press, 1995) pp. 47–79.

46 Beaumont, 'The Politics of a Divided Society', pp. 35–63.
47 Beaumont, *Broken Nation*, pp. 146–147.
48 'The women of Australia are now being put to a test, the result of which may be worldwide in its influence on the question of extending the franchise'. In the *Argus*, 4 December 1917, p. 6. Quoted in Bart Ziino, 'Great War, Total War', in Deborah Gare and David Ritter, eds., *Making Australian History. Perspectives on the Past Since 1788* (Melbourne: Thomson, 2008) pp. 335–344, p. 342.
49 Beaumont, *Broken Nation*, p. 223 and p. 242.
50 For a discussion of the legacy of loss, particularly as represented by the collective grief of Australian parents, see Jen Hawksley, ' "In the Shadow of War": Australian Parents and the Legacy of Loss, 1915–1935', *Journal of Australian Studies*, vol. 33, no. 2 (2009) pp. 181–194.
51 For instance, the United Women's Anti-Conscription Committee march in October 1916 was met with onlookers who disrupted events by throwing eggs and grabbing and breaking banners. See Beaumont, *Broken Nation*, p. 237.
52 For example, see John McQuilton's discussions about the campaigns in his study of the Great War and its impact on rural Victoria in John McQuilton, *Rural Australia and the Great War: From Tarrawingee to Tangambalanga* (Melbourne: Melbourne University Press, 2001).
53 In Brisbane, for example, at a meeting of the newly formed Women's Compulsory Service Petition League, a mass of women kicked and punched a young pacifist woman. Other women speakers were howled down, had objects thrown at them, or were set upon by male and female thugs. See Beaumont, *Broken Nation*, pp. 384–385.
54 Conscription was introduced in Britain in January 1916 and in New Zealand in May 1916 (for non-Maori men and then in June 1917 for Maori men too). See Beaumont, *Broken Nation*, pp. 219–220.
55 *Anti-Suffrage Review*, no. 99, January 1917, p. 3.
56 *Anti-Suffrage Review*, no. 99, January 1917, p. 3.
57 *Anti-Suffrage Review*, no. 99, January 1917, p. 3.
58 Joan Beaumont, 'Whatever Happened to Patriotic Women, 1914–1918?' *Australian Historical Studies*, vol. 31, no. 115 (2000) pp. 273–286, p. 276.
59 Beaumont, 'Whatever Happened to Patriotic Women, 1914–1918?'
60 See Joan Beaumont's and Pam McLean's individual chapters in Joan Beaumont, ed., *Australia's War 1914–1918* (Sydney: Allen and Unwin, 1995).
61 *Woman*, vol. 10, no. 2, 2 April 1917, pp. 47–49.
62 Irish anti-colonial nationalists were represented in Australia by those promoting the doctrines of the Irish separatist party Sinn Féin. As outlined in the book's introduction, Sinn Féin was a political party in Ireland whose aspirations for complete autonomy from Britain were clearly present in its title, translated from the Gaelic as 'We, Ourselves'.
63 *Woman*, vol. 10, no. 6, 1 August 1917, p. 185.
64 *Woman*, vol. 10, no 11, 1 January 1918, pp. 351–352.
65 *Woman*, vol. 10, no. 11, 1 January 1918, pp. 351–352.
66 *Woman*, vol. 10, no. 11, 1 January 1918, pp. 351–352.
67 *Woman*, vol. 10, no. 11, 1 January 1918, p. 373.
68 *Anti-Suffrage Review*, no. 11, October 1909, pp. 5–6. The Australian Labour Party changed the spelling of its name from the British 'Labour' to the American 'Labor' in 1912.
69 *Anti-Suffrage Review*, no .27, February 1911, pp. 25–26.
70 *Anti-Suffrage Review*, no. 27, February 1911, pp. 25–26.
71 *Anti-Suffrage Review*, no. 17, April 1910, pp. 3–4.
72 *Anti-Suffrage Review*, no. 103, May 1917, pp. 33–34.
73 *Woman*, vol. 12, no. 9, 1 November 1919, pp. 382–384.

74 This emphasis on the rest of the Empire was well founded because, by 1918, women in places like Britain and Ireland were qualified to vote. *Woman*, vol. 12, no. 9, 1 November 1919, p. 382–384.
75 *Woman*, vol. 12, no. 9, 1 November 1919, p. 382–384.
76 *Woman*, vol. 12, no. 9, 1 November 1919, p. 382–384.
77 *Woman*, vol. 12, no. 9, 1 November 1919, p. 382–384.
78 Beaumont, *Broken Nation*, pp. 233–235.
79 *Woman*, vol. 13, no. 10, 1 December 1920, pp. 291–299.
80 *Woman*, vol. 12, no. 10, 1 December 1919, p. 392.
81 *Woman*, vol. 12, no. 10, 1 December 1919, p. 392.
82 *Woman*, vol. 12, no. 10, 1 December 1919, p. 392.
83 *Woman*, vol. 12, no. 10, 1 December 1919, pp. 391–392.
84 *Woman*, vol. 10, no. 10, 1 December 1917, p. 383.
85 *Woman*, vol. 11, no. 1, 1 March 1918, p. 37.
86 *Woman*, vol. 12, no. 10, 1 December 1919, p. 392.
87 *Woman*, vol. 13, no. 1, 1 March 1920, pp. 11–12.
88 *Woman*, vol. 13, no. 10, 1 December 1920, pp. 291–299.
89 *Woman*, vol. 13, no. 10, 1 December 1920, pp. 291–299.
90 *Woman*, vol. 13, no. 10, 1 December 1920, pp. 291–299.
91 *Woman*, vol. 13, no. 10, 1 December 1920, pp. 291–299. For a discussion of the workings and the legacies of the White Australia Policy, see Laksiri Jayasuriya, David Walker, and Jan Gothard, eds., *The Legacies of White Australia: Race, Culture and Nation*, (Perth: University of Western Australia Press, 2003).

5 War and the Dishonourable British Feminist

In 1915, the British *Anti-Suffrage Review* (the *Review*) exposed the presence of the diabolical vampirish nurse—the woman, masquerading as a carer, who preyed on the pathetic gratitude of the broken and bleeding soldier in the field hospitals to secure for herself and her fellow feminists a promise to vote for woman suffrage should her patient survive the journey back to the homeland. The source of the leak was none other than Mrs Millicent Fawcett, leader of the National Union of Woman Suffrage Societies (NUWSS). Under Fawcett's direction, the NUWSS had raised an enormous £500,000 to support 14 all-female wartime hospital units.[1] It was, therefore, responsible for sending a significant number of female nurses to the front. This was certainly a laudable act of patriotism and yet, in an interview with the *Liverpool Daily Post*, Fawcett revealed that her nurses were managing to get a word in on the suffrage question while attending wounded soldiers. More than that, they were persuading these soldiers to promise that they would do what they could to secure the female franchise when the war was over. In the first place, the *Review* sternly objected to suffrage agitation when a truce had been agreed between the government and feminists at the outbreak of the war. Yet here were suffragist nurses acting with impunity. Secondly, accepting that feminists were carrying on with their campaign, the *Review* doubted that this political work could be classified as 'honest propaganda'. Wounded soldiers had impaired capabilities. They could not examine important political issues in a rational manner. 'Is there not something very unhallowed in exploiting in this fashion the natural gratitude of a wounded warrior for a kind lady who is nursing him?' the paper asked. It answered in the affirmative, 'It is hitting Tommy politically "when he is down"'.[2] Altogether, the political activism of wartime nurses was a 'nauseating spectacle'. It was tantamount to 'treachery to the public and blackmail on the troops'.[3]

As if this resort to political expediency was not bad enough, it seemed that Mrs Fawcett was actually proud of her nurses' endeavours. The unbelievable thing, the *Review* pronounced, is 'the *naiveté* with which Mrs Fawcett glories in the shame'.[4] It did not occur to her that there was anything 'illegitimate or dishonourable' in the actions of her followers.[5] This led the paper to declare that wartime feminists were incapable of embodying the masculine emotional virtues necessary for the proper conduct of politics, especially in a time of war. They had proven that they could not conduct themselves according to masculine codes of honour—drawing, as these did, on concepts of integrity, honesty, and fairness—that guided the gentleman's dealings in the worlds of business and politics. These codes also directed men's relations with each other during times of war. These women were, therefore, unmanly navigators of the male political sphere, especially the wartime political sphere.

In this chapter, I argue that anti-suffragists' bitter resentment of pre-war suffragist behaviour, particularly militant behaviour, and their suspicions about duplicitous wartime feminists, led them to regard the massive expansion of wartime women workers with great emotional unease. Traditionally, war served to clearly delineate male and female worlds—physical and emotional. Men went forth and fought, with honour, while women stayed home and waited and grieved. The phenomenon of total war threw all this into disarray. Men's and women's roles were converging. It seemed that total war was facilitating a temporary blurring of the gendered nature of emotional regimes. Feminists were capitalising on this by attempting to make this obscuring of emotional boundaries a permanent feature of British social life. Therefore, I examine how anti-suffragists attempted to expose the shame of the wartime feminist in order to oppose what they thought was her sustained attack on masculine honour codes. I analyse the degree to which concern for the returned soldier and worries about the nature of the emotional world he would be forced to come back to fed anti-suffragists' anxieties about the dishonest wartime feminist. I also look at the extent to which opposition to the wartime feminist was predicated on the fear that her shameful tactics would not be sufficiently exposed, and she would eventually win her goal—the vote—through dishonourable means.

Honour, Gender and the Wartime Political Sphere

In Chapter 2, I detailed the gendered nature of honour and its antithesis, shame. It suffices to summarise here. Whereas men's honour was tied to their performance in the male worlds of business, politics, and war, women's honour simply meant their chastity. Men's honour was tied to the public realm; women's honour was located in the private sphere. Both were social constructs. Both were about internalised reputations that were intimately tied to a society's or a community's judgement. Transgressing these gender-specific honour codes meant shame. To recount, shame is that painful emotion that arises from consciousness of having dishonoured one's sense of self—a sense of self that is tied to a particular and valued community of belonging.[6] Historically, only men had an active relationship with honour, meaning that a man could attempt to recover his lost honour, thereby removing the stigma or shame.[7] It also meant that only he had the power to assume an active role when it came to women's honour. She could not do so herself, confined as she was to the domestic realm. Strictly speaking, once lost, a woman's honour could not be restored. However, her menfolk could actively reassert their own honour in the face of her shame.[8] Histories of male duelling over a woman's lost honour testify to this.[9] Anti-feminists believed that women had no active relationship with honour; therefore, they had no place in a public world that was governed by codes of honour.

The onset of World War One served the paradoxical function of seemingly compounding the exclusively masculine nature of honour, on the one hand, and challenging this gender exclusivity, on the other. For the first time in Britain's history, a huge proportion of its manhood, including its working-class manhood, was directly implicated in the war effort. Traditionally, men of the elite classes were expected to adhere to honour codes. As explained earlier in the book, by the eighteenth and nineteenth centuries, this reach had extended to include men of the middle classes as that social group grew in prominence. Honour codes were increasingly imbued with middle-class values such as moral discipline, inner values, and the control of reproduction and sex.[10] These values did not replace traditional ones such as 'personal courage, loyalty, prowess in combat, and gallantry in love'. Rather, they existed together.[11] Working-class men's involvement in the war, then, meant that they too were expected to abide by emotional regimes previously closed to them. All men were expected to be courageous in the face of the enemy, fair in combat, and chivalrous even under fire. This mass expansion of potentially honourable men—a significant proportion of them being as yet untrained in these emotional codes—caused patriotic women some anxiety. The fear that British manhood would not prove itself up to the task of performing honour was ever-present; the fear that its manhood would be found wanting, bringing shame on the nation, lurked.[12] This fear only intensified as the war progressed and the need to replace a proud tradition of volunteerism with conscription for military service beckoned.

Yet the patriotic British women writing for the *Review* seemed less perturbed by the extension of honour codes to working-class men than they were about the influx of females of all classes into the public worlds of war work and wartime politics. The extension of honour codes to all eligible male soldiers during the war transformed the class character of that concept but not its gendered nature. However, extending the reach of those emotional regulations to women who performed public war work did serve to contest the masculine make-up of those codes.

The best that the *Review* could hope for was that women workers and feminist would-be politicians would acknowledge and respect the existing masculine emotional regime guiding men's usual participation in the public sphere. The paper regarded the influx of women into the public sphere during the war as a temporary initiative. Anti-suffragists hoped that, once the war ended, women would resume their positions in the domestic sphere. It was likely that the majority of female wartime workers would have to return to their pre-war occupations once the war was over and wartime industries disbanded. Yet there had been enough advancements in the preceding decades to indicate that women's participation in other non-wartime sectors, such as education and employment, would only grow. More than that, it was the hope of feminists that they would be enfranchised, thereby ensuring that they would become a permanent fixture in the public life of the country. The relationship between women and honour, then, grew increasingly ambivalent. If women were to assume more long-term public roles, would it not be necessary for masculine honour codes to transform permanently to accommodate them? Or perhaps women were already well placed to understand and abide by such emotional regulations. Suffragists, for example, had been common features in the nation's public life for a number of decades. If women's habitual presence in the public sphere had allowed them to familiarise themselves with honour codes, then the masculine character of honour no longer seemed relevant. The gendered nature of this emotional regime would be obsolete.

Of course, it was the actions of pre-war suffragists, especially the violent suffragettes, that had prompted anti-suffragist concerns about the state of honour in the first place. To anti-feminists, feminists were deficient 'gentlemen'.[13] As the war progressed, women opposed to the franchise grew increasingly convinced that feminist politicians were incapable of adhering to numerous aspects of modern honour codes. For example, feminists exhibited an inability to possess moral dignity and to demonstrate faithfulness to contractual arrangements with others, both modern middle-class additions to honour codes.[14] Their betrayal of the wartime political truce called between themselves and the government attested to this. Therefore, it seemed unlikely that these transgressive females were fit to adapt to existing masculine emotional codes.

An alternative outcome was that they corrupt those codes. If they were to do this irreversibly, then what would confront men when they returned from the front to assume their proper position in the public sphere? What state would honour protocols be in? How would men regulate their relations with each other? As Robert Nye has argued, through enforcing respectful behaviour between men, honour codes had traditionally safeguarded group cohesion. They had ensured that fiercely courageous and competitive men could exist in harmony.[15] Ute Frevert adds that by the beginning of the twentieth century, this was still the case. Honour was the 'glue' that bound a social group together and fostered cohesion among its members.[16] What would happen if public women corroded the codes that had been historically successful in preventing the stronger sex from descending into barbarism or chaos? It seemed that while men were drawing deeply on their emotional reserves to prove their masculinity on the battlefields of Europe, and treading a fine line between civilisation and barbarism, women at home were guilty of introducing a corrosive feminised element into masculine emotional regimes.

Importantly for tracing the dialogue between different groups of nationalist feminists on the issue of honour, the onset of the war prompted Irish nationalist women to agree with British anti-suffragists' claims that British feminists were dishonourable. However, the exact nature of their charge differed dramatically from those of British anti-feminists. Irish nationalist women accused British feminists of being dishonourable politicians for agreeing to a truce with an anti-feminist male government in the first place. The British feminists were guilty of dishonest dealings. They were guilty of attacking the integrity of the political community to which they belonged. They had attacked the values of the community that they had championed so ferociously before the war—namely, the feminist community. Now they were prioritising the objectives of male militarism over those of the feminist movement. Irish feminist nationalists entertained no such switch of alliances. They declared that they would not capitulate in the face of British male militarism. Rather, they would continue to campaign for the rights of all women subjected to the whims of the British parliament. In direct contrast to British anti-suffragists who thought that British suffragists were dishonest politicians for claiming to obey the truce while conducting an underground campaign for the vote, Irish nationalist suffragists considered their British sisters to be traitors to the feminist cause. In a way, this was not dissimilar to the accusations of slavish allegiance to male values over female objectives that Irish feminist nationalists had levelled at their nationalist feminist sisters as discussed in Chapter 2.

War as a Gendered and Gendering Experience

Women's relationship with war has received considerable scholarly attention in recent years. Doubtless, the recent centenary of the First World War has spurred some of this research. But, even before this, feminist historians probed the gendered dimensions of wartime experiences. War is a gendered and gendering activity. Numerous scholars attest to this. Kate Darian-Smith explains that war 'was, and continues to be a gendered activity because, more so than in peacetime, it delineates the function of men and women within their society'.[17] Men were expected to assume the role of warrior; women were supposed to play a support role at home. Therefore, war worked to reaffirm cultural constructions of men as soldiers and women as non-combatants.

However, relying on the groundbreaking theorising of Jean Bethke Elshtain, scholars such as Margaret Higonnet and Penny Summerfield have argued that while expectations of women's and men's wartime roles drew on pre-existing definitions of gender, the experience of war itself also worked to restructure gender relations.[18] At the same time that women were pressured to undertake ultra-feminine roles as wartime mothers and carers, war presented them with opportunities to assume traditionally masculine positions. Depending on the type and nature of the conflict, women could serve as propagandists, fundraisers, medical staff, and even combatants. The plurality and range of positions open to women—those that often crossed gender boundaries—has prompted Nicole Ann Dombrowski to assert that war is more complicated for women than it is for men.[19] The opportunity for women to act in unfamiliar positions introduced a level of ambivalence into understandings of gender that were already complex and sometimes contested. As Higonnet et al. explain, war highlights the workings of gender because it reveals a system of gender in flux.[20] However, they point out that this is a state of flux or fluidity that is often only temporary, confined as it is to the period of the conflict. Women may assume masculine roles, but they tend to be forced back into those that are traditionally feminine once the fighting has abated.

Margaret and Patrice Higonnet have usefully employed the metaphor of the double helix to explain the relationship between women's work and power relations during the war. Physical roles may alter throughout the course of the war, but the power relations between the sexes does not. They imagine men's and women's wartime experiences in terms of each sex climbing the opposing strands of a double helix and sliding back down again once the war comes to an end; they each keep an equal distance from the other, never converging. Therefore, Higonnet and Higonnet argue, despite the altered physical conditions during the war, the nature of gender relations remains the same during and after the war. Women remain the restricted and subordinate sex.[21]

Not all feminist historians agree with the double helix example, although few fail to reference it when explaining the nature of gender relations during war. For instance, Penny Summerfield believes that it is too 'rigid' a model, arguing that as they viewed the extraordinary blurring of the visual boundary between masculinity and femininity during the Great War, few contemporaries believed that they were maintaining a gender divide. Summerfield also discounts Elshtain's assertion that as a gendering activity, war further polarised gender relations rather than drawing them closer together.[22] She cites early twentieth-century men's hostility to what they perceived to be female encroachments of their territory as evidence of this. The subjects of this book certainly believed that war had the potential to alter gendered power relations, which is why radical feminists promoted women's participation in some of the more masculinised wartime activities and anti-feminists vehemently opposed such moves.

Women Participating in the Public World of the Great War

However long- or short-lived women's experiences of transgressing gender divides and transforming traditional power relations were, one thing that can be said is that the First World War forced those at the time to confront the fact that war was no longer simply a man's business. It defied the myth that men went forth and women and children stayed safe at home. Women were implicated in the conflict too. In keeping with the feminine tradition of philanthropy, care, and support, female patriots organised themselves to provide material comforts for the troops at the front—foodstuffs, literature, socks, and other goods such as cigarettes. Through working in the armaments industry, women expanded men's capacity for war.[23] As nurses in the battlefields, they repaired men's bodies so that they could resume their places on the frontlines. As members of wartime societies, they coped with rationing, shortages, bombings, and evacuations. As active patriots, they were incorporated into wartime politics. The supposedly safe home front could no longer be imagined as an inviolate space.[24]

Dombrowski asserts that World War One marked women's definitive entry into the war machine. For some, she writes, the war eased their entry into the political realm, incorporating them into wartime propaganda.[25] Modern conflicts, she states, have demanded that women play an integral role in supporting and sustaining masculine military cultures and campaigns.[26] Women were invoked to motivate men to enlist. However, this does not mean that real women were called on to organise themselves into physical recruitment drives. Military authorities often attempted to discourage such moves. Yet groups of women defied such male resistance and organised themselves, which created tensions between them and male military leaders. Nicoletta Gullace's research into attitudes towards the white feather shaming campaigns ably demonstrates this, for example.[27] Rather, authorities wanted women to perform a passive metaphorical role in recruitment campaigns. They wanted men to be inspired to fight for their loved ones at home based on images of the vulnerable women and children so pitifully depicted in wartime propaganda as being in desperate need of defence. Women, real or imagined, became an integral aspect of wartime politics.

A substantial proportion of British women worked in wartime industries despite considerable resistance—especially emanating from the anti-suffrage side of politics—to women performing any other roles than fundraising and providing comforts for the troops.[28] Women provided the much-needed labour force that replaced the men who went to the front. They also served in industries that expanded only for the life of the war. Over the course of the war, the number of British women in the industrial labour force grew from 3,276,000 to 4,808,000—an increase of approximately 1.5 million women since 1914. Approximately half a million of these women had previously been employed in domestic positions.[29] Around 23,000 women comprised the women's Land Army, helping with agricultural production.[30]

The female worker who arguably captured the public's attention more than any other was the woman in armaments production. Perhaps one million, mostly working-class women were employed to work in British munitions factories—a source of female employment that all but disappeared after the war.[31] These women—referred to as 'munitionettes' or 'Tommy's sisters'—challenged public perceptions of women's capabilities and their place in the war. Their masculine dress mesmerised and discomforted the public in varying doses. They worked in extremely dangerous and volatile conditions. Hundreds of women died in these factories. More were maimed or suffered the effects of TNT poisoning for the rest of their lives.[32] Their work and their sacrifices confirmed their pivotal place in the masculine war machine. As Angela Woollacott points out, these female workers facilitated the first stage in 'the production line of death that ended at the front'.[33] The physical nature of their work and their willingness to sacrifice themselves to the sometimes fatal dangers of war also worked to muddy the appropriateness of the physical force argument that anti-suffragists relied on when opposing the woman vote—namely, that women could not fight to defend their country at a time of war; therefore, they did not deserve to be enfranchised. The female munitions worker was an inconvenient necessity which blurred the lines existing between men's and women's physical and emotional spheres.

The female munitions worker was a typically British icon. However, Irish women also worked in the British wartime industries. Back in Ireland, support for the war was split. Unionists supported the British war effort. Moderate nationalists supported it in the hope that their loyalty would be rewarded with the implementation of the Home Rule Bill, which would see a parliament established in Ireland again. Radical nationalists opposed any Irish involvement in the war and instead proposed complete separation from all things British.[34] However, Irish men did fight in the war, and women there did contribute to the war effort. For example, elite women often organised fundraising activities and food and comforts drives.[35] Other women were involved in providing the needs of wartime hospitals. For example, 6,000 women across sectarian divides volunteered to manufacture equipment for the Irish War Hospital Supply Depot. In Dublin, 300 women knitted 20,000 pairs of socks and 10,000 scarves for soldiers.[36] But the opportunity for earning unusually high wages for working-class females tempted many Irish migrant women to undertake work in British factories. As Susan Grayzel point out, considering the intensifying strength of anti-war and anti-British propaganda in nationalist Ireland, it cannot be argued that Irish women's motivations to take up such work were the same as English women's.[37] In many cases, financial necessity rather than imperial loyalty pushed Irish women to work in British wartime industries. In some instances, the presence of nationalist Irish women in these wartime factories served to exacerbate tensions existing between nationalist Ireland and imperial Britain.[38]

British women also managed to actively support the war effort by infiltrating the medical services in larger numbers than previously. Numbers vary, but Claire Tylee writes that by 1917, there were 100,000 extra volunteer nurses and 45,000 nurses serving in military hospitals. The armed forces were also supported by a body of uniformed auxiliaries numbering about 40,000 women. Perhaps 8,500 of these women served abroad, in addition to 5,000 nurses and Voluntary Aid Detachments (VADs).[39] Since the Crimean War, which showcased the work of Florence Nightingale and her nurses, nursing was gradually becoming a more acceptable profession for women. However, the very obvious links between wartime nursing and British feminism meant that many anti-feminists looked on the profession with distrust.

As mentioned earlier, no other British organisation built its reputation for heroic womanly self-sacrifice more effectively during the war than the NUWSS. The NUWSS raised the enormous sum of £500,000, which it used to fund 14 all-female hospital units abroad, which were all under the direction of Scottish woman doctor Dr Elise Inglis.[40] Initially, British authorities barred women from serving in British wartime medical organisations stationed abroad under the auspices of protecting these women. Therefore, British women who wanted to serve overseas had to do so by enlisting with the French, Belgian, Russian, or Serbian Red Cross, which were desperate enough to appoint female medical staff. The NUWSS established one permanent hospital behind French lines; however, the greater number of British nurses were stationed in places close to conflict, for example, at Calais Corsica, Troyes, Salonica, and a number of towns in Serbia and Russia. Their positions there were precarious, as they often had to retreat with the military units they were attached to as they were forcibly beaten back. They were, therefore, at risk of being overtaken by the enemy army.[41] Wartime nurses risked injury and death, alongside men, on the field of battle. Like men, they were required to exhibit the more manly emotions of courage, loyalty, and sacrifice. Like the woman munitions worker, then, battlefield nurses represented an uncomfortable wartime reality for those who desired to protect the boundaries guarding the masculine and feminine emotional regimes.

Whereas wartime societies such as Britain offered women opportunities for an array and diversity of paid employment like factory or nursing work, Australia did not. As discussed in Chapter 4, Australians were overwhelmingly in favour of their country's participation in the war. Australian women endeavoured to contribute to that cause. Their significant contribution to the war was often via volunteer support organisations rather than paid employment.[42] For the most part, women's volunteer organisations were staffed by middle-class women and led by 'local political and social elites'.[43] They also tended to defer to male leaders.[44] Joan Beaumont has argued that wartime Australian society's emphasis on women's subsidiary and voluntary rather than paid contributions to the war effort induced a sense of discomfort among later feminists.[45] The memory of what has been termed patriotic feminism there is complicated for two reasons: for what it apparently reveals about women's blind homage to male militarism and the simultaneous devaluing of women's economic worth to the state.[46]

Australian women's contribution to the war effort was largely voluntary, but that is not to claim that no Australian women served in roles that challenged stereotypical gendered divisions of labour or gendered emotional regimes. In a limited way, similar to Britain, the Australian Red Cross provided avenues for women in Australia to challenge typical wartime gendered roles through the formation of VADs. However, as Melanie Oppenheimer explains, the tasks women were appointed to were usually 'domestic and quasi-nursing duties' in hospitals and convalescent homes set up to receive the increasing number of wounded returned solders.[47] After the Gallipoli campaign in 1915, VADs also worked in military hospitals.[48]

There were also a restricted number of possibilities for women to undertake more expansive wartime opportunities. Like Australian soldiers, for example, women travelled overseas to places such as Egypt and France working for the Red Cross, including its Prisoners of War branch run by Mary Chomley, and for Vera Deakin's Australian Wounded and Missing Inquiry Bureau.[49] Nursing also offered a relatively small number of only fully trained nurses the chance to aid the military by travelling overseas, thereby witnessing the conflict. Katie Holmes states that 2,229 Australian women served overseas as Australian Army Nursing Service nurses. Women who had qualified as doctors in the Australian Commonwealth, on the other hand, had no official pathway to overseas wartime service, for they were not permitted into the Australian Army Medical Corps. The alternative for women doctors was to travel to the United Kingdom at their own expense and join organisations there such as the Scottish Women's Hospitals.[50] Given that Australian women were already enfranchised and that they continued to advise the Mother Country to bestow similar rights on their womenfolk, it is likely that the British anti-suffragists' criticisms of wartime nurses extended to those Australians serving in the field hospitals too.

Wartime nurses—whatever their nationality—transgressed respectable notions of femininity and womanhood as they negotiated the deadly dangers of the war zone. As we will see later in the chapter, nurses' position of power over the broken male body means that, despite performing in the traditional role of carer, they were also viewed with suspicion, regarded as threats to the gender and sexual status quo. Their links to disruptive pre-war British feminism and enfranchised Australian feminism did not help ease anxieties about the status and objectives of wartime nurses. These nurses jeopardised the integrity of gendered emotional regimes on multiple fronts then. Their position on the battlefields required them to exhibit the courage, loyalty, and sacrifice required of the male soldier. As feminist activists, they also threatened to appropriate elements of masculine honour codes, such as honesty and fairness in contractual dealings, as they navigated the public sphere.

Irish Feminists and the Absurdity of Australian Women Voting on Matters of War

Anti-suffragists were worried about women performing public roles during the war. Not surprisingly, women's public contributions were often applauded by feminists who had long been campaigning for expanded public opportunities for women. However, suffragists found that they were ambivalent about certain groups of women who were endowed with public wartime responsibilities. Australian women were a case in point.

Somewhat ironically, at the time that Australian women were experiencing severely restricted access to wartime service, they formed one of the most powerful groups of women in the Empire in terms of wartime politics. Much discussion abounded in the British *Review* about women's lack of emotional suitability for matters of war. They would either be swayed by emotional arguments for intervening in conflict situations they had no right to be in. The *Review* declared that men would be compelled by women voters to put their lives at risk for causes only emotional women believed in. Or women would give into their renowned pacifist leanings, avoiding war at all costs, and placing Britain at a severe disadvantage in relation to the rest of the rational world.[51] Yet the fact of the existence of the Australian woman voter and Australia's simultaneous commitment to the war effort was held up by other groups of nationalist feminists as evidence of the enfranchised woman's ability to adopt a judicious approach to matters of war. Irish feminists, for instance, had no qualms about holding the wartime Australian woman up as a model of wise enfranchised womanhood.[52]

Enfranchised Australian women had previously intervened in Irish suffrage politics. To Irish suffragists, these were welcome interventions. Before the war, Australian feminists had not only instructed politicians in the British Motherland to enfranchise their women as Australian men had done.[53] Through renowned Australian feminist Vida Goldstein, they had also recognised the distinctiveness of Irish women by advising Irish politicians to include Irish women's enfranchisement in their dealings with the British over the Home Rule Bill. In 1912, for example, the Irish nationalist suffragist paper, the *Irish Citizen* (the *Citizen*) published a letter from Vida Goldstein to John Redmond's Irish Party, protesting against the 'undemocratic' nature of the proposed Home Rule Bill. At the same time that she delivered her protest, Goldstein reminded Irish nationalist politicians that women voters could be trusted to do the right thing. After all, she claimed, Australian women voters had always 'subscribed liberally' to Irish Home Rule funds. On behalf of the Women's Political Association of Australia, Goldstein wrote, 'We submit that Irishmen should not attempt to obtain political justice at the expense of Irishwomen, who have suffered equally with their men folk, and stood shoulder to shoulder with them in fighting for Home Rule'.[54] Her ploy was to remind Irish men of the debt they owed their sisters, to bring to their attention the simple fact of their belonging to the same community of dedicated patriots. Not unlike the tactic employed by Irish women discussed in Chapter 2, she invoked a traditional notion of chivalry to remind Irish men to safeguard the interests of their womenfolk.

Australian and Irish suffragists may have been united in their feminist aspirations, but the onset of the war also highlighted for Irish women their subordinate position in relation to other women in the Empire. It created something of a rift between them and their enfranchised sisters in the far-flung colonial outposts. War stressed women's supreme function as mothers of the nation and the 'race'. Irish feminist nationalists used widespread acknowledgement of this reverential attitude to motherhood—especially in times of war—to try to motivate their nationalist brothers to honour the bonds they shared with their womenfolk. They did so by referencing what they alleged was the Australian man's obvious regard for his Australian sister in their attempt to awaken the Irish man's sense of chivalry. In 1915, the *Citizen* reproached Irish men:

> Are Irishwomen inferior to Australian women who have got the vote? Are the mothers of Irishmen not worthy of the same liberty as mothers of Australian men? Or are Irishmen not the equals of Australian men—that they are afraid or jealous to give the vote to Irishwomen? If so, Australian mothers have cause to be more proud of the children they have borne than Irishwomen have to be proud of their children; and so, too, Australian men, who have given their women the same measure of justice that they claim for themselves, have, because of their truer sense of love and liberty—a claim to be loved by their womenfolk with a greater and more reverential love.[55]

The article concluded with the hopeful assertion that Irish men would soon awaken to 'their birthright and win this greater love and joy of comradeship'.[56]

As the war highlighted their separation from Australian feminists, it also cast light, however temporarily, on how intertwined British and Irish feminist woes and aspirations were. Relations between Irish nationalist feminists and British imperial feminists had been strained, especially since British suffragists had enacted militancy in Ireland in 1912 without consulting Irish suffragists as to the expediency of doing so.[57] As discussed next, the war further exacerbated divisions between Irish suffragists who championed anti-colonial nationalism and British suffragists who supported their country's imperial ambitions. Yet both communities of nationalist womanhood were united by their political inferiority to Australian womanhood. One contributor to the *Citizen* in 1915 pointed out that Australian women were voting on imperial matters:

> The Colonies count women as citizens. The absurdity of consulting Australian women as to the terms of peace, and contemptuously ignoring their own wives and mothers, cannot much longer be defended by English and Irish politicians.[58]

This was a transnational comparison that did not favour women in the imperial centre nor those in its neighbouring isle. The existence of the wartime enfranchised Australian woman raised the indignation of the Irish nationalist suffragist, revealing just how complicit anti-colonial Irish women were with British imperialists in promoting the superiority of the 'old' world over the 'new'.

At this stage, the Irish *Citizen*'s espousals of an alliance—accidental or otherwise—with British feminism was unusual. The war did little to promote unity between feminists on each side of the Irish Sea. Instead, competing nationalist allegiances exposed by the international conflict and an intensifying nationalist campaign in Ireland combined to almost sever any connections Irish feminists had shared with their British counterparts before 1914. The truce that British feminists and the British Government had called at the beginning of the war served to highlight how irreconcilable the differences between both communities of patriotic womanhood were. On this point, Irish suffragists formed an unlikely alliance with British anti-suffragists as they declared wartime British feminists to be dishonourable politicians. Their rationale for doing so differed, however. Whereas British anti-suffragists accused the wartime feminist of bringing dishonour to the community of patriotic British womanhood, Irish feminists accused British suffragists of shaming the transnational community of feminism, which they had formerly valued.

The Political Truce and Accusations of Feminist Dishonour

In Britain in 1910, in anticipation of the coming war, the *Review* reasserted that war was not women's business.

> Can women build or man battleships? Can women take them into action in the day of Armageddon? Can she serve as an able-bodied seaman in the humblest tramp steamer of the mercantile marine on the high seas? Take the War Office and the same principle applies.[59]

In April 1914, in a reappraisal of British ideals prompted by the pending conflict, the *Review* drew British womanhood directly into discussions about the country's readiness for war. Reaffirming its attitude of scepticism explored in Chapter 1, the paper declared that the actions of suffragists—militant and non-militant—were responsible for crushing 'the ideal of womanhood'.[60] This had implications for gender relations within Britain, and fed into anxieties about the British population's capability for performing as expected under duress. 'The times in which we live are critical, and our country has need of strong men', the *Review* asserted. The paper did not cast aspersions on British manhood's ability to step up to the task but it did recognise that masculinity did not exist in a vacuum. For its manhood to reach its full potential, it depended on the support offered to it by its womanhood. However, the paper expressed doubt that British womanhood would be up to the task of inspiring its manhood at times of supreme national crisis. It asked if the 'women who live for amusement, or the women frantically striving for imaginary equality', were qualified to 'inspire the men to do deeds of self-sacrificing patriotism, such as may be called for ere long'. 'We fear not' was the response.[61] By the time Britain had declared war on Germany, British anti-suffragists had lost faith in the proper functioning of the emotional regime directing women's actions, at least. Women selfishly pursuing amusement or political power were hardly positioned to assume the womanly function of guiding and inspiring the nation's manhood to perform honourably at a time when that manhood's masculinity was facing its ultimate test.

The actions of suffragists, especially the NUWSS and the Women's Social and Political Union (WSPU), in the early months of the conflict cemented anti-suffragists' views of women's general inadequacies. More specifically, anti-suffragists watched anxiously as political women seemed determined to adopt a dishonourable approach to wartime politics—a form of wartime dishonour that had the potential to border on treachery. Consequently, the *Review* spent considerable time voicing its opposition to a suite of highly objectionable feminist wartime claims and activities. In the first place, anti-suffragists accused suffragists of disobeying the political truce called at the beginning of the war. By not adhering to the truce they had initially agreed to, they corrupted honour codes that dictated that members of the public world had to possess moral dignity and were required to demonstrate faithfulness to contractual arrangements with others. They reneged on their contractual obligations. They were not 'gentlemen'. Secondly, feminists performing war work seemed to be doing so only in the hope of a reward—namely, the vote. More than that, they were doing so while also claiming that of all the nation's women, they were the most patriotic. They claimed prestige and selfish rewards for work they should have carried out willingly. Their displays of misplaced pride and selfishness at a time when the community of national womanhood was expected to behave with a generous willingness for personal sacrifice rendered them supremely unwomanly. Wartime exposed the feminist as both an unmanly and an unwomanly citizen. Feminists had proven that they could not adhere to masculine or feminine emotional standards. They were shamefully deficient.

Very early in the war, the *Review* stressed the need for national unity and social cohesiveness to optimise Britain's chances of success in the conflict. It reported that all political associations had agreed to stop their respective campaigning for the duration of the war in order 'that the country might present an undivided front to the enemy and that public men might the better perform what was required of them at a time of grave crisis'.[62] However, by as early as October 1914, it appeared as if feminists were not obeying the truce but were in fact continuing with their suffragist propaganda work. The paper decided, as important as it was to maintain the rhetoric of unity, it was more important to expose the duplicity of suffragists in order to avert a national crisis. The paper accused feminists who were claiming to be undertaking war work of actually 'turning the nation's need to the purposes of self-advertisement'.[63] The *Review*, although indignant, did not express surprise at this uncovering of feminist deceit. It claimed that suffragists were merely continuing a pre-war penchant for self-advertisement and for applying 'a moral code to the political world' that was hardly likely to 'uplift' British politics.[64]

In order to compound the wartime feminist's shame, the *Review* explained to its readers just how suffragists were going about rationalising what was clearly a betrayal of the political truce. Apparently, the NUWSS justified its recourse to feminist propaganda work by quibbling over the exact terminology of the political truce. The *Review* reported that the NUWSS claimed that it had abandoned all '*ordinary*' political work. However, it was now undertaking '*extraordinary*' political work—and 'with excellent results'. This distinction in the suffragist vernacular, the *Review* said, is 'worthy of the German Press Bureau'. There was no reason whatsoever to question the accuracy of suffragists' claims.[65] Suffragists were incapable of embodying the moral dignity required of masculine honour codes.

The *Review* continued to express itself torn over promoting national unity and exposing the duplicity of the wartime feminist. In an article titled 'The Broken Truce', the paper issued barbed observations regarding suffragists' love of feminism over patriotism.

> No pleasure can be taken at carping at any patriotic endeavours at the present crisis. But when the great majority of women are silently and without ostentation doing all that in them lies to help their country in her need, it is a matter for regret that the idea should be allowed to gain ground that their efforts are in reality stimulated by love of notoriety or a passion for propaganda work.[66]

'It would be a sorry spectacle if it were true', the paper continued, 'that one-half of the nation in seeking to do its simple duty at this time, considered it necessary to make its services to the country subservient to political propaganda.'[67] What disturbed anti-suffragists was the fact that suffragists were 'perfectly capable of reasonable endeavour'. However, they were refusing to act selflessly for the common good, even at this dire time. The *Review*'s indictment was that feminists' 'obsession [for the vote] is so strong that it stultifies even their patriotism'.[68] Suffragists were shamefully un-British.

Within months of the *Review*'s initial charge that suffragists were committed to fulfilling their own political desires over those of the nation, it appeared that, time and again, feminists were to be found confirming their devotion to feminism over patriotism. In a 1914 article optimistically entitled 'When the War Is Over', the paper declared that suffragists had definitely 'not subordinated their patriotic endeavours to political propaganda work without a definite object in view'.[69] That definite object was, of course, the vote. Anti-suffragists were irritated, even incensed, by the fact that suffragists were claiming that their contribution to the war effort was worth more than that of all other citizens to the point that they deserved a specific reward for their work. Of course, all women were doing good war work, the *Review* affirmed: 'It would be a monstrous thing if they did not'. The point was that while some women greedily clamoured for personal reward, others were simply content that their contribution should lead to an Allied victory.[70]

As exasperated with feminists' tactics and as keen to continue exposing them as they were, British anti-suffragists also understood the need to stress the desire for national unity. Indeed, this seemed ever more important in the face of attacks on social cohesion emanating from the feminist ranks. Therefore, rather than employing shame for the purpose of ostracising feminist women from the community of British patriots, the *Review* attempted to emphasis the unity of purpose across feminist and anti-feminist politics. Britain's 'helpers, like her fighters', the paper stated,

> come from every class, from every shade of political opinion; and the bulk of them ask that, just as they leave behind them their politics, so they should be freed from the taint of self-advertisement and from the appearance of doing good solely for the sake of the reward to be claimed when the war is over.[71]

However, despite its attempts at inculcating a single sense of purpose, feminist dishonesty led the paper to condemn suffragists for trying to 'place themselves first in patriotic endeavour', thereby creating a separate identity for themselves as ultra-patriots.[72] Later in 1915, when it seemed that the war was going to be a much more prolonged affair than initially thought, suffragists were continuing to perform war work while advertising their political objectives. Therefore, the *Review* took the decisive step of confirming the shame, and therefore the exclusion, of the deceitful feminist. British suffragists, the paper assured its readers, refused to see anything 'degrading or dishonourable' in their 'un-English' and 'unpatriotic' vice of self-advertisement at a time of national danger.[73] Anti-suffragists were under no such illusions. They recognised their opponents' shame.

Anti-suffragists at the time and historians since have demonstrated that suffragists were proficient self-advertisers throughout the course of the war.[74] The *Review* was constantly attuned to what it said was patriotic suffragists' abhorrent practice of claiming that their devotion to Britain's war effort was better than that of other female citizens. However, the temptation to allow self-satisfaction to trump self-sacrifice was not confined to feminists alone. By June 1915, anti-suffragists professed that they found it difficult to resist advertising the superb war work of the National League for Opposing Woman Suffrage (NLOWS). It was becoming 'a hundredfold harder not to associate the League in the public eye with some great philanthropic work, which might cover it with glory or advertisement', the *Review* stated. The difference was that, in contrast to dishonourable feminists, it remained true to its objective of not singling out the contribution of any one group, even if it thought that some self-advertisement would assist its own anti-suffragist agenda.[75] It was not honourable for it to do so in the context of the political truce called to engender unity at the outbreak of war.

As the war went on, tensions between anti-suffragists and suffragists only escalated, as demonstrated by the fact that the *Review* felt it expedient to pull the disruptive Irish into the conversation to explain its point about the deviancy of British feminists. In April 1917, exactly one year after the failed Irish insurrection against Britain, the *Review* declared that British feminists were worse even than the Irish. At least the Irish had observed the truce right up until 1916 when the radical nationalists gained the majority. In contrast, British suffragists had 'at no time complied with the spirit or even the letter of the truce', the *Review* stated. At no time, had they conducted 'an honourable observance' of the truce.[76] Irish politicians had been manly enough to abide by masculine codes of honour, at least until the nationalist allegiances trumped loyalty to the transnational community of manhood to which they belonged. Suffragist women had always existed beyond the pale of this male community that was guided by masculine emotional standards. It should not be surprising that feminists who had proved themselves unmanly and unwomanly found it difficult, if not impossible, to adhere to emotional standards that were foreign to their gendered emotional make-up.

Indeed, the only honour British feminists possessed—one that the Irish now shared with them—was the 'the doubtful honour of seeking to split the country at a time when it needs all the strength that unity can give it', the *Review* stated.[77] In making this statement, anti-suffragists were guilty of overlooking the fact that dividing the United Kingdom was exactly what radical Irish nationalists wanted to do, whatever the intentions of British feminists.

The Shame of the Feminist Wartime Nurse

Anti-suffragists accused British feminists of dishonesty by continuing to campaign for the vote under the guise of performing patriotic war work. But, as outlined in the opening of this chapter, suffragists took this deceitful conduct even further by exploiting their positions as wartime nurses to continue their propaganda campaigns. These women shamed themselves as women because they capitalised on men's gratitude for their feminine care and attention to secure a selfish reward. That was unwomanly. By continuing their campaign for the vote in the face of the political truce, they continued to demonstrate that they could not adhere to masculine codes of honour. They were dishonourable participants in the political life of wartime Britain.

In 1915, the *Review* announced that feminist nurses were guilty of 'dishonest propaganda' as they bent over sick and wounded bodies in the wartime hospitals and enticed men to promise a vote for woman suffrage should they make it home. At this stage, it looked like the male electorate would be expanded so that currently disenfranchised working-class men could be rewarded for their military service. Therefore, feminist nurses were being strategic in their endeavours. The spectacle of the empowered nurse preying on her prostrate male patient to capitalise on his potential enfranchisement sickened patriotic anti-suffragists, however.

The relationship between the wounded male body and the female nurse was ambiguous enough without these feminist overtures. Wartime nurses occupied an ambivalent position in the public imagination. Holmes has argued that for a long time the nurse occupied an ambiguous place in Australia's remembering of the Great War, for example, because of uncertainty surrounding the issue of her sexuality.[78] Given the intimate connection between the single and therefore supposedly virginal nurse and her vulnerable wounded patient or alternatively her convalescing yet rakish young soldier, interactions between nurses and soldiers were carefully monitored. Post-work interactions between nurses and patients or nurses and male members of the medical staff were severely curtailed. Yet surveillance could do little to manage sexual fantasising. Holmes asserts that whereas the nurse's uniform represented her desexualised professionalism and distance from the male patient, that stark uniform could also serve as a blank canvass for the projection of male fantasies.[79] Perceptions of the respectability of her position then were often beyond her control.

Sexual fantasies aside, nurses were also seen to occupy a dangerously powerful position in relation to the men they nursed. This was particularly so at a time of war when multitudes of broken male bodies received the attention of female nurses. Men in the hands of wartime nurses were 'weak, powerless, castrated', Holmes elucidates. They were dependent on their 'ministering angels' for their 'most fundamental and intimate needs'.[80] What this state represented, then, was a direct reversal of gendered power roles—a reversal of chivalry. It was no longer man's task to protect the weak and vulnerable woman. Rather, it was the female nurse's job to restore the weakened man to a state of masculinity.

Sandra Gilbert has written that there was a growing sense during the war that, 'as if by some uncanny swing of history's pendulum', women had become 'ever more powerful'.[81] To some men, embittered by their experiences of war, and fuelled by the knowledge that women at home had recruited men for the war through their propaganda work, this swing in the balance of power was imagined as a monstrous inversion of gender norms. Nurses were imagined as being representative of a monstrous form of 'victorious femininity' that loomed over the embattled male soldier.[82] The embattled male soldier was highly dependent on the female nurse—a far cry from the manly warrior of wartime propaganda. Such dependence could result in two very different outcomes. On the one hand, this dependence could lead to the formation of intimate attachments between soldiers and nurses. Female nurses did not always welcome these intimate attachments.

On the other hand, such reversals of power relations could also lead to male soldiers harbouring negative emotions such as resentment and anger. These negative emotions were prompted by the lurking suspicion that the nurse was somehow benefiting from men's pain and injury.[83]

It was not only nurses who were the subjects of such masculine misgivings. Women in uniforms 'at home'—those working as munitions workers, bus drivers, and soldiers in the 'land army', for example—could also be imagined as monstrous replacements of men. These 'former subservient creatures' loomed 'malevolently larger' in some men's imaginations. Indeed, as Gilbert has clarified, places such as London came to be epitomised by a sea of women in uniform—a transgressive, even subversive image of gender inversion.[84]

Still, as threatening as women in wartime uniforms were, the specific image of the woman in a nurse's uniform abusing her position of power nauseated contributors to the *Anti-Suffrage Review*. There were two reasons for this. One was that such actions violated the supposed sanctity of nursing as a woman's vocation. The other was that this behaviour transgressed sexual norms.

Capitalising on the male soldier's gratitude presented an 'unhallowed' vision precisely because it defiled the sanctity of the nursing profession, which, the *Review* asserted, was much more a feminine vocation than a female profession.[85] The feminist nurse, then, was no 'Tommy's sister', referring to the name given to female munitions workers. Instead, she was the female war worker who was guilty of 'hitting Tommy politically "when he is down"'.[86] This was a gross misuse of her power. It was a gross transgression of the emotional regimes guiding men's and women's conduct during the war. Feminist nurses brought shame to the community of patriotic womanhood, as they failed to perform their war work with the selfless devotion required of that collective in that time of need. By attempting to 'contaminate' men, they had 'degraded their own womanhood'.[87] Their shameless actions, the *Review* lamented, amounted to 'the undoing of England; the death-blow to woman's dignity, woman's position, woman's power'.[88]

The *Review* presented the feminist nurse as a woman who lacked a womanly sense of spirituality, but it also constructed her, more insidiously, as a sexual abomination. The paper depicted wartime nurses as a sexually suspicious class—a body of potential harassers waiting to use their now dominant sexual position to lure unsuspecting and vulnerable soldiers into their political fold. A series of articles printed in the *Review* in 1916 further expounded the nurse's treacherous sexuality. Prominent anti-suffragist Edith Milner reiterated that under Mrs Fawcett's direction, suffragist nurses were continuing to visit hospitals to make 'shameless bids for the vote'.[89] The paper painted a vivid picture of the exploitation. These 'frenzied viragos', the *Review* stated, were guilty of bending 'over the sick and suffering soldiers and ask[ing] them when they get the vote to promise a vote for Woman Suffrage'.[90] They used not only their sexuality but also the wounded man's vulnerability to feminine care and attention, the paper accused, to tempt weakened men to vote for woman suffrage. This was not in keeping with feminine codes of honour where chastity and modesty prevailed. They were dishonourable women.

It was not only the nurses affiliated with the NUWSS who were accused of such horrendous behaviour. As Gullace has pointed out, Dr Louisa Garrett Anderson and her medical partner Dr Flora Murray, who worked together in Paris and London, were regarded as one of the most successful medical teams of the war. Yet, and much to the chagrin of anti-suffragists, these two women offered their services to their patients while flaunting their WSPU sympathies. They were guilty, anti-suffragists affirmed, of prominently displaying a banner bearing the WSPU motto 'Deeds not Words' in their hospitals; wearing suffragette colours of purple, green, and white; and preaching to their soldier patients about why women should have the vote.[91]

Still, it was NUWSS leader Millicent Fawcett's shameless indulgence in self-advertisement that drew the particular wrath of the *Review*. In applauding the actions of her nurses, this renowned suffragist astounded anti-suffragists who decreed that 'the *naiveté* with which Mrs Fawcett glories in the shame' was what was unbelievable about the whole sham. It did not occur to her, the paper argued, that there was anything 'illegitimate or dishonourable' in the actions of her followers.

Moreover, that the actions of these feminists were tolerated—that the government was looking more and more likely to give in to their demands for the vote—meant that these women were not being judged by the same emotional standards as men. In demanding personal rewards for work they were carrying out under the banner of ordinary wartime citizens, suffragists were again claiming 'exemptions from honour which would not be tolerated for a moment in the case of ordinary male politicians', the paper insisted.[92] All these female 'politicians' had done was to prove to patriotic citizens 'that women generally take to underground methods as readily and as congenially as a duck takes to water'.[93] This was not to be applauded, for all this proved was that wartime feminists were unmanly navigators of the male political sphere. They bought dishonour to British men through the dishonour they brought to the running of their national politics.

Wartime nurses represented a particular type of emotional ambiguity. Anti-suffragists depicted them as unwomanly. They shamefully exploited their sexual power over weakened men. They also presented them as unmanly, as they defied the wartime political truce. They corrupted feminine and masculine forms of honour. Yet those nurses who served in hospitals in the theatre of war proved that they were capable of embodying other elements of masculine honour codes. Like male soldiers, they were courageous under fire, for example. Therefore, the wartime nurse confounded the anti-feminist who was keen to preserve the integrity of gendered emotional regimes, especially at this time of supreme national and international crisis. Of all wartime women, duplicitous nurses were to be detested.

Whatever British anti-suffragists thought of duplicitous feminist strategies—whatever they thought of the dishonourable wartime nurse—it was becoming increasingly more apparent that British women's wartime service was likely to result in their enfranchisement. As Gullace has argued, the 'spectacle of women's willingness to fight, to serve, to work, and to die for the war effort had a powerful effect on feminists' ability to justify their claim to citizenship'.[94] Although not entirely traditional or respectable, during wartime at least, nursing was accepted as a means of channelling female patriotism into useful, if dangerous avenues. Her displays of active patriotism doubtless influenced British politicians' decision to enfranchise women before the close of the war.

Dishonourable Tactics Win the Vote

Historians have confirmed the accuracy of anti-suffragists' wartime forecasts that continuing feminist propaganda, under the guise of patriotic war work, would eventually lead to the woman vote. In countering Susan Kingsley Kent's assertion that the NUWSS made a knee-jerk reaction to the war that resulted in their members turning to forms of war work that only worked to re-emphasise gender divisions, Jo Vellacott has argued that this large body of suffrage societies made a calculated turn towards war work that enhanced the reputation of suffragists as British patriots.[95] That the NUWSS continued to keep 14 political organisers across the country in their employment during the war is indicative of the fact that suffrage work was not entirely disbanded in the face of women's involvement in wartime propaganda and work.[96] Instead, Vellacott attests, for many feminists, a genuine dedication to the war effort went hand in hand with a deep commitment to the cause of suffrage.[97]

Gullace concurs. She has argued that, contrary to the notion that war disrupted the campaign for the woman vote, there is greater evidence that the war provided a context in which feminist claims seemed increasingly persuasive.[98] Both the WSPU and the NUWSS effectively used 'the spectacle of female patriotism' to legitimise their push for the vote.[99] Despite the 'tremendous ideological break' for many suffragists, marked by the shift for many from feminist pacifism to nationalistic support of war, British suffrage organisations retained a remarkable degree of coherence. Suffragists continued to undertake a whole range of political activities while performing war work, including regularly publishing papers, maintaining connections with their provincial branches, holding meetings, and running fundraising campaigns. They used their 'extraordinary notoriety'—combined with their penchant and skill for spectacle—to not only draw the public's attention to women's patriotic service but also to juxtapose this dedicated war service to examples of male cowardice.[100] By highlighting male wartime deficiencies and emphasising women's exceptional patriotism, British women helped to re-orientate citizenship away from maleness and towards Britishness.[101] Through staging parades, granting interviews to the popular press, and organising mass meetings and rallies, radical and constitutional suffragists together helped to disrupt notions of the gendered nature of citizenship—a disruption that would eventually lead to enfranchisement.[102] Their efforts worked to promote women's reputation for patriotism in the eyes of many and suspicion in the eyes of some, but however successful they eventually proved to be, such tactics also worked to expose the divisions between the feminisms that made up the early twentieth-century campaign for the vote in British parliament.

The ushering in of women's enfranchisement in the final year of the war saw British anti-suffragists lose all deference for unity in the face of the need for self-expression. The *Review* gave voice to renewed anger and fierce disappointment:

> Well, well, the Suffragist section of the women of the country, eluding all test as to whether they are the majority or not, and exploiting the war with the cry of unity when they themselves have created the division, are getting their way by the aid of sentiment, cowardice and political expediency.[103]

Suffragists were disingenuous citizens and politicians. They were also incapable of embodying prominent elements of masculine honour codes such as honesty and courage. Yet here they were being admitted into the masculine domain of parliamentary politics. To British anti-suffragists, feminists had waged an unnecessary underground war against gendered values and gendered emotional standards at a time when the nation and the Empire were fighting for their survival in what was the 'real' war. Anti-suffragists admitted the defeat of their own just cause and in doing so appropriated the rhetoric of warfare. For years, they had 'withstood successfully the direct assault of a subtle appeal to self-interest, reinforced by the vulgar challenge of intimidation'.[104] Yet this was to no avail, for now their position had 'been taken in the flank by a wave of sentimentality'.[105]

One of the most damaging aspects of this defeat was the particular role played by prominent anti-suffragists and that bastion of British conservatism, the House of Lords, in bringing it about. On 10 January 1918, the House of Lords voted 134 to 71 in favour of the inclusion of the woman suffrage clause. Ironically, it was the anti-suffrage creed of unity during the war that signalled the demise of anti-suffrage objectives. Lord Curzon, a president of the NLOWS, enjoined his anti-suffragist peers to abstain from voting against the clause for the sake of ensuring national security and peace with the lower house.[106]

Once the woman vote had been achieved, former anti-suffragists signalled their intent to switch their focus from opposing the franchise to educating the expanded electorate to perform their citizenly duties in a manner that protected the integrity of both the national community and gendered emotional regimes. The *Review* declared,

> There will be a better opportunity now for emphasising the constructive side of the Anti-Suffrage attitude—the reasoned, intelligent concern for the good of the community, as shown in the insistence upon the identity of interests of men and women; the strong belief in the capacity for women for work that must be done, if the nation as a whole is to prosper; the desire to see national efficiency raised to the highest possible level by the allocation of work in accordance with the suitability of the workers and the avoidance of overlapping and the duplication of effort that does not increase the resultant output.[107]

In many ways, former anti-suffragists' remit now resembled closely that of the Australian Women's National League (AWNL). However, whether British post-war anti-suffragists would be successful in this enterprise or not depended on each sex's ability to obey appropriate emotional regimes and moral codes. British anti-suffragists' fears were that feminists would not. Wartime feminists had demonstrated that they were unmanly navigators of the masculine sphere of action. They were immoral politicians. They were dishonourable in their political dealings. There was nothing, then, to suggest that their behaviour would become any more honourable in the post-war era. It seemed that by invading man's realm while he was drawing on his emotional reserves to prove his masculinity on the fields of battle, feminists had indeed introduced a corrosive feminised element into masculine emotional regimes back home. An uncertain fate awaited returning soldiers.

Irish Feminists Direct Accusations of Dishonour at British Suffragists

During the war, patriotic Irish women joined in the attack on British suffragists. Irish feminist nationalists, members of the militant Irish Women's Franchise League (IWFL), did not believe in supporting male militarism in Ireland or in Britain. As discussed in Chapter 2, they decried the auxiliary woman in Ireland. They detested her seemingly slavish need to act as the military man's support. They adopted the same attitude towards British suffragists—represented most spectacularly by the former leaders of the WSPU, Emmeline and Christabel Pankhurst—who they believed had dropped their feminist campaigning to support the British war effort. Before the war, the strident militancy of the WSPU represented a challenge to the exclusively masculine nature of honour codes. Women were proving that they too could challenge the honour of male opponents and that this challenge was underpinned by the threat, and often even the act, of physical force. The IWFL were bitterly disappointed that the Pankhursts had abandoned that noble duty in order to prop up male militarism. Instead of demonstrating that honour codes extended to women, these former militants lauded the traditional relationship between men and women in times of war—namely, men as fighters and women as supporters. They had rebadged honour as an exclusively male emotional virtue, then. In doing so, they rejected a belief that they had previously shared with other members of the community of militant feminists that directed that women were capable of embodying honour; therefore, they could take their rightful place alongside men in the public sphere. They shamed that community by their betrayal of that shared value.

As mentioned earlier, British anti-suffragists accused Irish nationalists of being as dishonourable in their political dealings as wartime British suffragists. Many members of the IWFL welcomed such an assignation on the basis that it confirmed their nationalist integrity. The majority of the nationalist IWFL were also proud of the fact that their feminist integrity remained intact because they had not joined what they perceived to be British feminists' 'stampede away from suffrage'.[108] It seemed that the IWFL was one of the few suffrage societies across Ireland and Britain that had remained truthful to its feminist goals in the face of the international war.[109] It filled the gap left in Ireland by the other vacating British and Irish societies. For instance, when the WSPU shut down its Belfast branch, the IWFL established its Ulster Centre there.[110] In 1915, the IWFL opposed the wartime political truce arguing, if British feminists had not agreed to this ceasefire, the campaign for the vote would have been much further advanced by now.[111] They further disagreed with the *Review*'s tactic of trying to shame British suffragists by pronouncing that Irish nationalists had honoured the truce up until the movement's radicalisation in 1916. At no point had nationalist or Unionist men observed the ceasefire, the IWFL's paper, the *Citizen* asserted. The proof was in the fact that both sides continued to arm in the event of war—international or civil.[112]

Perhaps surprisingly given the IWFL's and the WSPU's shared militancy, the Irish organisation agreed with British anti-suffragists that the WSPU was indeed a dishonourable body of politicians. But it did not cite the same reasons as these anti-suffragists. The *Citizen* accused the WSPU of not honouring its bond with the political community to which it owed its primary allegiance—namely, the transnational feminist community. Initially, it viewed prominent members of the WSPU—particularly Emmeline and Christabel Pankhurst—to be traitors to the suffrage cause, seeing their organisation as being 'almost indistinguishable from a Government Recruiting and Propaganda Department'.[113] The situation was different for the IWFL. Irish suffragists, and certainly radical Irish nationalist suffragists, were not as closely implicated in the war effort as British suffragists were. Many of them decided that they did not owe allegiance to either the British Government or to the Irish Parliamentary Party, both of whom were committed to the war effort and each of whom had rejected women's appeals for the franchise. Therefore, the IWFL felt little or no compulsion to abandon its feminist campaign in favour of obeying any political truce.

Since its inception, the *Citizen* reflected the fractured state of Irish feminist politics by accommodating opposing points of view in its pages. Now, during the war, it continued to do so, but it also felt compelled to insert editorial negations of any claims that ran counter to its increasingly strident Irish nationalist outlook. In October 1914, the paper published a letter criticising Irish suffragists' attacks on members of the WSPU and on the Pankhurst family in particular. The letter instructed that Irish feminists should feel grateful for the teachings and guidance of the WSPU over the years. That organisation, the letter went on, had taught Irish women about a number of important subjects including

> sacrifice, the glory of it, self-control, independence in thought and deed, and that a woman can be of the greatest value to her country; she can awake the sluggard to his sisters' pains and hardships, and a woman can die to help her country.[114]

Why should an Irish paper be the one to condemn the militant societies that have helped Irish women during the suffrage campaign? Instead, the writer argued, we owe these English militants 'our best loyalty and gratefulness'.[115]

The *Citizen* may have allowed these pro-WSPU sentiments to be expressed within its pages, but it challenged them. An editorial note directed readers' attentions to the fact that the *Citizen* was not in the habit of exalting individual leaders over the collective. It also reminded its audience that the WSPU, led by Emmeline and Christabel Pankhurst, had abandoned feminism in the face of the male-dominated war machine. Besides, Christabel Pankhurst was not and never had been a leader of the Irish suffrage movement. She had shown herself to be completely out of touch with the exceptional circumstances in Ireland—those circumstances that separated the Irish feminist movement from that in England. 'It is therefore difficult', the article went on, 'to understand on what grounds an Irish Suffrage paper should be obliged to refrain from publishing criticisms of her public action.'[116] Another article published the following year further affirmed the seemingly unbridgeable divisions between the suffrage movements in England and Ireland. It also, more specifically, attacked the credentials of Christabel Pankhurst as a leader of Irish suffragists. 'I would like to also point out', the *Citizen* stated, 'that Miss Pankhurst, though admirable in her own country, which she thoroughly understood, has never founded or led anything in Ireland.'[117]

Between 1914 and 1917, the *Citizen* published a series of attacks on the misguided ethics of the WSPU that the paper believed had led the British organisation to abandon feminism for the sake of militarised English nationalism and British imperialism. Nearing the end of 1914, the paper declared that the WSPU were akin to Irish women who prioritised the male-led nationalist movement over that for the woman vote. Mirroring accusations emanating from the British anti-suffrage camp, the *Citizen* declared that these former militants seemed to be only doing what they were doing for the sake of notoriety. It looked at that stage as if they had abandoned their true feminist mission 'merely in order to ride into popularity on the crest of the war-wave'.[118]

The following year, in an even more damning indictment, these British suffragists were labelled the new Antis.[119] The *Citizen* also drew attention to the British press's reference to the WSPU as 'ex-militants', which it thought was 'a stinging coinage'.[120] Now members of the WSPU were slavishly obeying the men they had previously fought and 'whose injustices they exposed so magnificently'. It was 'humiliating'. There was much 'cringing' by those writing for this still proud feminist paper for 'the once-proud fighting van of the women's army of justice'.[121] This cringing was intensified when the WSPU's Christabel Pankhurst published a call for all disloyal elements of British society to be imprisoned in the pages of her re-titled paper the *Suffragette*.[122] Pankhurst's call prompted another contributor to the *Citizen* to declare that the fact that this once renowned feminist leader

> should travesty and misrepresent the militant suffrage movement by doing so in a paper miscalling itself the *Suffragette*, which has frankly and unashamedly dropped the woman's suffrage movement, surely calls for protest from the real suffragettes, who have not become Government mouthpieces.[123]

The former British militants threatened to bring shame to the very name, suffragette, now and to those few women's associations continuing the militant feminist struggle.

By 1917, the IWFL's sense of disillusionment at the abandonment of the militant suffrage campaign in the face of the international conflict increased. The difference was that the woman suffrage bill was now on the cards. It looked like British suffragists were about to get what they wanted, but through what sacrifices? British feminists' tactics had seemingly won out, yet the *Citizen* claimed that in adopting the tactics they had, the Pankhursts and their followers were guilty of what could only be described as 'shameful conduct'. Their

> slavish pandering to, and lauding up of, Lloyd George—the man who, but a few years ago, they held up to the world as the lying, hypocritical, and dishonourable politician that he is, and with whom they have now joined hands

had embarrassed the feminist community.[124] The WSPU had transgressed feminist rules of engagement by supporting an ultra-masculine system of militarism to achieve their goal of enfranchisement rather than remaining true to feminist campaigning. They should have known better.

More than that, now in the post-war era, the *Citizen* declared that former militants appeared to be rejoicing in their capitulation. British suffragists had accepted what male politicians deigned to give them as a form of 'gift'— that is, a limited form of the franchise and one that omitted a large bulk of the women who campaigned with them before and during the war—namely, those women under 30 years old. British feminists succumbed to the condescending patronage of man, 'joyously accept[ing] the meagre crumb of war comfort' 'from the hands of a group of men who only a few years before sanctioned the brutal forcible feeding of women and the smashing of the bodies of the bearers of the human race in their struggle for citizenship'.[125] 'One had hoped much from the "leaders"', the *Citizen* confessed, but 'alas, they sold the organisation for a mess of pottage and led their bewildered followers up a blind alley.'[126] Or as another contributor to the paper put it a little later in the year, they 'prostituted their movement to militarist uses'.[127] In 1919, the *Citizen* was to be found reiterating what it had sensationally declared at the outbreak of the war: British militants had been found paying homage to the gods of 'jingoism'—'naked and unashamed'.[128]

The bitter disappointment for the Irish nationalist suffragists was that, during the war, British feminists had not challenged the gendered nature of the emotional standards guiding men's and women's participation in the public life of the nation. They had supported the masculine honour codes that regulated relations between men in wartime. They had lauded masculinised notions of courage and chivalry that were deemed necessary for men's participation in the theatres of war. They had helped to secure the franchise—yes—but by not affecting any real change to the emotional regimes governing men's and women's actions. Women were still suspended in a similar state as their pre-war and pre-enfranchised selves. Honour to former British militants still meant the masculine rules that conducted men's behaviour. If these militants had paid homage to a conceptualisation of honour that regulated women's' relations with each other, they would never have abandoned the campaign they shared with fellow feminists.

By 1918, some British feminists were indeed arguing that the abandonment of militant suffragism was responsible for winning women the vote. This triumphant narrative said that reformed militants had elicited the 'gift' of the franchise from male benefactors who were grateful that transgressive women were now playing the game their way. But others, like Irish militants, countered this by arguing that by abandoning disruptive feminist militancy, former militants were responsible for losing all the other hard-fought gains achieved during the war, such as women's access to traditionally masculine occupations and equivalent wages to men's.

> It is poor consolation to think that the fault, in this case at least, is not man's mainly, but woman's. It was women who sold out, abandoned their feminist constructive activities and set up instead masculine

destructiveness as their god. Their daughters and daughters' daughters will pay the price.[129]

In a way, the response of Irish feminist nationalists to winning the woman vote aligns with Higonnet and Higonnet's double helix metaphor mentioned earlier in the chapter. To their thinking, the concept of female citizenship had changed in that it had been accepted that women were fit for masculine forms of employment and political duties, but relations between the sexes were still hierarchically structured, and women's conduct in this newly expanded public sphere was still bound to be guided by the same pre-war gendered emotional regimes. By joining in with men in paying homage to the overwhelmingly masculine priorities of male militarism, British militant feminists had helped to ensure that, although the physical landscape had changed, emotionally men and women were still trapped within existing paradigms. The achievement of the vote had affected little change to the separate nature of the emotional regimes guiding men's and women's participation in the political life of their nations.

Conclusion

The Great War confirmed for British anti-suffragists that feminists were incapable of understanding or embodying the emotional qualities deemed necessary for participating in the public life of the nation. Women had been relegated to the domestic sphere; therefore, they were not trained in the ways of honour codes. Their clumsy attempts to appropriate masculine emotional standards before the war were shameful. During the war, when the British man's collective masculinity was under extreme duress, their transgressions of emotional regulations were even more shameful. They added to the British man's considerable stresses. While his adherence to honour codes was being severely tried on the fields of battle abroad, his womenfolk should have been protecting the integrity of those codes at home. Not only had feminist actions during the war served to corrupt the nature of masculine emotional regimes but also for anti-suffragists, the eventual admittance of women over 30 years old into the parliamentary franchise had confirmed the permanency of that corruption. If honour was indeed the 'glue' that bound a masculine social group together and fostered cohesion among its members, then what was in store for returning British soldiers and for postwar British society now that women had affected changes to honour codes?

Irish militant feminists, on the other hand, did not perceive that British feminists had enacted any transformation of masculine honour codes. Instead, their abandonment of the militant feminist campaign to actively support the male militaristic machine worked only to confirm the exclusive masculinity of those emotional codes. This bitterly disappointed Irish militants who believed that, along with the militant WSPU, they had been in the process of altering the gendered nature of honour codes. Attacking the gendered nature of those codes was what would allow women to take an equal place alongside their national manhood in carrying out the public affairs of the nation. The difference between Irish and British militant feminists, it seemed, was that while Irish feminist nationalists alleged that they shared a heritage of equality in politics and in arms with Irish men, British women claimed no such legacy. Militancy for British women was a matter of expediency only. Therefore, while it was in the Irish feminist's interests to undermine the masculinity of honour codes that were underpinned by the threat of violence, it was less so for British feminists whose recourse to militancy was only temporary, as demonstrated by their suspension of it during the war. I will discuss differing views on women's militancy further in Chapter 7.

Notes

1. Nicoletta Gullace, *'The Blood of Our Sons': Men, Women and the Renegotiation of British Citizenship During the Great War* (New York: Palgrave Macmillan, 2002) p. 151; and Claire Tylee, *The Great War and Women's Consciousness: Images of Militarism and Womanhood in Women's Writings, 1914–64* (Basingstoke: Macmillan, 1990) p. 7.
2. *Anti-Suffrage Review*, no. 75, January 1915, pp .4–5.
3. *Anti-Suffrage Review*, no. 75, January 1915, pp .4–5.
4. *Anti-Suffrage Review*, no. 75, January 1915, pp .4–5.
5. *Anti-Suffrage Review*, no. 75, January 1915, pp .4–5.
6. John Hollander, "Honor Dishonorable: Shameful Shame", *Social Research*, vol. 70, no. 4 (2003) pp. 1061–1074.
7. See Ute Frevert, *Emotions in History—Lost and Found* (Budapest and London: Central European University Press, 2011) p. 67.
8. Frevert, *Emotions in History*, p. 88.
9. See Nye for a historiography of duelling. Robert Nye, *Masculinity and Male Codes of Honor in Modern France* (Oxford: Oxford University Press, 1993).
10. Nye, *Masculinity and Male Codes of Honor in Modern France*, p. 32.
11. Nye, *Masculinity and Male Codes of Honor in Modern France*, p. 32.
12. I discuss the shame of the male coward in Chapter 6.
13. For description of a gentleman's conduct, Ute Frevert cites the *Encyclopaedia Britannica* in 1856, which states that a gentleman was regulated by honour. His character was mild and inoffensive, and yet he stood up for his convictions, values, and beliefs. He defended them through vigorous action and did not shirk sacrificing his health or life to defend his principles. See Frevert, *Emotions in History*, p. 58. For other studies of the notion of the gentleman and gentlemanly conduct in nineteenth-century British culture and literature, see, for example, Marc Girouard, *The Return to Camelot: Chivalry and the English Gentleman* (New Haven and London: Yale University Press, 1981), and Shirley Robin Letwin, *The Gentleman in Trollope: Individuality and Moral Conduct* (Basingstoke: Macmillan, 1984).
14. Nye explains that these were middle-class additions to existing honour codes. See Nye, *Masculinity and Male Codes of Honor in Modern France*, p. 16.
15. Nye, *Masculinity and Male Codes of Honor in Modern France*, pp. 19–20.
16. Frevert, *Emotions in History*, p. 42.
17. Kate Darian-Smith, 'War and Australian Society', in Joan Beaumont, ed., *Australia's War, 1939–1945* (Sydney: Allen and Unwin, 1996) pp. 54–81, pp. 61–72.

18 Summerfield cites Elshtain's 1987 book, *Women and War*. See Penny Summerfield, 'Gender and War in the Twentieth Century', *The International History Review*, vol. 19, no. 1 (1997), pp. 3–15, p. 4. Also see Margaret Randolph Higonnet, Jane Jenson, Sonya Michel and Margaret Collins Weitz 'Introduction', in Margaret Randolph Higonnet, Jane Jenson, Sonya Michel and Margaret Collins Weitz, eds., *Behind the Lines: Gender and the Two World Wars* (New Haven and London: Yale University Press, 1987) pp. 1–17, especially pp. 1–4.
19 Nicole Ann Dombrowski, 'Soldiers, Saints, or Sacrificial Lambs? Women's Relationship to Combat and the Fortification of the Home Front in the Twentieth Century', in Nicole Ann Dombrowski, ed., *Women and War in the Twentieth Century: Enlisted with or without Consent* (New York and London: Routledge, 1999) pp. 2–37, pp. 3–4.
20 Higonnet, Jenson, Michel and Collins Weitz, 'Introduction', p. 5.
21 See Margaret Randolph Higonnet and Patrice L.R. Higonnet, 'The Double Helix', in Margaret Randolph Higonnet, Jane Jenson, Sonya Michel and Margaret Collins Weitz, eds., *Behind the Lines. Gender and the Two World Wars* (New Haven and London: Yale University Press, 1987) pp. 31–47.
22 Summerfield cites Elshtain's 1987 book, *Women and War*. See Penny Summerfield, 'Gender and War in the Twentieth Century', p. 4.
23 Higonnet, Jenson, Michel and Collins Weitz, 'Introduction', p. 1.
24 Higonnet, Jenson, Michel and Collins Weitz, 'Introduction', p. 6.
25 Dombrowski, 'Soldiers, Saints, or Sacrificial Lambs?', pp. 7–8.
26 Dombrowski, 'Soldiers, Saints, or Sacrificial Lambs?', p. 3.
27 This issue is discussed in Chapter 6. See Nicoletta Gullace, 'White Feathers and Wounded Men: Female Patriotism and the Memory of the Great War, *Journal of British Studies*, vol. 36, no. 2 (1997) pp. 178–206, and Gullace, '*The Blood of Our Sons*'.
28 Jenny Gould, 'Women's Military Services in First World War Britain', in Margaret Randolph Higonnet, Jane Jenson, Sonya Michel and Margaret Collins Weitz, eds., *Behind the Lines. Gender and the Two World Wars* (New Haven and London: Yale University Press, 1987) pp. 114–125, p. 117.
29 Claire Tylee, *The Great War and Women's Consciousness: Images of Militarism and Womanhood in Women's Writings, 1914–64* (Basingstoke: Macmillan, 1990) p. 8.
30 Gould, 'Women's Military Services in First World War Britain', p. 117.
31 Tylee, *The Great War and Women's Consciousness*, p. 11.
32 See Gullace, *The Blood of Our Sons*, pp. 161–164, and Susan R. Grayzel, *Women and the First World War* (Abingdon and New York: Routledge, 2002) pp. 28–35. In these pages, Grayzel provides an overview of women's factory work in many of the belligerent countries. For a much more detailed analysis of British female factory workers, see Angela Woollacott, *On Her Their Lives Depend: Munitions Workers in the Great War* (Berkeley: University of California Press, 1994). For a discussion of the dangerous conditions munitions factory workers coped with, see Woollacott's Chapter 3, ' "Industrial Work is Good for Women": Health, Welfare, Deaths, and Injuries', pp. 59–88.
33 Woollacott, *On Her Their Lives Depend*, p. 2
34 Perhaps as many as 210,000 men served in the British Army and Navy during the war. Until recent years, ongoing conflict in Northern Ireland and postcolonial nationalist embarrassment at the memory of fighting for the imperial master in the Republic has allowed Unionist contributions to the war effort to overshadow that of nationalists. For a comprehensive account of Ireland's experiences of World War One, see Keith Jeffery, *Ireland and the Great War* (Cambridge: Cambridge University Press, 2000). For contended figures of those

serving and dying, see also 'Irish Soldiers in the First World War (Somme)', Department of the Taoiseach, Dublin, www.taoiseach.gov.ie/eng/Historical_Information/1916_Commemorations/Irish_Soldiers_in_the_First_World_War.html, accessed 4 April 2017.
35 Members of the titled and upper ranks of Irish society formed the non-political and non-sectarian Irish Women's Association in London in 1915 for the purpose of providing food and comforts for prisoners of war belonging to Irish regiments. (Eileen Reilly, 'Women and Voluntary War Work', in Adrian Gregory and Senia Pašeta, eds., *Ireland and the Great War: 'A War to Unite Us All'?* (Manchester: Manchester University Press, 2002) pp. 49–72, p. 65.)
36 For a discussion of women war workers in Ireland, see Jeffery, *Ireland and the Great War*, pp. 28–34. Given the divisive political cultures of Ireland at the time, it is perhaps surprising that most women's wartime societies organised themselves across political and religious divides. Eileen Reilly, for instance, cites the example of the Cavan Women's Patriotic Committee (CCWPC), consisting of Unionist and nationalist members, which was formed to undertake fundraising and the collecting and dispatching of comfort packs to troops at the front. Reilly asserts that the CCWPC was typical of most of the women's support organisations that were established during the war with the notable exception of the Ulster Women's Unionist Council, which openly projected its 'separatist political stance' and focused on the 36th Ulster Division (primarily based on membership of the Ulster Volunteer Force) as the sole beneficiary of their efforts. See Reilly, 'Women and Voluntary War Work', pp. 63–64.
37 Grayzel, *Women and the First World War*, p. 30.
38 She cites tensions and conflicts between English and Irish factory workers revealed in Angela Woollacott's work to exemplify this point. In 1917 at a shell-filling factory in Hereford, for example, conflicts broke out between Irish workers who sang nationalist songs and insulted soldiers and English ones who objected to this. The Irish workers were dismissed. See Grayzel, *Women and the First World War*, p. 30.
39 Tylee, *The Great War and Women's Consciousness*, p. 11. Numbers tend to vary a little across the large body of scholarship that exists on this subject. For example, Paul Ward states that by the war's end, 300 women had served in the Queen Alexandra's Imperial Military Nursing Service, 3,000 in the Territorial Force Nursing Service, and 50,000 in the VADs. (Paul Ward, ' "Women of Britain Say Go": Women's Participation in the First World War', *Twentieth Century British History*, vol. 12, no. 1 (2001), pp. 23–45, p. 28.)
40 Inglis had initially applied to the War Office to offer her services abroad. Under the auspices of the need to protect women from the dangers of the conflict zones, British authorities rejected her application. See Gullace, *The Blood of Our Sons*, p. 151. See also Tylee, *The Great War and Women's Consciousness*, p. 7.
41 Dr Inglis was the first woman to be awarded the Serbian Order of the White Eagle—presented by the crown prince—for her decision to stay with the wounded Serbian soldiers as her hospital was overrun with enemy soldiers during the retreat through Dobrudja. Gullace notes, tragically, that she died of advanced cancer shortly after evacuating wounded soldiers under her care from Archangel in a manoeuvre aided by the British. She was buried with full military honours at St Giles Cathedral, Edinburgh, on 29 November 1917. See Gullace, *The Blood of Our Sons*, pp. 151–152.
42 Bruce Scates and Raelene Frances note that there were approximately 10,000 volunteer women's clubs, societies, and sewing circles established during the war. (Bruce Scates and Raelene Frances, *Women and the Great War* (Cambridge: Cambridge University Press, 1997) especially pp. 45–46.) Melanie Oppenheimer

reports that by 1918 there were perhaps 82,000 women and 20,000 men and boys working for 2,200 Red Cross branches across the country. Their activities included organising goods for the troops abroad ('comforts', medical supplies, clothing, cooking equipment, and recreational equipment). See Melanie Oppenheimer, '"The Best P.M. for the Empire in War"? Lady Helen Munro Ferguson and the Australian Red Cross Society 1914–1920', *Australian Historical Studies*, vol. 33, no. 119 (2002) pp. 108–124, p. 117.
43 Joan Beaumont, *Broken Nation: Australians and the Great War* (Sydney: Allen and Unwin, 2013) p. 95.
44 Beaumont, *Broken Nation*, p. 100.
45 For example, there were over 80,000 women in unpaid positions in Australia during the war. In 1917, however, only 55,164 women were recorded to be in paid employment. See Beaumont, *Broken Nation*, p. 95.
46 See Joan Beaumont, 'Whatever happened to Patriotic Women?', *Australian Historical Studies*, vol. 31, no. 115 (2000) pp. 273–287.
47 Melanie Oppenheimer, 'Shaping the Legend: The Role of the Australian Red Cross and Anzac', *Labour History*, no. 106 (2014) pp. 123–142, p. 130.
48 Only those who were over 18 years old and trained in first aid and home nursing could apply to be VAs. See Oppenheimer, 'Shaping the Legend', p. 131.
49 Oppenheimer, '"The Best P.M. for the Empire in War"?', pp. 118–119.
50 Beaumont, *Broken Nation*, p. 100.
51 *Anti-Suffrage Review*, no 21, August 1910, pp. 6–13. As Dombrowski argues, it was not only anti-suffragists who argued that women were not suited to war. Liberal feminists have also argued that women, by nature, are not suited to war. See Dombrowski, 'Soldiers, Saints, or Sacrificial Lambs?', p. 4.
52 *Irish Citizen*, vol. 3, no. 15, 29 August 1914, p. 114.
53 I discuss this in detail in Chapter 3.
54 *Irish Citizen*, vol. 1, no. 3, 1 July 1912, p. 17. Goldstein reminded Irish men of the debt they owed to past women activists: 'In the name of justice and chivalry, pay the debt that Ireland owes to Anna Parnell and the Ladies' Land League by enfranchising Irishwomen on the same terms as Irishmen'. For more on Anna Parnell and the Ladies' Land League, see Patricia Groves, *Petticoat Rebellion: The Anna Parnell Story* (Cork: Mercier Press, 2009).
55 *Irish Citizen*, vol. 3, no. 13, 15 August 1914, p. 101.
56 *Irish Citizen*, vol. 3, no. 13, 15 August 1914, p. 101.
57 The strained relationship between Irish and British feminists was mentioned in the book's introduction. I will discuss the issue of women's militancy further in Chapter 7.
58 *Irish Citizen*, vol. 4, no. 14, 21 August 1915, p. 77.
59 *Anti-Suffrage Review*, no. 21, August 1910, pp. 18–19.
60 *Anti-Suffrage Review*, no. 66, April 1914, p. 48.
61 *Anti-Suffrage Review*, no. 66, April 1914, p. 48.
62 *Anti-Suffrage Review*, no. 72, October 1914, p. 162.
63 *Anti-Suffrage Review*, no. 72, October 1914, p. 162.
64 In April 1914, for example, the *Review* exposed suffragists' deplorable practice of boycotting shops which refused to advertise its aims and publications in their window and of sending 'scurrilous letters and postcards to Anti-suffragists whose names and addresses appear with their correspondence in the public press'. See *Anti-Suffrage Review*, no. 66, April 1914, p. 44.
65 *Anti-Suffrage Review*, no. 72, October 1914, p. 162.
66 *Anti-Suffrage Review*, no. 72, October 1914, p. 162.
67 *Anti-Suffrage Review*, no. 72, October 1914, p. 162.
68 *Anti-Suffrage Review*, no. 72, October 1914, p. 162.

War and Dishonourable British Feminist   163

69 *Anti-Suffrage Review*, no. 73, November 1914, p. 171.
70 *Anti-Suffrage Review*, no. 73, November 1914, p. 171.
71 *Anti-Suffrage Review*, no. 75, January 1915, pp. 3–4.
72 *Anti-Suffrage Review*, no. 75, January 1915, pp. 3–4.
73 *Anti-Suffrage Review*, no. 83, September 1915, p. 67.
74 For example, see Lisa Tickner, *The Spectacle of Women: Imagery of the Suffrage Campaign, 1907–14* (London: Chatto & Windus, 1987).
75 *Anti-Suffrage Review*, no. 80, June 1915, p. 42–3.
76 *Anti-Suffrage Review*, no. 94, August 1916, pp. 57–59.
77 *Anti-Suffrage Review*, no. 102, April 1917, pp. 25–26.
78 Katie Holmes, 'Day Mothers and Night Sisters: World War I Nurses and Sexuality', in Joy Damousi and Marilyn Lake, eds., *Gender and War: Australians at War in the Twentieth Century* (Cambridge: Cambridge University Press, 1995) pp. 43–59, p. 43.
79 Holmes, 'Day Mothers and Night Sisters', p. 52.
80 Holmes, 'Day Mothers and Night Sisters', p. 44.
81 Sandra M. Gilbert, 'Soldier's Heart: Literary Men, Literary Women, and the Great War', in Margaret Randolph Higonnet, Jane Jenson, Sonya Michel and Margaret Collins Weitz, eds., *Behind the Lines: Gender and the Two World Wars* (New Haven and London: Yale University Press, 1987) pp. 197–226, p. 200.
82 Gilbert, 'Soldier's Heart', p. 200.
83 Gilbert, 'Soldier's Heart', pp. 211–212.
84 Gilbert, 'Soldier's Heart', p. 200.
85 *Anti-Suffrage Review*, no. 75, January 1915, pp. 4–5.
86 *Anti-Suffrage Review*, no. 75, January 1915, pp. 4–5.
87 *Anti-Suffrage Review*, no. 101, March 1917, p. 20.
88 *Anti-Suffrage Review*, no. 94, August 1916, pp. 63–64.
89 *Anti-Suffrage Review*, no. 87, January 1916, pp. 6–7.
90 *Anti-Suffrage Review*, no. 87, January 1916, pp. 6–7.
91 Gullace, *The Blood of Our Sons*, p. 156.
92 *Anti-Suffrage Review*, no. 75, January 1915, pp. 4–5.
93 *Anti-Suffrage Review*, no. 75, January 1915, pp. 4–5.
94 Gullace, *The Blood of Our Sons'*, p. 149.
95 See Jo Vellacott, *Pacifists, Patriots and the Vote: The Erosion of Democratic Suffragism during the First World War* (Basingstoke: Palgrave Macmillan, 2007) pp. 17–18, and Susan Kingsley Kent, *Making Peace: The Reconstruction of Gender in Interwar Britain* (Princeton: Princeton University Press, 1993) pp. 15–16.
96 Vellacott, *Pacifists, Patriots and the Vote*, p. 19.
97 Vellacott, *Pacifists, Patriots and the Vote*, p. 32.
98 Gullace, *The Blood of Our Sons*, p. 6.
99 Gullace, *The Blood of Our Sons*, p. 6.
100 Gullace, *The Blood of Our Sons*, pp. 5–6.
101 Gullace claims that men opposed to the war, like one of the Labour leaders Ramsay MacDonald, 'cast a shadow over the public perception of maleness as a sufficient quality of citizenship'. See Gullace, *The Blood of Our Sons*, p. 119.
102 Gullace details the parades organised by the Pankhursts and other members of the WSPU, funded and aided by the government. (Gullace, *The Blood of Our Sons*, Chapter 'Reinventing Womanhood. Suffragettes and the Great War for Citizenship', pp. 117–144.) The Pankhursts were not the only suffragists to lead marches. In April 1917, when suffrage was again on the government's agenda, Millicent Fawcett led a massive deputation to 10 Downing Street. The

march gathered together women and men from diverse corners of the nations, including Emmeline Pankhurst, representatives from 30 other suffrage societies, actresses, agricultural workers, ambulance drivers, bus conductors, policewomen, and VADs. See Gullace, *The Blood of Our Sons*, p. 160.
103 *Anti-Suffrage Review*, no. 112, February 1918, pp. 12–13.
104 *Anti-Suffrage Review*, no. 113, April 1918, pp. 17–18.
105 *Anti-Suffrage Review*, no. 113, April 1918, pp. 17–18.
106 Gullace, *The Blood of Our Sons*, p. 168.
107 *Anti-Suffrage Review*, no. 113, April 1918, pp. 17–18.
108 *Irish Citizen*, vol. 3, no. 16, 5 September 1914, p. 122.
109 *Irish Citizen*, vol. 3, no. 16, 5 September 1914, p. 122.
110 In Ireland, the Irish Women's Suffrage Federation stopped its suffrage activity, for example. See *Irish Citizen*, vol. 3, no. 15, 29 August 1914, p. 114. See also Grayzel, *Women and the First World War*, pp. 81–82.
111 *Irish Citizen*, vol. 3, no. 44, 20 March 1915, p. 340.
112 *Irish Citizen*, vol. 3, no. 44, 20 March 1915, p. 340.
113 *Irish Citizen*, vol. 3, no. 30, 12 December 1914, p. 236.
114 *Irish Citizen*, vol. 3, no. 20, 3 October 1914, p. 155.
115 *Irish Citizen*, vol. 3, no. 20, 3 October 1914, p. 155.
116 *Irish Citizen*, vol. 3, no. 20, 3 October 1914, p. 155.
117 *Irish Citizen*, vol. 3, no. 38, 6 February 1915, p. 290.
118 *Irish Citizen*, vol. 3, no. 22, 17 October 1914, p. 171.
119 *Irish Citizen*, vol. 4, no. 9, 17 July 1915, p. 58.
120 *Irish Citizen*, vol. 4, no. 10, 24 July 1915, p. 62.
121 *Irish Citizen*, vol. 4, no. 10, 24 July 1915, p. 62.
122 From 1912, the official organ of the WSPU was the *Suffragette*, which was established and edited by Christabel Pankhurst until the war broke out. Reflecting its heavily inflected wartime patriotic content, the *Suffragette* was relaunched as *Britannia* in 1915. See June Purvis, *Emmeline Pankhurst: A Biography* (London: Routledge, 2002) p. 195.
123 *Irish Citizen*, vol. 4, no. 17, 11 September 1915, p. 89.
124 *Irish Citizen*, vol. 4, no. 53, December 1917, p. 390.
125 *Irish Citizen*, vol. 7, no. 4, August 1919, p. 17.
126 *Irish Citizen*, vol. 7, no. 4, August 1919, p. 17.
127 *Irish Citizen*, vol. 7, no. 6, October 1919, p. 36.
128 *Irish Citizen*, vol. 3, no. 31, 19 December 1914, p. 244.
129 *Irish Citizen*, vol. 6, no. 4, September 1918, p. 622.

6 Shaming Manhood to Embody Courage

In 1916, in a series of purported 'Voices from the Front' printed in *Woman*, the paper of the conservative Australian Women's National League (AWNL), Australian men who avoided enlisting for the Great War were shamed. One soldier allegedly wrote to the women's journal to say that he wanted to 'ride a few Australian duffers up and down Collins-street, and use the spur'.[1] Another swore to give a number of fellows he knew—'chaps who ought to have gone but for their white livers'—'a daddy of a hiding'. 'White livers want to be kicked into a proper colour', he stated. Despite being exhausted from the demands of war, this soldier declared that he could 'go on kicking wasters for sixty or eighty hours at a stretch without turning a hair'.[2] The fate of the male shirker was to be a violent and ignominious one.[3]

Physical courage was an integral aspect of masculine codes of honour. Physical force, or the threat of it, underpinned honour codes. In times of war, courage was overwhelmingly constructed as masculine. This was the time in which manhood's courage was put to its ultimate test. Men who demonstrated that they were incapable of physical courage, generally, were shamed. Men who proved they were not up to the task of embodying this emotional virtue during the war were not only shamed but also subject to the threat of physical retaliation. They were vulnerable to the threat of male-on-male violence.

The women of the AWNL respected the separateness of gendered emotional regimes. They were empowered to vote, but, as the pages of *Woman* show, they passionately maintained the distinctiveness of the emotional standards guiding men's and women's undertaking of their political responsibilities. How then did these women feel justified in intruding sufficiently into masculine emotional regimes to attempt to shame cowardly men into action during the war? In this chapter, I look at the strategies the AWNL adopted to rationalise the fact that threats of violence aimed at male shirkers emanated from their women's paper. I analyse the way in which they defended their appropriation of elements of the codes that regulated men's engagements with physical courage and physical force. I also examine whether or not different groups of patriotic womanhood—British and Irish—deployed shaming tactics to expose their menfolk's potential or confirmed cowardice with the aim of rearming that manhood for war. How far did they transgress the gendered emotional regulations they claimed to adhere to while undertaking this shaming?

In Australia, for example, patriotic women were painfully keen for their menfolk to prove their young white nation's honour on overseas battlefields. Their fears that this manhood would prove itself inadequate—that it would demonstrate lethargy and cowardice—propelled these women to dangerously encroach on masculine emotional regimes in the attempt to shame their men into action. In Britain, however, at the heart of the Empire, patriotic women in the National League for Opposing Woman Suffrage (NLOWS) considered all attempted shaming of men on the part of non-combatant women to be not only distasteful but also a gross intrusion into masculine emotional regimes. Women's physical courage was not tried on the battlefields as men's was. How then could women shame men on the basis of cowardice?

In Ireland, matters differed again. Many patriotic Irish women alternated between affirming the Irish man's physical courage and shaming him for his deficient moral courage. That is, he had a natural capacity for jumping into the fray, but he was prone to lethargy and an unwise reliance on politicians rather than soldiers to do the job for him. Therefore, he had to be chided into action. Moreover, those men who were exercising their natural aptitude for militancy were doing so for the wrong reasons and for the wrong people. In the context of colonised Ireland, too many Irish men were to be found serving the needs of a hostile Imperial Army, for example. To nationalist women who claimed to share a proud heroic Celtic warrior past where men and women were equal in combat, affirming the Irish man's physical bravery was strategic. It demonstrated the integrity of their shared heritage. This tactic also worked to support Irish women's assertions—militant suffragists and militant nationalists—that they had an aptitude for physical force. They had the capacity to exercise a typically masculine form of courage.

During times of war, courage was a highly gendered concept and, although each community of patriotic womanhood studied in this book promoted their national manhood's actions in defence of their respective nations, not all approached the issue of masculine cowardice and shame in the same way. In this chapter, I analyse how different groups of nationalist womanhood challenged or confirmed the exclusively masculine nature of courage during World War One.

Courage and the Masculine Body

As I outlined in Chapter 2, the notion of honour developed over time but certain elements of it remained constant. When honour as a concept originated in the context of knighthoods and oaths of loyalty, it was tied to performance in military, political, and national matters. From the seventeenth to the nineteenth centuries, honour had grown to embrace the values and ideals of the influential middle classes. For example, by the Victorian era, it also denoted a man's sense of integrity or his moral dignity.[4] At this time, honour moved further away from its previously integral associations with the body and with violence.[5] However, as Robert Nye has argued, it never lost its connections to the old martial values of courage and strength.[6] This was never more apparent than when war broke out in 1914.

Throughout its history, honour continued to be gendered. Men's honour was tied to their performance in the public world, women's to the private. Only men had an active relationship with honour. Men could use violence to restore their own honour. Women could not. Women could not act in honour's name, but they could feel the pain of a man's dishonour. Their association with a shamed man compromised their shared reputation. This was important when it came to the issue of the honour of the nation.

Traditionally, adherence to codes of honour protected an individual man's reputation. But, as nation-states proliferated, honour also increasingly came to be linked to the reputation of the nation. An individual's actions had an impact on the regard in which the nation was held.[7] The nation's honour had to be protected at all costs, including through recourse to war.[8] The gendered nature of honour became even more pronounced at times of war when men were directed to exhibit an expansive capacity for courage and sacrifice to prove their individual honour while protecting that of their nation. Man's personal honour was tied to the nation's honour. If a man lacked courage, he shamed both himself and the nation to which he belonged.[9] Patriotic women felt keenly the threat and fear of national dishonour as exhibited through male cowardice. As I pointed out in Chapter 2, it was in their interests to protect the manly qualities of the nation: its integrity, courage, dignity, and pride. Yet the gendered relationship between womanhood and honour made it unclear as to whether or not this was within women's remit.

Courage was a vital component of honour codes. As such, it too changed over time. By the outbreak of the Great War, courage was considered to be both an atavistic and an evolved concept. As Nye explains it, courage was understood at the time to be the primitive biological instinct that ensured our ancestors' survival. This explained its atavistic dimensions. However, through modernity, courage had also grown to embrace a moral sensibility. This moral sensibility was encapsulated by the notion of heroism. Individuals were considered brave and heroic when they rose above egoism and sacrificed themselves for the good of the collective.[10] The collective was increasingly defined as the nation or society. Ordinary and extraordinary individuals who sacrificed their interests for society at large were hailed as heroes.[11] The moral and physical dimensions of courage developed alongside each other. Moral and physical courage intertwined to promote the cult of the hero. The extent to which homage was paid to the cult of the hero in the early twentieth century helps us to understand why society expected so many men to sacrifice themselves for the greater good by subjecting themselves to the horrors of war.

In order to facilitate the growth of this moral and physical notion of courage—to promote and accommodate the cult of the hero—new opportunities for demonstrating these combined values emerged. Sport was developed, for example, to provide one such avenue for the display of moral and physical courage. The ethos of Muscular Christianity—embodying the virtues of Christian manliness and exhibiting spiritual, moral, and physical purity—permeated the nineteenth- and early twentieth-century playing field.[12] Male players could abide by the rules of the gentleman—playing with fairness and honesty—while also exhibiting physical prowess and courage. The links between sport and the military strengthened. Sport, then, became a means of 'socially producing the moral and psychological conditions of the battlefield'.[13] In turn, modern notions of courage soon figured prominently in the list of values defining the modern armed forces.[14] Courage's antithesis—cowardice—was increasingly used by the military to regulate men's behaviour. That is, the military used men's fear of being labelled a coward as a way of ensuring their physical courage.[15] To conform to the honour codes regulating men's relations with each other, man had to deny or overcome fear and cowardice. As Ute Frevert elucidates, 'A man of honour was, in short, anything but a coward'.[16]

Nye argues that on the eve of the Great War, 'courage was absurdly overdetermined and performed an astonishingly wide variety of ideological tasks'. At the onset of the war, many nations' manhood felt the 'burden of courage'.[17] The military had adopted courage as one of its defining virtues. This emotional virtue was, therefore, to have an enormous influence on the millions of men enlisting for and being drafted into the armed forces during the international conflict. But courage was co-opted for reasons beyond the needs of the military. More generally, physical and moral courage was called on to counteract a range of reigning and intensifying social, political, and physical anxieties 'at home'. For example, concerns about the health of the material nation—its material and industrial progress—became inseparable from concerns about the strength and endurance of the human body.[18] Physical and moral courage was lauded as a solution to physical decadence. Also, courage became 'part of a complex male reaction to the crisis of masculinity provoked by the challenge of feminism'.[19] In the face of increasing displays of female empowerment, timidity in a man was considered femininely weak and shameful. By the beginning of the World War One, then, courage had become 'a universally prized quality'—for men.[20]

Shaming Irish Men: Physical Courage or Moral Courage?

Long before the advent of the Great War, nationalist women lauded the Irish man's natural capacity for physical courage in the face of combat. In the 1890s, the *Shan Van Vocht*[21]—a nationalist women's paper edited by two Belfast poets, Alice Milligan and Anna Johnson—declared that the Irish who possessed 'the reckless courage of their race want to be in the front of any fight'.[22] Years later, in 1910, another nationalist women's paper, the *Bean na hEireann* (the *Bean*),[23] assured readers that the Irish were a 'fighting race'. The 'love of battle . . . is in every Irishman's soul', it continued.[24] The Irish man's physical courage did not seem to be in doubt. On the contrary, it was accepted as a natural consequence of his ethnicity and his history. What was more dubious, however, was the strength and extent of his moral courage.

The Irish male may be naturally imbued with the spirit of battle, but this spirit was not yet awakened in every man. He had not yet chosen to fight for what was right—namely, Ireland's freedom from British rule. The *Shan Van Vocht* accused too many 'sons of Ireland' of going about their daily business instead of 'making ready to serve their Motherland'.[25] 'Could they but realize', the paper asserted, 'that theirs is the shame, that in the eyes of all the world their manhood is disgraced and their honour lost because in cowardly apathy they acquiesce in the subjection of their country.'[26] Driving the point home, the writer continued,

> For the man worthy of the name there cannot be even a moment of doubt; the path of duty is plain, *there is no other way to freedom*, and he who turns his face from it brands himself a coward and a slave.[27]

A few years later, the paper was moved again to invoke the ancient Celtic warrior to motivate Irish men to pick up arms in the name of Irish nationalism. The time had come for men of the nation to either make a commitment to or to bow out of the race for freedom. It was the time to decide: 'Action or inaction! submission or resistance!'

> Men of Ireland, what is your decision? Ponder on the facts submitted, count the odds, calculate your strength, realise the momentous question involved, think of the sacrifices of the past, the 'wild welter of a chaos' of the present, and like men decide, and, having decided, like men act. On your decision and your action rests the future of your race and nation.[28]

Irish nationalist women had thrown down the gauntlet. Irish men had to prove themselves worthy of their nation and of the legacy of its ancestral manhood. It was to their shame if they could not do so. Again, the Irish man's physical courage was not in doubt. Once he decided to go into battle, his physical courage was assured. Accusations of cowardice, then, related to his lack of moral fortitude.

Further accusations of moral lassitude emerged when Maude Gonne, renowned nationalist feminist actress and 'Ireland's Joan of Arc', criticised Irish men, not for their unwillingness to fight, but rather for their misguided choice of which army to enlist in.[29] In one of her highly controversial political pamphlets, 'The Famine Queen' (1900), Gonne declared that British imperialists were vampires who needed an army to help them to protect the plunder they siphoned off their victims.[30] The elite members of Britain's own manhood were decadent, as they feasted on the rich spoils of its empire. All that was left were a weakened and exhausted mass of workers who fed Britain's industrial machine and an emasculated middle class who administered its empire. Soldiers were needed. Therefore, it turned to Ireland, one of its possessions, to raid its as yet unspoilt manhood.[31]

Irish men were already proving their masculinity in international battle. They were fighting in the Second Boer War (1899–1902). However, this was not uncontentious. Irish men were demonstrating their manly courage by engaging in physical combat but too many were fighting on the wrong side. English news agencies, Gonne revealed, were busy telling the world that there were 16,000 Irishmen fighting on the side of the English in the Boer War. As a result, she wrote, 'the world is crying shame on Ireland, and saying that the Irish were miserable slaves and deserved to remain so'. The 'black sheep' who joined the English Army and wore the uniform of their oppressors, she argued, were committing an 'awful crime' against 'the Motherland'. They were guilty of bringing 'disgrace on their people'.[32]

Thankfully, a group of Irish men were proving that the Irish were not merely the servants of the British. Some were also fighting on the righteous side of the Boers in the war against British imperialism. Gonne portrayed John MacBride (Gonne's future husband and one of the executed leaders of the 1916 Easter Rising) and his Irish Brigade who were fighting against the English in the Transvaal as the men who had managed to 'save Ireland's honour at a time when there was great need'. The 'wonderful courage' exercised by these men and witnessed by the world would be responsible for restoring Ireland's reputation for physical and moral fortitude.[33] Gonne directed Irish men not to shame themselves by further wearing the livery of their oppressor. They were directed to find another outlet for their displays of bravery and physical prowess other than serving the needs of the Imperial Army.[34]

A decade later, the *Bean* saw need to reprint Gonne's anti-enlisting tracts, this time alongside the pleas of other prominent female nationalists, like Constance Markievicz. Markievicz warned Irish boys against enlisting in the Imperial Army 'under the spell, as it were, of the drunken swagger of the "Tommy"'. She cautioned Irish girls against falling prey to 'scarlet fever' (that is, stepping out with the 'Tommy').[35] Indeed, the *Bean* later asserted that, far from giving in to scarlet fever, Irish girls were to 'look upon the British soldier as an active enemy to her own people standing upon the other side of an impassable gulf, and to shrink from the burning dishonour of his touch if he touches against her on the footpath'.[36] Her fear of contracting his shame was imagined as visceral. Irish women were also to 'shun, hate and despise' those females who ignored this warning and instead kept company with British soldiers.[37] Shame was the only fate awaiting the Irish girl who fraternised with the enemy.

The need to reaffirm that Irish men were not lacking in physical courage reappeared in the pages of the *Bean*. This time it was joined by a confirmation of the Irish man's patriotism. 'It is not love for the British Army, or lack of patriotism that drives our men into English ranks', the editors of the paper argued, 'but just poverty and want.'[38] This poverty and want were the direct consequences of British imperial policies on the island. Women were called on to be especially strong in offering 'moral help and advice' to their menfolk who were wavering between the security of a military income and the insecurity of the civil world. They were called on to be the bulwarks against their menfolk succumbing to the devastations of colonisation and the trappings of imperialism.

The *Bean* declared that it shrank 'from accusing our countrymen of this slavishness'.[39] However, it felt it had little choice but to do so. Irish men were directed to arm themselves to take back their liberty.[40] Too many, the paper said, were relying on 'moral force'—on political persuasion. That was ineffective. The moral force pathway had reduced Irish politicians to 'flunkeyism', a slavish form of pandering to the British Government in order to secure Home Rule—a modest form of political autonomy.[41] The Irish man's challenge, then, was to recognise the limits of diplomacy as far as Britain was concerned and embrace his natural capacity for physical daring and courage instead. 'Physical Force', the *Bean* asserted, was really 'nothing more than a name for that privilege which is their [men's] inherited right'— that is, 'the right to die for Ireland on the field of battle'.[42] The words of nineteenth-century patriot John Mitchel were evoked: 'Let the man amongst you who has no gun sell his garment and buy one'.[43]

Irish nationalist women felt that it was acceptable to attempt to shame men out of their lethargy. It was their responsibility to show Irish men the errors of their ways and to reacquaint them with the legacies of their proud warrior past, one characterised by feats of physical and moral courage. They professed that they shrank from accusing their brothers of any form of cowardice, but they did it nonetheless. Perhaps their reason for not being more hesitant about doing this was because Irish women believed that they too shared that heritage. Irish men and women had once been subject to the same physical and emotional standards. The idea of separate, gendered emotional regimes was a foreign one. It was imposed on the Irish by the British during the colonising process. Irish nationalist women had taken on the challenge of shrugging off British impositions, including the idea that men and women should adhere to different emotional standards. Therefore, they did not believe that they were transgressing when they directed men to adopt the same emotional standards that they felt all Irish people—men and women—should abide by.

Of course, as discussed in Chapter 2, Irish women were realistic enough to understand that men were more equipped to actively seek to restore Ireland's honour. They had political power. They also had more avenues for demonstrating their military zeal. Irish nationalist feminists believed that the impediments in the way of them demonstrating emotional equality with their menfolk were merely physical. Given the same avenues as men, they could prove themselves emotionally up to the task. As we will see next, they used these assertions of equality to argue that they too could pick up arms whether in defence of their country or their sex.

Defending the Masculinity of British Manhood: The Feathers

Far from being hesitant to shame men for cowardice like members of the NLOWS, some British women embraced the notion—and the action—enthusiastically. For example, before conscription was introduced into Britain through the Military Service Act of 1916, a number of zealously patriotic women began attempting to shame men who had not enlisted in the British Army into doing so by handing out white feathers—symbols of cowardice.[44] These women acted under the influence of wartime propaganda, and celebrities such as Baroness Orczy, author of the popular *The Scarlet Pimpernel*, led them. However, if those women who doled out white feathers to men out of uniform expected their fellow female patriots to applaud them unanimously, they were to be disappointed. In many instances, fellow patriotic women instead accused them of being unwomanly. They were deemed guilty of shaming patriotic womanhood. This was a far cry from expectations of patriotic endorsement.

The official organ of the NLOWS, the *Anti-Suffrage Review* (the *Review*), was overwhelmingly in support of the war and of men enlisting to aid the war effort. However, this did not prevent it from opposing moves on the part of patriotic British women to try to shame men into enlisting. The *Review* opposed such moves on the grounds that women existed beyond the pale of men's emotional regimes. They could not, therefore, understand how those regimes operated. They could not embody the emotional virtues required of men whose actions were guided by honour codes. Here I refer to virtues like courage and chivalry. How then could they police the embodiment of those emotions?

In condemning women's policing of masculine emotions, the paper was drawing on a tactic that it had used time and again to block women's entry into the public world of politics. It countered feminists' demands for the vote by claiming that women were not trained in masculine emotional regimes. They could not understand the emotional virtues that composed men's honour codes, for instance. Those honour codes guided men's participation in the public world. Women, therefore, could not participate in a sphere regulated by emotional standards they could not adhere to.

In 1915, the *Review* noted that here 'in this beautiful western country which has done so well in recruiting there has been much indignation at the women who permitted themselves to hand white feathers to young men of whom they knew nothing'.[45] Such acts amounted to 'a gross insult, an impertinence'. 'There has', the article continued, 'been altogether too much scolding and hectoring on the part of women.'[46]

The *Review* echoed the sentiments of other indignant witnesses to this rising trend. For example, in her article on female patriotism and the white feather campaign, Nicoletta Gullace cited the case of correspondent for the *Times* Michael MacDonagh, who likewise expressed dismay as he watched this attempted shaming of British masculinity. He saw three young women trying to 'dishonour' young men on a tram. A look of contempt spoiled the 'lovely face' of one 'pretty wench' handing out the feathers, MacDonagh attested—a facial distortion that mimics the 'monstrous distortion of her femininity', according to Gullace.[47] There was nothing feminine or beautiful about publicly humiliating unknown men so that they would agree to enact violence in the name of the state.

These expressions of discomfort with certain forms of female patriotism fed into what Gullace has identified as an existing 'deep suspicion about female patriotism'. The white feather campaign hinged on 'a masculinized sexual identity policed by women'.[48] Its aim was to motivate men to enlist at the risk of appearing unmanly. Such men would appear unmanly if it looked as if they were unable or unwilling to live up to the demands of masculine honour codes and if it looked as if they were deficient in virtues such as courage and chivalry.

Yet, again, women did not share in the emotional world of men. How then could they police those emotions? War was not testing their honour as it was men's. They were not under the same intense pressure to prove their capability for physical bravery. Attempting to deprive men of their honour in this instance, then, was not an act of courage but a distortion of it. British women's attempts to impose shame on British manhood—instead of gently guiding it to fight for what was right, to draw on notions of Victorian gender idealism—brought shame only to those women for not being true to their womanhood. These women betrayed long-cherished notions of femininity. It was to their shame that they betrayed the community of womanhood to which they belonged in their misguided attempts to impose shame on the community of manhood to which they did not belong or understand. Their attempted incursion of masculine emotional spaces threatened to destabilise both masculine and feminine emotional regimes.

Australian Women Shaming Australian Men

As discussed in Chapter 4, patriotic Australian women believed that war was essential, not only for Australia to prove its manhood on the international stage but also for it to deliver a display of might that would work to deter any would-be invaders, particularly from Asia. They exerted considerable pressure then on Australian men to realise masculine ideals on the overseas battlefields. However, they feared that their manhood would not prove itself up to the task. Too many men were not enlisting for the war.

The shame of the cowardly shirker lurked. These women endeavoured to inspire Australian men to perform as they should. However, when it seemed that womanly guidance and inspiration was not enough, they resorted to shaming. As equal members of the Australian community, they felt justified in shaming Australian men for not honouring the values of Australia, for being un-Australian.

Patriotic Australian women attempted to shame unenlisted men for cowardice, but they displayed a level of ambivalence about doing so. The women of the AWNL had pledged to protect the distinctly gendered nature of the emotional regimes guiding men's and women's behaviour. How could they shame men without appearing unwomanly? How could they criticise Australian manhood for being cowardly and unmanly at the exact time that that manhood needed to prove its masculinity internationally? The quandary for these conservative women was how to attack the emotional fabric of Australian masculinity in order to spur it into action without affecting any lasting damage to masculine or feminine emotional regimes.

The AWNL's official organ, *Woman*, adopted particular strategies for addressing this dilemma. It directed itself to fellow women to ignite their patriotism. The paper appealed to women to inspire their menfolk to take their place at the front. It also targeted seemingly transgressive females—emotional mothers especially—who looked like they were not up to the task of performing patriotism at this crucial moment in the young white nation's history. *Woman* also directed itself to Australian men. In order to navigate the line dividing masculine and feminine emotional regimes, the paper adopted the strategy of appropriating male voices. Not only would that help to solve the problem of conservative women's discomfort with shaming men, but it might also prove more effective. Surely, men accusing other men of shameful cowardice would be more likely to motivate those transgressors to undertake a shameful self-assessment than shaming emanating from those situated outside that community of manhood? Therefore, *Woman* published letters and poems purportedly from men serving at the front. These letters and poems addressed themselves to shirkers at home. In this way, this exclusively female paper attempted to shame the male slacker who was either too dishonourable or too cowardly to do his manly duty. It also relied on these male testimonies to provide reluctant female patriots with a glimpse into the extraordinary difficulties facing Australia's manhood in the hope that this would spark their allegiance to selfless patriotism over realising selfish interests.

When the war broke out, the AWNL sent a greeting to Expeditionary Forces in Victoria: 'Quit you like men' for 'Australia's honour lies greatly in your hands'.[49] It then published periodic affirmations of Australian manhood's success in protecting the nation's honour. For example, within a year, in recognition of the supreme sacrifices made by Australian soldiers at the front and the mothers who sacrificed their sons to the war effort, *Woman* declared that 'this hour of trial has proved the mettle of our nation'.[50] Later still, the paper affirmed that the war had 'revealed to the hearts of the women of the Empire that every woman's son is capable of becoming a hero'. 'Every woman in this war has learnt the worth of a man—she has discovered him', *Woman* continued. 'He is once again her hero, her knight-errant.'[51] Chivalry, courage, and honour were proven to be very much alive amid the body of soldiers defending the nation and the Empire on the overseas battlefields.

Not surprisingly, this sense that Australia had proven itself was not isolated to members of the AWNL. As Joan Beaumont has argued, heroic reports of Australians' conduct during the war, particularly at Gallipoli, produced jubilant public responses. Headlines like 'Heroic Work, Holding Firm, Thrilling Narratives', 'How Australians Fight, "Extraordinarily Good Under Fire"', and 'Wonderful Dash and Bravery' worked to confirm what Beaumont says many Australians were waiting to hear—namely, that 'Australian men, though reared in a young nation in the Antipodes, were as good as the fighting men of old Europe. Possibly they were even better!'[52] As a body of manhood, its capacity for courage under fire seemed assured.

However, no matter how certain *Woman* professed itself to be on the issue of the nation's honour, fears that Australian manhood would prove itself deficient constantly surfaced in its pages. Throughout the war, the paper made continuous pleas for greater numbers of men to enlist to serve at the front. There are 'still hosts of virile young men', the paper argued early in 1915, 'to whom it has not yet been brought home that, in Lord Kitchener's words, the Empire "wants men, more men, and still men"'.[53] If these virile young men had no respect for the demands of Kitchener, would they at least listen to the 'piteous' appeals from their fellow Australians at the front? How many 'gallant lives' have been unnecessarily sacrificed for want of 'more men'?

> We in Australia, so far distant from the war zone, have been lulled into a false lethargy—a false sense of security, because we have known nothing of the fear and terror and horrors of an invasion. Protected by the strong right arm of the Motherland, our infant nation has grown to manhood, enjoying the priceless privilege of peace.[54]

Yet the suspicion that Australia had not yet grown into its manhood prevailed. We can no longer afford to live in 'a fool's paradise', *Woman* entreated. Its cry was 'we *can* do more, we *should* do more, we *must* do more'.[55] Instead, too many Australian citizens were demonstrating that they were 'slack' citizens of the nation and the Empire.[56] At this point, it seemed that *Woman*'s complaints were less about the Australian man's capacity for physical bravery and rather his lack of moral courage. He did not seem to know to fight for what was right.

The following year, this problematic situation had still not abated. There continued to be a disconcertingly visible and superfluous presence of able-bodied men on the Australian landscape. 'Strong, lusty young men (in many cases not married)' were opting to stay by their farms, president of the AWNL Eva Hughes remarked. Sometimes, these young men had brothers also claiming the same exemptions from active service. Such a collection of farm workers was unnecessary and wasteful at this time of supreme national crises, she declared.[57] Men needed to sacrifice themselves for war. Women needed to sacrifice their men for the sake of the war, for 'the honour of the British Empire, for the honour of our beloved Australia'.[58] This was a damning indictment of the young nation's response to its first chance to prove its manhood on the global stage.

As in Britain, female patriots across Australia formed part of the wartime propaganda machine as they encouraged or tried to shame men into enlisting. Women distributed literature on trains and trams, threw baked goods with messages in them encouraging men to enlist (what Beaumont calls a kind of fortune cookie), hassled individual 'shirkers' (without enquiring as to their personal circumstances), and ostracised non-enlisted men by refusing to socialise with them. In Australia, male sports were targeted in particular. For example, women were instructed by other women and by the jingoistic press to refuse to participate in any sporting activity with men who wasted their time with such frivolous ventures while their brothers risked their lives at the war front. In another notable exhibition of women's sports shaming, newspapers reported that over one thousand black armband-wearing women lined the approach to an Australian race-course, forming what was referred to as 'a guard of dishonour', while 20 drums beat a tattoo in order to deter male race-goers from prioritising entertainment over patriotic service.[59] Shaming was not left only to the country's women. Some places of employment sacked workers whom they deemed to be 'shirkers', for instance. The State also assumed a leading role in targeting shirkers. It closed down leisure and sporting facilities and suspended competitive sports when it seemed that those places were harbouring slackers and idlers.[60] Still, no matter how broad-ranging wartime shame and shaming were, the image of the patriotic female shamer captures the historical imagination for what Gullace previously asserted was the 'monstrous distortion of her femininity' caused by her shaming.[61]

It was not only Australian men letting the country down. While many women—like those of the AWNL—continued to demonstrate that they were up to the task of sacrificing themselves and their sons up to the war effort, other women did not. *Woman* drew readers' attention to the supremely womanly sacrifice of mothers who gave their sons up to war and lost them eternally. For instance, the paper cited the example of one mother from the Riverina district of New South Wales 'who had sent six sons to the war'. Two sons were already dead, it reported. Her husband had died before this. Despite these tragedies, and as a sign of her devotion to the nation and the Empire, this grieving mother said she would not do things differently. Her boys were doing their duty to her and to their country. 'She was as truly a heroine as those who had won the Victoria Cross', *Woman* asserted.⁶² Such stories were intended to inspire women's selflessness, but, as we will see next, they were not always successful. Some women, through a misguided application of maternal or wifely love, still refused to allow their sons and husbands to prove their courage, and therefore their masculinity, on the battlefields. Hence the paper's resort to the more negative tactic of shaming.

Individual men and individual women were guilty of letting Australia down, but, more generally, it also seemed as if the young Commonwealth was determined to prove itself incapable of acting honourably. In 1915, *Woman* asked, 'Has our Empire's need fully gripped our heart as a nation? Do we realise how deeply our interests and our honour are bound up in the successful prosecution of this war?'⁶³ By 1916, the paper responded in the negative. It revealed that Australia was about to renege on the number of troops it had promised to deliver up for the war effort because it did not have enough enlisted men. The Australian Government was about to lower the number of reinforcements it promised Britain from 300,000 to just over 200,000. *Woman*'s appeal to the government was to restore the initial figure and by doing so 'not allow the fair name of Australia to be besmirched by the disgrace of a promise unfulfilled, a great obligation ignored'; the plea was to see 'that Australia's name is not dishonoured'.⁶⁴ This was a matter, the paper said, that would surely 'make Australia blush!'⁶⁵ The shame would be Australia's not only for failing to honour a contractual agreement but also for refusing to force its manhood to demonstrate its capacity for valour on the battlefield.

Woman's Shaming Tactics: Appropriating Male Voices and Male Threats of Violence

Woman had little sympathy for women who hesitated to send their menfolk to war. As a paper by and for women, it addressed itself to those females who shirked their duty to their country, generally, and their menfolk, specifically—or at least to women who might know those shirking women. It adopted several different strategies in the process. In the first place, in a series of 'Voices from the Front' or from 'the Trenches', it appropriated male voices. In this way, it seemed to offer its female readers a sneak peek into how men regulated their relations with each other—an otherwise inaccessible glimpse into the operation of masculine honour codes. The paper continued this approach in its 'children's pages'. Women and older children were invited to use this privileged access to masculine worlds to influence those around them to improve their patriotic performances. Secondly, *Woman* used humiliating images of male-on-male violence to write male shirkers out of existing honour codes and, therefore, out of masculinity. And, thirdly, the paper exposed the shame of those women who attempted to disrupt the proper operation of masculine honour codes. Mothers, sisters, and sweethearts, *Woman* said, were guilty of influencing their menfolk to shame themselves—and Australian manhood more generally—by begging them to not sign up for the war. These women were guilty of interfering with the proper running of masculine emotional regimes when they prevented men from exercising their right to prove their courage on the field of battle.

Woman was adamant about the shame of the man who refused to enlist. Shame emasculated the shirker. It robbed him of his manhood: 'Any man who shirks the call does not deserve the name'.[66] Come 'play the man' before it is too late was the paper's 1915 directive.[67] By 1916, the call was the same.

> For the able-bodied man of military age to shirk his duty to defend his country now is also a scandal and a sin against humanity—against his better self, which may be will one day in the future rise up and confront him—when it is too late.[68]

The message was that it was not too late for the male shirker to redeem himself and his manhood. He was offered the chance to reform, thereby reversing his shame. Australia still needed him.

Doubtless, those contributing to *Woman* considered that this message to shirkers, and to the women who supported them, would be more effective if it came from the mouths or pens of men who were already serving at the front. Accordingly, throughout 1916 and 1917, years that were dominated by the fiery debate over conscription (discussed in Chapter 4), the paper published a series of letters and articles that were purportedly written by Australian soldiers. Whether real or imagined, these male soldiers offered readers insight into supposed feelings of 'good' Australian men. The letters were largely addressed to mothers, sisters, and sweethearts. They were characterised by expressions of disbelief, anger, and resentment. They were also filled with images of and inducements to violence. They affirmed the masculinity of the soldier and the shame of the shirker while exposing the selfish emotionalism of those women who refused to sacrifice their happiness—and their sons—for the war. Women were directed to understand that their pride in their serving sons would make them happy. They were also asked to understand that their menfolk's happiness lay in the chance offered to them to prove their courage alongside the men of the Allied nations as they fought to protect democracy. In war, the only avenue to happiness for men and women was through exhibitions of male courage.

For example, one 1916 letter declared, 'Mother, if I go down, you know you would rather have me die a man than live as your cold-footed boy, now, wouldn't you?'[69] Cold-footed referred to cowardice. Another letter from a soldier to his mother expressed relief that by enlisting he had managed to avoid shaming the multiple intersecting communities to which he belonged: 'I'm glad that I've not disgraced the family name, nor the Australian name, nor the British name'.[70] In the lead up to the second conscription referendum in December 1917, *Woman* endorsed such sentiments: 'Liberty could not live where there was not valor. It was the prerogative of the brave, and was never held by cowards. Shame and dishonour were worse than death'.[71]

Yet, it seemed that too many 'cold-footed rotters' were refusing to bolster the ranks in the trenches and were instead to be found playing football back home.[72] By this stage in the war, when Australian men had been offered countless opportunities to enlist and Australia's desperate need for enlistments was well advertised, all shirkers were considered cowards. It was no longer enough to simply label them unpatriotic. Poetry was deemed an appropriate vehicle for exposing the cowardly shirker's shame.

A soldier who had been invalided at Gallipoli and was now suffering from shell shock wrote a poem addressed to his compatriots who were evading their duty, *Woman* reported. Why, he asked the shirker, 'should you funk and refuse to go?' He continued,

> You left us there on that fire-swept beach,
> Where death reigned supreme.

There was little to do but try to motivate them into action or, failing that, paint a picture of their future of ignominy:

> So tread lightly, boys, as you pass the graves
> Of heroes lying here.
> Deserted they died as at Sari Bair,
> Betrayed by their own, who had left them there
> To the lyddle's blast and the shrapnel's tear,
> And a grave on Aghyl Dere.[73]

In another piece entitled 'Is It Nothing to Them? A Soldier's Opinion of Australian Shirkers', a soldier asked if the sacrifices of Australian men were nothing to those refusing to enlist:

> What is wrong with Australia?
> Surely there are some MEN left.[74]

The conclusion was that shame was the only reward for those who 'had not taken their places amongst the MEN of the world'.[75] The shame of the coward who did not embrace the opportunity to demonstrate his bravery confirmed his exclusion from the community of manhood.

Not all shaming voices were male. Female poets, too, joined the crusade:

> Thou dost tarry, while laggards are still in our midst
> Who tarnish Australia's name—
> Caring naught, though the glory of 'Anzac' should end
> In a sequel dark with shame.[76]

Again, the warning was that exclusion from the community of brave manhood faced the man who gave in to cowardice:

> No part may they have in the joy of Thine advent
> Who heard not their Country's call—
> No part in the honour awaiting our heroes
> Who willingly offered all.[77]

Even non-Australians took on the mission of motivating Australian men to enlist. Anglo-Irish polar explorer, Sir Ernest Shackleton, made a direct appeal to Australians, as reported in the children's pages of *Woman*. He entreated Australian men to 'fight because you have the hearts of men, and because if you fail you will know yourselves in your own inner consciousness to be forever shamed'. To Australian women, Shackleton said: 'Be as the women of Rome, who said to husbands, brothers, and fathers, "Come back victorious or on your shields" '.[78]

Violence underpinned masculine honour codes so it is not surprising that violence was also a consistent feature of these shaming 'Voices from the Front'. Women existed beyond the pale of male honour codes; therefore, they could not threaten violence against men who transgressed those codes. Men could, though. By appropriating male voices, *Woman* could threaten or imagine violence being done to men's bodies in a way that ordinary women could not.[79] Women with male relatives serving in the war often expressed anger at shirkers who had abandoned those men to meet their fate. Their refusal to enlist reduced the possibility of those male relatives returning home alive or uninjured. Therefore, including threats of violence in their writing was also a likely means for patriotic women to channel any anger or aggression they harboured towards men they considered cowardly—violent feelings for which there were few respectable avenues of expression.

For example, and as outlined in the opening paragraph of this chapter, in 1916 *Woman* published a letter from a soldier supposedly serving at the front. He expressed his desire to inflict violence on those men who were too afraid to test the limits of their courage on the battlefields. He desired to 'ride a few Australian duffers up and down' a busy Melbourne street in order to advertise their ignominy. Furthermore, he wanted to 'use the spur'.[80] *Woman* vividly painted a picture of the public spectacle of man's shame.

Another 'soldier' promised to return home to enact violence on the bodies of those cowardly men—men with 'white livers'—who ought to have gone to the war. He wanted to give those 'chaps' 'a daddy of a hiding'. 'White livers want to be kicked into a proper colour', he stated. Then, in a statement that was as ludicrous as it was angry, he added that despite being exhausted from the demands of war, he could 'go on kicking wasters for sixty or eighty hours at a stretch without turning a hair'.[81] The only thing that could deliver this assertion from the depths of absurdity was the fact that the threatened violence was to be inflicted on a cowardly shadow of manhood by a courageous model of manhood—one which was currently testing its capacity for heroism in the theatres of war.

In the gathering pace of the campaign leading up the second conscription referendum in 1917, more male voices were appropriated. This time their remit was to convince women that they must vote 'yes' for conscription. In September of that year, for example, 'Voices from the Front' reported another soldier affirming that war was 'man's game, and a man's death'.[82] The same soldier wrote to his mother informing her that a friend that he had enlisted with had just been killed. In painting a heroic picture of the dead man, the soldier reported that the dying man's last directives to his comrades in battle were to turn him around on his stretcher to face the enemy lines so that he could die facing his enemy. He was granted his wish. 'I wonder', the son wrote to his mother, 'if the shirkers out there heard his last words would it shame them?'[83] The implication was that it was much more desirable to be the mother of a dead hero than a living idler and coward.

Word of the shame of the slacker in Australia also travelled through the trenches, *Woman* reported. In another letter purported to be from a soldier to a mother—this time an English soldier to his mother—Australia was depicted as a place where things were 'extremely bad'. Australian soldiers returning to the trenches brought tales of Australian shirkers. These tales were so shameful, they made even the non-Australian soldier's 'blood boil'. 'Poor old Aussie is certainly being ruined', the English soldier lamented, 'while we are over here doing our best for her.'[84] Violence again pervaded the letter. However, this time the threat of violence had escalated. Now it was less the pain and the humiliation of the spur and more the execution of the coward or the deserter that was evoked:

> Why they don't shoot a few of them I don't know. Wait till the A.I.F. gets back, and things will begin to hum then, and we'll jolly soon get rid of these out-and-out shirkers and anti-conscriptionists. It makes me too wild, mother. I can't say any more. It seems that Aussie is not a very inviting place to go to at present.[85]

Woman evoked a sense of empire manhood that some Australian men were exempting themselves from through their cowardice and lack of adherence to manly duty. For their transgressions, these men were to be subject to the violence that underpinned honour codes. Whereas earlier in the war, it appeared as if they might redeem themselves after being exposed to humiliating aspects of male-on-male violence—namely, the public parade and the spur. Now, in 1917, the sense was that there was little or no chance of reform. By this late stage in the game, through evocations of military execution, the emphasis was less on shaming them into redeeming themselves and more on ostracising them, removing them, physically and emotionally, from the community of Australian and empire manhood.

Woman's Shaming Tactics: Allowing Women a Glimpse Into Masculine Emotional Regimes

Australian men were coming up short in the eyes of the women of the AWNL, but Australian women were also subject to their judgment. As mentioned earlier, women could interfere with the proper working of honour codes too. Through feminine weakness, for example, they could hold their men back from acquitting themselves like men/MEN. In the attempt to make those women realise the destructive impact that they were having on Australia's manhood, *Woman* produced stories of mothers and wives who undertook the journey away from indulgent displays of feminine weakness and selfishness towards the redemption that came with self-sacrifice.

The irreparable damage to a man's soul and psyche caused by a woman 'keeping him back' was made clear in the 'Children's Corner' of *Woman*. A potential soldier lamented the fact that he succumbed to his sweetheart's desire that he avoid the dangers of war. He was dishonoured from that day, he said.

> Oh Mothers, Sweethearts, Sisters, Wives,
> Think of this thing you do!
> Who hold us here in shameful peace,
> Dishonoured—shamed—untrue.
> Crowned by your brave, unflinching hands,
> We longed to win or fall,
> Or die, at Duty's call!
> Had you but thought of Honour then,
> Needing your courage too,
> You had not heard that bitter cry,
> Accusing—Was it you?[86]

One word from her, and he would have gladly marched off to war. Then his soul and his pride would have been redeemed. He was capable of courage—moral and physical. He was ready to exercise his right as a man to test his physical courage and, more than that, to do so while fighting on the side of right. But his 'sweetheart' held him back. She interfered with the proper working of the gendered emotional regime he was subject to. Through her lack of womanly courage, she made a coward of a man who had the expansive capability for exhibiting valour on the battle field.

Another 'Children's Corner' story, this one written by a 16-year-old boy, revolved around the notion that 'The Mother' was the 'Greatest Hero of the War' because she helped her son to overcome his initial hesitancy about enlisting. The narrative ended triumphantly with her son returning and taking part in a jubilant motorcar ride through the city.[87] His courage was paraded publicly. In yet another story, this one between a wife and a husband, the errant wife, who initially held her man back, responded to his unhappiness over the fact that he would have to tell their boy that he 'hid behind his mother's skirts' by letting him go to war. Even though she missed her husband, she was 'a happier woman' because he had restored his sense of honour. She had enabled him to test his courage. Each had 'done their bit'. The moral of this story was 'to-day a man **should** think of **self**, and where his direct duty lies. A woman must **forget** herself and know where **her** duty lies' (bold in original).[88] Masculine courage ensured men's and women's happiness.

Women who did not 'do their bit' during the conscription referenda found the pathway to redemption much more difficult than the errant wife in the pages of *Woman* because the results of national elections were not as easily overturned as a wife's decision to let her husband enlist. For example, in a letter apparently written before the first referendum but published in the paper afterwards, one soldier at the front appealed to his mother and sister to influence their friends do the right thing:

> Mother, you and Cis, for God's sake, influence everybody you can. Of course you'll vote 'Yes' yourselves, I know, but do try and secure some waverers. We must have more men to relieve us oftener, and to take the places of the sick and wounded. There are always some folks who can be roped in easily. Do your share for my sake, and for the sake of Australia. Surely Australia won't turn us down! If she does, then it is no place for any of us to return to. I shouldn't want to see it again for one.[89]

The editor, it seemed, was privy to more than simply the letter from the soldier to the mother and sister because she included the postscript:

> (The receipt of this letter has plunged a mother and sister into great distress, for they had been 'roped in' by the anti-conscriptionists, and had voted No!)[90]

Published in December 1916, there was still time—and given the follow-up referendum—there was still opportunity for 'Mother' and 'Cis' to redeem themselves. For women voting 'no' in the 1917 plebiscite, there would be no reprieve. As another 'soldier' assured his mother after the failed second referenda, 'You and our sisters will never have the finger of scorn pointed at you like some of the Australian mothers will'.[91] By denying their menfolk the opportunity to demonstrate their courage, these women shamed themselves and their men.

Irish Women Challenge the Gendered Nature of Courage

The pages of the Australian *Woman* were rife with allusions to the masculine nature of courage. This assurance suited their patriotic purposes during wartime. Only men could fight, therefore courage was badged as manly. Irish feminist nationalists, however, were not content to allow assumptions about the intrinsic link between courage and the masculine body to go unchallenged. The war threw up examples of women's courage that fed these feminists' theories about the malleability or even the inappropriateness of gendered emotional regimes. One such example was that of executed British nurse, Edith Cavell.

In 1915, the Germans executed Cavell, a British nurse working in a Belgian hospital, for being part of an operation that sheltered enemy soldiers and then guided them into neutral Holland.[92] Accounts of Cavell's death varied across many of the Allied countries, but one common thread connected these narratives and that was that 'chivalrous understandings of patriarchal warfare surmised that it was essentially wrong to kill a woman'.[93] In her study of the memory of Cavell, Katie Pickles asserts that by the 1970s, amid the women's movement's claims for equality, reactions to Cavell's execution had transformed from initial views of it as the unchivalrous murder of a woman to it forming an accepted if tragic aspect of wartime culture.[94] From the time of her death, however, Irish feminist nationalists had already argued this point. They also used the British nurse's experience to argue that women were as capable as men of displaying of moral and physical courage during wartime, and beyond.

In 1916, the British *Review* used the example of Cavell to juxtapose her womanly martyrdom to the shameless disruptiveness of wartime suffragist nurses who were using their power over wounded soldiers to continue campaigning for the vote (discussed in the previous chapter). To make its point, the paper recalled the transgressive behaviour of the pre-war suffragette. Nothing has been more offensive, the article declared, than

> the braying of trumpets, the processions, the meetings of Militant Suffragettes, who horrified the civilised world by their wanton destruction of property, their attempts, in some cases too successful, to destroy sacred buildings, their threats to the clergy, their profane interruptions of God's services in fine, these forerunners of the Huns, who only stopped short of taking the human lives their antics had certainly endangered.[95]

And yet here, amid death and destruction on a mass and tragic scale, suffragists were to be found preying on sick and maimed male bodies. Their form of womanhood was diametrically opposed to that exhibited by Cavell. Cavell, the paper attested,

> in the full flower of her splendid womanhood she passed on, murdered by the perpetrators of such acts as the Suffragettes have not been ashamed to commit, and she will live forever, not only in the Courts above, but in the memory of her sister women and the true manhood of the whole world.[96]

Cavell was exalted as a supreme model of womanliness by the anti-suffragist paper. Her act of self-sacrifice in order to support male soldiers ensured for her this mantle of sanctified femininity.

As mentioned, women did not have to wait for the 1970s to participate in feminist debates about the rightness or wrongness of the manner of Cavell's death. The gendered nature of chivalry and war formed part of feminist debates at the time. For example, Irish feminist nationalists used the Cavell case to argue that women were as capable of courage as men. They also used responses to her death to object to constant references to cowardice as feminine. Not only were these references demeaning to women, they were also woefully inaccurate.

The *Irish Citizen* (the *Citizen*), official organ of the Irish Women's Franchise League (IWFL), was almost amused at the male press's expressed shock when confronted with stories of women's bravery. Why was the male press so perplexed that Cavell reportedly accepted the extreme penalty 'like a brave woman, without flinching or whining'?[97] It 'does not surprise anyone who knows anything of womankind', the paper responded. 'Women have far more of the cold, two-o'clock-in-the-morning courage than men: had they not, the race would long since have perished.'[98]

As suffragists and feminists, the contributors to the paper declared that they were not going to become sentimental about Cavell's fate. They knew the horrors of war. They also knew the unique horrors facing women—disenfranchised women who had no say in engaging in mass conflict in the first place. 'Many women indeed', one article stated, 'are compelled through their sex to suffer exquisite tortures in war, compared with which Edith Cavell's death was clean and merciful.'[99] The sentimental squeamishness and 'heroics' of the men who were now going about preaching about the Cavell atrocity left the *Citizen* a little cold. These were the same men—'honourable members' and members of the press—who not that long ago were to be seen standing and 'jeering behind closed gates to see the police kick and batter' suffragist women. These were the same men who were found 'suggesting refinements of torture for suffragettes'. Yet here they were now engaging in grief-stricken histrionics. 'One vote', the paper avowed, was 'worth a bushel of this kind of chivalry.'[100]

Continued media attention given to Cavell pressed the *Citizen* to hold her up as an example of women's capabilities for embodying emotional qualities that were purportedly masculine. Women were told constantly that they could not fight. They were to benefit from men's physical protection. Yet Cavell died for men. She was not sheltered by men; on the contrary, she sheltered them. And she knew the consequences if she were caught. 'The Germans say that', the *Citizen* affirmed. Moreover, 'inasmuch as Miss Cavell showed herself truly "masculine" in her courage and capacity, it would have been a derogation of dignity to have given her any but a masculine death'.[101]

Commentators from renowned Irish feminist pacifist Louie Bennett to Irish playwright and suffragist George Bernard Shaw were used to support the assertion that feminists did not hide behind their sex when they claimed equal rights. They expected equal penalties for their actions. They did not ask for 'chivalry'.[102] Shaw was cited as claiming that to go on and on about 'chivalry' was a false tactic, for had Cavell survived and returned to England and demanded her rights by breaking windows, she would have been 'mobbed, insulted, and subjected to gross physical violence with the full approval of many of the writers who are now canonising her'. What we can do, the article argued, is to enfranchise her sex in recognition of her 'valour'.[103] That would be a more fitting recognition of women's capabilities for typically 'masculine' qualities than mere sentimental homage. Woman's displays of manly valour surely demonstrated her capability for assuming the masculine role of fully enfranchised citizen and fulfilling all the responsibilities that came with that. Armed service in wars that women voted for would be one of those expected responsibilities.

Besides, the *Citizen* argued that countries such as France and England should not be up in arms at the Germans' treatment of women in wartime. The French executed two German women in 1915, the paper asserted.[104] And, quoting a 'German semi-official organ', the paper directed the English to 'recall the treatment of Boer women under Lord Kitchener in the Boer War'.[105] It was not only German and French but also English chivalry that war cast into doubt.

The *Citizen* took its critique of the links between sex and courage further. It issued strong objections to the common and mindless coupling of cowardice with femininity. Even before Cavell's death, the paper reported that Mr T. M. Healy, M.P.—amid laughter and applause—labelled as cowardly men who were avoiding enlisting, and suggested that they should have fled the country 'in petticoats'.[106] Whatever we think of their actions, the author said,

> the method of expressing Mr Healy's disapproval every self-respecting woman will take exception to. The view that cowardice is essentially feminine: that courage is the attribute and monopoly of the male, is surely benighted in a country whose womanhood has always been famous for its heroic qualities.[107]

The *Citizen* invoked the right to recall Irish women's ancient warrior heritage to argue that Irish women were capable of embodying courage. But they also argued this point for women more generally.

The following year, the *Citizen* published a similar protest, this time against the use of the term 'Petticoat Brigade'. Why was this the worst form of abuse that some men felt they could fling at fellow men?

> Are women, the petticoat wearers, synonymous with slackness and cowardice; is there no viler epithet to be flung at a man than a reminder

if his mother's sex? Do men fancy they have a monopoly of courage, of heroism, of the civic virtues? They might take a lesson in the same from the sex that wears the petticoat.[108]

One such mundane, non-war example of woman's courage that men could learn from was that exhibited by a young girl who died after jumping into a Dublin canal to save her drowning sister. The *Citizen* claimed that the jingoistic press represented bravery as 'a precarious virtue, only preserved by men murdering their fellows in war. Without war, it is hinted, bravery must perish'.[109] And yet, here was proof that courage existed beyond the pale of male warfare. Women performed courage on a daily basis. More than that, women performed bravery without expectation of any reward. This girl's 'heroic deed', the *Citizen* stated, was one for which there were no medals. The girl's heart-broken mother would receive no Victoria Cross for her efforts and sacrifice.[110] If women were as capable as men of embodying courage—of performing 'heroic' deeds—then surely honour codes, of which courage was an essential component, should be open to them. Surely, then they could take their place as enfranchised citizens alongside their menfolk.

Conclusion

It suited the purposes of many groups of patriotic womanhood to deem courage a solely masculine attribute from the outset of the war. Pro-war propaganda applauded man's capability for heroism. Heroism required moral and physical courage. Men worldwide were directed to acquit themselves like men/MEN. They were instructed to prove their valour on the battlefields. Courage and masculinity were represented as synonymous. The male-only battlefield was promoted as the ultimate sphere for the testing of man's courage.

In Britain, conservative women continued to work to protect the boundaries around the masculine emotional regime. Pre-war militant suffragists had already attempted to erode the gendered nature of those regimes by using physical force to argue that they could exercise the same political responsibilities as men. Now, during times of war, it was ever more important to protect the integrity of those regimes so that British men could acquit themselves in a manly way on the battlefields. Interfering with the workings of gendered emotional regimes would not help men to face the ultimate test of their manliness. Women should refrain from attempting to impose shame on men whose interiorities they had no insight into.

In Australia, patriotic women considered that they had no choice but to interfere with masculine emotional regimes. Their national manhood was a masculine community that was still under development. The manliness and the maturity of their young white nation was still a work-in-progress. The war had provided Australians with their first real opportunity of demonstrating their manly virtues. To ensure a successful 'baptism by fire', which patriotic women so dearly desired, their menfolk had to prove their courage under that fire.[111] Conservative women, then, took it upon themselves to instruct Australian men about how to go about doing that. However, the degree of ambivalence they felt about intruding in masculine emotional regimes was demonstrated by the shaming strategies they adopted. For example, by appropriating men's voices (apparently those of soldiers from the front) to deliver the words of shame, they attempted to justify their female-on-male shaming. This technique also allowed these women to evoke the threat of violence that honour codes dictated would be the fate of any man transgressing reigning codes of honour. By not embodying courage—by proving themselves to be cowards—male shirkers deserved to be the targets of such threats. Women could not threaten violence because they existed beyond the pale of masculine honour codes. Therefore, male voices were employed to do so. By appropriating male voices to deliver these threats, patriotic Australian women interfered with masculine emotional regimes without seeming to do so.

In Ireland, matters were different. Irish nationalist women alternated between affirming the Irish man's physical courage and shaming him for his deficient moral courage. British colonisation had created a situation whereby Irish men were tempted to channel their natural aptitude for bravery and skill for fighting into the service of the British Imperial Army. Too often, the Irish man exhibited a lack of moral courage by giving in to this temptation—donning the livery of his enemy—and fighting for what was clearly not in Ireland's best interest. However, Irish nationalist women's approach to bravery and gender went well beyond confirming man's capacity for acting heroically, whether guided by moral courage or not. These women also drew on stories about the proud warrior past that they shared with their menfolk to argue that they were emotionally equality to Irish men. In doing so, they challenged the assumed masculine nature of courage. They used these assertions of emotional equality to promote their claim that women—Irish women at least, but doubtless women in general too—were absolutely justified in picking up arms in defence either of their sex or their country.

Notes

1 *Woman*, vol. 9, no. 9, 1 November 1916, p. 247.
2 *Woman*, vol. 9, no. 9, 1 November 1916, p. 247.
3 Joanna Bourke states that shirking in wartime was regarded as 'an evasion of man's duty to the state and to other men'. See Joanna Bourke, *Dismembering the Male. Men's Bodies, Britain and the Great War* (London: Reakton Books, 1996) p. 78.
4 Charles Stewart, 'Honor and Shame', in James D. Wright, ed., *International Encyclopedia of the Social and Behavioral Sciences*, 2nd ed., vol. 11 (Amsterdam: Elsevier, 2015) p. 181.

Shaming Manhood to Embody Courage 189

5 See Pieter Spierenburg, 'Masculinity, Violence, and Honor: An Introduction', in Pieter Spierenburg, ed., *Men and Violence: Gender, Honor, and Rituals in Modern Europe and America* (Columbus: Ohio State University Press, 1998) pp. 1–29, p. 6. Both Spierenburg and Stewart support an uneven history of honour-violence globally. See Spierenburg, 'Masculinity, Violence, and Honor', and Stewart, 'Honor and Shame'. For a specific discussion of honour and violence in relation to the construction of modern masculinity, see Robert Shoemaker, 'Male Honour and the Decline of Public Violence in Eighteenth-Century London', *Social History*, vol. 26, no. 2 (2001) pp. 190–208. Also see Carolyn Strange, Robert Cribb, Christopher E. Forth, eds., *Honour, Violence and Emotions in History* (London: Bloomsbury Academic, 2014).
6 Robert A. Nye, *Masculinity and Male Codes of Honor in Modern France* (Oxford: Oxford University Press, 1993) p. 16.
7 Pieter Spierenburg, 'Masculinity, Violence, and Honor', pp. 11–12.
8 Ute Frevert, 'Wartime Emotions: Honour, Shame, and the Ecstasy of Sacrifice', *International Encyclopedia of the First World War* (1914–1918 Online) encyclopedia.1914–1918-online.net/article/wartime_emotions_honour_shame_and_the_ecstasy_of_sacrifice, accessed 15 June 2017, p. 4.
9 Ute Frevert, 'Wartime Emotions', p. 9.
10 For a more nuanced discussion of the evolution of courage, see Nye, *Masculinity and Male Codes of Honor in Modern France*, pp. 216–228.
11 Nye, *Masculinity and Male Codes of Honor in Modern France*, p. 218.
12 Andrew Parker and Nick J. Watson, 'Sport and Religion: Culture, History and Ideology', *Movement and Sport Sciences*, vol. 86 (2014) pp. 71–79.
13 Nye, *Masculinity and Male Codes of Honor in Modern France*, p. 219.
14 Peter Olsthoorn, 'Courage in the Military: Physical and Moral', *Journal of Military Ethics*, vol. 6, no. 4 (2007) pp. 270–279, p. 270.
15 Olsthoorn, 'Courage in the Military: Physical and Moral', p. 275.
16 Ute Frevert, *Emotions in History—Lost and Found* (Budapest and London: Central European University Press, 2011) p. 58.
17 Nye, *Masculinity and Male Codes of Honor in Modern France*, p. 226.
18 Nye, *Masculinity and Male Codes of Honor in Modern France*, p. 222.
19 Nye, *Masculinity and Male Codes of Honor in Modern France*, p. 226.
20 Nye refers specifically to France between the years 1890 and 1914, but in this chapter, I argue that the same can be said of Britain during the same time. See Nye, *Masculinity and Male Codes of Honor in Modern France*, p. 217.
21 As explained in Chapter 2, the *Shan Van Vocht* was a cultural-nationalist and often explicitly feminist paper published from 1896 to 1898. It was motivated by the desire for Irish women to 'have a voice in directing the affairs of Ireland'. A large proportion of the contributors were women. See C. L. Innes, ' "A Voice in Directing the Affairs of Ireland": *L'Irlande Libre*, *The Shan Van Vocht* and *Bean na h-Eireann*', in Paul Hyland and Neil Sammells, eds., *Irish Writing: Exile and Subversion* (Basingstoke: Macmillan, 1991) pp. 146–158, pp. 150–151.
22 *Shan Van Vocht*, vol. 1, no. 7, 3 July 1896, p. 130.
23 The *Bean na hEireann*, translating as *Woman of Ireland*, ran from 1908 to 1911 and pronounced itself the first Irish nationalist-feminist paper. See the 'introduction' in this book for more details.
24 *Bean na hEireann*, vol. 2, no. 22, December 1910, pp. 5–7.
25 *Shan Van Vocht*, vol. 1, no. 7, 3 July 1896, p. 130.
26 *Shan Van Vocht*, vol. 1, no. 7, 3 July 1896, p. 130.
27 *Shan Van Vocht*, vol. 1, no. 7, 3 July 1896, p. 130.
28 *Shan Van Vocht*, vol. 3, no. 11, 7 Nov 1898, pp. 229–230.

29 She was labelled this for her dramatic calls to arms. See Margaret Ward, *Maud Gonne. Ireland's Joan of Arc* (London: Pandora, 1990).
30 This pamphlet referred to Queen Victoria's complicity in the tragic famines of the 1840s and stridently opposed the upcoming visit to Ireland of the British monarch. The British Government confiscated all available copies of the article on the grounds that it was libellous.
31 Maud Gonne, 'The Famine Queen', *United Irishman*, 7 April 1900, in Karen, ed., *Maud Gonne's Irish Nationalist Writings, 1895–1946* (Dublin and Portland: Irish Academic Press, 2004) pp. 54–56.
32 Maud Gonne, 'Ireland and her Foreign Relations', *United Irishman*, 22 December 1900, in Steele, *Maud Gonne's Irish Nationalist Writings*, pp. 177–181.
33 Maud Gonne, 'Ireland and her Foreign Relations'.
34 Maud Gonne, 'Ireland and her Foreign Relations'.
35 *Bean na hEireann*, vol. 1, no. 7, May 1909, pp. 6–7.
36 *Bean na hEireann*, vol. 1, no. 21, November 1910, p. 14.
37 *Bean na hEireann*, vol. 1, no. 21, November 1910, p. 14. These were women who were guilty of 'betraying their country and their sex'. See *Bean na hEireann*, vol. 2, no. 22, December 1910, pp. 5–7.
38 *Bean na hEireann*, vol. 1, no. 21, November 1910, p. 14.
39 *Bean na hEireann*, vol. 1, no. 7, May 1909, p. 8.
40 *Bean na hEireann*, vol. 1, no. 11, September 1909, p. 35.
41 This is discussed in Chapter 2.
42 *Bean na hEireann*, vol. 1, no. 11, September 1909, p. 35.
43 *Bean na hEireann*, vol. 1, no. 11, September 1909, p. 35.
44 See, for example, Nicoletta Gullace, 'White Feathers and Wounded Men: Female Patriotism and the Memory of the Great War', *Journal of British Studies*, vol. 36, no. 2, 1997, pp. 178–206.
45 *Anti-Suffrage Review*, no. 76, February 1915, p. 13.
46 *Anti-Suffrage Review*, no. 76, February 1915, p. 13.
47 Gullace, 'White Feathers and Wounded Men', p. 187.
48 Gullace, 'White Feathers and Wounded Men', p. 184.
49 *Woman*, vol. 7, no. 9, 1 November 1914, p. 249.
50 *Woman*, vol. 8, no. 3, 1 June 1915, pp. 385–387.
51 *Woman*, vol. 9, no. 7, 1 September 1916, pp. 173–174.
52 Joan Beaumont, *Broken Nation. Australians and the Great War* (Sydney: Allen and Unwin, 2013) p. 91.
53 *Woman*, vol. 8, no. 1, 1 March 1915, pp. 313–315.
54 *Woman*, vol. 8, no. 1, 1 March 1915, pp. 313–315.
55 *Woman*, vol. 8, no. 1, 1 March 1915, pp. 313–315.
56 One short poem in the same edition of the paper referred to 'slack' and 'slackness' perhaps seven or eight times for emphasis. See 'We Must Do More' (Poem) by Gertrude Hart in *Woman*, vol. 8, no. 1, 1 March 1915, p. 315.
57 *Woman*, vol. 8, no. 12, 1 February 1916, p. 583.
58 *Woman*, vol. 8, no. 12, 1 February 1916, p. 583.
59 Carmel Shute, 'Heroines and Heroes: Sexual Mythology in Australia 1914–18', in Joy Damousi and Marilyn Lake, eds., *Gender and War: Australians at War in the Twentieth Century* (Cambridge: Cambridge University Press, 1995) pp. 23–42, p. 26.
60 Beaumont, *Broken Nation*, p. 375.
61 Gullace, 'White Feathers and Wounded Men', p. 187.
62 *Woman*, vol. 8, no. 12, 1 February 1916, pp. 578–583.
63 *Woman*, vol. 8, no. 1, 1 March 1915, pp. 313–315.
64 *Woman*, vol. 9, no. 2, 1 April 1916, p. 39.

65 *Woman*, vol. 9, no. 2, 1 April 1916, p. 50.
66 *Woman*, vol. 8, no. 6, 2 August 1915, p. 429.
67 *Woman*, vol. 8, no. 6, 2 August 1915, p. 429.
68 *Woman*, vol. 8, no. 12, 1 February 1916, p. 577.
69 *Woman*, vol. 9, no. 8, 2 October 1916, p. 209.
70 *Woman*, vol. 9, no. 9, 1 November 1916, p. 247.
71 *Woman*, vol. 10, no. 11, 1 January 1918, pp. 358–359.
72 *Woman*, vol. 9, no. 8, 2 October 1916, p. 209. For other allusions to inappropriate indulgence in sports, see *Woman*, vol. 8, no. 1, 1 March 1915, p. 336, and *Woman*, vol. 8, no. 6, 2 August 1915, p. 429.
73 *Woman*, vol. 10, no. 2, 2 April 1917, p. 57.
74 *Woman*, vol. 10, no. 6, 1 August 1917, p. 180.
75 *Woman*, vol. 10, no. 6, 1 August 1917, p. 180.
76 *Woman*, vol. 10, no. 4, 2 July 1917, p. 135.
77 *Woman*, vol. 10, no. 4, 2 July 1917, p. 135.
78 *Woman*, vol. 10, no. 2, 2 April 1917, p. 67.
79 I discuss women's views of gender and violence in Chapter 7.
80 *Woman*, vol. 9, no. 9, 1 November 1916, p. 247.
81 *Woman*, vol. 9, no. 9, 1 November 1916, p. 247.
82 *Woman*, vol. 10, no. 7, 1 September 1917, p. 223.
83 *Woman*, vol. 10, no. 7, 1 September 1917, p. 223.
84 *Woman*, vol. 10, no. 7, 1 September 1917, p. 223.
85 *Woman*, vol. 10, no. 7, 1 September 1917, p. 223.
86 *Woman*, vol. 8, no. 12, 1 February 1916, p. 601.
87 *Woman*, vol. 9, no. 1, 1 March 1916, p. 1.
88 *Woman*, vol. 9, no. 4, 1 June 1916, pp. 90–91.
89 *Woman*, vol. 9, no. 10, 1 December 1916, p. 279.
90 *Woman*, vol. 9, no. 10, 1 December 1916, p. 279.
91 *Woman*, vol. 10, no. 11, 1 January 1918, p. 359.
92 Katie Pickles, *Transnational Outrage: The Death and Commemoration of Edith Cavell* (Basingstoke and New York: Palgrave Macmillan, 2007) p. 3.
93 This is despite the fact that many of these Allied nations executed women The French shot two nurses in 1915 for the same offence as Cavell. And between 1914 and 1918, they executed at least 11 women for espionage. Note that Cavell was not executed for espionage. See Pickles, *Transnational Outrage*, p. 43, p. 52, and p. 202.
94 Pickles, *Transnational Outrage*, p. 57.
95 *Anti-Suffrage Review*, no. 87, January 1916, pp. 6–7.
96 *Anti-Suffrage Review*, no. 87, January 1916, pp. 6–7.
97 *Irish Citizen*, vol. 4, no. 24, 30 October 1915, p. 144.
98 *Irish Citizen*, vol. 4, no. 24, 30 October 1915, p. 144.
99 *Irish Citizen*, vol. 4, no. 24, 30 October 1915, p. 144.
100 *Irish Citizen*, vol. 4, no. 24, 30 October 1915, p. 144.
101 *Irish Citizen*, vol. 4, no. 25, 6 November 1915, p. 149.
102 *Irish Citizen*, vol. 4, no. 25, 6 November 1915, p. 151.
103 *Irish Citizen*, vol. 4, no. 26, 13 November 1915, p. 157.
104 *Irish Citizen*, vol. 4, no. 27, 20 November 1915, p. 165. Katie Pickles states that the French shot two nurses in 1915 for the same offence as Cavell and between 1914 and 1918, they also executed at least eleven women for espionage (Pickles, *Transnational Outrage*, p. 52). See also Susan R. Grayzel, *Women and the First World War* (Abingdon and New York: Routledge, 2013) pp. 43–45.
105 The German paper cited in *Irish Citizen* named the two German women executed by the French as Margaret Schmidt at Nancy in March 1915 and Ottilie

Moss at Bourges in May 1915 see *Irish Citizen*, vol. 4, no. 27, 20 November 1915, p. 165.
106 *Irish Citizen*, vol. 3, no. 26, 14 November 1914, p. 201.
107 *Irish Citizen*, vol. 3, no. 26, 14 November 1914, p. 201.
108 *Irish Citizen*, vol. 4, no. 22, 16 October 1915, p. 125.
109 *Irish Citizen*, vol. 3, no. 41, 27 February 1915, p. 313.
110 *Irish Citizen*, vol. 3, no. 41, 27 February 1915, p. 313.
111 As reported in Chapter 4, in 1911, anticipation of the coming war, *Woman* stated, 'A "baptism of fire," much as it may be deplored, is *the* force, above all others, which welds a nation into one and arouses its patriotism to an effective degree'. See *Woman*, vol. 3, no. 12, 1 February 1911, p. 749.

7 The Shame of the Violent Woman

In Britain in 1909, militant suffragist Theresa Garnett publicly whipped politician Winston Churchill with a riding switch saying, 'Take that, in the name of the insulted women of England'. In an inversion of gendered norms, the male Churchill was reported in the feminist paper, *Votes for Women*, as pale and afraid, and the female Garnett as forceful and courageous. She had undertaken 'a piece of cool daring'.[1] Churchill and his 'cowardly' government would not accept deputations of suffragists. They endorsed state violence against campaigning feminists. This man, *Votes for Women* declared, was a 'statesman who has dishonoured British statesmanship by his dishonest conduct to the women of Great Britain'.[2] 'Moved', another article declared, 'by the spirit of pure chivalry, Miss Garnett took what she thought to be the best available means of avenging the insult done to womanhood by the Government to which Mr. Churchill belongs'. The writer added, 'A woman has at last humiliated the man who has humiliated women for so long'.[3] Yet another article represented Garnett's actions as 'a knightly and chivalrous thing'.[4]

In feminist reports about this incident, the male politician embodied the weaker feminine emotional values of fear, dishonesty, and humiliation. The female protester embodied the more masculine ones of courage, chivalry, and retribution. It seemed that through exercising physical force publicly, women were able to challenge the gendered nature of the emotional regimes underpinning the traditional honour codes of men.

In this chapter, I analyse a range of issues related to female displays of violence and the exclusivity of the masculine honour codes that directed men's participation in violent conflict, but not women's. I examine how British anti-suffragists constructed their arguments against female militancy—whether in the suffrage campaign or in World War One—on the basis that women's violence eroded honour codes and that led to social and emotional instability. I also look at fears about the prevalence of male-on-female violence. Women's violence did not exist in a vacuum. It invited reciprocal violence from men whether in the form of male hecklers or representatives of the police force or enemy army. British anti-suffragists were highly sensitised to the issue of male-on-female violence. Therefore, they often predicated their hostility to female uses of physical force on the basis that women exercising violence would interfere with the normal operation of codes of chivalry. Theoretically, chivalry protected women from male acts of aggression. If women proved they were as capable of violence as men, what would compel men to exercise restraint against women? Irish women, however, took a different route into this issue. In this chapter, I also explore how Irish nationalist women challenged the gendered nature of reigning emotional regimes by claiming a special relationship with violence. I analyse their endeavours to revise modern or British understandings of chivalry to accommodate their claims of male-female parity on the issue of exercising physical force.

Physical Force and Gendered Implications of Honour and Chivalry

Anti-suffragists had long premised their opposition to the woman vote on the basis of physical force. Women could not join the military. They could not defend the nation; therefore, they should not be able to vote on matters of national security. By performing militancy publicly, militant suffragists challenged this assertion. Suffragists, such as members of the National Union of Women's Suffrage Societies (NUWSS), advocated constitutional means to assert women's right to citizenship. Militant suffragists, on the other hand, used a variety of more contentious techniques. Members of the Women's Freedom League (WFL), formed in 1907 after breaking away from the dominant Women's Social and Political Union (WSPU), exercised militancy by resisting the government and its laws until they were acknowledged as full citizens.[5] The more recognised and sensationalised members of the WSPU—those typically referred to by the title 'suffragette'—employed a more violent form of militancy. They used physical force with the intention of damaging property and, later, injuring human beings.[6]

The WSPU's use of violence was strategic.[7] Their public and strategic uses of physical force departed from the more womanly employment of moral force tactics by mainstream suffragists. Such a disruptive departure from moral force tactics shocked conservative commentators—female and male—who considered violence in men an essential if often inconvenient characteristic. They viewed violence in women to be a degradation of womanhood.

Scholars affirm the prodigiously gendered nature of violence throughout history. Pieter Spierenburg argues that in 'practically every historical setting, violent crime has been overwhelmingly a male enterprise'. Today is no different, he asserts.[8] Robert Shoemaker agrees. In his study of masculinity and the decline of violence in eighteenth-century Britain, Shoemaker declares that, historically, violence was not seen as a feminine activity. He states that this was 'not because women were assumed to be weaker than men'. Rather, it was 'due to the expectation that women were more passive and submissive, as well as more sensitive to the needs of others'.[9] Violence in a woman was deemed to be out of synch with her feminine character. For instance, a woman who committed a particularly violent crime in the era Shoemaker analysed tended to be labelled a 'masculine woman'.[10] Violent women were also accused of being emotionally disturbed, of being 'passionate and temperamental'.[11] This emotional imbalance accounted for their incursion into a traditionally masculine domain.

Historically, the masculine domain of violence was policed by honour codes. The profound association that honour maintained with masculinity means that 'males, overwhelmingly, have been the chief antagonists in violence inflicted in its name'.[12] Indeed, in many instances, masculine resort to violence was considered not only honourable but also essential.[13] In some societies—those with pronounced ideas about honour and shame—men remaining passive in violent situations was viewed as 'a cardinal feminine virtue'.[14] For example, in many European cultures it was deemed unmanly not to react aggressively to personal insults.[15] Although masculine honour codes changed over time, they continued to denote the capacity for violence to be a manly trait—an integral aspect of masculine identity. Violence offered men the opportunity of proving their gender identity.[16] Rules were intended to govern men's violent engagements with each other. Honour codes directed men to fight fairly and courageously. Honour, then, inspired many men's public acts of violence, and it also guided their participation in those acts.

Women's exclusion from male cultures of violence is partially explained by their exclusion from honour codes. Women were not permitted to assume an active relationship with honour and its codes. However, they were not entirely absent from those codes. A passive function was conferred on women through the notion of chivalry, an integral aspect of honour codes. Honour codes directed men to be chivalrous in their behaviour towards women or to correct the attitudes of those men who rejected such chivalry. Historically, chivalry incorporated a broad set of cultural norms. The elevation of honour above all virtues, the promotion of strict sex roles subordinating women, and class limits were chief among these.[17] Chivalry regulated honour violence. Women could not earn honour through physical violence or martial prowess. Consequently, woman's place was in the home. The public world, guided as it was by men's violence and martial codes of honour, was too dangerous for the female sex.[18]

Chivalry, then, was an exemplary example of benevolent sexism. It revealed what René Moelker and Gerhard Kümmel explain as the

> construction of a gender order in which the male is the strong one, the protector, the active one and also the courting one, while the role of the weak and passive one, those in need of protection, and the courteously treated and courted one is attributed to the female. Women here are the applauding and caring spectators only.[19]

Honour codes excluded women from male cultures of violence and in the process allowed men to assert 'their difference from and superior position over women'.[20]

Women were much more likely to be victims of violence than perpetrators of it, especially at the hands of men.[21] Some of this violence was legally endorsed. Males were already permitted to use acceptable forms of violence against their womenfolk, children, and servants, for example.[22] Other forms of male-on-female violence, such as domestic violence, were much less acceptable but still prevalent. Honour played various roles in these varied forms of aggression. Historically, male heads of households were permitted to defend their honour by upholding their positions and reputations as masters of their households. Therefore, they were permitted to exercise their judgment in meting out punishment to those who threatened their position, including, as I stated before, their womenfolk, children, and servants. However, too much violence against those below them could also be considered dishonourable. For instance, 'irrational and unjustified violence against women was viewed as dishonourable'.[23]

Shoemaker argues that as public forms of male violence declined throughout the eighteenth century, women might have become even more vulnerable to men's violence. He cites the 'privatization of violence' in support of this assertion. Public displays of violence became less socially acceptable in response to the growing popularity of middle-class values, such as politeness. Men had to find new ways of conducting their disputes with each other in the face of growing intolerance for public violence. This caused the link between honour and violence to weaken, although not disappear. Men's violence declined but did not vanish. Rather, Shoemaker argues, it retreated behind closed doors.[24] Behind closed doors, honour codes, which traditionally governed participation in fights between male equals, did little to prevent male-on-female violence. These were not equal fights but one-sided attacks.[25]

The shift towards public violence becoming less socially acceptable forced men to readdress the nature of their actions towards other men, but they were not compelled to reappraise relations between men and women. Therefore, relationships with women remained or even grew more problematic. The emergence of the effeminate middle-class clerk and the masculinised feminist or New Woman brought about a blurring of boundaries between the sexes.[26] This blurring of gender distinctions publicly meant that some men might have felt the need to assert themselves over women privately.[27] Whatever the exact nature of the relationship between modernity, sex distinction, and domestic violence, many women at the time certainly articulated their concern about their vulnerability to male violence. As I will outline next, anti-suffragist women expressed deep concern that whatever protection they had from male aggression would be eroded by militant suffragists' displays of physical force. If women were to prove themselves as capable of violent acts as men, what need would there be for men to protect women from men's violence? Honour codes did not guarantee women protection from male violence, but they were supposed to act as a deterrent. Given their vulnerability to male aggression, it is hardly surprising that women clung to whatever form of protection they could find, effective or not.

A Feminist Ethics of Violence?

British anti-feminists were committed to the idea that the female sex was the pacifist sex. They were not alone in their support of this viewpoint. Many feminists at the time—and since—argued likewise. Therefore, before examining the nature and extent of the British *Anti-Suffrage Review*'s (the *Review*) opposition to female acts of violence, I want to briefly explore feminist interest in and debates about the nature of woman's relationship with violence.

Recent studies of women's violence—emanating mainly from feminist scholars within disciplines such as political science and international relations[28]—tend to begin their projects by acknowledging the reigning supposition that women are the peaceful sex and that most forms of violence perpetrated by a woman are aberrations.[29] For example, Caron E. Gentry and Lara Sjoberg argue that many women globally participate in political acts of violence, including 'organizing attacks, leading insurgent groups, perpetrating martyrdom, engaging in sexual violence, committing war crimes, hijacking airplanes, or abusing prisoners'.[30] Yet, despite the extent and range of women's violent activities, they point out that the public continues to be shocked by what is deemed the aberrant violent woman. Paige Whaley Eager attests that societies, regardless of their religious or ethnic make-up, 'seem especially uncomfortable with women who are violent'. Women who commit violence outside the acceptable scope of female physical force—an acceptable scope which includes fending off an attacker (such as a rapist or a physically abusive husband), defending their children, and, to a degree, engaging in sporting or endorsed military activities—are viewed overwhelmingly as aberrant or 'less than a woman', she asserts.[31] Drawing on the groundbreaking work of political scientist, Jean Bethke Elshtain,[32] Gentry and Sjoberg argue that this is because the image of the female combatant runs counter to traditional images of womanhood 'as pure, maternal, emotional, innocent and peace-loving'.[33] They add that this figure of the violent woman also disrupts many feminists' conceptions of the liberated woman as 'capable and equal, but not prone to men's mistakes, excesses or violence'.[34] Violent women, therefore, are often viewed as 'bad women'. Not only are they bad because they are violent, but they are also bad at being women because they fail expectations of womanhood—they fail some feminist as well as non-feminist understandings of womanhood.[35]

A body of feminist scholarship dealing with the history of women's participation in violent conflicts—including the two world wars—emerged in the 1980s and 1990s.[36] A great deal of this literature deconstructed the myth that war was a man's business only. The total wars of the twentieth century defied the accuracy of that statement. As detailed in Chapter 5, women were pulled in to serve in those conflicts whether they desired it or not. Moreover, these histories showed that many women supported war. In the introduction to their edited collection on gender and the two world wars, for example, Higonnet et al. questioned the long-standing assumption that men were 'naturally fierce and warlike' and women, as mothers, had 'an affinity for peace'. Such a differentiation, they asserted, existed because it served the function of maintaining a distinction between battlefront and home front that helped to guarantee social stability.[37] In her 1990 chapter 'Why the Pursuit of Peace Is No Part of Feminism', Janet Radcliffe Richards argued that feminists who maintained the distinction between warlike men and peace-loving women were guilty of buying into exactly the separate spheres notions that anti-feminists had traditionally peddled.[38] If peace is good for all, then it is not a women's issue, she argued, because it is not for women. Feminists who argued that pacifism was a woman's issue did so, she said, on the grounds of a 'women's values kind of feminism' rather than an equal rights model of feminism.[39]

Other feminist historians took a different path. For instance, in 1999, Nicole Ann Dombrowski pointed out that many feminists who championed women's entry into male institutions such as the military were often contradictory or inconsistent in their approaches. Some liberal feminists asserted that women were not necessarily less aggressive than men. They did not necessarily assume a different physical relationship with violence than men did. On the other hand, some argued that if women were to gain entry to such bastions of masculinity, they could affect a radical transformation. Being ethically superior, they could civilise the military. Such arguments about women's physical or ethical difference or sameness could not be paired unproblematically.[40] Were feminists who promoted women's entry into the military, for example, claiming that women were equal to or different from men?

Despite feminist discussions about the nature of the relationship between women and violence, assumptions that women are naturally the more peaceful sex continues to appear in histories of violence. In her 2014 book on violence, militarisation, and weapons, Joanna Bourke noted that on hearing about her research, friends asked her if she was being 'gender-blind'. 'Aren't women either innately or culturally more peaceable?'[41] While she supported the assertion that males were more likely to be drawn to 'all things martial', Bourke pointed out that women were hardly lacking in complicity in sustaining the militarisation of society. Wars were routinely fought in the name of protecting woman or women, women's taxes funded military campaigns, and women, she said, are as likely as men to be co-opted by militarist values and practices through, for example, watching movies and playing on games consoles.[42] To what degree, then, were women historically as drawn to and supportive of violence compared with men?

Writing in 2012, Setsu Shigematsu acknowledged that there were studies of women involved in acts of political violence—in protest movements as well as wars—but she argued that these had not led to a theorisation of women's relationship with violence.[43] Shigematsu declared that she was 'disturbed by the relative hesitation, if not reluctance, of feminists to theorize capacities, complicities, and desires for power, domination, and violence *in women*' (italics in original).[44] This was despite, she said, the very obvious support shown for state-orchestrated violence by high profile American women at the time.[45] She posited a number of reasons for feminist hesitancy in this regard. Generations of feminist activists worked to affect changes that have since enabled women to enter into formerly male-only institutions such as the military, prisons, and police force. Feminist critiques of women's relationship with violence might undermine those achievements, inviting further discrimination against women. Globally, the women's movements of the 1960s and 1970s made visible particular forms of violence that have been used against women, including domestic violence and wartime violence against women. Casting light on women's complicity in violent activism—State-endorsed or otherwise—might overshadow the very real status of many women as victims of male aggression.

Still, Shigematsu's concern was to interrogate how women have both resisted and been complicit in acts of violence. She argued that only by moving aside from the general focus on women's victimhood could feminist scholars take more seriously 'the problem of women's complicity and agency in the perpetuation of violence against other women, children, and men and how these circuits are maintained and reproduced geopolitically through gendered and racialized economies'.[46] The 'relative feminist mutedness about violence among women', she asserted—due perhaps to the tendency to universalise discourses of women's victimhood in the face of patriarchy and sexism—threatened to prevent adequate theorisations of women's investments in systems of power and violence. Shigematsu posited the need for a new understanding of feminist ethics of violence.

In this chapter, I focus on anti-suffragist opposition to women's militancy and violence. I trace anti-feminist reactions to radical feminists' adoption of militant tactics and, therefore, in the minds of their conservative opponents, their simultaneous appropriation of masculine emotional traits, values, and codes. However, by examining intersecting suffragist/anti-suffragist debates in Britain and Ireland, I also go a little way towards exploring what Shigematsu labels a feminist ethics of violence. Irish women responded to women's actual or suggested involvement in suffrage militancy, nationalist militancy, and the onset of the Great War in ways that departed radically from British conservatives. Many of them invoked gender and nationalist politics to champion the woman warrior. How did attitudes to gender, violence, and emotional regimes connect or divide patriotic women—suffragists or anti-suffragists—across Britain and Ireland?

A Word About Australia and Suffrage Militancy

Australian women are largely absent from this chapter. Before examining British anti-feminist responses to female militancy, I want to make some brief comments about this relative absence. As outlined earlier in the book, the Australian suffrage campaigns, although contentious and divisive, lacked the violence and civil disobedience of the British campaigns.[47] The British *Review* made much of this when attempting to render irrelevant suffragists' references to Australian suffrage 'experiments' as fitting precedence for the British case. The woman vote in Australia was nothing more than 'an idle compliment Australian men have paid their women', one contributor wrote.[48] The attitude of Australian women to the political franchise was one of 'supreme indifference'.

> There were never any militant suffragettes 'down under.' No Minister was attacked with a dog whip, or even heckled by women. No deputations waited on him to demand votes for women. No constable had his face slapped for merely doing his duty, neither was his helmet knocked from his head. There was not even a quiet, self-respecting, ladylike league for the promotion of the franchise to women.[49]

Oblivious to the often heated and discordant nature of the various suffrage campaigns that had taken place in the Australian colonies in the late nineteenth- and early twentieth centuries (as outlined earlier in the book), the *Review* declared that Australia was an irrelevant case study of the female franchise.

Yet Australia was not entirely free of association with suffrage militancy. Women from around the Empire participated in the suffrage movement in Britain more generally—tied as their interests were to British political outcomes. This was exemplified by the 1911 Women's Coronation Procession organised by the WSPU, which included marching women from places such as India, Australia,[50] and Ireland in its attempt to create what Rebecca Cameron terms 'an impressive spectacle of international, transhistorical female solidarity'.[51] However, the militant side of the campaign more specifically also attracted outsiders. As Barbara Caine explains, the British militant movement acted as a magnet for feminists from places like North America,[52] Europe, and Australia.[53] I will reiterate here what I have already explained in the 'Introduction'. A number of prominent Australian activists travelled to the United Kingdom and joined in the militant movement. Among these were Dora Montefiore, Nellie Martel, Jessie Street, and the more spectacular Muriel Matters (who is renowned for an infamous escapade during which she threw out suffrage pamphlets from an airship over London not long after she had been released from prison for chaining herself to the Ladies' Gallery grille in the House of

Commons). Perth-based Bessie Rischbieth, who became very conservative in later life, was also swept up by the energy of the militant movement when she visited London in 1913. Still others journeyed to Britain to offer their general support, most famously, Victoria's Vida Goldstein who championed the movement on her tour there in 1911.[54]

Despite this record of Australian involvement with suffrage militancy, the Australian journal, *Woman*, rarely commented on the activities of pro-militant Australians. Perhaps the paper considered that being seen to pass judgement on British suffrage militancy would have rendered their already ambivalent position as reluctant suffragists even more so. As it were, they wanted to encourage British authorities to validate the Australian example by offering other Empire women the power to cast their vote too. Therefore, Australian women's views on militancy and violence do not form a significant part of this chapter. For an analysis of Australian women's attitudes towards gender and violence, see the section of Chapter 6 that discusses women's support for male threats of violence against other men—mostly virile, courageous solders' threats of violence against cowardly, wartime shirkers.

British Opposition to Female Acts of Violence: Shame and Degradation

The British *Review* had no qualms about declaring the militant suffragist to be a creature of no sex—a gender abomination. Even before militant tactics were to escalate to include inflicting property or personal damage, anti-suffragists expressed outrage at the militant strategy of disrupting public events. Indeed, interrupting public meetings to demand politicians pledge themselves to the suffragist cause or explain why they would not do so was to become one of the movement's most common tactics. In January 1909, the paper used the example of suffragists interrupting an Albert Hall meeting at which Cabinet Minister Lloyd George was speaking to articulate their indignation at length.

Women, the *Review* stated, had come to the event to commit 'ugly violence'. What resulted were 'disgraceful scenes' in which men were prevented from exercising their right to free speech. This was 'an aggressive attack' on British values and freedoms perpetrated by 'riotous women' who had given in to 'lunacy and hysteria'.[55] The paper recreated the scene:

> Grown women and young girls, timid shrinking creatures as their friends describe them, fought, screamed, bit, and scratched like the termagants of the slums. We are told of one lady being carried from the platform on the shoulders of four stewards, her clothing disarranged, her hair streaming, her face purple with rage. Another is seen wildly struggling to remove the hands that gag her, and utilizing her sounds of freedom to shriek insults at Mr. Lloyd-George. In one of

the boxes a woman of the new model is slashing right and left with a dog-whip.[56]

This assortment of disturbing images led the *Review* to conclude,

> The most degrading spectacle on this planet is generally supposed to be the ejection of a drunken female from a public house, but the Maenads at the Albert Hall had not even the excuse of inebriety; and these are the special champions of the Suffrage movement, bent on showing that women can approach great national questions, calmly, with dignity and common sense.[57]

The paper warned that if women were granted the right to vote, such scenes would ensue. Chaos would pervade the political life of the great nation.

Giving full scope to female capacities for excitement and hysteria in the realm of national politics would irretrievably injure and degrade English public life, the *Review* stated. It also added that such a move would result in 'the loss of English womanhood first and foremost'. The Albert Hall meeting had brought this latter message home to England. The article continued, 'As women we record it with shame and regret'.[58] Women bore the brunt of fellow women's violent behaviour.

> No one could look at these faces full of wild excitement; no one could hear the storm of offensive clamour from women's mouths without shame and sorrow.[59]

As explained in the first chapter of this book, the integrity of British womanhood was at risk.

Also at risk was the nature of relations between the sexes. The Albert Hall scenes were, the paper asserted, 'only the climax in a long process which has been undermining that old chivalrous respect for woman as woman which used to be our national pride'. Women were guilty of poisoning the well from which springs trust and pity for the unenfranchised sex, the article went on to say. Not only that, but these transgressive acts also jeopardised woman's rightful place in politics. The *Review* said that there was a time when 'the presence of a woman on a platform could restrain the roughest crowd'. Now, 'Ladies with bells and dog-whips have changed all that'. Through the militant suffragist, violence had entered more forcefully into the already precarious world of politics. The pity of all of this, the paper asserted, was that 'the innocent must suffer with the guilty'.[60] Bringing the reader back to the impact that violent women were having on the community of British womanhood, the article affirmed that women had shamed other women by bringing the community to which they all belonged into disrepute. This was an accusation that the paper was to repeat until the WSPU ceased its militant tactics with the onset of war in 1914.

Further into 1909, the *Review* reported that these feminists were still to be found 'slapping policemen's faces and knocking off their helmets in the middle of a crowd of all the hooligans in London'.[61] It then juxtaposed the political ineffectiveness of such disreputable tactics in the face of the potential efficacy of more womanly methods employed by the non-militant side of the campaign. A section of the suffrage movement were to be found sitting outside parliament 'meekly' asking to be heard, the paper reported. Anti-suffragists 'trembled' in the face of such tactics. The *Review* considered this 'display of sweet patience and feminine gentleness' to be 'far more likely to melt the hearts of susceptible legislators than a hundred crusades led by Boadiceas on horseback'.[62] Besides, unlike the original Boadicea who was a patriot who died fighting against foreign occupation, modern-day versions of the warrior woman were motivated only by their selfish desire for political power.

Militant feminists brought shame to British womanhood. Good British women resented this. 'Women', especially', the paper asserted, 'are burning with a deep latent shame at the behaviour of the unwomanly women who disgrace the sex while purporting to "emancipate" it.' Women did not need the suffragette's form of emancipation. They needed to be emancipated 'from the Suffragettes'.[63] The following year, in the face of continuing feminist disruption, the *Review* pleaded for such emancipation. It called for a halt to the demeaning of British womanhood perpetrated by a radical section of that community. It asked,

> Cannot some restraining influence be brought to bear on those who would renew the sickening policy which has degraded British womanhood, and has gone far towards stirring up the animosity between the sexes which is fraught with the certainty of social disaster?[64]

Womanly women attempting to shame unwomanly women was not yielding the desired results. Transgressive women were not undertaking the shameful self-assessment demanded by anti-suffragist women. Other methods were needed, then, to halt the erosion of British womanhood's reputation.

In 1912, the paper published a cartoon that made explicit the connection between shame and female militants—those they referred to as 'latter-day specimens of the old-fashioned nagging woman'.[65] Entitled 'Desperate Cases and Despar(d)ate Remedies'—referencing Anglo-Irish leader of the militant Women's Freedom League Charlotte Despard—the cartoon consisted of a series of images that juxtaposed the 'Relative Importance of the Suffragist and the True Woman'.[66] The final image, of relevance only to the suffragist, contained those historic instruments of public humiliation, the Stocks, and, specifically for women, the Scold's Bridle. If women refused to internalise shame, then the only recourse it seemed was to inflict public shame on them as in days of old.

As militant tactics escalated, the *Review* felt compelled to call on the support of other anti-suffragists in the wider community. In 1913, the paper reasserted the link between female militancy and shame. It reprinted an account of an anti-suffragist lecture given by Father Day, S. J. at Manchester that made explicit the links between women's violence and the degradation of womanhood. The cleric was reported as saying,

> On the subject of militant methods there is no need to enlarge. Violence in woman is an ethical degradation of her being. The man who strikes a woman is a coward. The woman who strikes a man is lost to shame.[67]

The emotional regimes governing engagements with violence were gendered. By transgressing these regulations, men and women destabilised their identities. By striking a female, men positioned themselves beyond the pale of masculine honour codes, particularly where those codes related to courage and chivalry. They proved themselves unmanly. By using violence against men, women ostracised themselves from the community of true womanhood. They brought shame to themselves. Anti-suffragist women, however, feared that that stigma would mark them too.

Revisiting and Revising Codes of Chivalry: Britain and Ireland

Suffragette violence forced those writing for the *Review* to revisit and clarify their understanding of the relationship between gender and violence. Relatively early in the militant campaign, the paper confirmed that there were times when women could justifiably resort to the use of physical force. To slap the face of a 'too-aspiring admirer' has 'the charm and piquancy of comedy'. The woman 'who resorts to the use of weapons of war to defend her home or her children, possesses the state and dignity of tragedy'. However, the suffragette 'who slaps a policeman's face because he is doing his duty, displays only the extravagant absurdities of burlesque'.[68] Her public violence was a ridiculous and vulgar imitation of man's legitimate recourse to physical force.

The act of inflicting a feminine slap did not translate well when enacted publicly. Such an action was not in tune with gendered emotional regimes. The slap that protected her honour in private, led only to dishonour and shame in public. That is because, the private slap was intended to protect a feminine conception of honour—namely, chastity—whereas the public slap was a gross misappropriation of a masculine notion of honour—namely, honour in battle and in politics.

Such a confusion of gendered emotions and actions did not bode well for women. As the *Review* affirmed, the 'very qualities which are respectively attractive and imposing in woman's own sphere, become distorted and ridiculous when translated into the sphere of public and political life'. Moreover, if woman insists on 'laying down her most irresistible weapon'—no doubt referring to her charm and influence—and instead arms herself with 'man's clumsier panoply of war', 'then, instead of increasing her influence in the State, she will greatly diminish it'.[69] By proving herself both unwomanly and unmanly, the violent suffragist wrote herself out of any role in relation to the political life of the country.

The *Review* cited historical cases to show that women's violence demeaned not only womanhood but also the political cause at stake. Through their participation in revolutions globally—in places such as Russia, Poland, Italy, and France—women 'cheapened' not simply the relevant cause but also the very term 'revolution', the paper averred.[70] A few years later, in response to escalating militant tactics, the *Review* returned to the argument that through their participation in violent campaigns, women demeaned those campaigns. 'Women took part in the French Revolution', a 1912 article stated, 'but it has never been claimed that they raised the tone of that great movement'. Instead, it went on, 'women in the aggregate were guilty of the worst excesses and took the lead in most of the riots and outrages of those times'.[71] The paper's claim was that, historically, the mixture of women perpetrating violence and their inability to be emotionally disciplined had only ever produced a negative outcome for the political cause at stake.

Violent women demeaned otherwise just political causes. They also affected a negative transformation of relations between the sexes. The *Review* argued that militant women brought entire codes of chivalry under threat. In 1909, feminists disrupted politicians playing golf in order to draw attention to their demands. In doing so, they brought the concept and practice of chivalry under scrutiny. The personal attacks orchestrated by these 'brazen' women were 'revolting', but they were also 'cowardly', the *Review* declared. Everyone knew that men could not hit back at a lady—even if provoked. The militant movement was sustained by what the paper identified as a 'rising tide of hooliganism'. Members of organisations like the WSPU were not men and women any longer. They simply constituted 'a whirlwind'.[72] Their tactics were dishonourable because they were unfair. This was not an equal playing field, guided as it was by rules that protected women from men's physical retaliations, no matter how justified these might be. Notions of chivalry designed to protect women from men's excesses were instead being used to safeguard the excesses of women. This was a gross corruption of gendered emotional standards.

Initially, the *Review* expressed a sense of hope that society would yet correct itself and normal relations between the sexes would resume. In 1910, it stated,

> The days of chivalry are not over; never will be as long as men are men and women are women; but the moment that women cease to be women, and range themselves alongside of men in the arena of political life, then the days of chivalry and of the reign of womanhood alike will

be numbered, and the actual and intolerable subjection of woman will begin.[73]

However, by 1912, its optimism waned in the face of an intensification and expansion of suffrage militancy. British men's reactions to feminist violence also deflated anti-suffragists' hopes of a resumption of normalcy. 'Suffragism and its by-products are exercising a demoralising effect upon the nation', the *Review* declared. It was referring to a suffrage meeting in Wales that had turned violent—an event that suffragists had labelled 'Black Friday'. Today, the article continued, 'we have the repeated spectacle of women being roughly handled by a crowd—only, of course, when they have deliberately courted their punishment'.[74] As it conjured up images of women's bodies being manhandled, the paper asserted that today the 'dignity and the modesty of womanhood is being trampled in the dust'.[75]

Men manhandled women, yet the fault for doing so was not entirely or even largely theirs, the *Review* stated. Violent women brought out the worst in man. They forced him to reconsider or abandon his traditional adherence to codes of chivalry. 'The blame and the shame for the disgraceful scenes at Wrexham', the paper stated, 'lie with those presumably educated and enlightened women, not only with the rough uncontrolled mob whose passions they provoked.'[76] Violent women debased men: 'For the brute in man cannot be uncovered without exposing the serpent in woman who tempts him to his own undoing'.[77] Such viragos could not 'thus dare and rouse the brute in man without taking shame and humiliation to their hearts'.[78] Despite the confidence of this assertion, there was little evidence that such would be the case. There was little evidence that violent women would internalise the shame the *Review* directed at them and amend their disruptive ways. The tide of hooliganism looked set to continue rising.

Forcing men to review or deny chivalry also put women at risk of real physical harm. Consequently, the *Review* issued warnings of almost apocalyptic proportions directed at suffragettes.

> Let them seek 'martyrdom' for themselves, if they will, in their own way; but let them beware how they open the floodgate of man's violence upon their sex. Once these are opened nothing can stem the tide by which all women must be overtaken.[79]

The hope was, then, that the unrestrained violence of this Welsh incident might have 'brought it forcibly home to these women what their fate may be at the hands of men from whom provocation has released the restraints of civilised life'.[80] Instead of safeguarding against regression, as was woman's vocation, violent women brought it on. They initiated a decivilising force that morally degraded the nation's manhood and corroded long-standing codes of chivalry. The utterly frustrating thing for anti-suffragist women was their recognition of the fact that 'women *need* the chivalry of men (a quality which Suffragettes are doing their level best to destroy), and are not ashamed to own it'.[81] Violent women were blindly dismantling emotional regimes that were supposed to ensure their protection from male acts of violence. They were guilty of placing women in harm's way. Despite the rather grandiose language employed to bring the point home to its readers, the *Review*'s approach to male-on-female violence demonstrated that it felt keenly the very real physical threat represented to women by the erosion of codes of chivalry.

For all their insistence on chivalry as a means of protecting women from male violence, anti-suffragists proved themselves complicit with the wider body of British men in endorsing the use of certain acts of physical force against women. By 1909, the issue of the imprisonment of women's bodies, and soon after the force-feeding of hunger-striking suffragette prisoners, received considerable media attention. These issues certainly coloured the discussions taking place in feminist periodicals like the WSPU's *Votes for Women* and the *Irish Citizen* (the *Citizen*). The *Review* discussed the controversy surrounding the cyclic imprisonment, release, then re-arrest, and later force-feeding of hunger-striking women. It asserted that 'a great deal of nonsense has been talked about the unfairness meted out by a government of men to these latter-day specimens of the old-fashioned nagging woman'.[82] Not surprisingly, the paper argued, all this attention given to women 'indulging in a few days' fasting' in prison was frustrating and angering men. The paper targeted working-class men in particular. 'The good-humoured tolerance which originally greeted the suffragettes in working-class constituencies', it claimed, 'is rapidly giving way to a feeling of passionate anger.'[83] The main reason for this was the working man's intolerance for nagging. 'The peculiar form of "nagging" which the suffragettes have introduced into public life', the *Review* stated, 'is little calculated to prepossess him, and the next young lady who tries to silence a Cabinet Minister with a hand bell will have a rough time of it.'[84] The militant woman affected a transformation of gender relations, but through her actions, she also brought class relations into doubt.

In another article, the *Review* supported similar claims that nagging women invited violence from men. The 'Suffragette, who tries to goad a policeman into losing his temper, is like nothing so much as the wife who nags at her husband till he hits her, and then calls him a brute'.[85] Some women—nagging wives and now nagging militant suffragists—were undeserving of men's protection. By not adhering to the emotional standards deemed appropriate for their sex—by not allowing feminine emotional regimes to direct their interactions with members of the opposite sex—these women were not guaranteed protection by the emotional standards guiding men's behaviour. They were not assured protection from male acts of aggression. Indeed, they were accused of provoking legitimate physical retaliation from the men they wronged. The physical and emotional consequences of such a provocation did not favour either sex.

The *Review* claimed that through their militancy, suffragettes had alienated the once sympathetic English working class. By 1912, it added the Irish population to the group of people the militant feminists had estranged. In July of that year, three English militant suffragists and members of the WSPU travelled to Ireland where, in what is now a renowned display of suffragette activism, they threw a small hatchet at Herbert Asquith, visiting British prime minister, and John Redmond, leader of the Irish Parliamentary Party, who had gathered to discuss the issue of Irish Home Rule.[86] Later, they also set fire to Dublin's Theatre Royal where Asquith was due to speak. The English suffragettes had not consulted Dublin-based militant suffragists, members of the Irish Women's Franchise League (IWFL), before undertaking either action. Members of the IWFL, far from simply condoning the actions of their British counterparts as expected, were angered and frustrated that members of the British organisation had conducted a brief violent campaign in Ireland without recourse to either the volatility of nationalist and Unionist relations there or the leanings and strategic outlook of Irish suffragists. The events put even more strain on the already fragile relationship between suffragists on either side of the Irish Sea.[87]

In reporting these incidents and other acts of militancy in Ireland, the British *Review* chose to focus on the negative impact on gender relations wrought by the introduction of feminist violence there. The July incident was not the beginning of suffrage militancy in Ireland, however it was the most spectacular. Two months before that event, the paper had detailed the intensification of the Irish suffrage campaign. Redmond's nationalist Irish Party's decision to block the passing of the Conciliation Bill through the British parliament had excited passion and hysteria among suffragists in his home country. When those suffragists attempted to gain entry to a nationalist convention, there was an outbreak of violence. The *Review* pointed out that, as in England and Wales, women had been manhandled by a jostling crowd. The fear of more crowd violence against these women meant that they had to be protected and escorted away by the police. The paper declared that the whole episode would have been 'ludicrous if it had not worn an ugly aspect'.[88] These women, it asserted, 'had completely lost control of themselves and fought, literally, tooth and nail, suffered some very rough handling, for some of which the pressure of the exasperated crowd was responsible'.[89] The appearance of the violent suffragist in Ireland offered the British paper the chance to utter afresh the indignation spurred by the spectacle of the militant woman, this time in a different national setting.

Violent suffragism in Ireland also allowed anti-suffragists across the United Kingdom to once again draw attention to the attempted erosion of codes of chivalry on the part of violent women. This ' "militant" nonsense', whether enacted in Britain or Ireland, was 'unwomanly and degrading'. However, the new Irish example provided for the exercise of a slightly different anti-suffragist tactic. This time, the more archaic Irish temperament—in contrast to the robust and progressive English one—was used to further expose the insidious capabilities of transgressive womanhood. Female political violence, the British paper affirmed, had a profound impact on the Irish way of life. The Irish character, the *Review* stated, was essentially chivalric and conservative. Given their supposed innate conservativeness, it was hardly surprising that 'the spectacle of these women unsexing themselves in this manner' aroused 'feelings of utter repugnance' among the Irish population.[90]

Later in 1912, the *Review* noted that episodes of suffragette violence were continuing in Ireland. In response to a spate of window-breaking escapades by Dublin-based suffragists, the paper declared, 'Dublin residents of all classes were highly indignant at this outrage which brought discredit upon a country where Suffragists had up to this time, remained uninfected by the hysteria of their kind in England'.[91] It seemed that Dublin was now shackled to the militancy that had for years terrorised and shamed England. Returning to the Asquith hatchet incident, the *Review* pointed out that the Irish city was 'to have the unenviable distinction of being the scene of the worst outrages which have yet been associated with the more discreditable side of the Female Suffrage movement'.[92] Not only that, but it also noted that feminist militancy there was escalating dangerously. The paper decried 'the wanton nature of this outrage'—an outrage that had moved beyond mere heckling and interrupting political gatherings to acts of window-breaking, life-threatening arson, and the 'even more dastardly' hatchet-throwing incident.[93] It is only fair to say, the *Review* stated, that the hatchet and theatre incidents were perpetrated by English women. However, the very fact that Irish suffragists—through their paper, the *Citizen*—did not repudiate these acts of aggression demonstrated that they were complicit in the 'conspiracy'. 'Indeed', the British paper added, the IWFL could hardly have done so considering that 'their whole propaganda rests upon violence, and is a direct incitement to violence'.[94]

Whatever the nationality of the perpetrators of these dangerous outrages in Ireland, the *Review* was adamant that the Irish way of life, and Irish women in general, suffered as a consequence. Since the extension of suffrage violence to the island, Irish women had found that they could not walk the streets at night without being molested by men. Men who have since been charged with violence against these women in courts of law have claimed that they were provoked to do so because they assumed their victims were suffragettes, the paper explained. However, it continued, in 'every case she turned out to be nothing of the kind'.[95] Drawing attention again to the supposedly chivalric and conservative character of the Irish people, the paper declared,

> Dublin used to be the only capital, perhaps in the world, where a woman was safe at any hour from insult or molestation in the streets. Women were supposed to be more respected in Ireland than in any other country in Europe. In less than three months, the Suffragists have succeeded

in destroying that traditional respect. If no other achievement stood to their credit, that fact alone would be enough to rand their cause with shame.[96]

As unsubstantiated as their claim that Dublin was the safest city in the world as far as protection from male acts of violence was, the point that the *Review* drove home was that the intrusion of feminists' modern-day political tactics into a sphere that the British paper had constructed as archaic and conservative had served to corrupt and corrode those archaic values. Those archaic values, the paper directed, had protected women from male violence. Now Irish women were on equal footing with women in England. That is, whether guilty of feminist transgressions or not, the female population had been put at risk of men's violence. That fellow women, while professing to be the champions of women's affairs, were in fact responsible for lifting existing veils of protection was to their shame. The *Review* used a romanticised notion of Ireland to further reveal just how responsible women were for the disintegration of chivalry, womanliness, and the bonds that connected not only the community of womanhood but also the community of male and female patriots.

The advent of the Great War, although it saw an end to the violent campaign of the WSPU, provoked more heated discussions about gender and violence, not least because of Irish nationalist women's continued advocacy of feminist militancy and the well-meaning though thoroughly misguided offers on the part of patriotic British women to establish women's military organisations to assist with the war effort. Honour, shame, and related emotional concepts continued to be located at the heart of these discussions.

World War One, Women's Militancy and Gendered Emotional Regimes

The onset of the war in 1914 prompted further discussion about the relationship between gender, violence, and honour codes. During the war, emotional values such as honour, courage, chivalry, and their antithesis, shame and cowardice, became a common feature of civilian and military discourse.[97] For example, across all the belligerent states, wartime propaganda was at pains to urge men to fight to protect their personal honour as well as the honour of their nation. At the same time, it depicted the enemy soldier as barbaric and entirely lacking in honour.[98] Woman's honour was invoked as a reason to go to war. Men's courage and chivalry were appealed to in terms of correcting atrocious wrongs such as the real rape of women in war and the metaphorical rape of a country by invading armies. The much-cited 'Rape of Belgium' is a case in point here.[99] Drawing on the topic of sexual violence against women in nationalist propaganda served a highly symbolic function, because rape did not just humiliate women and injure men's self-perception, it also targeted and damaged the honour of the masculine nation.[100]

To invoke honour, Ute Frevert reminds us, was to call to action. Historically, honour was considered to have held such emotional power that it imperatively called for action. Violence underpinned this call to action. Personal and national shame threatened if a man or the nation's manhood proved that it was not up to the task. If it proved itself weak and cowardly, then all honour was lost.[101] Cowardly behaviour on the part of a man could only, Frevert asserts, be perceived 'as utterly dishonourable, shameful, and unchivalrous'.[102] During times of war, then, the nation's honour became inextricably tied to the active and violent performance of its manhood. Women were accorded a passive position in line with understandings of chivalry. Therefore, women agitating to enter into active spheres directed by masculine honour codes jeopardised an already precarious balance between honour, masculinity, and violence. The *Review*'s passionate response to such attempted incursions of male wartime spaces—particularly the theatres of violence—demonstrates just how aware anti-suffragists were of the increased pressure that the violent conflict exerted on the ongoing operation of gendered emotional regimes.

As outlined in the previous chapter, women reacted to the commencement of the international conflict in a myriad of ways.[103] In Britain, some women became outwardly jingoistic. The WSPU's Emmeline and Christabel Pankhurst are renowned examples of this. Others used the occasion to morally police the general population. For instance, young women in particular deemed it appropriate to shame men out of uniform for not being manly enough to enlist to fight. Pacifists—such as Emmeline Pethick-Lawrence in Britain, Vida Goldstein in Australia, and Hanna Sheehy Skeffington in Ireland—came out in opposition to the war. Feminist pacifists evoked the image of the mother and the nurturer in their attempts to influence more women to oppose what they saw as the relentlessness of male militarism and the senseless slaughter of human life. Anti-imperialist feminists pointed out that the war served only the imperial elite not the thousands of men dying on the battlefields daily. Still other women—both on the conservative and the radical sides of politics—used the example of the war to argue that the female sex could do its bit on the battlefield. Women, this minority asserted, were as useful as men in the realm of modern warfare, where technological innovation eliminated the need for brute strength. Military strategy trumped brute strength. Discussions taking place between women about the war and women's perceived roles in war unsettled pre-war political affiliations and divisions. Whereas many on both sides of the general political divide—left-wing and right-wing—united under the banner of patriotism, others who had formerly aligned with each other—for example, members of the feminist community—split over their allegiances to the war effort and to international pacifism.

212 *The Shame of the Violent Woman*

World War One and Female Combatants

Since the outbreak of war, the British *Review* looked on the behaviour of patriotic women with some trepidation. As we saw in Chapter 5, the paper accused feminists of carrying on their campaigning under the guise of carrying out their patriotic war work. These duplicitous women were guilty of the unpatriotic act of corrupting the emotional regimes guiding men's and women's experiences at a time when performances of masculinity and femininity were under intense scrutiny. Anti-suffragists were irritated and angered but not entirely shocked by the fact that feminists' pre-war deviancy continued into wartime. But they were exasperated that patriotic women generally were threatening to transgress the boundaries dividing men's and women's traditional wartime roles, thereby eroding wartime gendered emotional standards.

One year into the war, for example, anti-suffragists professed their profound embarrassment at seeing women performing war work in military uniform. Susan Grayzel notes that British contemporaries were struck by women workers taking on roles previously closed to them—like bus and tram conductors, guards and ticket collectors on trains, and postal workers—and wearing uniforms, often masculine uniforms, while doing so.[104] This influx of uniform-wearing women workers was jarring enough, but the sight of women in military garb was positively disconcerting. By 1915 in Britain, for instance, organisations such as the Women's Emergency Corps and Women's Voluntary Reserve had begun to wear khaki uniforms and practice drilling and parading.[105] These were patriotic women whose enthusiasm for working for the State, ordinarily, would have been applauded. However, instead of performing their patriotism in an appropriately feminine manner, they were guilty of weakly imitating the male soldier by donning his uniform. Their actions forced more knowing British patriots to experience vicarious embarrassment. As explained in Chapter 3, vicarious embarrassment is described as the feelings of humiliation people experience on behalf of those close to them who have had cause to embarrass themselves.[106] Patriotic women had committed a minor *faux pas* by dressing as men. They were not soldiers. They embarrassed themselves by not knowing this when all others did.

In a 1915 article entitled 'A Question of Taste', the *Review* pointed out that these female military uniforms were not bloodstained khakis from the war front. The wearing of military uniform and adoption of military titles by women was striking what the paper said was a 'wrong and jarring note'. Ultimately, it was a 'question of taste'.[107] Later, the paper again felt compelled to object to this questionable habit. While it was true that women were doing their war work, 'neither that nor the wearing of khaki livery makes them soldiers'.[108] The duty and the right to exercise physical force divided the two patriotic communities—masculine and feminine. Appropriating masculine uniform only drew attention to women's inadequacy as soldiers. It highlighted the fact that they were denied entry into the sphere of direct action where those wearing the uniform legitimately were serving.

Initially, uniform-wearing women patriots embarrassed the patriotic community to which they belonged. After all, these were just over-zealous patriotic women who valued belonging to their collective. However, as it became more apparent that these women were actually proposing to assume an active role in the theatres of combat—at home in case of invasion or even on the overseas battlefields—anti-suffragists' expressions of emotional discomfort alternated between embarrassment and shame. In proposing that they mobilise—and perhaps even take up arms—in defence of Britain, patriotic women did not simply blunder. Rather, they attacked the emotional standards guiding men's and women's experiences in war. They attempted an incursion of masculine physical and emotional spaces, and they did this, again, at a time when the masculinity of the nation was under extreme duress. They proposed that they were as capable as men of defending the nation. In doing so, they undermined men's ability to safeguard the nation as was their duty. These ultra-patriotic women were now proving themselves dangerously and shamefully unpatriotic.

In January 1915, the *Review* reported that a body of British women were proposing 'a Women's Volunteer reserve'. The proposed Women's Volunteer Corps was 'not to be so Amazonian as its name implies and its founders hoped'. Rather than arming, women members were to be organised and disciplined so that they could perform duties such as carrying dispatches and taking control of transport in the unlikely event that the country is invaded. Still, there were some more ominous references to 'rifle practice'.[109] 'It is fortunate that the Briton is a good fighter, for we are a hopelessly unmilitary nation', the *Review* stated ironically. Then, with more earnestness, the paper went on to explain,

> The lack of military instinct is displayed in the supposition that organised defence will be deficient in what the Women Volunteers have to offer, will take the field without transport and without dispatch riders. The patriotism of these women is magnificent, but it is to be hoped that the country is in a better state of organisation than their scheme implies. There remains the more serious aspect that women who might be employed in the capacities indicated would become ipso facto combatants. Great Britain would not be making a contribution to the cause of civilisation when she pressed her women into any other form of military service than that of Red Cross work.[110]

At stake was Britain's position at the head of the 'civilised' world. At stake were international codes of chivalry.

British anti-suffragists were already concerned that women enacting suffragette violence would dismantle codes of chivalry that had until now, they said, protected women from men's aggression. These were domestic codes, intended to regulate relations between the sexes, they explained. However, if women were to now propose enacting physical force on the international stage, then entire international codes of chivalry would be brought under scrutiny. The event that prompted this renewed interest in chivalry was the paper's report in March 1915 that the Women's Volunteer Corps had dropped attempts to include taking up rifles as part of their remit and were instead turning towards the idea of establishing a Women Signallers' Territorial Corps. Equality for the Sexes before this has been treated as a folly, but is now entering on the criminal, the *Review* asserted.[111] These women claimed that they were ready to face the enemy and to put up with the penalties potentially inflicted on them as wartime belligerents. But who, the *Review* asked, is going to inflict penalties on these potential female belligerents? Not the Germans, was its response:

> Certainly not the Germans, for they would refuse to recognise women as anything else than non-combatants, and if they were found assisting in military operations the infuriated invaders would consider themselves justified in regarding their enemies as outside the pale of civilized warfare. Is the British Government going to the next Hague Conference to announce that in future it proposes to employ women as soldiers?[112]

The Germans might have what another article declared was a 'Teutonic lust of world power' that rivalled the suffragette's violent lust for domestic power. Certainly, infamous suffragist women were the ones proposing 'drilling' women and readying them for violent conflict, the *Review* reported.[113] The paper continued, however desirous of power the Germans were, at least they knew the limits of civilised and uncivilised behaviour, particularly as it directed relations between men and women.[114] It seemed that over-zealous patriotic women and feminists harbouring an unseemly and irrational lust for power through calls for equality—including physical equality—did not.

To make its point about international codes of chivalry, the *Review* chose to ignore accusations of rape and other atrocities that were circulated by the British propaganda machine and which would have affirmed for readers that the Germans were barbarians. This was also months before the execution of British nurse Edith Cavell, which, for many British citizens, did indeed confirm that German soldiers existed beyond the pale of civilisation.[115] Therefore, the paper persisted with the task of elucidating just what damage violent patriotic women could do to international war conventions.

Women combatants were unnatural and their proposed actions could only provoke undesirable consequences. As the *Review* explained,

> Such a kicking against the limits imposed by nature and by civilization can only result in one of two alternatives: either these military women will be shot and bayoneted by the enemy, or they will take advantage of their sex so as to put the enemy's soldiers into an unfair and impossible

position, at any rate until the unnatural behaviour of such amazons has driven international usage to reconsider and revise its code of chivalry.[116]

However, there was yet another alternative, the paper stated. 'If the enemy regards such armed women as non-combatants, they may bring massacre on the whole civil population of the locality', it concluded.[117] Violent women would only serve to dismantle entire codes of chivalry that many believed protected against decivilising forces. Despite stories and images of the blatant horrors of the battlefield that flooded into the home front, many continued to subscribe to the view that chivalry stemmed some of the savagery of war.

As it seemed more and more likely that the government was going to give into feminist demands to extend the franchise to women, the *Review* published a flurry of articles that reaffirmed its belief in the physical force argument. At least three long years of violent bloodshed and the seemingly endless loss of male lives fuelled the paper's panicked reaction to a political move that now seemed imminent. The war had demonstrated that men's and women's physical and emotional worlds remained separate. Why then would their political duties merge to become inextricable from the other? Men's bodies were sacrificed for the war effort. Men were compelled to exhibit courage and chivalry and honour, not women. Why then would women be granted the right to exercise the vote—a vote that would inevitably mean power over whether or not a country went to war? Nothing about men's and women's experiences during the war had convinced those writing for the *Review* that women were capable of adhering to the masculine emotional regimes that necessarily guided men's participation in war. Anti-suffragists were not convinced that it was even appropriate for women to contemplate their fitness for emotional regimes that had never regulated their behaviour.

In December 1917, the *Review* reasserted some well-known facts:

> Now, when war occurs, it is the men of this country who make a wall with their bodies against the foe; who suffer every torture of bodily discomfort that can be imagined, and who pay the supreme sacrifice. Those who pay the piper have the right to call the tune. Women do not pay the piper.[118]

Women suffered during war. That was undisputed. One article pointed out that '*some* women have been killed and wounded at the front, or through air raids at home'. But women were not asked to sacrifice their lives during war.

> The nation can and does ask its manhood to give life up in the defence of a just cause; men, therefore, knowing their responsibilities, should have the vote. That many have faced danger gladly and have given up

all to the cause of right, does not alter the fact that the nation cannot compel women to undergo anything in the nature of military service. It would take too long to explain why this cannot be done, but one word will suffice. Health. The health of potential mothers and of actual mothers must be protected or the nation would cease to exist.[119]

As this passage outlines, a woman's willingness to display courage did not seem to be under doubt. However, the appropriateness of her doing so in the field of conflict certainly was. On the battlefield, her courage was misplaced. This was a place for the exhibition of man's valour exclusively.

One month later in January 1918, the paper affirmed that 'when fighting is in the air, the occasion belongs to man, and that the Amazon is not the highest ideal of womanhood'.[120] That month, the *Review* also devoted a number of pages to renowned anti-suffragist, Sir Almroth E. Wright's plea to the House of Lords to deny the woman vote on the basis of reigning views of physical force. Wright opposed suffrage on the grounds that men's and women's bodies would become indistinguishable from each other, particularly in relation to the exercise of physical force. The woman vote would result in, he said,

> A State in which the governing power—that is, the power of physical compulsion by the communal force—was committed to man and woman equally; in which such State compulsion was brought to bear equitably upon the two sexes; and in which man applied physical compulsion to a woman, and she to a man, without distinction. Of sex. In a State organised upon this pattern woman, if physically fit, would, like man, be subject to military conscription and active fighting. She would also be enrolled in the police force, and would be employed as an arm of the law to apply physical compulsion without distinction to man and woman.[121]

He invoked shocking images of male-female violence—of 'men and women shooting each other down and falling upon each other with bayonets' and 'of the female body shot and run-through'. He went further to include the pregnant body in his repertoire of bloody and violent imagery. There surge into the mind 'visions also of the possibility of women soldiers fighting and killed in a condition of pregnancy; and worst nightmares'.[122] The woman's body as a sight of reproduction, life, and nurture was glaringly incongruous with the deadly intent of the battlefield.

Significantly, however, it was not the wrong done to female bodies that Wright was most worried about but rather the impact that these visions would have on the masculine mind. Such images of male-on-female violence may be dismissed as romanticised, he said, as fantastical. However, he added, 'it would, without doubt, be arguable that their appeal is to the sentimental masculine, rather than to the matter-of-fact feminine intellect'.[123] It was men's emotional regimes that violent women threatened to invade at the same time that they altered their own. To allow women to exercise physical force—surely an appendage of the vote—was to make both sexes subject to the same moral law. To do so, then, would be to instil in women the idea that 'it is moral and reputable of her to resort to the weapon of force'. It is to invite her to use violence against men. Yet, civilisation, he added, relied on it 'being maintained as a settled moral principle between the sexes that neither shall turn against the other the weapon of physical compulsion'.[124] Again, however, Wright returned to the matter of masculine emotional regimes. To allow or ask woman to use violence against the male body would be to ask him to transform his entire way of thinking and being. Wright posited that asking women to alter their emotional make-up was significant but that it was 'an even greater matter' to instruct men to do so because that involved going 'to work to uproot out of man's mind the instinctive feeling that it is culpable to use physical force against woman. And it is to make bad blood in man's heart against woman and in woman's heart against man'.[125]

This call to enter into the realm of politics and political violence was an attempted incursion into male worlds—physical and emotional—such as the country had never before seen. It was also a clumsily miscalculated one that revealed just how far outside the pale of the male emotional and physical world, women were. Women proposing such shocking measures did not simply affect a transformation of gendered emotional standards. Corrupting these emotional standards naturally promised dire physical consequences. To Wright—and to the women contributing to the *Review*—the dismantlement of emotional regimes that had traditionally protected women from men's violence promised only a future of unrestrained male-on-female violence. The international war had just revealed how utterly destructive and devastating male violence could be. Why would Britain sanction such a prospect?

Irish Feminists and Physical Force

The commencement of the war and the normalisation of male violence on a mass scale prompted many suffragists too to revisit discussions that had taken place earlier in the suffrage campaign about women's resort to physical force. Therefore, before concluding, I want to necessarily briefly return to the notion that I raised near the beginning of this chapter about a feminist ethics of violence.

Irish militant suffragists had often used the example of the increasing militarisation of early twentieth-century Irish society to distinguish between reactions to male and female displays of militancy. In October 1914, the *Irish Citizen* reported the arrest of feminist activists, Mrs Sheehy Skeffington and Mrs Connery, for trying to address a crowd in the vicinity of visiting British Prime Minister Asquith. At the same time, nearby male socialist activists, Mr Larkin, Mr Connelly, and Mr Daly, addressed a crowd and were protected by a large body of men from the socialist Irish Citizen Army with rifles which they apparently discharged into the air from time to time. No attempt was made by the police to interfere with these meetings. The article concluded that the effectiveness of shows of male political violence exposed the ineffectiveness of peaceful, though militant, female protest.[126]

Not all suffrage militants in the country agreed with exercising typically masculine forms of force, however. As with the British suffragists, the militant movement in Ireland was split between those who advocated the destruction of property and those who promoted more active forms of violence, such as violence against the person.[127] The appropriate nature of woman's weapons of war was a highly contentious subject. This was even so in two countries which were variously embroiled in domestic and international conflict; where displays of mass, organised violence were increasingly accepted as normal.

The onset of the Great War advertised the versatility and effectiveness of violence for those women who had previously advocated political violence, whether for feminist, nationalist, and/or general military campaigns. For example, in the first year of the war, advocate of Irish and Indian feminism and nationalism, Margaret Cousins, issued the call, 'One man, one gun; one woman, one gun.'[128] If fighting was wrong, she argued, it was for men and women equally. If it was justifiable then it was equally so for both sexes too. 'Modern warfare', she declared,

> depends more on skill and endurance than on brute strength. Physiology proves conclusively that woman's power of endurance is greater than man's. Her success in sports proves woman's equality of skill and aim. Powers of magnetic leadership have constantly been acknowledged in women.[129]

Cousins was quite rational in her approach to the issue. It made more sense to her to send single women to war where they risked death than to send married men who had wives and children dependent on them. Sex did not delineate capability for exercising physical force. Morally, emotionally, and physically now—in the era of technological warfare—men and women were equally suited to and equipped for war.

Besides, as Cousins pointed out, women were already arming in anticipation of civil strife between nationalists and Unionists in Ireland. This was in evidence through women's involvement with the Unionist Ulster Volunteer Force and the nationalist Cumman na mBan, the Women's Council of the Irish Volunteers (later the Irish Republican Army). As outlined in Chapter 2, prominent nationalist feminists, including Constance Markievicz, claimed that Irish women had a special ancestral relationship with violence. Markievicz was a nationalist, socialist, and feminist politician and soldier. She trained boys and young men for armed combat through the militant Fianna na hÉireann, a nationalist version of the Boy Scouts, which she co-founded in 1909.[130] She fought in the failed nationalist uprising in 1916 and was sentenced to be executed only to have that sentence commuted to life imprisonment because of her sex. While incarcerated in 1918, she was elected to the British parliament but refused to take her seat. In 1919, she was elected to the first Dáil Éireann (Irish parliament). She was appointed the minister for labour, thereby taking her place as the first woman minister of any European parliament. Markievicz endured more imprisonments during the Anglo-Irish War or Irish War of Independence (1919–1921). During this time, she was appointed president of the Cumann na mBan, the militant women's organisation supporting the armed separatist group, the Irish Volunteers.[131]

Markievicz was a vocal advocate of women arming in defence of their country. Prior to the war, her views had been aired through public speeches and in the pages of women's periodicals like the *Bean na hEireann* (the *Bean*) and the *Citizen*. At the outset of the international war, the *Citizen* republished one of Markievicz's earlier, well-circulated call to arms. Markievicz instructed Irish women to arm themselves with 'noble and free ideas'. 'And if in your day the call should come for your body to arm', she added, 'do not shirk that either.'[132] It was preferable that women arm themselves than that they rely on the 'problematic chivalry' of men.[133] Too many women existed in 'domestic ruts', armed only with 'feminine pens'. Hers was a call to direct action. As a radical Irish nationalist and a separatist, Markievicz was not a friend of the British war effort. But she considered that the war was useful because it had helped to shake 'women out of old grooves' by forcing different responsibilities on them.[134] She lauded the feminist consciousness-raising that war could bring about for women.

Like many of her fellow nationalist feminists, Markievicz asserted that Irish women in particular had a proud tradition of militancy to live up to. 'I have never heard in the early history of any country so many stories of great fighting women as I read in the history of Ireland', she declared. Here she was referring to the stories of Maeve, of Macha, of Granuaile, of Fleas, and many others.[135] Fighting was in the Irish woman's blood. 'Ancient Ireland bred warrior women, and women played a heroic part in those days', she asserted.[136] Here she was supported by prominent feminist nationalist Hanna Sheehy Skeffington. Sheehy Skeffington declared that in ancient times, Irish men and women were equal in arms, as in other professions.[137]

Irish women had lost their way since these ancient times but it was not impossible for them to reacquaint themselves with their proud warrior tradition. They only had to invoke the spirit of more modern specimens of Irish warrior women, for example, those who fought in the United Irishmen's Rebellion of 1798.[138] Markievicz explained that, in that 1798 conflict, many women 'actually fought in the ranks, like Ireland's Amazon women of the past'. Even those who did not—those who 'were not of the old martial nature, and who shrunk from the clash of arms'—were not idle. They played their part by sending 'their mankind to battle with a brave word, and many earnest heart-deep prayers'. The 'timidest' of Irish women 'were ever ready to nurse the wounded, hide the fugitive, and to strain every nerve to serve the National cause and the Nation's heroes', she said.[139]

Since then, too many Irish women had been seduced by the comforts and familiarities of daily life. Too many were

> so utterly indifferent to the struggle that is going on around them; caring very little for the National cause, provided they can be amused, well fed, and prosperous enough to live in the same style as their friends and contemporaries.[140]

Women were to blame, but they were aided by men and colonialism. By accepting the imposition of the soulless, middle-class gender ideals of the modern world that were introduced and imposed on the Irish by the British—those that banned women from spheres of action that they had enjoyed in the past, such as combat—modern Irish women had been 'civilised'. Indeed, the successful implementation of sex segregation had severely endangered women's very existence, Markievicz accused, adding, 'To-day we are in danger of being civilised by men out of existence'.[141] The difference, she instructed readers, between the warrior women of old and women today is that the women of old owed 'no allegiance to any man'.[142] Only the suffragette and the woman trade unionist seemed to still embody the spirit of the warrior women of old.[143] But, again, Markievicz saw it as one of her duties to reawaken that spirit in the Irish women of her day. Her strategy was to hold a mirror up to the Irish woman who had been seduced by the luxuries and ease of British-imposed modernity in order to reflect her shameful state. She wanted to shame fellow Irish women into honouring their warrior women ancestry.

Along with the other women who had participated in the 1916 Rising, for example, Markievicz had shown that women could fight. More than that, a *Citizen* contributor declared, she was also responsible for overturning the myth that women could not assume a leading military role because men would be too ashamed to be found following a woman into battle. 'It has been my lot during the last few weeks', the author continued, 'to meet several men who were "on the Green with the Countess,"[144] and I have entirely failed to observe on their part any feeling of disgrace at being led by a woman; their wives, too, seem to regard that fact with pride.'[145] The warrior woman was not shameful and neither was the warrior woman leader—leader of men as well as women.

Markievicz understood the power of training. She drilled the boys of the Fianna in the use of arms. Women too could be trained in such skills. But her testament to women's combat capabilities went beyond mere technical skill. The desire and the right to bear arms was, she claimed, the Irish woman's privilege. Courage underpinned that privilege. Courage was an emotional virtue shared by Irish men and Irish women. It was their shared heritage. Markievicz's legacy has always been highly contested and controversial. Immediately after her death—and indeed since, for the controversy continues—commentators have variously criticised her for her flamboyant style and passionate manner, and for the fact that she trained young men and instilled in them a desire to kill and die for Ireland.[146] Yet one thing that has not been disputed is her capacity for courage. Even writer and socialist compatriot, Sean O'Casey, who condemned Markievicz for what he said was a superficial personality and lack of commitment, declared that she had physical courage, with which 'she was clothed as with a garment'.[147] This female combatant's physical courage may not have been in doubt. But its exercise in the field of battle was out of character with the times.

Patriotic Irish women, such as Markievicz, constructed an ethics of violence that pertained to Irish women specifically. Irish women, nationalist feminists declared, had a proud past of shared warrior status with their manhood. Men and women had adhered to the same emotional standards, engaging as they did in the same physical activities, combat included. Back then, there was nothing shameful about the violent woman. British colonisation, through the imposition of modern or civilised notions of separate spheres, had corroded the historic nature of relations between Irish men and women. It had sentenced men and women to different physical spheres guarded over by different emotional regimes. It was up to nationalist women to instigate a decivilising process that would allow them to return to a pre-British and pre-civilised world. Then they could take their place alongside men in the public worlds of politics and war. Recollections of that proud past of gender equality had been deployed to awaken Irish women's nationalism. However, it had also been used by nationalist feminists and feminist nationalists to justify their recourse to militancy.[148] Margaret Cousins may have argued along more universal lines that women could fight if men were fighting. If fighting was good for men, it was good for women. However, the overwhelming sense emanating from the community of nationalist Irish women was that their specific ethnic heritage rendered them fit for militancy. The ethics of violence that they constructed, then, was less exclusively feminist than it was nationalist feminist. The fighting Irish woman was not shameful, but the woman who denied her heritage and instead embraced British models of passive femininity was.

Conclusion

British anti-suffragists were adamant that violence degraded womanhood. Women were not fit for active engagement with violence. Physically, they were not suited to the exercise of physical force. Women's bodies were built to facilitate the more nurturing and less destructive function of childbirth. Emotionally, they were not trained to engage in legitimate forms of violence as men were. Honour codes directed men's use of physical force. Men were directed to adhere to standards of courage, chivalry, and fairness when engaging in physical combat with each other. Women were not brought up to embody these virtues. Therefore, when women demanded access to the battlefield—or when they performed violence publicly in the name of feminism—they attacked the make-up of the different gendered emotional regimes. They brought shame on womanhood when they abandoned their life-giving instincts for the destructive capacities of masculine violence. They threatened to corrupt the nature of manly emotional virtues like courage and chivalry when they attempted to embody those virtues. For example, by demanding to stand alongside their brothers in the country's defence during the Great War, patriotic women cast aspersions on British men's ability to perform their manly duty of protecting the nation. They cast doubt on his ability to embody the emotional qualities required of him to perform this function at this crucial time.

More than that, by enacting violence publicly, women jeopardised the existence of codes of chivalry that were established to protect them—the weaker sex—from the violent actions of men—the stronger sex. They provoked a reappraisal of codes of chivalry to the detriment of both women and men. Women were already vulnerable to male violence but militant women brought the very real threat of male-on-female violence much closer to home than it had been previously. If women were capable of combat then why would men need to adhere to emotional regulations that were intended to protect the supposedly weaker sex? By forcing men to react violently towards women—by provoking men's anger and violence as they disturbed public meetings and threw hatchets at prime ministers—violent women also forced men to confront that part of themselves that they worked to control. They awoke man's inner brute. No one benefitted from such an awakening.

By threatening to fight alongside men for the nation's defence, violent women also provoked the wrath of the international soldier. She jeopardised entire international codes of chivalry that were designed to protect women from some of war's barbarity and depravity. The violent woman in the theatre of war put all women at further risk of wartime male violence. Moreover, men could not abide by notions of chivalry that required them not to strike a woman when women were pointing guns at them. To ask them to do this would be unfair. It would put them at a disadvantage. Women entering conflict zones destabilised the gendered character of international emotional regimes.

Indeed, suffragist violence compelled British anti-suffragists to re-examine their views on legitimate forms of male-on-female violence. Anti-feminists expanded the category of womanhood which was undeserving of the physical protection promised to women by codes of chivalry to accommodate feminists. Nagging suffragettes were added to nagging wives as women who deservedly provoked men's wrath and their violence. The inability of suffragettes—or 'latter-day specimens of the old-fashioned nagging woman'[149]—to internalise shame revitalised the need for pre-modern forms of public shaming. For example, British anti-suffragists recalled the effectiveness of the torturous Scold's Bridle as a means of imposing shame on those women who refused to amend their ways. In the modern age, violent women served no other function than to return society to its pre-civilised state.

Irish women, however, justified their recourse to violence on the grounds that what they desired was indeed a return to this pre-civilised state. They wanted to reinstate gender relations that had existed in Ireland before the onset of British colonisation and the so-called civilising process. This meant reinstating an emotional regime that directed men's and women's actions equally. Drawing on stories of ancient Irish equality, Irish nationalist women championed the recreation of a permanent national context in which men and women could engage equally in the public worlds of politics and war. They proposed an ethics of violence that was feminist in nature but that was largely directed by nationalist concerns.

Notes

1 *Votes for Women*, 19 November 1909, p. 116.
2 *Votes for Women*, 19 November 1909, p. 116.
3 *Votes for Women*, 19 November 1909, p. 120.
4 *Votes for Women*, 26 November 1909, p. 138.
5 Laura E. Nym Mayhall presents a nuanced analysis of militancy in her article where she places the less-recognised militancy of the WFL and the more infamous militancy of the WSPU into the longer tradition of radical protest in the country. Both the WFL and the WSPU understood themselves to be 'Suffragettes' at the time. However, the WFL rejected violence unlike the WSPU. See Laura E. Nym Mayhall, 'Defining Militancy: Radical Protest, the Constitutional Idiom, and Women's Suffrage in Britain, 1908–1909', *Journal of British Studies*, vol. 39, no. 3 (2000) pp. 340–371, pp. 343–349.
6 As outlined in the Introduction to this book, from 1905 to 1912, the militant campaign—largely through the WSPU—took the form of heckling politicians, noisily disrupting political meetings, and a willingness to go to prison rather than paying fines for 'unruly' behaviour. From 1912 until their cessation with the beginning of the Great War in 1914, suffragettes, as members of the WSPU were labelled, moved on to more violent and often illegal forms of activity such as mass window-breaking raids, vandalising post boxes, attacking public property, including setting fire to buildings and going on hunger strike. See June Purvis, 'Fighting the Double Moral Standard in Edwardian Britain: Suffragette Militancy, Sexuality and the Nation in the Writings of the Early Twentieth-Century British Feminist Christabel Pankhurst', in Francisca de Haan, Margaret Allen, June Purvis and Krassimira Dasklova, eds., *Women's Activism: Global Perspectives from the 1890s to the Present* (New York: Routledge, 2013), pp. 121–135, p. 121. For a recent, revisionist history of the nature and origins of suffragette militancy see Laura E. Nym Mayhall, The *Militant Suffrage Movement. Citizenship and Resistance in Britain, 1860–1930* (Oxford: Oxford University Press, 2003).
7 Violence is defined as behaviour that involves physical force and is intended to 'hurt, damage, or kill' according to the *Oxford English Dictionary*. Gemma Clark, therefore, argues that all violence is mindful because violence is, by definition, the intended infliction of injury on people or property. See Gemma Clark, *Everyday Violence in the Irish Civil War* (Cambridge: Cambridge University Press, 2014), p. 1.

8. Pieter Spierenburg, 'Masculinity, Violence, and Honor: An Introduction', in Pieter Spierenburg, ed., *Men and Violence. Gender, Honor, and Rituals in Modern Europe and America* (Columbus: Ohio State University Press, 1998) pp. 1–29, p. 1.
9. Robert Shoemaker, 'Male Honour and the Decline of Public Violence in Eighteenth-Century London', *Social History*, vol. 26, no. 2 (2001) pp. 190–208, p. 202.
10. For example, he quotes the *London Evening Post*, 29 March 1735 in relation to a woman committing robbery with violent assault in Shoemaker, 'Male Honour and the Decline of Public Violence in Eighteenth-Century London', p. 202.
11. Shoemaker, 'Male Honour and the Decline of Public Violence in Eighteenth-Century London', p. 202.
12. Carolyn Strange and Robert Cribb affirm that the profound association that honour maintained with masculinity means that 'males, overwhelmingly, have been the chief antagonists in violence inflicted in its name'. See Carolyn Strange and Robert Cribb, 'Historical Perspectives on Honour, Violence and Emotion' in Carolyn Strange, Robert Cribb, Christopher E. Forth, eds., *Honour, Violence and Emotions in History* (London: Bloomsbury Academic, 2014) pp. 9–38, p. 8.
13. Spierenburg, 'Masculinity, Violence, and Honor', p. 1.
14. Spierenburg, 'Masculinity, Violence, and Honor', p. 1.
15. Spierenburg argues that this is not a characteristic of some non-European cultures. See Spierenburg, 'Masculinity, Violence, and Honor', p. 3. Duelling was one way for more elite members of a society to react to personal insult. For an example of a study of duelling in European society, see Ute Frevert, 'The Taming of the Noble Ruffian: Male Violence and Duelling in Early Modern and Modern Germany', in Pieter Spierenburg, ed., *Men and Violence: Gender, Honor, and Rituals in Modern Europe and America* (Columbus: Ohio State University Press, 1998) pp. 37–63.
16. Certain forms of violence, such as duelling before its demise through the eighteenth and nineteenth centuries, also offered gentlemen the means by which to prove their superiority standing. See Shoemaker, 'Male Honour and the Decline of Public Violence in Eighteenth-Century London', p. 200.
17. Steven F. Shatz and Naomi R. Shatz, 'Chivalry is Not Dead: Murder, Gender, and the Death Penalty', *Berkeley Journal of Gender, Law & Justice*, vol. 27, no. 1 (2012) pp. 64–112, p. 67.
18. Shatz and Shatz, 'Chivalry is Not Dead', p. 68.
19. René Moelker and Gerhard Kümmel, 'Chivalry and Codes of Conduct: Can the Virtue of Chivalry Epitomize Guidelines for Interpersonal Conduct?', *Journal of Military Ethics*, vol. 6, no. 4 (2007) pp. 292–302, p. 298.
20. Shoemaker, 'Male Honour and the Decline of Public Violence in Eighteenth-Century London', p. 196.
21. As Angela Woollacott argues, violence against women has been used historically to maintain men's privileges. Globally, women continue to be highly vulnerable to male violence, whether domestic violence, sexual assault, wartime violence (including sexual violence), and workplace violence (for example, trade union violence when women enter male dominated industries). Violence against women continues to be a transnational as well as national issue. See Angela Woollacott, 'A Feminist History of Violence: History as a Weapon of Liberation?', *Lilith*, vol. 16 (2007) pp. 1–11, pp. 1–4.
22. Shoemaker, 'Male Honour and the Decline of Public Violence in Eighteenth-Century London', p. 203.
23. Shoemaker, 'Male Honour and the Decline of Public Violence in Eighteenth-Century London', p. 206.
24. For example, Shoemaker points out that by the end of the eighteenth century, more homicides by men were reported as taking place in place 'in private houses,

taverns, coffee-houses, and shops'. See Shoemaker, 'Male Honour and the Decline of Public Violence in Eighteenth-Century London', p. 206.
25 Shoemaker, 'Male Honour and the Decline of Public Violence in Eighteenth-Century London', p. 203.
26 It is widely accepted that the term 'New Woman' was first coined in 1894 by the novelist Sarah Grand, pseudonym of Frances Elizabeth Belleuden Clarke, author of *The Heavenly Twins*, 1893. Grand's article entitled 'The New Aspect of the Woman Question,' in which she uses the term 'New Woman,' was published in 1894, in the *North American Review*. (David Rubinstein, *Before the Suffragettes: Women's Emancipation in the 1890s* (Brighton: Harvester, 1986) pp. 15–16.) See also Barbara Caine, *Victorian Feminists* (New York: Oxford University Press, 1992) p. 252. For an extensive discussion of Grand and the New Woman novel see Teresa Mangum, 'New Strategies for New (Academic) Women', *Nineteenth-Century Gender Studies*, vol. 3, no. 2, (2007) pp. 1–19.
27 Shoemaker, 'Male Honour and the Decline of Public Violence in Eighteenth-Century London', p. 208.
28 While some of these analyses of female combatants make use of historical case studies to demonstrate their arguments about the relationship between gender and violence, they are guided by the research agendas and theories of the political sciences rather than those of historical studies. See, for example, Caron E. Gentry and Lara Sjoberg, *Beyond Mothers, Monsters, Whores: Thinking about Women's Violence in Global Politics* (London: Zed Books, 2015); Siphokazi Magadla, 'Women Combatants and the Liberation Movement in South Africa: Guerrilla Girls, Combative Mothers and the In-Betweeners', *African Security Review*, vol. 24, no. 4 (2015) pp. 390–402; Swati Parashar, *Women and Militant Wars: The Politics of Injury* (Abingdon: Routledge, 2014); Paige Whaley Eager, *From Freedom Fighters to Terrorists: Women and Political Violence* (Aldershot: Ashgate, 2008); and Miranda Alison, 'Women as Agents of Political Violence: Gendering Security', *Security Dialogue*, vol. 35, no. 4 (2004) pp. 447–463.
29 Miranda Alison acknowledges just how widespread this assumption is and devotes her article to debunking this myth through case studies of female militants in Sri Lanka and Northern Ireland. See Alison, 'Women as Agents of Political Violence: Gendering Security', p. 448.
30 Gentry and Sjoberg, *Beyond Mothers, Monsters, Whores*, p. 2. Angela Woollacott draws on research that demonstrates that girls (under 18), voluntarily and involuntarily, have been part of fighting forces in 55 different countries between 1990 and 2003. These countries include developed (including the United States, Israel, Denmark, France, Ireland, Sweden, Britain, Australia, and Japan) as well as less developed (for instance, Mozambique, northern Uganda, and Sierra Leone). See Angela Woollacott, 'A Feminist History of Violence: History as a Weapon of Liberation?', p. 7.
31 Eager, *From Freedom Fighters to Terrorists*, p. 3.
32 In her groundbreaking work on women, feminism and war, Jean Bethke Elshtain argued that, despite accumulating evidence of women's participation in modern conflicts, the notion of woman as a static symbol of peace continues to exert a hold over the popular imagination. Women have been used time and again to exemplify qualities that work to keep the barbarism of war at bay. (See Jean Bethke Elshtain, 'Women as Mirror and Other: Toward a Theory of Women, War, and Feminism', *Humanities in Society*, vol. 5, no. 2 (1982) pp. 22–44, p. 32.) They represent the possibility of a return to normality once the conflict has ended. (Margaret Randolph Higonnet, Jane Jenson, Sonya Michel and Margaret Collins Weitz, 'Introduction', in Margaret Randolph Higonnet, Jane Jenson, Sonya Michel and Margaret Collins Weitz, eds., *Behind the Lines:*

226   *The Shame of the Violent Woman*

    Gender and the Two World Wars (New Haven and London: Yale University Press, 1987) pp. 1–17, p. 2.)
33 Gentry and Sjoberg cite Elshtain's 1987 book, *Women and War*. See Jean Bethke Elshtain, *Women and War*, (New York: New York University Press, 1987).
34 Gentry and Sjoberg, *Beyond Mothers, Monsters, Whores*, p. 2.
35 See Gentry and Sjoberg, *Beyond Mothers, Monsters, Whores*, p. 3.
36 Important contributions to the study of women and the military, pacifism and women, and, gender and war were made in the 1980s and 1990s and include, for example: Margaret Randolph Higonnet, Jane Jenson, Sonya Michel and Margaret Collins Weitz, eds., *Behind the Lines. Gender and the Two World Wars* (New Haven and London: Yale University Press, 1987); Cynthia Enloe, *Does Khaki Become You? The Militarization of Women's Lives* (London: Harper Collins, 1988); Jean Bethke Elshtain and Sheila Tobias, eds., *Women, Militarism, and War: Essays in History, Politics, and Social Theory* (Savage: Rowman and Littlefield, 1990); and Ruth H. Howes and Michael R. Stevenson, eds., *Women and the Use of Military Force*, (Boulder: Lynne Reiner Publishers, 1993). Nira Yuval-Davis also deals with the gendered nature of the military and war in her book, *Gender and Nation*. See Nira Yuval-Davis, *Gender and Nation* (London: SAGE Publications, 1997).
37 Randolph Higonnet, Jenson, Michel and Collins Weitz, 'Introduction', p. 1.
38 In this chapter, Richards was questioning why the Greenham Common camp had to be entirely female. See Janet Radcliffe Richards, 'Why the Pursuit of Peace is No Part of Feminism', in Jean Bethke Elshtain and Sheila Tobias, *Women, Militarism, and War* (Savage: Rowman and Littlefield, 1990) pp. 211–225.
39 Richards, 'Why the Pursuit of Peace is No Part of Feminism', p. 223.
40 Nicole Ann Dombrowski, 'Soldiers, Saints, or Sacrificial Lambs? Women's Relationship to Combat and the Fortification of the Home Front in the Twentieth Century', in Nicole Ann Dombrowski, ed., *Women and War in the Twentieth Century. Enlisted with or without Consent* (New York and London: Routledge, 1999) pp. 2–37, p. 4.
41 Joanna Bourke, *Deep Violence: Military Violence, War Play and the Social Life of Weapons* (Berkeley: Counterpoint, 2015) p. 4.
42 Bourke, *Deep Violence*, p. 5.
43 Specific examples of histories of women's engagements with war exist. However, they do not tend to theorise about women's or feminists' ethics of violence. Rather, they plot women's participation in violent campaigns. See, for example, Lisa Lines, 'Female Combatants in the Spanish Civil War: *Milicianas* on the Front Lines and in the Rearguard', *Journal of International Women's Studies*, vol. 10, no. 4 (2004) pp. 168–187, and Jeffrey J. Roberts, 'On John Keegan, Soviet "Amazons", and the Issue of Women in Combat', *Minerva: Quarterly Report on Women and the Military*, vol. 14, nos. 3-4 (1996) pp. 11–28.
44 Setsu Shigematsu is a scholar of Asian and gender studies. Her book, *Scream from the Shadows*, is a history of the Japanese Women's Liberation Movement. See Setsu Shigematsu, *Scream from the Shadows: The Women's Liberation Movement in Japan* (Minneapolis: University of Minnesota Press, 2012) p. x. In 2007, Lee-Ann Monk, who has written on women asylum warders' use of violence against their patients, noted that histories of women as violent tended to depict these women in ways that denied their agency and status as responsible moral citizens. She directed that a feminist history of violence should seek to explain unsettling complexities of women's agency in violent situations, such as colonising processes. See Lee-Ann Monk, 'A Feminist History of Violence: History as a Weapon of Liberation?', *Lilith*, vol. 16 (2007) pp. 12–14, p. 13.

45 She cites American politicians, Madeleine Albright, Condoleezza Rice, and Hilary Rodham Clinton for their support of state-sanctioned imperialist violence, especially in the name of saving women. See Shigematsu, *Scream from the Shadows*, p. x.
46 See 'Preface' in Shigematsu, *Scream from the Shadows*, pp. ix-xiv.
47 Joy Damousi, 'Socialist Women and Gendered Space: Anti-Conscription and Anti-War Campaigns 1914–1918', in Joy Damousi and Marilyn Lake, eds., *Gender and War: Australians at War in the Twentieth Century* (Cambridge: Cambridge University Press, 1995) pp. 254–273, p. 257.
48 *Anti-Suffrage Review*, no. 27, February 1911, pp. 25–26.
49 *Anti-Suffrage Review*, no. 27, February 1911, pp. 25–26.
50 In an inversion of accepted hierarchies within the family of nations that made up the Empire—namely, an understanding which placed the imperial centre at the top—already enfranchised Australian women marching carried a banner which instructed their imperial mother to 'Trust the women Mother as I have done'. The issue of how the British responded to such suggestions emanating from its former colonies are examined in detail in Chapter 3.
51 The 'transhistorical' element refers to the inclusion of women dressed as iconic female figures from the past. See Rebecca Cameron, 'From Great Women to Top Girls: Pageants of Sisterhood in British Feminist Theatre', *Comparative Drama*, Vo. 43, No. 2 (2009) pp. 143–166, p. 153.
52 For example, by 1915, the National Woman's Party (NWP) as an amalgam of the more militant American suffrage bodies led by activists such as Alice Paul, Lucy Burns and Harriot Stanton Blatch—all of whom either had connections with or experience in the British militant movement—adopted more visually arresting and disruptive techniques including the infamous 1913 march held in Washington, D.C., the day before the inauguration of Woodrow Wilson as president. From 1917, they deployed the 'Silent Sentinels' tactic of conducting a campaign of silently picketing outside the White House. For more on the militant tactics of the Silent Sentinels, see Belinda A. Stillion Southard, 'Militancy, Power, and Identity: The Silent Sentinels as Women Fighting for a Political Voice', *Rhetoric & Public Affairs*, vol. 10, no. 3 (2007) pp. 399–417.
53 Barbara Caine, 'Australian Feminism and the British Militant Suffragettes', Paper presented to the Department of the Senate Occasional Lecture Series at Parliament House, Canberra, Australia, 31 October 2003: www.aph.gov.au/binaries/senate/pubs/pops/pop41/caine.pdf, accessed 21 January 2016.
54 Barbara Caine, 'Australian Feminism and the British Militant Suffragettes'. For an account of an exchange Goldstein had with a British commentator over the comparative value of the Australian women's and British man's vote when she visited England, see Sharon Crozier-De Rosa, 'The National and the Transnational in British Anti-Suffragists' Views of Australian Women Voters', *History Australia*, vol. 10, no. 3 (2013) pp. 51–64. This exchange is also discussed in Chapter 3.
55 *Anti-Suffrage Review*, no. 2, January 1909, p. 1.
56 *Anti-Suffrage Review*, no. 2, January 1909, p. 1.
57 In Greek mythology, Maenads are the 'demented', 'mad' or 'raving' female followers of Dionysus. *Anti-Suffrage Review*, no. 2, January 1909, p. 1.
58 *Anti-Suffrage Review*, no. 2, January 1909, p. 1.
59 *Anti-Suffrage Review*, no. 2, January 1909, p. 1.
60 *Anti-Suffrage Review*, no. 2, January 1909, p. 1.
61 *Anti-Suffrage Review*, no. 8, July 1909, pp. 1–2.
62 Boadicea was queen of the Iceni people of Eastern England and led a major uprising against occupying Roman forces. *Anti-Suffrage Review*, no. 8, July 1909, pp. 1–2.

228 The Shame of the Violent Woman

63 *Anti-Suffrage Review*, no. 11, October 1909, pp. 5–6.
64 *Anti-Suffrage Review*, no. 15, February 1910, p. 3.
65 *Anti-Suffrage Review*, no. 9, August 1909, pp. 1–2.
66 *Anti-Suffrage Review*, no. 43, May 1912, p. 105.
67 *Anti-Suffrage Review*, no. 51, January 1913, pp. 321–322.
68 *Anti-Suffrage Review*, no. 22, September 1910, pp. 5–6.
69 *Anti-Suffrage Review*, no. 22, September 1910, pp. 5–6.
70 *Anti-Suffrage Review*, no. 11, October 1909, pp. 1–2.
71 *Anti-Suffrage Review*, no. 46, August 1912, pp. 179–180.
72 *Anti-Suffrage Review*, no. 41, April 1912, p. 63.
73 *Anti-Suffrage Review*, no. 22, September 1910, pp. 5–6.
74 *Anti-Suffrage Review*, no. 48, October 1912, p. 230.
75 *Anti-Suffrage Review*, no. 48, October 1912, p. 236.
76 *Anti-Suffrage Review*, no. 48, October 1912, p. 236.
77 *Anti-Suffrage Review*, no. 48, October 1912, p. 236.
78 *Anti-Suffrage Review*, no. 48, October 1912, p. 236.
79 *Anti-Suffrage Review*, no. 48, October 1912, p. 236.
80 *Anti-Suffrage Review*, no. 48, October 1912, p. 236.
81 *Anti-Suffrage Review*, no. 47, September 1912, p. 219.
82 *Anti-Suffrage Review*, no. 9, August 1909, pp. 1–2.
83 *Anti-Suffrage Review*, no. 11, October 1909, pp. 3–4.
84 *Anti-Suffrage Review*, no. 11, October 1909, pp. 3–4.
85 *Anti-Suffrage Review*, no. 9, August 1909, pp. 1–2.
86 The English suffragettes were Mary Leigh, Gladys Evans, and Lizzie Baker (Jennie Baines).
87 *Irish Citizen*, vol. 1, no. 17, 17 September 1912, p. 130.
88 *Anti-Suffrage Review*, no. 43, May 1912, pp. 102–103.
89 *Anti-Suffrage Review*, no. 43, May 1912, pp. 102–103.
90 *Anti-Suffrage Review*, no. 43, May 1912, pp. 102–103.
91 *Anti-Suffrage Review*, no. 46, August 1912, p. 188.
92 *Anti-Suffrage Review*, no. 46, August 1912, p. 188.
93 *Anti-Suffrage Review*, no. 46, August 1912, p. 188.
94 *Anti-Suffrage Review*, no. 46, August 1912, p. 188.
95 *Anti-Suffrage Review*, no. 47, September 1912, p. 217.
96 *Anti-Suffrage Review*, no. 47, September 1912, p. 217.
97 Edward Madigan, ' "Sticking to a Hateful Task": Resilience, Humour, and British Understandings of Combatant Courage, 1914–1918', *War in History*, vol. 20, no. 1 (2013) pp. 76–98, p. 78.
98 Madigan, ' "Sticking to a Hateful Task"', p. 88.
99 The use of the 'Rape of Belgium' as a means of ensuring support for the Allied war effort went beyond the borders of Britain and Europe. For example, see Judith Smart, ' "Poor Little Belgium" and Australian Popular Support for War, 1914', *War and Society*, vol. 12 (1994) pp. 23–42.
100 Ute Frevert, *Emotions in History—Lost and Found* (Budapest and London: Central European University Press, 2011) p. 74. See Chapter 2 for a discussion about the nationalisation of honour.
101 The relationship between masculinity and violence is discussed in much greater detail in Chapter 6.
102 Ute Frevert, 'Wartime Emotions: Honour, Shame, and the Ecstasy of Sacrifice', *1914–1918 Online. International Encyclopedia of the First World War*, Last Updated 8 October 2014: http://encyclopedia.1914-1918-online.net/article/wartime_emotions_honour_shame_and_the_ecstasy_of_sacrifice, accessed 21 May 2017. For an extended discussion of honour, also see Frevert, *Emotions in History*.

103 For a general and comprehensive guide to women's involvement in and reactions to World War One, see Susan Grayzel, *Women and the First World War* (London and New York: Routledge, 2013).
104 Grayzel, *Women and the First World War*, p. 36.
105 Grayzel also notes that even in far-off, Australia, women who wanted to serve in the military established the Australian Women's Service Corps. By January 1917, this group had 700 members who practised marching and drilling. Grayzel, *Women and the First World War*, p. 54.
106 Laura Müller-Pinzler, Lena Rademacher, Frieder M. Paulus and Sören Krach, 'When Your Friends Make You Cringe: Social Closeness Modulates Vicarious Embarrassment-Related Neural Activity', *Social Cognitive and Affective Neuroscience*, vol. 11, no. 3 (2016) pp. 466–475, p. 467.
107 *Anti-Suffrage Review*, no. 82, August 1915, p. 59.
108 *Anti-Suffrage Review*, no. 99, January 1917, p. 4.
109 *Anti-Suffrage Review*, no. 75, January 1915, p. 4.
110 *Anti-Suffrage Review*, no. 75, January 1915, p. 4.
111 *Anti-Suffrage Review*, no. 77, March 1915, pp. 20–21.
112 *Anti-Suffrage Review*, no. 77, March 1915, pp. 20–21.
113 In 1915, the Review reported that 'the more blatant extravaganza in the service of the "cause" comes out in the offer of a notorious Suffragist lady to raise a battalion of fighting women, and in the organisation for the "drilling" of women by a woman'. See *Anti-Suffrage Review*, no. 77, March 1915, p. 21.
114 *Anti-Suffrage Review*, no. 77, March 1915, p. 22.
115 Edith Cavell's execution is discussed in Chapter 6.
116 *Anti-Suffrage Review*, no. 77, March 1915, p. 21.
117 *Anti-Suffrage Review*, no. 77, March 1915, p. 21.
118 *Anti-Suffrage Review*, no. 110, December 1917, p. 98.
119 *Anti-Suffrage Review*, no. 110, December 1917, p. 98.
120 *Anti-Suffrage Review*, no. 111, January 1918, pp. 7–8.
121 *Anti-Suffrage Review*, no. 111, January 1918, pp. 4–5.
122 *Anti-Suffrage Review*, no. 111, January 1918, pp. 4–5.
123 *Anti-Suffrage Review*, no. 111, January 1918, pp. 4–5.
124 *Anti-Suffrage Review*, no. 111, January 1918, pp. 4–5.
125 *Anti-Suffrage Review*, no. 111, January 1918, pp. 4–5.
126 *Irish Citizen*, vol. 3, no. 20, 3 October 1914, p. 153.
127 This debate was exemplified by an exchange taking place in the paper in 1915 between two well-known correspondents: Lilian Suffern and M. E. Duggan. Suffern argued that when 'reason and persuasion' did not work. Physical force via the destruction of property would get male politicians to sit up and listen. Duggan, on the other hand, asserted that militancy was a betrayal of the female emotional community—'a betrayal of that very instinct of motherhood' that militants claimed they cared about. Property destruction was an apt political tool for women. See *Irish Citizen*, vol. 3, no. 31, 19 December 1914, p. 243, and *Irish Citizen*, vol. 3, no. 35, 9 January 1915, p. 267.
128 *Irish Citizen*, vol. 3, no. 17, 12 September 1914, p. 132.
129 *Irish Citizen*, vol. 3, no. 17, 12 September 1914, p. 132.
130 For more on Na Fianna Éireann, see Marnie Hay, 'An Irish Nationalist Adolescence: Na Fianna Éireann, 1909–23', in Catherine Cox and Susannah Riordan, eds., *Adolescence in Modern Irish History* (Basingstoke: Palgrave Macmillan, 2015) pp. 103–128.
131 For more on Markievicz, see, among others, Sinéad McCoole, *No Ordinary Woman: Irish Female Activists in the Revolutionary Years* (Dublin: The O'Brien Press, 2003), pp. 185–6; Ann Matthews, *Renegades: Irish Republican Women*

1900–1922 (Cork: Mercier Press, 2010); Karen Steele, 'Constance Markievicz and the Politics of Memory', in Louise Ryan and Margaret Ward, eds., *Irish Women and Nationalism: Soldiers, New Women and Wicked Hags* (Dublin: Irish Academic Press, 2004), pp. 62–79.

132 *Bean na hEireann*, vol. 1, no. 9, July 1909, p. 8.
133 *Irish Citizen*, vol. 4, no. 23, 23 October 1915, p. 137.
134 *Irish Citizen*, vol. 4, no. 23, 23 October 1915, p. 137.
135 *Irish Citizen*, vol. 4, no. 25, 6 November 1915, p. 150.
136 *Irish Citizen*, vol. 4, no. 23, 23 October 1915, p. 137.
137 *Bean na hEireann*, vol. 1, no. 13, November 1909, pp. 5–6.
138 The Irish Rebellion of 1798 was staged by the Society of United Irishmen (established 1791) which was inspired by the Enlightenment ideals of the American and French revolutions. The Society advocated parliamentary reform and the elimination of British rule in Ireland.
139 *Irish Citizen*, vol. 4, no. 25, 6 November 1915, p. 150.
140 *Irish Citizen*, vol. 4, no. 25, 6 November 1915, p. 150.
141 *Irish Citizen*, vol. 4, no. 23, 23 October 1915, p. 137.
142 *Irish Citizen*, vol. 4, no. 23, 23 October 1915, p. 137.
143 *Irish Citizen*, vol. 4, no. 23, 23 October 1915, p. 137.
144 During the Rising, she was positioned in St Stephen's Green, Dublin.
145 *Irish Citizen*, vol. 4, no. 40, October 1916, p. 230.
146 For example, journalists have more recently labelled her a woman of beauty but no substance, 'a snob, fraud, show-off, and murderer' who dangerously 'brainwashed' children into believing that they should kill and die for their country. See Nicola Tallant, 'She was a Snob, Fraud, Show-Off, and Murderer', *Irish Independent*, 29 October 2006, and Kevin Myers, 'FF Celebratory Plans for the Easter Rising a Load of Claptrap', *Irish Independent*, 20 April 2011.
147 Sean O'Casey, 'Drums Under the Window' in *Autobiographies 1* (London: Papermac, 1963), pp. 596–597, quoted in Matthews, *Renegades*, pp. 73–76. There were other examples of male commentators noting Markievicz's courage. For example, in his 1919 book, *The Irish Republic*, Charles Newton Wheeler declared that she was a revolutionary who was courageous, impulsive and reckless; a soldier who, if 'all tales be true', kissed her gun before surrendering to the British. Likewise, Richard Michael Fox, who claimed Markievicz as a personal acquaintance, extolled the Countess's courage and passion. Her inspiration was actual as well as spiritual, he wrote. See Charles Newton Wheeler, *The Irish Republic: An Analytical History of Ireland, 1914–1918, with Particular Reference to the Easter Insurrection (1916) and the German "plots." Also a Sketch of De Valera's Life by Harry J. Boland, his Private Secretary: A Close-Up View of Countess Markievicz, and a Defense of Ulster by Ulstermen* (Chicago: Cahill-Igoe Company, 1919) pp. 243–246: http://babel.hathitrust.org/cgi/pt?id=loc.ark:/13960/t3514hr60;view=1up;seq=9, accessed 21 October 2015, and Richard Michael Fox, *Rebel Irishwomen* (Dublin: Progress House, 1967 [1935]), p. 18.
148 For a more nuanced discussion of the differences between nationalist feminist and feminist nationalist in the Irish context, see Chapter 2.
149 *Anti-Suffrage Review*, no. 9, August 1909, pp. 1–2.

Conclusion

Historically, shame has proven to be a highly versatile emotion. Part of its versatility has been due to the fact that it is supported by a large family of related emotions. There are numerous variants and connected emotions, like humiliation, disgrace, indignation, dishonour, and embarrassment. There are, therefore, many ways of articulating shame and shame-related feelings. There are also many emotional virtues that, if transgressed, can elicit shame, for example, honour, courage, and chivalry. This means that there have been countless situations in which shame can, and has arisen. For instance, it has been deemed appropriate to attempt to elicit shame and shame-related feelings on the basis of displays of cowardice, a lack of patriotism, selfishness, misplaced pride, or undignified servility. We have examined many of these in this book.

Shame's historic versatility has also been supported by the fact that shame is an ever-present emotion. As Thomas Scheff has explained, shame is 'the feeling of a *threat to the social bond*'.[1] In this study of the bonds connecting members of three different communities of patriotic womanhood, shame was ever-present not only because individual members had brought shame to those collectives through their transgressive actions but also because the fear that they would do so always existed. Shame was always anticipated because the fear of being judged defective always lurked. The reasons for worrying about being found wanting varied from community to community.

Patriotic women worried about two intersecting sets of social bonds. They were concerned that fellow members of their gendered and their national communities would not demonstrate allegiance to group values. At the heart of their concerns were the gendered nature of emotional regimes. Patriotic women understood that the emotional standards that men and women were expected to adhere to in any particular national setting were different for each sex. These different sets of emotional rules were established to guide the actions of each sex as they performed the roles expected of them in relation to the nation. Gendered emotional regimes directed individuals to be 'good' men and women as well as 'good' national citizens.

In line with nineteenth- and early twentieth-century gender ideals, men were the active doers in society. They participated in the public worlds of business, politics, and when it was required, war. The emotional rules that regulated their behaviour in these public worlds were encapsulated by the concept of honour. Men were required to use the emotional virtues comprising honour codes—courage, chivalry, and moral dignity—to guide their relations with other men. Violence underpinned codes of honour. Therefore, if a man was to judge another to be guilty of deviant or dishonourable behaviour, he could rightly use violence against the deviant.

According to these same gender ideals, women were the passive repositories of national values. They were confined to the private sphere. They were not permitted to participate fully in the public worlds of business, politics, and war. Accordingly, they were not allowed to assume an active relationship with honour. As befitted their place in the domestic realm, their honour existed only in the form of the private notion of chastity. Women could not legitimately use violence to regulate their relations with others of their sex because they existed beyond the pale of the honour codes that directed individuals' engagements with violence. Men could use violence if a woman was dishonoured. But his use of violence was to restore his own reputation from the taint of being associated with an unchaste woman. Once her honour was lost, she was shamed. The emotional standards that guided women's participation in the domestic world, then, were different to those directing men's activities in the public sphere. Women were expected to adhere to feminine emotional virtues such as selflessness, purity, kindness, and gentle influence as they gave birth to and brought up the next generation of national citizens.

In early twentieth-century Britain, women agitating to enter the public sphere threatened to destabilise or corrupt the gendered nature of the separate emotional regimes that governed men's and women's actions. This was particularly pertinent to the realms of politics and war. Feminists campaigned for equal political rights with men. Therefore, they were not only demanding access to the physical sphere that traditionally men participated in, they were also asking for access to the emotional regimes that typically guided men's performance in that sphere. Those opposed to feminist demands did not believe that women could adequately adhere to those masculine standards. Feminists had not given them any reason to challenge this perception. By reneging on wartime political truces, for example, they had demonstrated that they were unmanly navigators of masculine realms. They had dishonoured the rules that normally guided men's public interactions with other men. They corrupted the nature of the emotional standards that men were expected to adhere to.

Those feminists who advocated women's use of physical force, for feminism and/or for nationalism, were deemed guilty of enacting a gross misappropriation of masculine honour codes. Only men were permitted to use physical force to fight for their rights. It was man's responsibility to fight to protect the integrity of democracy, for instance. It was not woman's remit to use violence to corrupt the nature of that democracy as suffragettes were doing. Violent and dishonourable feminists brought shame to both the feminine and the masculine national communities. As unwomanly women, they threatened the integrity of the emotional regimes underpinning the community of womanhood. As unmanly women, they endangered the survival and integrity of exclusively masculine emotional virtues. In both cases, these feminists proved themselves unpatriotic too. They brought shame to the national community through jeopardising the workings of the gendered physical and emotional regimes that, until then, had ensured the nation's stability. More than that, the welfare of the immense British Empire depended on the stability of the imperial centre. The success of the Empire rested on transporting British values and transplanting them in its colonial outposts. By upsetting the integrity of those values and the general political and emotional balance 'at home', feminists threatened the disintegration of this vast imperial network. They were shamefully un-British.

Anti-suffragists used shame in the attempt to repel feminist threats of shame. Shame performed a number of ideological functions. It was used to variously bind members of a group together and exclude undeserving individuals from belonging to that group. However, its effectiveness as a form of social control was limited. As feminist theorist Jill Locke has argued, shaming relies on the target's or intended recipient's 'ability to engage in shameful self-assessment'.[2] If a woman did not value her connection to the community of 'good' patriotic womanhood, she was unlikely to amend her ways because of shaming emanating from members of that community. Therefore, in this instance, shame could only perform the function of confirming the belonging to that community of those loyal to the values of that collective. If shaming transgressive women did not compel them undertake shameful self-assessment and bring about their reform—and there was nothing to say that it would—then at least it worked to draw a tighter, more defined border around the rightful members of that community.

As this book has demonstrated, different communities of patriotic womanhood did always not undertake the shameful self-assessment that British anti-suffragists demanded of transgressive feminists. But they rarely omitted to acknowledge the existence of that attempted shaming. Instead, they often used acknowledgement of accusations of shame as a basis for clarifying the values of their specific community of patriotic womanhood. Diverging national priorities and national narratives played a prominent role in shaping different patriotic women's reactions to anti-feminist calls for shame.

In Australia, for example, patriotic women believed that they had been successful in ensuring that the values of the British Motherland had been maintained in the former colonies, now young white Commonwealth. However, these women also acknowledged that different conditions in their new nation meant that they had to amend some of those values. Conservative Australian women had not wanted the vote. But now that they were entrusted with it, they realised that they had to amend their conception of proper notions of womanliness and womanly duties. These transformed notions of womanliness did not accord with anti-suffragist opinions in

Britain. In Britain, the notion of womanhood championed by those in the former colonies was shameful. Australian women denied the legitimacy of this shame as they defined the parameters of good womanly citizenship.

Moreover, whereas some groups of patriotic British women declared that it was wrong to interfere in emotional regimes guiding men's behaviour—women could not try to shame men into enlisting in a war, for example, because they were not part of the emotional regime guiding men's participation in violent conflict—patriotic Australian women disagreed. Generally, they respected the separate nature of emotional standards, but they deemed it necessary to intrude into masculine emotional spheres when it looked like their nation's manhood was not up to the task of proving itself internationally.

World War One provides a good example of this. Too many Australian men were demonstrating apathy and perhaps even cowardice at a crucial time in the young white nation's history. Given their relative newness, this was a white manhood and white nation still under formation. Australian women had a unique responsibility for extending and improving the British 'race'. However, they were aware that they were settler-colonial dispossessors in a seemingly hostile Asia-Pacific environment. They could only realise their racial vocation if their manhood and their nation proved itself capable of defending themselves against potential Asian invasion. Therefore, patriotic Australian women affected an incursion of traditionally gendered emotional regimes. They directed Australian men to acquit themselves like men during the war. They attempted to shame those who did not. However, the strategies that they adopted in order to affect such an incursion are telling about how ambivalent they were about the legitimacy of their intrusion. The fact, for example, that they felt that they had to appropriate male voices in the attempt to shame men into performing masculinity reveals how uncomfortable they were about transgressing the boundaries separating emotional regimes.

Patriotic Irish women were directed by altogether different national and gendered concerns. The intensifying anti-colonial nationalist campaign there coloured Irish women's attitudes towards the legitimacy or otherwise of the lines dividing men's and women's spheres—physical and emotional. Nationalist Irish women referenced British anti-suffragists' warnings about the shame of intruding into masculine emotional regimes before denying that shame and establishing their own rules about the nature of the emotional standards guiding men's and women's experiences.

Patriotic Irish women desired to reverse the British colonising process. They promoted a nationalist narrative that declared that gender equality reigned in pre-colonised Ireland. Back then, men and women had participated equally in the public worlds of politics and combat. Both sexes, therefore, had been subject to the same emotional regulations. Therefore, these women charged themselves with the task of restoring pre-British and pre-modern gender relations. This meant reclaiming an emotional regime that directed men's and women's actions equally. By doing this, they could reinstate authentic Irish culture, genuine Irish practices, and therefore Irish pride. In this way, they could assist nationalist men to actively regain Irish autonomy.

Irish women were realistic enough to understand that in these modern times, because of the imposition of British values and institutions, only their men were equipped to actively restore national pride. Only Irish men were enfranchised and able to serve as politicians. They also had greater access to means of exercising military force. However, if their nationalist brothers looked like they were not up to the task of actively reclaiming this national liberty, then Irish women had every right to intrude into foreign-imposed masculine emotional regimes. They used stories of their shared emotional heritage—a lived past of being subject to the same emotional standards—to justify their attempted shaming of Irish men who looked like they were deficient in Irishness.

Transnationally, patriotic women across the British Empire acknowledged that separate emotional rules governed men's and women's different spheres of activity. However, as we saw earlier, the relative positioning of each nation on the imperial spectrum (for example, important imperial metropole or less significant colonial outpost) and the unique political contexts informing experiences within those nations (for instance, prevailing racial anxieties or nationalist conflict) shaped how patriotic women responded to attempts to maintain the integrity of these separate emotional regimes. Whatever their specific views about the links between shame and incursions into existing gendered emotional regimes, the threat of shame—the threat of their views and values being judged deficient—was ever-present across all national communities.

Militant Suffragists and the Embarrassment of Having Gotten it Wrong

Significantly, for historical evaluations of the tenacity of shame as an attempted means of social control, shame did not disappear once early twentieth-century feminist or nationalist campaigns ceased. Shame and its related emotions re-emerged in gendered remembrances of these once deviant women. For example, British anti-suffragists had to address the quandary of how to remember notoriously disruptive suffragette leaders, including Emmeline Pankhurst, once they had been proven right in their assertion that women deserved to be enfranchised. The embarrassment of opposing a political move that was eventually endorsed manifested itself in moves to remember Pankhurst.

In 1930, two years after Emmeline Pankhurst's death, and just before women were granted equal voting rights with men, a statue of her was erected in Tower Gardens, alongside the Houses of Parliament. A. G. Walker, who was also responsible for the Florence Nightingale monument in Waterloo Place, sculpted the memorial.[3] The statue depicts Pankhurst striking a respectable and commanding pose, as if about to address a crowd. The stone inscription accompanying the statue reads, 'This statue of Emmeline Pankhurst was erected as a tribute to her courageous leadership of the movement for the enfranchisement of women'. Through the construction of this physical monument, Pankhurst's valour was immortalised. Whereas once the statue stood in full view of formidable Westminster—commanding an impressive and uninhibited view of the Houses of Parliament that the the Women's Social and Political Union (WSPU) once terrorised—over the decades it has become somewhat obscured by growing foliage and the erection of a fence around Tower Gardens. The garden setting has worked to feminise Pankhurst; certainly, there is little about her statue that suggests militancy. Rather than recalling Pankhurst's disruptive militancy, the monument evokes a sense of solid citizenship.

This concept of solid and dependable citizenship goes a long way towards explaining how authorities could have authorised a public monument—to be situated beside the Houses of Parliament—dedicated to a dangerous feminist revolutionary who had previously declared war on that parliament. Historian Laura Nym Mayhall has argued that this statue to a former militant was only made possible because of Pankhurst's confirmed conversion from radicalism to conservatism.[4] As outlined earlier in the book, the Pankhursts abandoned their militancy and dedicated themselves to patriotic war work once war broke out. Emmeline went even further to prove her devotion to nationalism over feminism. In 1916, she argued publicly that the British Government should desist from putting a clause to enfranchise women in a proposed bill designed to extend the franchise to serving soldiers and sailors. She did not want to jeopardise granting serving men the vote by raising the ire and opposition of anti-feminists. As further evidence of her nationalistic devotion to the war, in 1917, she travelled to Russia to try to convince the country to continue supporting the Allied cause. In the post-war era, she unsuccessfully stood for election as a Conservative Party candidate—a long way away from the original WSPU's affiliation with the Labour Party.[5]

At the statue's dedication in March 1930, Conservative Prime Minister Stanley Baldwin worked to absolve himself and other anti-suffragists of any embarrassing wrongdoing by claiming that he and his peers were right to be suspicious of women's political capabilities and their female patriotism until they had the chance to observe women perform that patriotism. They were only granted this opportunity during World War One.[6] He then dealt with the shame of the militant feminist by revising history. He removed Pankhurst from her place in narratives of dangerous and radical protest movements, and instead inserted her into a long English tradition of gradual liberal reform. Although he acknowledged her earlier role as a revolutionary, he worked to situate her activism within a British tradition of 'gradual, peaceful reform, a tradition he viewed as evidence of Britain's distinctiveness from the rest of Europe'. He further pointed to the 'very English' nature of the dedication proceedings which he said had brought previous rivals together to now honour a controversial leader.[7] It was Pankhurst's self-directed reformation from shameful feminist to reliable and dedicated patriot that had affected a removal of the blot that she had previously cast on British history. By shifting the gaze from the potential post-suffrage embarrassment of the anti-suffragist to this transgressive woman's recovery from shame, Baldwin erased any potential discomfort for anti-suffragists brought about by this memorial to this once violent woman.

Militant Nationalist Women and Postcolonial Legacies of Shame

Perhaps even more fraught than remembering Emmeline Pankhurst and fellow suffragettes was the process through which the contributions of violent nationalist Irish women were remembered. After women had been granted the vote in Britain and in Ireland, these already disruptive Irish feminist nationalists and nationalist feminists were to participate in two major violent conflicts, the Anglo-Irish War (1919–1921) and the Irish Civil War (1922–1923). The large majority of these revolutionary women fought on the wrong side in the Civil War. They had fought against a treaty that had partitioned the country and imposed the status of Commonwealth rather than Republic on the part of the island now called the Free State. Therefore, they were deemed enemies of the new postcolonial Irish Free State, which was established in 1922.

Through colonisation, imperial Britain, as the supposedly superior, virile 'race', had emasculated the Irish by imposing on them a discourse of racial inferiority. They had constructed Irish men and Irish women as siblings in a childlike Celtic 'race' that was erratic, irrational, and emotional.[8] Once the Irish Free State was established, Irish nationalists attempted to re-masculinise the new postcolonial nation by invoking a mythological past characterised by an ancient brotherhood of proud and noble warriors. Revolutionary women had little place in this new national imagining. To remember the actions of these 'unmanageable revolutionaries',[9] to use the words of fellow revolutionary and future president of the Irish Republic, Éamon de Valera, threatened the new postcolonial nation's claims to masculinity. Remembering that they once relied on the active help of the weaker sex to achieve independence would not help Irish nationalists to shift the taint of feminisation from a once colonised manhood. Therefore, Irish nationalist men, those administering the new Free State, had to confront the issue of how to remember (or forget) the embarrassing existence of the revolutionary Irish woman. Through choosing how to remember her, they had to address the twinned issue of colonial shame and postcolonial embarrassment.

From 1922, one tactic postcolonial Irish men employed to reverse the shame of colonialism was to demean the role played by women throughout the country's freedom campaigns. During the Irish Civil War, for example, president of the new Free State, W. T. Cosgrave, belittled those women fighting on the Republican, anti-Treaty side by declaring that they 'should have rosaries in their hands or be at home with knitting needles'.[10] He was not the only dignitary during the life of that conflict attempt to inflict shame on combatant women. Cardinal Logue followed the Catholic Church's excommunication of all those fighting against the Treaty and the Free State by singling females out for particular condemnation. He deplored, he said, that women and girls were involving themselves in what he asserted was a 'wild orgy of violence'.[11]

The shame of the revolutionary woman—the woman who had persisted in fighting for a Republic on the whole island of Ireland—continued to be advertised in the writings of nationalist men throughout the 1920s.[12] In *The Victory of Sinn Féin*, writer P. S. O'Hegarty, for example, allowed himself 'a misogynistic rant' about revolutionary women, calling them 'practically unsexed' and incapable of understanding politics. He accused these women of only being motivated by 'swashbuckling and bombast and swagger'.[13] Another nationalist, journalist and politician, Ernest Blythe, saw Republican women as something akin to 'hysterical camp-followers'.[14] A particular tactic employed against Republican women in this decade was to label them 'furies'—'snaked headed avenging demons'.[15] Another high profile Church figure, Bishop Doorley, for instance, warned his congregation no one would respect or marry such furies. His advice to all females interested in politics was to never join organisations such as Cumann na mBan and to instead 'work as your grandmothers did before you'.[16] The shame of the armed woman was palpable.

Almost a century later and the shame of the violent woman continues to circulate in discussions about gender and nationalism in Ireland. For example, in 2006 writer Ruth Dudley Edwards was quoted as labelling renowned revolutionary politician and soldier, Constance Markievicz, 'a snob, fraud, show-off, and murderer' who 'who got a kick out of wearing uniforms'.[17] She proved she was 'bloodthirsty' when she 'brainwashed children into believing that they must die for Ireland'. She was, Dudley Edwards continued, 'physically brave to the point of recklessness', but she was also a 'bloodthirsty show-off' who did not understand the causes she championed. She may have been 'beautiful and flamboyant but she was all style and no substance along with other uncompromising green harpies of her generation'.[18] In what she considered a final damning indictment of Markievicz and the other 'green harpies', Dudley Edwards ludicrously concluded that they were to blame for postcolonial Ireland's notorious anti-feminist turn.[19] They were responsible for forcing men to do everything they could to keep women out of politics. 'Can you blame them?' Dudley Edwards asked. 'They turned off men for generations. We are all lucky that in due course some women came along and showed that they could be ordinary and not mad to get involved in politics.'[20] Mad revolutionary women, like Markievicz, shamed nationalist men through shaming nationalist politics.

Not unlike Emmeline Pankhurst, some acts of remembering Markievicz also worked to disarm and domesticate this violent woman. They thereby reduced her capacity to embarrass or shame those still troubled by the violent anti-colonial Irish woman. A number of physical monuments to Markievicz represent her militancy. For example, there is a memorial to her as a soldier in the Irish Citizen Army in St Stephen's Green, Dublin, that was officially unveiled by Éamon de Valera in 1932. More recently, an impressive sculpture of her in the Fianna na hÉireann (Irish Boy Scouts) uniform carrying a flag at an opened prison gate was erected in her home county, Sligo.[21] However, there is also the Poppet statue.

In 1998, a statue of Markievicz and her dog, Poppet, was created by Irish sculptor Elizabeth McLaughlin. It was erected outside a fitness facility in Dublin. The statue depicts Markievicz informally, out of full militant uniform, in a flowing skirt and militant blouse, and with her cocker spaniel by her side. It is a very tame, feminine portrait of the revolutionary. The twinning of Markievicz with her domestic pet has opened a gateway for observers to trivialise Markievicz's memory. For instance, writer Frank McNally used the knowledge that the statue had received divided reviews from locals to comment that it was fitting that the statue divided the people of Dublin because the dog, Poppet—inseparable from and indulged by Markievicz—divided all those she came into contact with.[22] McNally added to the farce by recounting a story about the cocker spaniel tearing the famous Irish flag that Markievicz had sewn for the 1916 Easter Rising concluding that had the dog faced a Republican court martial for treason, he might have evaded execution like his mistress.[23] Disarmed and domesticated—in the same year that the Northern Irish state that Markievicz had fought against was disarmed via the signing of the historic 1998 Good Friday Peace Accord—the Poppet statue provided no evidence that its central subject had ever been anything but a sentimentally popular local heroine. It removed the need for feelings of discomfort on the part of those who continued to feel the shame of the revolutionary woman, as articulated by Dudley Edwards. It bore no signs whatsoever of the postcolonial embarrassment wrought by the violent Irish woman.

Endings

Philosopher Michael L. Morgan has declared that many today think that it is a shame that shame exists. He used this to preface his assertion that a little more investment in the reformative abilities of this uncomfortable emotion would be a good thing for our global community. If as a collective, we undertook more shameful self-assessment, he claims, we could prevent the genocidal atrocities that plague our world.[24] Morgan subscribes to the reformative power of shame. Patriotic women at the beginning of the twentieth century likewise believed in the motivational capacity of shame. It could affect positive change by strengthening peoples' bonds with each other—by reinforcing group values. However, their perceptive articulations of the nature of shame also revealed their understanding of shame's limitations. Shame would only achieve the desired outcome of affecting the reformation of transgressive subjects if those subjects valued the bonds of the community to which they belonged, thereby agreeing to undertake shameful self-assessment. Even if the targets of shaming did not agree to undergo moral and emotional self-assessment, a positive outcome could still be realised for the community, if not the targeted individuals. Ostracising the reluctant recipient of shame could work to confirm group membership—to clarify group values and strengthen group belonging. In this way, communities of patriotic women globally affirmed and exhibited their understanding of the complex nature of shame and its possible ideological functions. These women participated in a global dialogue about shame, gender, and nationalism. They facilitated a global circulation of ideas about shame and its family of related emotions.

Notes

1 Thomas J. Scheff, 'Shame and the Social Bond: A Sociological Theory,' *Sociological Theory*, vol. 18, no. 1 (2000) pp. 84–99, p. 97.
2 Jill Locke, 'Shame and the Future of Feminism', *Hypatia*, vol. 22, no. 4 (2007) pp. 146–162, p. 156.
3 Statue of Mrs Emmeline Pankhurst' Historic England, National Heritage List for England: www.historicengland.org.uk/listing/the-list/list-entry/1357336, accessed 17 January 2016.
4 See Laura Nym Mayhall, 'Domesticating Emmeline: Representing the Suffragette, 1930–1993', *NWSA Journal*, vol. 11, no. 2 (1999) pp. 1–24. Laura Nym Mayhall, *The Militant Suffrage Movement: Citizenship and Resistance in Britain, 1860–1930* (Oxford and New York: Oxford University Press, 2003).
5 Mayhall, 'Domesticating Emmeline', p. 3.
6 See Mayhall, 'Domesticating Emmeline', p. 7.
7 Mayhall, 'Domesticating Emmeline', p. 6.
8 Begoña Aretxaga, *Shattering Silence: Women, Nationalism, and Political Subjectivity in Northern Ireland* (Princeton: Princeton University Press, 1997) and, Robert J.C. Young, *The Idea of English Ethnicity* (Oxford: Blackwell, 2008).
9 See Sarah Benton, 'Women Disarmed: The Militarization of Politics in Ireland 1913–23', *Feminist Review*, vol. 50. no. 1 (1995) pp. 148–172 p. 168.
10 Quoted in Louise Ryan, ' "Furies" and "Die-hards": Women and Irish Republicanism in the Early Twentieth Century', *Gender and History*, vol. 11, no. 2 (1999) pp. 256–275, p. 256.
11 Quoted in Ryan, ' "Furies" and "Die-hards" ', p. 256.
12 From the mid-1920s, male nationalists permitted themselves a 'series of angry outbursts' about revolutionary women that was highly influential in shaping how these activists were to be remembered in the coming decades. See Senia Pašeta, *Irish Nationalist Women, 1900–1918* (Cambridge: Cambridge University Press, 2013), p. 12.
13 P. S. O'Hegarty, *The Victory of Sinn Féin* (Dublin), 1924, quoted in Pašeta, *Irish Nationalist Women*, p. 12.
14 Pašeta, *Irish Nationalist Women*, p. 12.

15 Ryan, '"Furies" and "Die-hards"', p. 270.
16 Quoted in Ryan, '"Furies" and "Die-hards"', p. 270.
17 Quoted in Nicola Tallant, 'She was a Snob, Fraud, Show-Off, and Murderer', *Irish Independent*, 29 October 2006.
18 Tallant, 'She was a Snob, Fraud, Show-Off, and Murderer'.
19 For example, the long-awaited Republic did not guarantee civil rights to women. Instead, its 1937 Constitution appealed to 'a national character rooted in a rural Irish tradition' and was embedded in Catholic social doctrine, confining women to traditional roles of wives and mothers as it enabled legislation that curtailed the rights of working women. See Aretxaga, *Shattering Silence*, p. 147.
20 Aretxaga, *Shattering Silence*, p. 147.
21 On 21 April 2003, in recognition of the woman the *Enniscorthy Guardian* labels 'Sligo's most famous daughter', a 20-foot bronze figure of Markievicz raised on a stone plinth with stainless steel gates was unveiled in Rathcormac, Co. Sligo. ('Unveiling of Statue', *Enniscorthy Guardian*, 17 April 2003.)
22 Frank McNally, 'An Irishman's Diary', *The Irish Times*, 5 September 2015.
23 McNally, 'An Irishman's Diary'.
24 Michael L. Morgan, *On Shame* (New York: Routledge, 2008) pp. 1–7.

Bibliography

Women's Periodicals

Anti-Suffrage Review
Bean na hEireann
Irish Citizen
Shan Van Vocht
Woman

Other References

Alison, Miranda, 'Women as Agents of Political Violence: Gendering Security', *Security Dialogue*, vol. 35, no. 4 (2004) pp. 447–463.
Anderson, Benedict, *Imagined Communities: Reflections on the Origin and Spread of Nationalism* (London: Verso, 1983).
Aretxaga, Begoña, *Shattering Silence: Women, Nationalism, and Political Subjectivity in Northern Ireland* (Princeton: Princeton University Press, 1997).
Australian Women's National League, History of the Australian Women's National League, 50th Anniversary Publication, Melbourne, 1954.
Bastin, Coralie, Harrison, Ben J., Davey, Christopher G., Moll, Jorge and Whittle, Sarah, 'Feelings of Shame, Embarrassment and Guilt and Their Neural Correlates: A Systematic Review', *Neuroscience and Biobehavioral Reviews*, vol. 71 (2016) pp. 455–471.
Beaumont, Joan, 'The Politics of a Divided Society', in Joan Beaumont, ed., *Australia's War 1914–18* (Sydney: Allen & Unwin, 1995) pp. 35–63.
Beaumont, Joan, 'Whatever Happened to Patriotic Women?', *Australian Historical Studies*, vol. 31, no. 115 (2000) pp. 273–287.
Beaumont, Joan, *Broken Nation. Australians and the Great War* (Sydney: Allen and Unwin, 2013).
Bédarida, François, *A Social History of England 1851–1990*, translated by A. S. Forster and Geoffrey Hodgkinson (London and New York: Routledge, 1990).
Bell, Duncan S. A, 'Dissolving Distance: Technology, Space, and Empire in British Political Thought, 1770–1900', *The Journal of Modern History*, vol. 77, no. 3 (2005) pp. 523–562.
Biess, Frank, Confino, Alon, Frevert, Ute, Jensen, Uffa, Roper, Lyndal, and Saxer, Daniela, 'Forum: History of Emotions', *German History*, vol. 28, no. 1 (2010) pp. 67–80.

Bigland, Eileen, *Corelli: The Woman and the Legend* (London: Jarrolds, 1953).
Blom, Ida, 'Feminism and Nationalism in the Early Twentieth Century: A Cross-Cultural Perspective', *Journal of Women's History*, vol. 7, no. 4 (1995) pp. 82–94.
Blom, Ida, 'Gender and Nation in International Comparison', in Ida Blom, Karen Hagemann and Catherine Hall, eds., *Gendered Nations: Nationalisms and Gender Order in the Long Nineteenth Century* (Oxford: Berg, 2000) pp. 3–26.
Bourke, Joanna, *Dismembering the Male. Men's Bodies, Britain and the Great War* (London: Reakton Books, 1996).
Bourke, Joanna, *Deep Violence: Military Violence, War Play and the Social Life of Weapons* (Berkeley: Counterpoint, 2015).
Braithwaite, John, 'Shame and Modernity', *The British Journal of Criminology*, vol. 33, no. 1 (1993) pp. 1–18.
Brookes, Barbara, 'Shame and Its Histories in the Twentieth Century', *Journal of New Zealand Studies*, no. 9 (2010) pp. 37–54.
Brownfoot, Janice N., 'Goldstein, Vida Jane (1869–1949)', *Australian Dictionary of Biography*, National Centre of Biography, Australian National University, http://adb.anu.edu.au/biography/goldstein-vida-jane-6418/text10975, published first in hardcopy 1983, accessed online 13 April 2017.
Bullock, George, *Corelli: The Life and Death of a Best-Seller* (London: Constable, 1940).
Bush, Julia, 'British Women's Anti-Suffragism and the Forward Policy, 1908–14', *Women's History Review*, vol. 11, no. 3 (2002) pp. 431–454.
Bush, Julia, *Women Against the Vote: Female Suffragism in Britain* (Oxford: Oxford University Press, 2007).
Bush, Julia, 'National League for Opposing Woman Suffrage (act. 1910–1918)', *Oxford Dictionary of National Biography*, online ed. (Oxford: Oxford University Press, 2008) oxforddnb.com/view/theme/92492, accessed 13 November 2011.
Caine, Barbara, *Victorian Feminists* (New York: Oxford University Press, 1992).
Caine, Barbara, 'Australian Feminism and the British Militant Suffragettes', Paper presented to the Department of the Senate Occasional Lecture Series at Parliament House, Canberra, Australia, 31 October 2003: aph.gov.au/binaries/senate/pubs/pops/pop41/caine.pdf, accessed 21 January 2016.
Caine, Barbara, and Sluga, Glenda, *Gendering European History 1780–1920* (London: Continuum, 2004).
Cameron, Rebecca, 'From Great Women to Top Girls: Pageants of Sisterhood in British Feminist Theatre', *Comparative Drama*, vol. 43, no. 2 (2009) pp. 143–166.
Carey, Jane, 'White Anxieties and the Articulation of Race: The Women's Movement and the Making of White Australia, 1910s–1930s', in Jane Carey and Claire McLisky, eds., *Creating White Australia* (Sydney: Sydney University Press, 2009) pp. 195–213.
Castle, Gregory, *Modernism and the Celtic Revival* (Cambridge: Cambridge University Press, 2001).
Chadya, Joyce M., 'Mother Politics: Anti-Colonial Nationalism and the Woman Question in Africa', *Journal of Women's History*, vol. 15, no. 3 (2003) pp. 153–157.
Chatterjee, Partha, 'Colonialism, Nationalism, and Colonialized Women: The Contest in India', *American Ethnologist*, vol. 16, no. 4 (1989) pp. 622–633.
Clark, Gemma, *Everyday Violence in the Irish Civil War* (Cambridge: Cambridge University Press, 2014).

Cohen, Deborah, *Family Secrets: Shame and Privacy in Modern Britain* (Oxford: Oxford University Press, 2013).

Columbus, Brittany, 'Bean na h-Éireann: Feminism and Nationalism in an Irish Journal, 1908–1911', *Voces Novae: Chapman University Historical Review*, vol. 1, no. 1 (2009) pp. 3–30.

Comerford, Vincent, 'Grievance, Scourge or Shame? The Complexity of Attitudes to Ireland's Great Famine', in Christian Noack, Lindsay Janssen and Vincent Comerford, eds., *Holodomor and Gorta Mór: Histories, Memories and Representations of Famine in Ukraine and Ireland* (London: Anthem Press, 2012).

Corelli, Marie, *Woman, or—Suffragette? A Question of National Choice* (London: Arthur Pearson, 1907).

Corelli, Marie, Steel, Flora Annie Webster, Ardagh, Lady Susan Hamilton and Jeune, Baroness St Helier Susan Elizabeth Mary Stewart-McKenzie, *The Modern Marriage Market* (London: Hutchinson, 1898).

Cronin, Sean, *Irish Nationalism: Its Roots and Ideology* (New York: Continuum, 1980).

Crossman, Virginia, 'The Shan Van Vocht: Women, Republicanism, and the Commemoration of the 1798 Rebellion', *Eighteenth-Century Life*, vol. 22, no. 3 (1998) pp. 128–139.

Crozier-De Rosa, Sharon, 'Marie Corelli's British New Woman: A Threat to Empire?', *The History of the Family*, vol. 14, no. 4 (2009) pp. 416–429.

Crozier-De Rosa, Sharon, 'The National and the Transnational in British Anti-Suffragists' Views of Australian Women Voters', *History Australia*, vol. 10, no. 3 (2013) pp. 51–64.

Crozier-De Rosa, Sharon, 'Identifying with the Frontier: Federation New Woman, Nation and Empire', in Maggie Tonkin, Mandy Treagus, Madeleine Seys and Sharon Crozier-De Rosa, eds., *Changing the Victorian Subject* (Adelaide: University of Adelaide Press, 2014) pp. 37–58.

Crozier-De Rosa, Sharon, 'Marie Corelli, Shame and the "New Woman" in Fin-de-Siècle Britain', in David Lemmings and Ann Brooks, eds., *Emotions and Social Change: Historical and Sociological Perspectives* (Oxford: Routledge, 2014).

Crozier-De Rosa, Sharon, 'Shame and the Anti-Suffragist in Britain and Ireland: Drawing Women Back Into the Fold?', *Australian Journal of Politics and History*, vol. 60, no. 3 (2014) pp. 346–359.

Cullen, Mary, 'The Potential of Gender History', in Maryann Gialanella Valiulis, ed., *Gender and Power in Irish History* (Dublin: Irish Academic Press, 2009) pp. 18–38.

Cullen, Mary, 'Feminism, Citizenship and Suffrage: A Long Dialogue', in Louise Ryan and Margaret Ward, eds., *Irish Women and the Vote: Becoming Citizens* (Dublin: Irish Academic Press, 2007) pp. 1–20.

Cullen Owen, Rosemary, *Smashing Times: A History of the Irish Women's Suffrage Movement, 1889–1922* (Dublin: Attic Press, 1984).

Curthoys, Ann and Lake, Marilyn, 'Introduction', in Ann Curthoys and Marilyn Lake, eds., *Connected Worlds: History in Transnational Perspective* (Canberra: ANU E-Press, 2005) pp. 6–20.

Damousi, Joy, 'Socialist Women and Gendered Space: Anti-Conscription and Anti-War Campaigns 1914–1918', in Joy Damousi and Marilyn Lake, eds., *Gender and War: Australians at War in the Twentieth Century* (Cambridge: Cambridge University Press, 1995) pp. 254–273.

Darian-Smith, Kate, 'War and Australian Society', in Joan Beaumont, ed., *Australia's War, 1939–1945* (Sydney: Allen and Unwin, 1996) pp. 54–81.

Deane, Bradley, 'Imperial Barbarians: Primitive Masculinity in Lost World Fiction', *Victorian Literature and Culture*, vol. 38, no. 1 (2008) pp. 205–225.

Delap, Lucy, 'Feminist and Anti-Feminist Encounters in Edwardian Britain', *Historical Research*, vol. 78, no. 201 (2005) pp. 377–399.

Department of the Taoiseach, 'Irish Soldiers in the First World War (Somme)', Dublin, www.taoiseach.gov.ie/eng/Historical_Information/1916_Commemorations/Irish_Soldiers_in_the_First_World_War.html, accessed 4 April 2017.

Devereux, Cecily, 'New Woman, New World: Maternal Feminism and the New Imperialism in the White Settler Colonies', *Women's Studies International Forum*, vol. 22, no. 2 (1999) pp. 175–184.

DiCenzo, Maria, Delap, Lucy and Ryan, Leila, *Feminist Media History: Suffrage, Periodicals and the Public Sphere* (Basingstoke and New York: Palgrave Macmillan, 2011).

Dolan, Thomas, 'Demanding the Impossible: War, Bargaining, and Honor', *Security Studies*, vol. 24, no. 3 (2015) pp. 528–562.

Dombrowski, Nicole Ann, 'Soldiers, Saints, or Sacrificial Lambs? Women's Relationship to Combat and the Fortification of the Home Front in the Twentieth Century', in Nicole Ann Dombrowski, ed., *Women and War in the Twentieth Century. Enlisted With or Without Consent* (New York and London: Routledge, 1999) pp. 2–37.

Eager, Paige Whaley, *From Freedom Fighters to Terrorists: Women and Political Violence* (Aldershot: Ashgate, 2008).

Elias, Norbert, *The Civilizing Process: The History of Manners and State Formation and Civilization*, translated by Edmund Jephcott (Oxford, UK, and Cambridge, USA: Blackwell, 1994 [1939]).

Eller, Anja, Koschate, Miriam, Gilson, Kim-Michelle, 'Embarrassment: The Ingroup—Outgroup Audience Effect in Faux Pas Situations', *European Journal of Social Psychology*, vol. 41 (2011), pp. 489–500.

Elshtain, Jean Bethke, 'Women as Mirror and Other: Toward a Theory of Women, War, and Feminism', *Humanities in Society*, vol. 5, no. 2 (1982) pp. 22–44.

Elshtain, Jean Bethke, *Women and War* (New York: New York University Press, 1987).

Elshtain, Jean Bethke and Tobias, Sheila, eds., *Women, Militarism, and War: Essays in History, Politics, and Social Theory* (Savage: Rowman and Littlefield, 1990).

Enloe, Cynthia, *Does Khaki Become You? The Militarization of Women's Lives* (London: Harper Collins, 1988).

Enloe, Cynthia H., *Bananas, Beaches and Bases: Making Feminist Sense of International Politics* (Berkeley: University of California Press, 2014).

Federico, Annette R., *Idol of Suburbia: Marie Corelli and Late-Victorian Literary Culture* (Charlottesville and London: University Press of Virginia, 2000).

Fox, Harry, 'The Embarrassment of Embarrassment', in Tzemah Yoreh, Aubrey Glazer, Justin Jaron Lewis and Miryam Segal, eds., *Vixens Disturbing Vineyards: Embarrassment and Embracement of Scriptures* (Boston: Academic Studies Press, 2010) pp. 5–18.

Fox, Richard Michael, *Rebel Irishwomen* (Dublin: Progress House, 1967 [1935]).

Fraser, Hilary, Green, Stephanie and Johnston, Judith, *Gender and the Victorian Periodical* (Cambridge: Cambridge University Press, 2003).

Frevert, Ute, 'The Taming of the Noble Ruffian: Male Violence and Duelling in Early Modern and Modern Germany', in Pieter Spierenburg, ed., *Men and Violence: Gender, Honor, and Rituals in Modern Europe and America* (Columbus: Ohio State University Press, 1998) pp. 37–63.

Frevert, Ute, *Emotions in History—Lost and Found* (Budapest and London: Central European University Press, 2011).

Frevert, Ute, 'Wartime Emotions: Honour, Shame, and the Ecstasy of Sacrifice', *1914–1918 Online. International Encyclopedia of the First World War*, Last Updated 8 October 2014: http://encyclopedia.1914-1918-online.net/article/wartime_emotions_honour_shame_and_the_ecstasy_of_sacrifice, accessed 21 May 2017.

Gammerl, Benno, 'Emotional Styles—Concepts and Challenges', *Rethinking History*, vol. 16, no. 2 (2012) pp. 161–175.

Gellner, Ernest, *Nations and Nationalism* (Ithaca: University of Cornell Press, 1983).

Gentry, Caron E., and Sjoberg, Lara, *Beyond Mothers, Monsters, Whores: Thinking about Women's Violence in Global Politics* (London: Zed Books, 2015).

Gilbert, Sandra M., 'Soldier's Heart: Literary Men, Literary Women, and the Great War', in Margaret Randolph Higonnet, Jane Jenson, Sonya Michel and Margaret Collins Weitz, eds., *Behind the Lines: Gender and the Two World Wars* (New Haven and London: Yale University Press, 1987) pp. 197–226.

Girouard, Marc, *The Return to Camelot: Chivalry and the English Gentleman* (New Haven and London: Yale University Press, 1981).

Goodwin, Jeff, Jasper, James M., Polletta, Francesca, 'Introduction: Why Emotions Matter', in Jeff Goodwin, James M. Jasper, Francesca Polletta, eds., *Passionate Politics: Emotions and Social Movements* (Chicago: University of Chicago Press, 2001) pp. 1–24.

Gould, Jenny, 'Women's Military Services in First World War Britain', in Margaret Randolph Higonnet, Jane Jenson, Sonya Michel and Margaret Collins Weitz, eds., *Behind the Lines. Gender and the Two World Wars* (New Haven and London: Yale University Press, 1987) pp. 114–125.

Grayzel, Susan R., *Women and the First World War* (Abingdon and New York: Routledge, 2002).

Grimshaw, Patricia, Lake, Marilyn, McGrath, Ann, and Quartly, Marian, eds., *Creating a Nation, 1788–1900* (Ringwood: McPhee Gribble, 1994).

Groves, Patricia, *Petticoat Rebellion: The Anna Parnell Story* (Cork: Mercier Press, 2009).

Gullace, Nicoletta, 'White Feathers and Wounded Men: Female Patriotism and the Memory of the Great War', *Journal of British Studies*, vol. 36, no. 2 (1997) pp. 178–206.

Gullace, Nicoletta, *'The Blood of Our Sons': Men, Women and the Renegotiation of British Citizenship During the Great War* (New York: Palgrave Macmillan, 2002).

Hall, Catherine, *White, Male and Middle-Class: Explorations in Feminism and History* (New York: Routledge, 1992).

Harrison, Brian, *Separate Spheres: The Opposition to Women's Suffrage in Britain* (London: Croom Helm, 1978) pp. 13–24.

Hawksley, Jen, ' "In the Shadow of War": Australian Parents and the Legacy of Loss, 1915–1935', *Journal of Australian Studies*, vol. 33, no. 2 (2009) pp. 181–194.

Hay, Marnie, 'An Irish Nationalist Adolescence: Na Fianna Éireann, 1909–23', in Catherine Cox and Susannah Riordan, eds., *Adolescence in Modern Irish History* (Basingstoke: Palgrave Macmillan, 2015) pp. 103–128.

Higonnet, Margaret Randolph, and Higonnet, Patrice L.R., 'The Double Helix', in Margaret Randolph Higonnet, Jane Jenson, Sonya Michel and Margaret Collins Weitz, eds., *Behind the Lines: Gender and the Two World Wars* (New Haven and London, Yale University Press, 1987) pp. 31–47.

Higonnet, Margaret Randolph, Jenson, Jane, Michel, Sonya and Weitz, Margaret Collins, 'Introduction', in Margaret Randolph Higonnet, Jane Jenson, Sonya Michel and Margaret Collins Weitz, eds., *Behind the Lines: Gender and the Two World Wars* (New Haven and London: Yale University Press, 1987) pp. 1–17.

Hobsbawm, Eric, *Nations and Nationalism Since 1780* (Cambridge: Cambridge University Press, 1990).

Hollander, John, 'Honor Dishonorable: Shameful Shame', *Social Research*, vol. 70, no. 4 (2003) pp. 1061–1074.

Holmes, Katie, 'Day Mothers and Night Sisters: World War I Nurses and Sexuality', in Joy Damousi and Marilyn Lake, eds., *Gender and War: Australians at War in the Twentieth Century* (Cambridge: Cambridge University Press, 1995) pp. 43–59.

Howes, Ruth H. and Stevenson, Michael R., eds., *Women and the Use of Military Force* (Boulder: Lynne Reiner Publishers, 1993).

Hunt, Lyn, *The Family Romance of the French Revolution* (Berkeley: University of California Press, 1993).

Hutchinson, John, 'Myth Against Myth: The Nation as Ethnic Overlay', *Nations and Nationalism*, vol. 10, nos. 1–2 (2004) pp. 109–123.

Innes, C. L., '"A Voice in Directing the Affairs of Ireland": *L'Irlande Libre*, *The Shan Van Vocht* and *Bean na h-Eireann*', in Paul Hyland and Neil Sammells, eds., *Irish Writing: Exile and Subversion* (Basingstoke: Palgrave Macmillan, 1991) pp. 146–158.

Iriye, Akira, 'Transnational History', *Contemporary European History*, vol. 13, no. 2 (2004) pp. 211–222.

Jayasuriya, Laksiri, Walker, David, and Gothard, Jan, eds., *The Legacies of White Australia: Race, Culture and Nation* (Perth: University of Western Australia Press, 2003).

Jayawardena, Kumari, *Feminism and Nationalism in the Third World* (London, and Atlantic Highlands, NJ: Zed Books, 1994).

Jeffery, Keith, *Ireland and the Great War* (Cambridge: Cambridge University Press, 2000).

Johnson, Carol, 'From Obama to Abbott: Gender Identity and the Politics of Emotion', *Australian Feminist Studies*, vol. 28, no. 75 (2013) pp. 14–29.

Jusová, Iveta, *The New Woman and the Empire* (Columbus: The Ohio State University Press, 2005).

Kee, Robert, *The Green Flag: A History of Irish Nationalism* (London: Penguin, 2001).

Kemp, Sandra, Mitchell, Charlotte, and Trotter, David, *Edwardian Fiction: An Oxford Companion* (Oxford and New York: Oxford University Press, 1997).

Kent, Susan Kingsley, *Making Peace: The Reconstruction of Gender in Interwar Britain* (Princeton: Princeton University Press, 1993).

Kent, Susan Kingsley, *Sex and Suffrage in Britain, 1860–1914* (Princeton: Princeton University Press, 1987).

Kiberd, Declan, *Inventing Ireland: The Literature of the Modern Nation* (London: Vintage, 1996).

Kumar, Krishan, 'Nation and Empire: English and British National Identity in Comparative Perspective', *Theory and Society*, vol. 29, no. 5 (2000) pp. 575–608.

Lake, Marilyn, 'Mission Impossible: How Men Gave Birth to the Australian Nation—Nationalism, Gender and Other Seminal Acts', *Gender and History*, vol. 4, no. 3 (1992) pp. 305–322.

Lake, Marilyn, 'The Politics of Respectability: Identifying the Masculinist Context', Penny Russell and Richard White, eds., *Pastiche 1: Reflections on Nineteenth Century Australia* (Sydney: Allen & Unwin, 1994) pp. 263–271.

Lake, Marilyn, 'The Inviolable Woman: Feminist Conceptions of Citizenship in Australia, 1900–1945', *Gender and History*, vol. 8, no. 2 (1996) pp. 197–211.

Lake, Marilyn, 'Women and Nation in Australia: The Politics of Representation', *Australian Journal of Politics and History*, vol. 43, no. 1 (1997) pp. 41–52.

Lake, Marilyn, *Getting Equal: The History of Australian Feminism* (St Leonards, NSW: Allen & Unwin, 1999).

Lake, Marilyn, 'The Ambiguities for Feminists of National Belonging: Race and Gender in the Imagined Australian Community', in Ida Blom, Karen Hagemann and Catherine Hall eds., *Gendered Nations: Nationalisms and Gender Order in the Long Nineteenth Century* (Oxford and New York: Berg, 2000) pp. 159–176.

Lake, Marilyn, 'British World or New World?', *History Australia*, vol. 10, no. 3 (2013) pp. 36–50.

Lester, Alan, 'British Settler Discourse and the Circuits of Empire', *History Workshop Journal*, vol. 54, no. 1 (2002) pp. 24–48.

Letwin, Shirley Robin, *The Gentleman in Trollope: Individuality and Moral Conduct* (Basingstoke: Macmillan, 1984).

Lines, Lisa, 'Female Combatants in the Spanish Civil War: *Milicianas* on the Front Lines and in the Rearguard', *Journal of International Women's Studies*, vol. 10, no. 4 (2004) pp. 168–187.

Locke, Jill, 'Shame and the Future of Feminism', *Hypatia*, vol. 22, no. 4 (2007) pp. 146–162.

Lucas, John, 'Marie Corelli', in James Vinson, ed., *Great Writers of the English Language: Novelists and Prose Writers* (London and Basingstoke: Palgrave Macmillan, 1979) pp. 281–283.

Macintyre, Stuart, *A Concise History of Australia*, 3rd ed. (Cambridge: Cambridge University Press, 2009).

Madigan, Edward, ' "Sticking to a Hateful Task": Resilience, Humour, and British Understandings of Combatant Courage, 1914–1918', *War in History*, vol. 20, no. 1 (2013) pp. 76–98.

Magadla, Siphokazi, 'Women Combatants and the Liberation Movement in South Africa: Guerrilla Girls, Combative Mothers and the In-Betweeners', *African Security Review*, vol. 24, no. 4 (2015) pp. 390–402.

Magarey, Susan, 'History, Cultural Studies, and Another Look at First-Wave Feminism in Australia', *Australian Historical Studies*, vol. 27, no. 106 (1996) pp. 96–110.

Mangum, Teresa, *Married, Middlebrow, and Militant: Sarah Grand and the New Woman Novel* (Ann Arbor: The University of Michigan Press, 2001).

Mangum, Teresa, 'New Strategies for New (Academic) Women', *Nineteenth-Century Gender Studies*, vol. 3, no. 2 (2007) pp. 1–19.

Marks, Shula, 'History, the Nation and Empire: Sniping from the Periphery', *History Workshop Journal*, vol. 29, no. 1 (1990) pp. 111–119.

Masters, Brian, *Now Barabbas Was a Rotter: The Extraordinary Life of Marie Corelli* (London: Hamish Hamilton, 1978).
Matt, Susan, 'Current Emotion Research in History: Or, Doing History from the Inside Out', *Emotions Review*, vol. 3, no. 1 (2011) pp. 117–124.
Matthews, Ann, *Renegades: Irish Republican Women 1900–1922* (Cork: Mercier Press, 2010).
Mayhall, Laura E. Nym, 'Defining Militancy: Radical Protest, the Constitutional Idiom, and Women's Suffrage in Britain, 1908–1909', *Journal of British Studies*, vol. 39, no. 3 (2000) pp. 340–371.
Mayhall, Laura E. Nym, *The Militant Suffrage Movement. Citizenship and Resistance in Britain, 1860–1930* (Oxford: Oxford University Press, 2003).
McClintock, Anne, 'No Longer in a Future Heaven: Gender, Race and Nationalism', in Anne McClintock, Aamir Mufti and Ella Shohat, eds., *Dangerous Liaisons: Gender, Nation and Postcolonial Perspectives* (Minneapolis: University of Minnesota Press, 1997) pp. 89–112.
McClintock, Anne, 'Family Feuds: Gender, Nationalism and the Family', *Feminist Review*, vol. 44 (1993) pp. 61–80.
McCoole, Sinéad, *No Ordinary Woman: Irish Female Activists in the Revolutionary Years* (Dublin: The O'Brien Press, 2003).
McDowell, Margaret B., 'Marie Corelli', in Thomas F. Staley, ed., *Dictionary of Literary Biography, vol. 34: British Novelists, 1890–1929: Traditionalists* (Detroit: Gale Research Company, 1985) pp. 82–89.
McGregor, Russell, 'The Necessity of Britishness: Ethno-Cultural Roots of Australian Nationalism', *Nations and Nationalism*, vol. 12, no. 3 (2006) pp. 493–511.
McQuilton, John, *Rural Australia and the Great War: From Tarrawingee to Tangambalanga* (Melbourne: Melbourne University Press, 2001).
Meaney, Neville, 'Britishness and Australian Identity: The Problem of Nationalism in Australian History and Historiography', *Australian Historical Studies*, vol. 32, no. 116 (2001) pp. 76–90.
Mitchell, Sally, 'New Women, Old and New', *Victorian Literature and Culture*, vol. 27, no. 2 (1999).
Moelker René, and Kümmel, Gerhard, 'Chivalry and Codes of Conduct: Can the Virtue of Chivalry Epitomize Guidelines for Interpersonal Conduct?', *Journal of Military Ethics*, vol. 6, no. 4 (2007) pp. 292–302.
Monk, Lee-Ann, 'A Feminist History of Violence: History as a Weapon of Liberation?', *Lilith*, vol. 16 (2007) pp. 12–14.
Moore, Clive, 'Colonial Manhood and Masculinities', *Journal of Australian Studies*, vol. 22, no. 56 (1998) pp. 35–50.
Morgan, Greg, ' "Give Me the Consideration of Being the Bondsman": Embarrassment and the Figure of the Bond in the Sentimental Fiction of Samuel Richardson', *Eighteenth Century Fiction*, vol. 28, no. 4 (2016) pp. 667–690.
Morgan, Michael L., *On Shame* (New York and London: Routledge, 2008).
Mosse, George L., *Nationalism & Sexuality: Respectability and Abnormal Sexuality in Modern Europe* (New York: Howard Fertig Inc., 1985).
Müller-Pinzler, Laura, Rademacher, Lena, Paulus, Frieder M. and Krach, Sören, 'When Your Friends Make You Cringe: Social Closeness Modulates Vicarious Embarrassment-Related Neural Activity', *Social Cognitive and Affective Neuroscience*, vol. 11, no. 3 (2016) pp. 466–475.

250 Bibliography

Murphy, Cliona, *The Women's Suffrage Movement and Irish Society in the Early Twentieth Century* (New York and London: Harvester Wheatsheaf, 1989).

Murphy, William, *Political Imprisonment and the Irish, 1912–1921* (Oxford: Oxford University Press, 2016).

Murphy, Cliona, 'Suffragists and Nationalism in Early Twentieth-Century Ireland', *History of European Ideas*, vol. 16, nos. 4–6 (1993) pp. 1009–1015.

Myers, Kevin, 'FF Celebratory Plans for the Easter Rising a Load of Claptrap', *Irish Independent*, 20 April 2011.

Nash, David, 'Towards an Agenda for a Wider Study of Shame. Theorising from Nineteenth-Century British Evidence', in Judith Rowbotham, Marianna Muravyeva and David Nash, eds, *Shame, Blame and Culpability. Crime and Violence in the Modern State* (New York: Routledge, 2014) pp. 43–59.

Nash David, and Marie Kilday, Anne, *Cultures of Shame: Exploring Crime and Morality in Britain 1600–1900* (Basingstoke: Palgrave Macmillan, 2010).

Nettelbeck, Amanda, 'Introduction', in Catherine Martin, *An Australian Girl* (Oxford: Oxford University Press, 1999) pp. vii–xxxi.

Nic Congáil, Ríona, 'Agnes O'Farrelly's Politics and Poetry, 1918–27', in Tina O'Toole, Gillian McIntosh, and Muireann Ó'Cinnéide, eds., *Women Writing War: Ireland 1880–1922* (Dublin: University College Dublin Press, 2016) pp. 103–117.

Nye, Robert A., *Masculinity and Male Codes of Honor in Modern France* (Oxford: Oxford University Press, 1993).

Oldfield, Audrey, *Woman Suffrage in Australia: A Gift or a Struggle?* (Cambridge: Cambridge University Press, 1992).

Olsthoorn, Peter, 'Courage in the Military: Physical and Moral', *Journal of Military Ethics*, vol. 6, no. 4 (2007) pp. 270–279.

Oppenheimer, Melanie, ' "The Best P.M. for the Empire in War"? Lady Helen Munro Ferguson and the Australian Red Cross Society 1914–1920', *Australian Historical Studies*, vol. 33, no. 119 (2002) pp. 108–124.

Oppenheimer, Melanie, 'Shaping the Legend: The Role of the Australian Red Cross and Anzac', *Labour History*, no. 106 (2014) pp. 123–142.

Parashar, Swati, *Women and Militant Wars: The Politics of Injury* (Abingdon: Routledge, 2014).

Parker, Andrew and Watson, Nick J., 'Sport and Religion: Culture, History and Ideology', *Movement and Sport Sciences*, vol. 86 (2014) pp. 71–79.

Pašeta, Senia, *Irish Nationalist Women, 1900–1918* (Cambridge: Cambridge University Press, 2013).

Patmore, Coventry, *The Angel in the House* (1854–1856) (London: Cassell, 1887).

Paulus, Frieder M., Müller-Pinzler, Laura, Stolz, David S., Mayer, Annalina V., Rademacher, Lena, Krach, Sören, 'Laugh or Cringe? Common and Distinct Processes of Reward-Based Schadenfreude and Empathy-Based Fremdscham', *Neuropsychologia* (2017), https://doi.org/10.1016/j.neuropsychologia.2017.05.030, accessed 27 June 2017.

Pickles, Katie, *Transnational Outrage: The Death and Commemoration of Edith Cavell* (Basingstoke and New York: Palgrave Macmillan, 2007).

Porter, Bernard, *The Absent-Minded Imperialists: Empire, Society, and Culture in Britain* (Oxford: Oxford University Press, 2004).

Purvis, June, *Emmeline Pankhurst: A Biography* (London: Routledge, 2002).

Purvis, June, 'Fighting the Double Moral Standard in Edwardian Britain: Suffragette Militancy, Sexuality and the Nation in the Writings of the Early Twentieth-Century

British Feminist Christabel Pankhurst', in Francisca de Haan, Margaret Allen, June Purvis and Krassimira Dasklova, eds., *Women's Activism: Global Perspectives from the 1890s to the Present* (New York: Routledge, 2013) pp. 121–135.

Quartly, Marian, 'Defending "The Purity of Home Life" Against Socialism: The Founding Years of the Australian Women's National League', *Australian Journal of Politics and History*, vol. 50, no. 2 (2004) pp. 178–193.

Ransom, Teresa, *Miss Marie Corelli, Queen of Victorian Bestsellers* (Gloucestershire: Sutton, 1999).

Reddy, William M., *The Navigation of Feeling: A Framework for the History of Emotions* (Cambridge: Cambridge University Press, 2001).

Reilly, Eileen, 'Women and Voluntary War Work', in Adrian Gregory and Senia Pašeta, eds., *Ireland and the Great War: 'A War to Unite Us All'?* (Manchester: Manchester University Press, 2002) pp. 49–72.

Roberts, Jeffrey J., 'On John Keegan, Soviet "Amazons", and the Issue of Women in Combat', *Minerva: Quarterly Report on Women and the Military*, vol. 14, nos. 3-4 (1996) pp. 11–28.

Rosenwein, Barbara, 'Worrying About Emotions in History', *The American Historical Review*, vol. 107, no. 3 (2002) pp. 921–945.

Rosenwein, Barbara, 'Problems and Methods in the History of Emotions', *Passions in Context I: International Journal for the History and Theory of Emotions*, no. 1 (2010) pp. 1–32.

Rubinstein, David, *Before the Suffragettes: Women's Emancipation in the 1890s* (Brighton: Harvester, 1986).

Ruskin, John, Lecture II: 'Of Queens' Gardens', in *Sesame and Lilies: The Two Paths: & The King of the Golden River* (London: Dent, 1970 [1865]).

Ryan, Louise, 'The Irish Citizen, 1912–1920', *Saothar*, vol. 17 (1992) pp. 105–111.

Ryan, Louise, 'Traditions and Double Moral Standard: The Irish Suffragists' Critique of Nationalism', *Women's History Review*, vol. 4, no. 4 (1995) pp. 487–503.

Sanders, Valeria, *Eve's Renegades: Victorian Anti-Feminist Women Novelists* (London: Macmillan Press, 1996).

Scates Bruce, and Frances, Raelene, *Women and the Great War* (Cambridge: Cambridge University Press, 1997).

Scheff, Thomas J., 'Shame and the Social Bond: A Sociological Theory,' *Sociological Theory*, vol. 18, no. 1 (2000) pp. 84–99.

Scheff, Thomas J., 'Shame in Self and Society', *Symbolic Interaction*, vol. 26, no. 2 (2003) pp. 239–262.

Scheff, Thomas J., 'Elias, Freud and Goffman: Shame as the Master Emotion', in Steven Loyal and Stephen Quilley, eds., *Sociology of Norbert Elias* (New York: Cambridge University Press, 2004) pp. 229–242.

Scheff, Thomas, 'A Taxonomy of Emotions: How Do We Begin?' www.soc.ucsb.edu/faculty/scheff/main.php?id=47.html, accessed 26 January 2017.

Schudson, Michael, 'Embarrassment and Erving Goffman's Idea of Human Nature', *Theory and Society*, vol. 13 (1984) pp. 633–648.

Scott, Joan Wallach, *Only Paradoxes to Offer: French Feminists and the Rights of Man* (Cambridge, US: Oxford University Press, 1997).

Scott, William Stuart, *Corelli: The Story of a Friendship* (London: Hutchinson, 1955).

Shatz, Steven F., and Shatz, Naomi R., 'Chivalry Is Not Dead: Murder, Gender, and the Death Penalty', *Berkeley Journal of Gender, Law & Justice*, vol. 27, no. 1 (2012) pp. 64–112.

Bibliography

Shigematsu, Setsu, *Scream from the Shadows: The Women's Liberation Movement in Japan* (Minneapolis: University of Minnesota Press, 2012).

Shoemaker, Robert, 'Male Honour and the Decline of Public Violence in Eighteenth-Century London', *Social History*, vol. 26, no. 2 (2001) pp. 190–208.

Shute, Carmel, 'Heroines and Heroes: Sexual Mythology in Australia 1914–18', in Joy Damousi and Marilyn Lake, eds., *Gender and War: Australians at War in the Twentieth Century* (Cambridge: Cambridge University Press, 1995) pp. 23–42.

Shweder, Richard A., 'Toward a Deep Cultural Psychology of Shame', *Social Research*, vol. 70, no. 4 (2003) pp. 1109–1130.

Simms, Marian, 'Conservative Feminism in Australia: A Case Study of Feminist Ideology', *Women's Studies International Quarterly*, vol. 2, no. 3 (1979) pp. 305–318.

Smart, Judith, 'Eva Hughes: Militant Conservative', in Marilyn Lake and Farley Kelly, eds., *Double Time: Women in Victoria—150 years* (Melbourne: Penguin, 1985) pp. 179–189.

Smart, Judith, 'Hughes, Agnes Eva (1856–1940)', *Australian Dictionary of Biography*, National Centre of Biography, Australian National University, http://adb.anu.edu.au/biography/hughes-agnes-eva-6755/text11675, published first in hardcopy 1983, accessed online 29 May 2017.

Smart, Judith, '"Poor Little Belgium" and Australian Popular Support for War, 1914', *War and Society*, vol. 12 (1994) pp. 23–42.

Smith, Anthony D., *Theories of Nationalism* (London: Gerald Duckworth & Co., 1971).

Smith, Anthony D., *The Ethnic Origins of Nations* (London Wiley, 1991 [1986]).

Smith, Evan, and Marmo, Marinella, *Race, Gender and the Body in British Immigration Control: Subject to Examination* (Basingstoke: Palgrave Macmillan, 2014).

Southard, Belinda A. Stillion, 'Militancy, Power, and Identity: The Silent Sentinels as Women Fighting for a Political Voice', *Rhetoric & Public Affairs*, vol. 10, no. 3 (2007) pp. 399–417.

Spierenburg, Pieter, 'Masculinity, Violence, and Honor: An Introduction', in Pieter Spierenburg, ed., *Men and Violence: Gender, Honor, and Rituals in Modern Europe and America* (Columbus: Ohio State University Press, 1998) pp. 1–29.

Stearns, Peter N., 'Shame, and a Challenge for Emotions History', *Emotion Review*, vol. 8, no. 3 (2015) pp. 197–206.

Steele, Karen, 'Constance Markievicz and the Politics of Memory', in Louise Ryan and Margaret Ward, eds., *Irish Women and Nationalism: Soldiers, New Women and Wicked Hags* (Dublin: Irish Academic Press, 2004), pp. 62–79.

Steele, Karen, ed., *Maud Gonne's Irish Nationalist Writings, 1895–1946* (Dublin and Portland: Irish Academic Press, 2004).

Steele, Karen, *Women, Press and Politics During the Irish Revival* (Syracuse: Syracuse University Press, 2007).

Steele, Karen, 'Editing out Factionalism: The Political and Literary Consequences in Ireland's "Shan Van Vocht"', *Victorian Periodicals Review*, vol. 35, no. 2 (2002) pp. 113–132.

Stewart, Charles, 'Honor and Shame', in James D. Wright, ed., *International Encyclopedia of the Social and Behavioral Sciences*, 2nd ed., vol. 11 (Amsterdam: Elsevier, 2015).

Strange Carolyn, and Cribb, Robert, 'Historical Perspectives on Honour, Violence and Emotion' in Carolyn Strange, Robert Cribb, Christopher E. Forth, eds., *Honour, Violence and Emotions in History* (London: Bloomsbury Academic, 2014) pp. 9–38.

Strange, Carolyn, Cribb, Robert, Forth, Christopher E. eds., *Honour, Violence and Emotions in History* (London: Bloomsbury Academic, 2014).
Summerfield, Penny, 'Gender and War in the Twentieth Century', *The International History Review*, vol. 19, no. 1 (1997) pp. 3–15.
Tallant, Nicola, 'She Was a Snob, Fraud, Show-Off, and Murderer', *Irish Independent*, 29 October 2006.
Thackeray, David, 'Home and Steele Politics: Women and Conservatism Activism in Early Twentieth-Century Britain', *Journal of British Studies*, vol. 49, no. 4 (2010) pp. 826–848.
Thompson, Andrew, *The Empire Strikes Back: The Impact of Imperialism on Britain from the Mid-Nineteenth Century* (Harlow: Pearson Longman, 2005).
Tickner, Lisa, *The Spectacle of Women: Imagery of the Suffrage Campaign, 1907–14* (London: Chatto & Windus, 1987).
Tiernan, Sonja, 'Tabloid Sensationalism or Revolutionary Feminism? The First-Wave Feminist Movement in an Irish Women's Periodical', *Irish Communications Review*, vol. 12, no. 1 (2010) pp. 74–87.
Tylee, Claire, *The Great War and Women's Consciousness: Images of Militarism and Womanhood in Women's Writings, 1914–64* (Basingstoke: Palgrave Macmillan, 1990).
Tyrrell, Ian, 'Comparative and Transnational History', *Australian Feminist Studies*, vol. 22, no. 52 (2007) pp. 49–54.
Vellacott, Jo, *Pacifists, Patriots and the Vote: The Erosion of Democratic Suffragism during the First World War* (Basingstoke: Palgrave Macmillan, 2007).
Wagner, Tamara S., 'Introduction: Narratives of Victorian Antifeminism', in Tamara S. Wagner, ed., *Antifeminism and the Victorian Novel: Rereading Nineteenth-Century Women Writers* (Amherst, New York: Cambria Press, 2009) pp. 1–15.
Walby, Sylvia, 'Woman and Nation', *International Journal of Comparative Sociology*, vol. 32, nos. 1–2 (1992) pp. 81–100.
Ward, Margaret, *Unmanageable Revolutionaries: Women and Irish Nationalism* (London: Pluto Press, 1983).
Ward, Margaret, *Maud Gonne: Ireland's Joan of Arc* (London: Pandora, 1990).
Ward, Margaret, 'Conflicting Interests: The British and Irish Suffrage Movements', *Feminist Review*, vol. 50, no. 1 (1995) pp. 127–147.
Ward, Paul, ' "Women of Britain Say Go": Women's Participation in the First World War', *Twentieth Century British History*, vol. 12, no. 1 (2001) pp. 23–45.
Weltman, Sharon Aronofsky, ' "Be No More Housewives, but Queens": Queen Victoria and Ruskin's Domestic Mythology', in Margaret Homans and Adrienne Munich eds., *Remaking Queen Victoria* (Cambridge: Cambridge University Press, 1997) pp. 105–122.
Wheeler, Charles Newton, *The Irish Republic: An Analytical History of Ireland, 1914–1918, with Particular Reference to the Easter Insurrection (1916) and the German "plots." Also a Sketch of De Valera's Life by Harry J. Boland, his Private Secretary: A Close-Up View of Countess Markievicz, and a Defense of Ulster by Ulstermen* (Chicago: Cahill-Igoe Company, 1919). http://babel.hathitrust.org/cgi/pt?id=loc.ark:/13960/t3514hr60;view=1up;seq=9, accessed 21 October 2015.
Woollacott, Angela, *On Her Their Lives Depend: Munitions Workers in the Great War* (Berkeley: University of California Press, 1994).
Woollacott, Angela, 'A Feminist History of Violence: History as a Weapon of Liberation?', *Lilith*, vol. 16 (2007) pp. 1–11.
Young, Robert J.C., *The Idea of English Ethnicity* (Oxford: Blackwell, 2008).

Young, Robert J.C., *Empire, Colony, Postcolony* (Hoboken: John Wiley & Sons Inc., 2015).

Yuval-Davis, Nira, and Anthias, Floya, eds., *Woman, Nation, State* (Basingstoke: Palgrave Macmillan, 1989).

Yuval-Davis, Nira, *Gender and Nation* (London: SAGE Publications, 1997).

Yuval-Davis, Nira, 'Gender and Nation', *Ethnic and Racial Studies*, vol. 16, no. 4 (1993) pp. 621–632.

Ziino, Bart, 'Great War, Total War', in Deborah Gare and David Ritter, eds., *Making Australian History. Perspectives on the Past Since 1788* (Melbourne: Thomson, 2008) pp. 335–344.

Index

Aboriginal Australians 13, 31n47–49, 104n30, 109–110, 127n16, 127n21
Amazons 213–216, 219
anger: of anti-suffragists 40, 152, 212; of Australian women 117; at conscription 115; of Irish feminists 79, 208; at Irish revolutionary women 240n12; of men 222; at nurses 149; at shirkers 178, 180; at Sinn Féin 122; of working-class men 207
anti-feminism, definition 17–18
Anti-Suffrage Review, origins 16–17
anti-suffragism, definition 10, 16–18
Asquith, Herbert 208–209, 217
Australia: home front during World War One 112–115, 139–140; national identity 107–108, 124, 126n14; racial fears—Asia 13–14, 114, 173, 234; White Australia Policy (*see* White Australia Policy (Immigration Restriction Act 1901))
Australian girl, the 55–56
Australian Women's National League (AWNL), origins 20
Australian Women's Service Corps 117, 229
Australian woman voter: colonial women 101–102; disloyal 116–118, 118–120, 123–124; Irish views during World War One 52–54, 140–143; socialism 111–112, 115, 118–120, 125

Baldwin, Stanley 236–237
barbarism 29n27, 84n32, 92; German 213; Irish 61; violent women 222; World War One 134, 210, 225n32
Bean na hEireann, origins 19

Boadicea 203, 228n62
Boer War 8, 170, 186
British-Australia relations 14, 87–88, 90–91, 94–96, 98, 102–103
British Empire, anxieties of 7–8

Catholic Church: Australia 121; Ireland 238
Cavell, Edith 184–186, 191n93, 191n104, 214
chastity 62, 64, 132, 150, 204, 232
chivalry 26, 42, 148, 157, 172–173, 175; and Cavell, Edith 184–186; definition 195–196; international codes 213–215; Ireland 72, 76–77, 141–142, 162n54, 208–210; and Markievicz, Constance 219; violence against women 195–197, 204; violent women 26, 193–194, 196–197, 202, 205–207, 221–223
Churchill, Winston 193
citizenship: and Australian women 109–111, 126n14; concepts of 35–37, 56n3; and empire 90–91, 93; World War One and reconceptualization 151–152, 158, 163n101
civilisation 7–9, 44, 68, 87, 91–92, 124, 221; and feminism 56, 68–69, 100, 107, 124, 198, 206, 213–215, 217, 220, 223; and World War One 134, 213–214
Conciliation Bill (1912) 75–76, 208
Connery, M. K. 78–79, 217
conscription 129n54, 133, 216; Military Service Act of 1916 (Britain) 172; referenda in Australia 33n90, 51, 102, 108, 115–118, 121–122, 178, 181, 183

Corelli, Marie 1–2, 21, 26n3, 39–41, 54, 68
courage 25–26, 63–64, 165–167; and Australian men and war 182–183; and Edith Cavell 184–186; heroism, cult of 167–168; and the Irish man 168–172; Irish women warriors (*see* violence, Irish women warriors); masculine honour 133–134, 166–168; and the military 168; moral courage 73, 166–168, 168–172, 175, 182, 184, 188; and women 73, 119–120, 166, 182, 183–187; women and war 55, 139–140, 150
Cousins, Margaret 19, 30n41–42, 33n79, 218, 221
cowardice: British government 193; and challenge of feminism 168; challenges to feminine nature of 186–187; and the military 168; violence against shirkers 165–166, 177–181; wartime suffragist 152; white feathers (*see* white feather campaign)
Cumman na mBan 19, 78–80, 85, 218

Despard, Charlotte 203
de Valera, Éamon 237, 239
drunken women 202

Easter Rising (1916) 170, 239
emasculation of colonised man 24, 62, 65–66, 68, 70–75
embarrassment: of the apolitical woman 99–102; of Australian women voters 90–91, 93–97, 102; definition 5, 88–90; postcolonial embarrassment 237–239; post-suffrage embarrassment 235–237; and shame 5, 89; vicarious embarrassment 22, 88–91, 97, 99, 212
emotions: defining emotions 22–23; emotional communities 4–6; emotionalism of women 48, 56, 116, 141, 178, 205; emotional regimes 3–6, 10, 12; emotional regimes and World War One 132–134, 139–140, 144, 149–150, 153, 157–158, 182–183; emotional vocabularies 21–22; as feminine 4; locating emotions in text 21–23; and reason 4, 56n3

England: Englishness 28n23, 87, 104n19, 126n13, 126n24; reputation 1–2, 7–8, 91, 95, 213

families and voting 53
Fawcett, Millicent Garrett 8, 131, 149–150, 163n102
femininity, views of 39–44
Fianna na hÉireann 218–220, 239
Flunkeyism *see* slavish obedience, Irish men; slavish obedience, flunkeyism

Garnett, Theresa 193
gender: separate spheres (*see* separate spheres ideology); sex difference (*see* sex difference); and war 135–136, 210–212
gentleman: code of conduct 168; concept of during World War One 132, 134, 144, 159n13
Goldstein, Vida 14–15, 31n55, 97–99, 128n45, 141, 162n54, 201, 211, 227n54
Gonne, Maude 169–170
Good Friday Peace Accord (1998) 239

happiness: English nation 100; of the home 52; the Irish 62; and war service 178, 183; the woman vote 97
Home Rule Bill, Ireland 11–12, 71–72, 75–77, 81, 114, 123, 138, 141, 171, 208
honour: Australia 6–7, 24–25, 52, 107, 109, 112–120; Britain 88, 133–135; codes 2, 10, 25, 62–64, 82n6, 132–135, 194–197; and courage in war 132–134, 165–168; Ireland 7, 24, 61–62, 66–67, 69–74, 75–77, 82; loss of 63; and martial values 63, 166–167; and masculinity 2–3, 10, 62–64, 77; nationalisation of 63–64, 167; political truce (*see* World War One, political truce and dishonourable women); shame as antithesis 3, 83n17; and violence 25, 83n11, 165–167, 187–188, 189n5, 194–197, 210–211; women 2–3, 10, 25, 41–42, 52, 54–55, 61–64, 69–74, 77, 112–120, 131–135, 143–147, 151–153; World War One 77, 112–115, 132–135, 158–159, 168, 210–211; *see also* cowardice, violence against shirkers
Hughes, Eva 33n84, 51, 54, 176

Index 257

indignation: Australia 117; British 96, 172, 201, 208; Irish 73, 79, 143
Inghinidhe na hEireann 19, 73, 85n66
Ireland: Ancient Ireland 61, 71, 219; Anglicisation of 67–69; warrior legacy 166, 169, 171; *see also* violence, Irish women warriors
Irish-Australians 33n90, 108, 114–115, 117, 120–123
Irish Citizen Army 218, 239
Irish Civil War 237–238
Irish Free State 237
Irish National Volunteers (Irish Volunteers, later Irish Republican Army) 19, 78, 85n66, 218
Irish Parliamentary Party (Irish Party) 11, 75, 78–80, 141, 154, 208
Irish War of Independence (Anglo-Irish War) 19, 219, 237
Irish Women's Franchise League (IWFL): origins 19–20; views of WSPU 153–154

jingoism 75, 157, 176, 187, 211
Joan of Arc 169

Ladies' Land League (Ireland) 162n54
Lloyd-George, David 156, 201

Mannix, Archbishop 121–123
Markham, Violet 44, 96
Markievicz, Constance: Easter Rising (1916) 218–219, 220; Irish women warriors 71, 73, 218–219, 220–221, 238; remembering 230n146, 230n147, 238–239; and World War One 170, 219
marriage 16, 40, 42, 49, 55, 176, 238
masculinity: Australia 108, 113, 174, 177–178, 234; Britain 8, 134, 143–144, 153, 158, 172–173; Ireland 36, 70, 77, 159, 170, 237; and shame 64, 177; and violence 194–195, 211, 224n12, 234; and war 136, 148, 153, 168, 172–175, 177–178, 187–188, 212–213
Matters, Muriel 14, 200
medical doctors, female 55, 139, 140, 150, 161n41
middle class: and gender in Australia 9, 55, 57n5, 108–109; and gender in Ireland 170, 196, 220; and honour codes 63, 133–134, 159n14, 166–167, 196; and respectability 9, 108
militancy, nationalist Irish women *see* violence, Irish women warriors
militancy, suffrage: and Australia 14, 200–201; cowardice of 205; degradation of womanhood 194–195, 201–204; dog-whip 99, 193, 200, 202; hatchet incident 208–209, 222; hooliganism 205–206; in Ireland 10–11, 30n41, 142, 159, 208–210; tactics 8–9, 184, 193, 194; in USA 227n52
militarism, male 135, 139, 153, 156–158, 211, 221
Milner, Edith 149
modesty, womanly 1, 39–40, 150, 206
monstrous femininity: of wartime nurses 147–151; of wartime women workers 149; of white feather campaigners 173, 176
motherhood 43, 53, 100, 110, 135, 142, 174, 176–179, 181–183, 187, 198, 211, 216, 229n127, 232, 241n19; of the nation/race 1, 10, 100, 109–110, 142, 157
Muscular Christianity 168

nagging women 204, 207, 222
nation, and woman 64–66
nationalism, false: of Irish-Australians 121–123; of Irish women 78–79
National League for Opposing Woman Suffrage (NLOWS), origins 11, 18, 40–41, 58n31
National Union of Woman Suffrage Societies (NUWSS) 8, 11, 131, 194; nurses 139, 149–151; political truce (*see* World War One, political truce and dishonourable women); World War One 144–145, 149–151
National Woman's Party (NWP) 227n52
New Woman (modern women) 1, 9, 27n4, 42–43, 47–49, 88, 196
New World 13, 90, 92, 98, 107–108, 125n3
New Zealand: suffrage 35, 87, 93–96; and war 113, 115
nurses *see* Cavell, Edith; World War One, nurses

O'Casey, Sean 221

Pankhurst, Christabel 8; as a coward 153–156; Irish feminism 153–156
Pankhurst, Emmeline 8, 153–155, 235; remembering 235–236
patriotism, lack of proper: Australian men 174, 179; Australian women 110; British women 145–146, 172–173, 212–213, 233; Irish women 19
physical force argument 138, 194, 215
politics and shameful women: the apolitical Australian woman 51–52, 99, 107, 111–112, 125; dishonourable political woman, British views 143–147, 151–153; dishonourable political woman, Irish views 153–158; disloyal woman voter, Australia 115–120

race, construction of: Anglo-Saxon or British race 13, 90, 107–110, 124, 126, 234; Australian racial anxieties 13–14, 109–110, 114; Irish fighting race 168–169; Irish or Celtic race 61, 66, 168–169, 237; white Australia 14, 108–110, 125; *see also* Australia, racial fears—Asia
Redmond, John 11, 78–80, 141, 208
religion: Catholic Church (*see* Catholic Church); Catholicism 76, 121, 241n19; Catholic priests 36, 121; Catholics 33n90, 121; nuns and womanliness 42, 53; Protestantism 33n90, 76, 121
Revolutionary Irish women, Irish men's views 237–239

scarlet fever (Irish females and British soldiers) 170
Scold's Bridle 203, 223
Scott, Rose 101, 126n11
selfishness 2, 23, 35, 231; Australian woman voter 50, 101, 110, 174, 178, 182; British suffragists 35, 44, 203, 100–101, 144–145, 147; Irish feminists 45–46
separate spheres ideology 2, 35–37, 39, 42, 45, 50, 55–56, 57n5, 198, 204
sex difference 47, 54–5, 96, 196
sex-dignity 79, 82
shame: affective displays 22, 39, 41, 72, 117, 156, 170, 177, 203; definition 2–3, 5–6, 22, 37–39, 132–132; shameful self-assessment 39, 52, 76, 120–121, 123, 174, 203, 233, 239–240
Shan Van Vocht 67–68, 72, 84n33, 168, 189n21
Shaw, George Bernard 185–186
Sheehy Skeffington, Hanna 19, 30n41–42, 33n79, 71, 211, 219
Sinn Féin 11, 117–118, 122
slavery, USA 68
slavish obedience: Irish feminists 66, 74–75, 82; Irish Home Rule 71–72; Irish men, flunkeyism 71–74, 82, 171; Irish nationalist women 66, 77–80, 82, 153; WSPU 153–158
socialism: Australian Labor Party 51, 107, 112, 118, 120; Australian women voters (*see* Australian woman voter); Russian Revolution 8, 114, 119, 128n45, 205; threat of 8, 13, 112, 114–115, 125
spinsterhood 42–43
suffrage campaigns: Australia 12–13; Britain 8–10, 151–153; Ireland 10–12
Suffragette, the 156, 164n122
suffragettes 8–9, 27n5, 29n31; *see also* militancy, suffrage

transnationalism: and empire 92–93, 118, 142; and feminism 143, 154; and manhood 76, 147; methodology 3, 6, 15, 27n9, 92–93; and womanhood 24, 44, 56, 124–125, 235

Ulster Volunteer Force (UVF) 218
uniforms, women's wartime 212–213
Unionism, Ulster 10–11, 18, 33n90, 154, 218; and feminism 11, 18, 19, 30n38, 30n42, 46, 154, 208; nationalists appeasing Ulster Unionists 76; World War One 138, 160n34, 161n36
Unionist women 80–81
United Irishmen's rebellion (1798) 219, 230n138
unsexed women 43–44, 201, 209, 238

Victoria, Queen 67, 190n30
violence: chivalry (*see* chivalry, violence against women; chivalry, violent women); conscription, Australia

115–116 (*see also* cowardice, violence against shirkers); domestic violence 26, 196, 224n21; female bodies, battlefields 215–217; feminist ethics 197–199; honour codes (*see* honour, and violence); Irish women warriors 166, 171, 186, 188, 217–221; legitimate womanly violence 204–205; male violence against suffragettes 185, 206–210; Markievicz, Constance 219–221, 230n146, 230n147, 238–239; masculine nature of 194–195; and pregnancy 216; privatisation of 196; remembering violent women 235–239; sexual 210–211, 224n21; women in revolutions 205; women in war (*see* World War One, women as combatants)
viragos 39, 149, 206
Votes for Women 16, 40, 193, 207

war and gender 135–136
Westminster, British Parliament 9, 11–12, 14, 18, 45, 62, 66, 74–76, 135, 152, 208, 219, 236
White Australia Policy (Immigration Restriction Act 1901) 113, 124
white feather campaign 137, 172–173; monstrous femininity of 173, 176
Woman, origins 20–21

Women's Emergency Corps 212
Women's Freedom League (WFL) 29n31, 194, 203
Women's Peace Army (Australia) 117, 128n45
women's press 15–16, 32n73
Women's Signallers' Territorial Corps 214
Women's Social and Political Union (WSPU) 8–9, 16; Irish feminists' views of WSPU and the truce 153–158; political truce during World War One 143–147
Women's Voluntary Reserve 212
working class: Australia, tensions 121; men and honour codes 133; men and the vote 8, 148; men and women's suffrage 207; women and World War One 137–138
World War One: and Australian women 139–140; and British women 136–139; honour codes 132–135, 158–159; and Irish women 138; nurses 131–132, 138–140; nurses as sexual and emotional predators 147–151; political truce and dishonourable women 143–147, 151–158; women as combatants 212–217
Wright, Almroth 117, 216–217